LOUISA MAY ALCOTT

THE WOMAN BEHIND
LITTLE WOMEN

HARRIET REISEN

A JOHN MACRAE BOOK
HENRY HOLT AND COMPANY   NEW YORK

Henry Holt and Company, LLC
Publishers since 1866
175 Fifth Avenue
New York, New York 10010
www.henryholt.com

Henry Holt® and 🛅® are registered trademarks of
Henry Holt and Company, LLC.

Library of Congress Cataloging-in-Publication Data
Reisen, Harriet.
Louisa May Alcott : the woman behind Little women / Harriet
Reisen.—1st ed.
    p.   cm.
"A John Macrae book."
Includes bibliographical references and index.
ISBN-13: 978-0-8050-8299-9
ISBN-10: 0-8050-8299-9
1. Alcott, Louisa May, 1832–1888.   2. Authors, American—19th
century—Biography.   I. Title.
PS1018.R45 2009
813'.4—dc22
[B]   2009010637

Henry Holt books are available for special promotions and
premiums. For details contact: Director, Special Markets.

First Edition 2009

Designed by Kelly S. Too

Printed in the United States of America
1   3   5   7   9   10   8   6   4   2

LOUISA MAY ALCOTT

To Nancy Porter,

treasured friend and colleague

CONTENTS

PREFACE

Like so many other girls, I fell under the spell of Louisa May Alcott when my mother presented *Little Women* to me as if it were the key to a magic kingdom. I was taken into Louisa's story so completely that a book with covers and pages has no place in my memory of the experience. While I was there, by my mother's decree, normal life was suspended. Jelly omelets were delivered to my room on bed trays, and sleep was optional. At such a time, school was out of the question. Jo March was coming to take up residence in my heart, a companion for life, to endow me with a little something of Louisa Alcott's own wise, funny, sentimental, and sharply realistic outlook.

Coming to the end of *Little Women* left me feeling as Louisa did when she emerged from a vortex (one of her all-absorbing periods of writing): cranky, bereft, and lamenting that never again would I read *Little Women* not knowing how it came out. The next long rainy weekend my grandmother, tipped off by my mother, showed up for a visit bearing the remaining seven of Alcott's juvenile novels. I polished off one of them before the sun came out and Grandma went home; the rest by the end of the month. I had gobbled Alcott all up without coming close to satisfying my appetite for her work.

Later, my mother made me aware of Louisa Alcott, the woman behind *Little Women*. Mom felt deep sympathy for Louisa's losses, which resembled her own. Her fury on Louisa's behalf toward Bronson Alcott (Louisa's father, whose resemblance to her own father she never recognized) was as pure and freely expressed as any tirade she directed at a teacher she felt had done me wrong. So it was my mother's attachment to Louisa's story that kindled my own interest, and soon after I moved to the Boston area in my twenties I took myself to the Alcotts' modest doorstep in Concord.

Orchard House is chockablock with things the Alcotts made and ate from and wore and painted and used so much that I imagine their smell must still cling to them. Downstairs in Bronson's study are his books, his hat, his satchel, and the ingenious little mantel clock to be ignored when neighbor Ralph Waldo Emerson came by to philosophize, and to take from its stand and put in his pocket when he went off on lecture tours. In the entry are palimpsests of May's frieze of silhouettes of the famous friends and neighbors who visited. Lizzie's picture hangs by her melodeon in the dining room where Abby's green-and-white Coalport china set is displayed. Upstairs a trunk contains costumes the sisters made for their theatricals, including the russet boots that Louisa so prized she wrote a role requiring them for every production. But it was in her small bedroom, from the tiny semicircular writing surface where she wrote *Little Women* in ten weeks, that Louisa May Alcott emerged to make herself real and claim me.

Over the next decade I read whatever I could find of Alcott's scores of short stories, poems, and works of nonfiction such as *Hospital Sketches*, her account of her experience as an army nurse in the Civil War. Her rediscovered thrillers were coming out every year or two, at the rate of a popular living novelist, and three biographies—Ednah Cheney's, Madeleine Stern's, and Martha Saxton's—told a story as full of plot and character as any the author invented, although none of them gave me the woman I glimpsed in her writing.

Louisa's journals and letters were published at about the same time as the thrillers. In them I finally heard Louisa Alcott's voice—not Jo March's voice, or the authorial voice of Louisa May Alcott, but the voice of the woman who had lived and breathed and was as real to me as my friend Nancy Porter. Nancy, an Emmy Award–winning documentary filmmaker for PBS, shared my enthusiasm for Alcott and thought we should bring her story to film; no one ever had. Over the next twenty years I continued my study of Alcott's life, work, and times while we tried to put together funding for the film. By the time the National Endowment for the Humanities (and later the Corporation for Public Broadcasting, the Arthur Vining Davis Foundations, Audrey Simons and the Simons Foundation, and the National Endowment for the Arts) recognized the merit of our subject, I had read just about all of Louisa's hundreds of works and could sift them for the autobiographical elements we needed to tell her story without leaving her imagination out. Susan Lacy of the PBS series *American Masters* agreed to coproduce and broadcast a ninety-minute documentary biography, and my pleasant obsession with Louisa Alcott became a better-than-full-time job. With it came the opportunity also to fulfill my "long-held dream" (a phrase of Louisa's that came to me as easily as any words of my own) to tell her story in print.

Through writing and producing the film, I came to know the subject of this book in a way few biographers do. Nancy and I spent hours in Orchard House planning the filming, becoming as comfortable there as we would be at a friend's house. In the venerable New York apartment on East Eighty-eighth Street of Madeleine Stern and Dr. Leona Rostenberg, under the suspicious gaze of the last of the household's dachshunds named Laurie, we filmed the nonagenarian literary sleuths (and rare book dealers) who had discovered Louisa's pseudonym, A. M. Barnard, and with it the key to her secret literary life as a writer of pulp fiction. I became a literary sleuth myself in search of an Alcott scholar I never met—Madelon Bedell, the author of *The Alcotts: Biography of a Family.* In 1975 Bedell had interviewed ninety-six-year-old Lulu Nieriker Rasim, Louisa's niece and the only person then still alive to have known her personally. Bedell's account of the interview is in the preface to her 1980 book, but the interview itself was never published; the author died of cancer before she completed a second volume. I wondered what had happened to Bedell's interview with Lulu, had asked various Alcott scholars about it, had even tried calling Bedells listed in telephone books. One day I picked up a used copy of *The Alcotts*, and out of it tumbled a carbon copy of an August 1980 letter written by Bedell herself to Michael Sterne, then the travel editor of the *New York Times*, proposing a story. At the bottom of the letter was a return address in Brooklyn where, more than two decades later, Madelon Bedell's widower still lived.

Bob Bedell, it turned out, had trustingly loaned the papers to an eccentric author, who had been sitting on them for years. Nancy and I went to New York to take Bob and the author (mostly of books about nineteenth-century décor) to lunch, then went to her strangely wonderful Greenwich Village town house (its windows suffocated with fabrics, the walls and ceilings of each room papered in half a dozen exuberant Victorian patterns), where in the basement she kept the large battered boxes of Bedell's files. Since she was moving soon, she agreed to let us take the papers to New England. After we left, however, she answered none of our many phone messages, e-mails, and letters. It looked as if Bedell's work would stay in that basement—or worse, disappear in the impending move. Finally, after a good six months of anxious strategizing with the Bedell family and some blustery talk about lawyers, the papers were transferred. At present they take up half my study while en route to the Orchard House collection.

Shooting the dramatized scenes of the film was the most unusual aspect of my research. Casting actors as our subject and her family did wonders to focus them in my mind. Location filming in Orchard House, Emerson's house, and Fruitlands brought home the material and physical reality of Alcott's life and times. Seeing the costumes—especially the Fruitlands clothing, which had been described but never pictured—and watching them being worn, especially running at full throttle in the woods—made visible how it felt to be breathing under their weight. Eating an authentic plumcake baked by the film's prop-master made real the pain of three-year-old Louisa when she was asked to renounce the rare promised birthday sweet.

Now that the film and the book are done—having truly gobbled Louisa May Alcott all up—I confess to feeling just about as cranky and bereft as I did as a girl when I finished reading what I believed was everything she wrote. My hope is that readers of this book will be inspired to track down the dozen or more of Louisa May Alcott's works whose titles are known but whose whereabouts are not, to bring them forth from obscure periodicals in the backs of old local library shelves, attic trunks, even from inside the walls of old houses, as pages of Louisa's Fruitlands diaries were, so they may be published and read as widely as their most recent predecessors have been. If they do, I may never have to run out of new work from the prodigious pen of Louisa May Alcott.

—HARRIET REISEN,
March 2009

LOUISA MAY ALCOTT

BEHIND A MASK

For many girls, *Little Women* is a reading experience so stirring and lasting in impact that as adults they name their baby daughters after the characters. When they judge their daughters old enough, they press the book on their little Megs, Josephines, Beths, and Amys; often it is the same copy they read with their mothers, sometimes the one their mothers read with their grandmothers, occasionally an early or original edition that represents continuity through a hundred or more years. Louisa May Alcott wrote many works in every genre—conservatively, more than two hundred, over a career that spanned almost forty years—but *Little Women* was far and away her most successful. The story of the March sisters, which Alcott thought lifeless and flat as she was writing it, unexpectedly touching and true when she finished, struck a deep chord with readers when it appeared in 1868, just three years after the end of the Civil War. The sequel, *Little Men,* was a bestseller before it was even published. Readers anticipated Alcott's juvenile novels with a fervor not seen again until the *Harry Potter* series of J. K. Rowling.

One hundred forty years after the publication of *Little Women*, none of Louisa May Alcott's eight novels for what is now called the "young adult" audience has ever been out of print. Women around the world cite *Little Women* as the most treasured book of their childhoods—"magically the book told my story," as a writer for the *Philippine Inquirer* recently put it. Translated into more than fifty languages, *Little Women* crosses every cultural and religious border. It has been adapted for stage, television, opera, ballet, Hollywood, Bollywood, and Japanese anime. Its characters have been drafted for new versions set in California's Beverly Hills, Salvador Allende's Chile, and New York's Upper West Side.

Little Women is a charming, intimate coming-of-age story about family love, loss, and struggle set in a picturesque rendering of mid-nineteenth-century New England life. What sets it apart is the young woman at its center. Her name is Jo March, but her character is Louisa Alcott.

Jo March is a dazzling and original invention: bold, outspoken, brave, daring, loyal, cranky, principled, and real. She is a dreamer and a scribbler, happiest at her woodsy hideout by an old cartwheel or holed up in the attic, absorbed in reading or writing, filling page after page with stories or plays. She loves to invent wild escapades, to stage and star in flamboyant dramas. She loves to run. She wishes she were a boy, for all the right reasons: to speak her mind, go where she pleases, learn what she wants to know—in other words, to be free.

At the same time, Jo is devoted to the fictional March family, which was closely modeled on the Alcott family: a wise and good mother, an idealistic father, and four sisters whose personalities are a sampler of female adolescence. But while Jo March marries and is content within the family circle, Louisa Alcott chose an independent path.

Descriptions of Louisa by her contemporaries matched Alcott's first description of Jo March in *Little Women*: "Fifteen-year-old Jo was very tall, thin, and brown, and reminded one of a colt, for she never seemed to know what to do with her long limbs, which were very much in her way. She had a decided mouth, a comical nose, and sharp, gray eyes, which appeared to see everything, and were by turns fierce, funny, or thoughtful." Frederick Llewellyn Willis wrote that his cousin Louisa Alcott was "full of spirit and life; impulsive and moody, and at times irritable and nervous. She could run like a gazelle. She was the most beautiful girl runner I ever saw. She could leap a fence or climb a tree as well as any boy and dearly loved a good romp."

Another Louisa May Alcott lurked behind the spirited hoyden who wrote the March family books (*Little Women*, *Little Men*, and *Jo's Boys*), five other juvenile novels, and countless stories for children. The real Louisa Alcott was infinitely more interested in the darker side of human nature and experience than in telling polite stories to nice children. She was a protean personality, a turbulent force, a passionate fighter attracted to danger and violence.

The voice of the other Louisa is heard in writings that were unknown or unpublished for almost ninety years after her death. In pulp fiction written anonymously, or under the name "A. M. Barnard," she is villain, victim, and heroine, sometimes all of them at once.

An actress of professional caliber, Louisa played many roles in life and used them in her work. Much of her fiction is not fictional at all: Louisa Alcott held the jobs heroine Christie Devon holds in the gritty novel *Work*; loved the two men, Ralph Waldo Emerson and Henry David Thoreau, who inspired the characters Sylvia Yule loves in *Moods*; served in the Civil War as a nurse, as Tribulation Periwinkle does in *Hospital Sketches*; and displays her infinite variety in a lifetime of poetry, journals, and letters. She was her own best character.

In everything Louisa Alcott wrote she made use of the outward details and the hidden emotional currents of her life, and her life was no children's book. She knew not only family affection but also dangerous family disaffection; not just domestic toil but grueling manual labor; she knew gnawing hunger and the bloody aftermath of war. She was familiar with scenes of wealth and fashion from visits to privileged relatives, knew the famed sights of Europe from traveling as paid companion to a wealthy woman, and had vast vicarious experience from a lifetime of reading novels.

She wrote almost everything at high speed and for money. Works as different as *Little Women* and "Perilous Play" (a tale about the dangers and blessings of hashish) were written in the same year and brought to life from the same experiences. They are both filled with classical allusions and quotations from Shakespeare, both peppered with metaphysics and moral scrutiny. They provide tantalizing glimpses not of the New England spinster of popular conception, but of the real Louisa Alcott, a person we might recognize, someone so modern that she could pass at a dinner party as a woman born 150 years after her actual birth in 1832.

A Concord contemporary, Clara Gowing, described Louisa as "a strange combination of kindness, shyness, and daring; a creature loving and spiteful, full of energy and perseverance, full of fun, with a keen sense of the ludicrous, apt speech and ready wit; a subject of moods, than whom no one could be jollier and more entertaining when geniality was in ascendancy, but if the opposite, let her best friend beware."

Jo March resembles her creator most in the fertility of her imagination. Like Jo, the young Louisa May Alcott burned with genius, spinning tales of murder and treachery one minute, fairy tales and sentimental poetry the next. She told herself a dozen stories at a time, working out their plots in her head, sometimes for years. Spinning out her fantasies on paper, Louisa was transported, and liberated. Her imagination freed her to escape the confines of ordinary life to be flirtatious, scheming, materialistic, violent, rich, worldly, or a different gender. In her struggle to fulfill her childhood vow to be "rich, famous, and happy before I die," her imagination was her greatest comfort, and her refuge even in her last days, when she wrote in her journal, "Lived in my mind where I can generally find amusement. . . . A happy world to go into when the real one is too dull or hard."

ONE

FIT FOR THE
SCUFFLE OF THINGS

She has "a fine foundation for health and energy of character," Bronson Alcott wrote to his father-in-law within hours of the birth of his second daughter on November 29, 1832. "[She] is a very fine healthful child, much more so than Anna was at birth." He had wished for a boy, but he was linked to Louisa by a coincidence rarer than a common gender: "She was born at half-past 12 this morning on my birthday (33)."

Although they shared a birthday, Louisa May Alcott and her father were born under different stars. From the first, Louisa displayed her mother's moody, passionate temperament. She was an autumn hurricane arriving twenty months after Anna, a veritable March lamb, a paragon of a baby with her father's calm temperament. Louisa's version of her vexed beginnings matched her sense that life had been one long battle from the start. "On a dismal November day I found myself, & began my long fight," she wrote on her twenty-third birthday. Her first fight would be for supremacy over her sister. Her mother would be her best ally.

Abigail May Alcott's family was a distinguished one, especially on her mother's side. Dorothy Sewall May was the daughter of Samuel Sewall, the deacon of Old South Church, from whose steps Samuel Adams had signaled the start of the Boston Tea Party in 1773. The Sewalls were related to the Quincys and the Adamses; Abigail's aunt Dorothy Quincy's second marriage was to John Hancock. Born in 1800, Abigail (called Abby or Abba) was the youngest of the May family's eight surviving children.

Colonel Joseph May, Abigail's father and Louisa's grandfather, came from a humbler line. (The title "colonel" was a memento not of wartime service but of his rank in a teenage cadet corps during the Revolution.) The son of a modestly successful lumber dealer, Joseph May met Dorothy Sewall when he was a thirteen-year-old apprentice in her uncle's store. Enterprising and ambitious, by age thirty Colonel May was a rich and gregarious man known for his honesty, his love of learning, his charitable works, and his support of liberal causes. He was one of the best informed men of his day, according to a family biographer. Outside the family he was distinguished by his snuff habit and for wearing outmoded black silk stockings and knee buckles. All Boston knew of Colonel May's vanity about his shapely legs, which he claimed were the models for George Washington's in the full-length Gilbert Stuart portrait.

The Colonel's easy course through life hit a snag in 1799, the year before Abigail was born, when he was involved in a disastrous investment. To clear his debts and his name, thirty-eight-year-old Joseph May gave up everything he owned, selling even the gold rings on his fingers. He vowed never again to pursue wealth, took a part-time salaried job in a shipping insurance office, and sold his grand mansion on Atkinson (now Congress) Street. He moved his family to a modest place on Federal Court. May's was by all accounts a happy household, alive with music and intellectual engagement.

Abby was very attached to her father, although she later felt she could never live up to his high expectations. She was a much loved and indulged child, yet near the end of her life, she began her brief memoir on a deeply mournful note: "I was the youngest of twelve children, born sickly, nursed by a sickly mother." The roots of Abigail's lifelong melancholy and sense of having been shortchanged may lie in a childhood dominated by her mother's declining health, the ghosts of siblings she never knew, and the subsequent deaths of other siblings she had known and loved.

Abby idealized her mother as Louisa would in turn idealize Abby as "Marmee" in *Little Women*. "She adored her husband and children," Abby wrote of Dorothy. "She loved the whole human family." Dorothy May had twelve pregnancies in sixteen years, several times burying an infant and giving its name to a successor: two Charleses, two Louisas, and three Samuels. When Abby was only a year old, her six-year-old brother

Edward—"a fair-haired boy, with blue eyes, bright, playful, affectionate" in his younger brother Sam's recollection—impaled himself on a post while playing in the backyard and bled to death in his mother's arms. Two of Abby's married sisters preceded her mother to the grave; only Abby, Charles, and Sam would live to see their own children grow up.

In her earliest years Abby was allowed to tag along after her older brother Sam to school in Boston's High Street; later she was given private lessons. Both Sam and her older sister Louisa took an active interest in Abby's intellectual development. From Harvard Sam corresponded with Abby about his readings in philosophy, while at home Louisa urged Abby to concentrate on her studies.

Abby shared her father's love of music and reading, and favored him in appearance—the same thick eyebrows above deep-set brown eyes, the same sloping nose, fine upper lip, and vivid complexion. But where her father was steady and careful, Abby was mercurial and rash. By her own account, Abby "was a good child—but willful."

When her parents suggested she marry one of her May cousins, Sam Frothingham, she resisted the idea; she wanted a love match. Her brother and ally Sam proposed to their parents that Abby spend a year studying with a Reverend Allyn in Duxbury, about thirty-five miles south of Boston. The courses in moral philosophy, natural theology, science, history, and Latin left Abby with a fleeting sense of possibility that she and her sister Louisa might together open a school. "I may yet earn my bread by the knowledge this year has afforded me. I am not willing to be thought incapable of anything," she wrote, as honest a self-assessment as she would ever make. Aware of his sister's inclination to despondency, Sam wrote to her of the importance of "a cheerful habit of mind. Cheerfulness is a kind of oil to the springs, and wheels of life. . . . Without it they may move, but they will move [badly and] all our duties will be performed with pain."

It was advice she was constitutionally unable to follow. Her Duxbury sojourn did not make her happier, and, living under threat of an unwanted marriage, Abby could scarcely believe in any of her schemes for an independent life. Then, in August 1819, Sam Frothingham died unexpectedly. Abby insisted she be excused from any obligation to pay or receive calls. "If I incur the epithet pedantic or unsocial or misanthropic, I must bear it patiently," she wrote, but patience was not a virtue she possessed. Louisa Alcott would not have it either.

·Abby's dream of starting a school with her sister ended with Louisa

May's marriage in 1823. She turned to her brother Sam, now a Unitarian minister embarking upon a distinguished career as a radical reformer as eloquent and fierce as he was sweet-tempered. Abby became a regular visitor at his home in the town of Brooklyn in eastern Connecticut, cheering on Sam's efforts to reform education, and taking to his wife, Lucretia ("Lu"), as a sister.

Abby's mother, Dorothy Sewall May, died in 1825; less than a year later Colonel Joseph May remarried. His new wife was just fourteen years older than his only remaining unmarried daughter. As a spinster of twenty-five, Abby could have hoped and expected to take on the role of lady of the house to her widowed father. Instead, disaffected with her father for remarrying and displaced by her stepmother, she paid a visit of indefinite length to her brother and congenial sister-in-law. On a hot afternoon in July of 1827, she was alone at the parsonage when a towering blue-eyed young man appeared at the door looking for Sam. Abby was almost twenty-seven and ripe for a serious attachment. After five minutes alone with Bronson Alcott, she was sure she had found it.

Of the small band of radical thinkers who defined the Transcendentalist movement of the early nineteenth century, Bronson Alcott was possibly the most original, certainly the most improbable. He was born Amos Bronson Alcox in the last year of the eighteenth century, into an isolated clan of farmers long settled in the northwestern corner of Connecticut. Their only news came in small weekly doses of the *Connecticut Courant*, read by the few literate to the many illiterate members of the family, among the latter Joseph Alcox, Bronson's father. Bronson's mother, Anna Bronson Alcox, though a genuine rustic who smoked a corncob pipe, could read, and taught her eager son to write the alphabet on the wood kitchen floor of the home they called Spindle Hill. She praised his gift for drawing too. Bronson was the first of Anna Alcox's eight children (of ten) to live past infancy; mother and son adored each other.

Bronson's years of rudimentary country education, interrupted for spring planting and the fall harvest, ended when he was thirteen. He and his cousin William Alcox, also avid for knowledge, embarked upon an ambitious plan of private study. Their self-improvement program extended to their surname: their common paternal grandfather, a Revolutionary War veteran, was Captain John Alcock, not Alcox. The pun-inviting family name was spelled several different ways, and none conjured the image of a cultivated gentleman. Young Bronson and William came up with the more refined "Alcott." William took up a middle name, "Andrus," and Bronson further improved his handle by reducing the plain "Amos" to its initial *A*. They assembled their own library of stray books hoarded by relatives, now and then scraping together enough money to purchase a volume. They acquired the poems of Pope, a volume of Milton, a copy of *Robinson Crusoe*, and more Bibles than they could use. They began a correspondence for their mutual edification, with marked success. Bronson succeeded in honing his intellect to the point where his friend Ralph Waldo Emerson opined that he could have talked with Plato. Dr. William Andrus Alcott wrote two of America's earliest modern-style marriage manuals: *The Physiology of Marriage* and *The Moral Philosophy of Marriage*.

"Eli's Education" is Louisa's romanticized account of her father's struggle to better himself with learning. She pictures him reading quietly "under the trees or by the fire" every chance he got, studying "as he went with the cows to and from the pasture, [sitting up] late in his little room, ciphering on an old slate, or puzzling his young brain over some question which no one could answer for him."

The farm boy sought in erudition a route to illumination, finding it first in a cousin's edition of John Bunyan's *Pilgrim's Progress*. Bunyan's 1678 allegory is a solemn picaresque whose everyman hero, Christian, makes a journey riddled with obstacles, burdens, and sacrifices (he leaves his wife and children), to go from the City of Destruction to the Celestial City. Christian's journey served as the template of Bronson's own, however many subsequent philosophies he piled upon it. He used *Pilgrim's Progress* to instruct his children, and Louisa in turn picked up the leitmotifs of burdens and pilgrim journeys in *Little Women* and *Work*, another largely autobiographical novel.

At fifteen, encouraged by his mother, Bronson won admission to Cheshire Academy, six miles from Spindle Hill and a near-certain path to Yale. He was homesick and uncomfortable among the better-dressed boys and left after a few weeks. For the next two years he worked for the Seth Thomas clock company in one of the factories that had sprung up in Connecticut's rocky fields. Although schoolteachers were paid less than factory workers, at seventeen Bronson took and passed the exam for his teaching certificate. When he was not given the post he hoped for, he became a Yankee peddler, first within his native Connecticut and later throughout the South.

Bronson, now a pilgrim-peddler, followed a path of learning. The Quakers of Albemarle Sound, North Carolina, instilled in him a belief in a direct personal relationship with God, a conviction of man's great intellectual and moral possibilities, and a material asceticism to coexist with his native appetite for beauty. In the South, Bronson's rough Yankee manners softened and grew more elegant when plantation owners admitted him to their elegant homes and fine libraries; when they didn't, he observed slavery intimately during nights sharing the crowded quarters of the field workers.

In five years as a peddler, Bronson's debts exceeded his profits. On his final trip, he walked the five hundred miles home to Connecticut, six hundred dollars in debt to his father.

At last Bronson landed a teaching job at the Cheshire public school. Eagerly he set out to overturn education as he had known it. He transformed the Spartan schoolroom along Athenian lines, dignifying his students as he added backs to the uncomfortable benches, improved the lighting and heating, and provided individual slates for writing, paying for it all himself. He banished the rote learning and memorization that suffocated curiosity, and avoided corporal punishment in favor of more respectful forms of social organization, including an honor system. He elicited his pupils' opinions, guiding their discussions along Socratic lines, posing questions rather than imparting facts.

Bronson's radical teaching practices were admired in the small circle of freethinking educators in New England, among them Abby's brother Sam May. In the spring of 1827, May wrote to Alcott, asking about his methods and philosophy. An invitation to visit May soon followed.

Bronson, not quite twenty-eight to the lovestruck Abby's not quite twenty-seven, projected a patrician grace and confidence completely at odds with his country upbringing. Her opposite in coloring, temperament, background, and education, Bronson was also the first eligible man Abby recognized as her intellectual and spiritual equal. Her pent-up thoughts on education, social reform, women's nature, and moral growth came spilling forth in a torrent. "I found . . . an intelligent, philosophic modest man . . . whose reserved deportment authorized my showing many attentions," she would explain. Abby found his "views on education . . . very attractive," although he was "not an educated man himself." Indeed, Samuel May "soon saw the indications of a mutual attraction." He, too, was dazzled by the young educator. "I have never been so taken by any man.

He seemed like a born sage and a saint." Bronson returned to Cheshire, and Abby proceeded to throw herself at his feet by mail. Excerpts from their journals and letters to others form twin soliloquies. Bronson: "An interesting woman [I] had often portrayed in imagination. In her [I] ... saw its reality." Abby: "I have been conquered by moral power, I serve moral excellence, I love moral rectitude." Bronson: "All was openness, simplicity itself. Everything seemed to favor an acquaintance of a sentimental kind." Abby: "I have something to live for."

The Yankee parents of Cheshire saw Bronson's teaching methods as lax and indulgent. By the time he met Abby, he had lost their children to a traditional school. After his next school went the same way, he took the advice of Sam May to join forces in Boston with Scottish-born William Russell, founder of the *American Journal of Education*. Russell expounded on the educational theories of Johann Pestalozzi, a Swiss follower of Jean-Jacques Rousseau, who believed that children were born with the seeds of understanding. A benign facilitator could cultivate and bring them to fruition. Here was a philosophical steed for Bronson Alcott, whose stable of intriguing new ideas would be stocked with a new favorite every year or two.

On his way to Boston to meet up with Russell, Bronson stopped to visit the May household again. Abby thought Bronson's manner formal and distant after ten months of flirtatious correspondence; perhaps Bronson, aware that he was in no financial position to propose, was afraid to encourage the forward Miss May. His reserve, wrote Abby, prompted her resolution to "avoid him as much as possible." Ten days later, however, she was on a carriage to Boston.

When Bronson Alcott first set foot in Boston in April 1828, the city was in a financial and intellectual boom. Armed with introductions from Sam May and his growing reputation in progressive education circles, he quickly landed a job as headmaster of a school for children on Salem Street in the North End. He boarded with William Russell at Mrs. Newall's on Franklin Street and mixed with the reform-minded crowd.

He met twenty-four-year-old Elizabeth Peabody, a brilliant protégée of Dr. William Ellery Channing, the influential Unitarian preacher. At a second job running the Chauncy Place Sunday School he heard young Ralph Waldo Emerson preach, and judged his sermon "a very respectable effort." By autumn, within five months of his arrival in Boston, Bronson Alcott had his own elementary school—sixteen scions of Boston's best families aged three to seven, paying seven dollars a quarter—for an annual wage equal to a third of his debt to his father.

In June Abigail May, eager for employment and hoping to melt Bronson's chilly demeanor by proximity, applied for a job as Mr. Alcott's teaching assistant and renewed their acquaintance. Realizing that her feelings for him were also renewed, and evidently his for her, she had second thoughts about her application; her boldness might cause tongues to wag. Sam cautioned his sister to withdraw. But Abby's overture got Bronson thinking about marrying the well-born Miss May. "We are unwilling she should engage in this school," Bronson noted in his journal, using the editorial *we* of the day, ". . . she should assist in the more desirable situation that we propose."

Abby accepted without consulting her brother or father, in keeping with her prickly independence and singular rules. "[Father] must approve what I have done, " she asserted. "He must receive [Mr. Alcott] as a son, [and] make him acquainted with my relations and friends. . . . They must cultivate his acquaintance for my sake; they will love him for his own."

His betrothed's "take no prisoners" state of mind was not lost on Bronson. "I cannot look with complacency on . . . that spirit of individualism which sometimes assumes the form of pride," he wrote her.

"I will modify it, if not eradicate it," she replied—and complained in her diary that Bronson had "delicately sketched what the object of his affection should be rather than what she is." It was a portent of decades of struggle to come.

Contrary to Abby's expectation, her family welcomed Bronson. "Mr. Alcott's visits afford us pleasure as we get more acquainted with him," Colonel May wrote his daughter, "but he is a man who must be drawn out."

Abby confided her hopes for the marriage in a letter to Sam. "I have something to love," she told him. "I have felt a loneliness in this world that was making a misanthrope of me in spite of everything I could do to overcome it."

That November, Abby's sister Louisa died, leaving behind two small children. Wedding plans were suspended for two years while Abby mothered Louisa's children at Sam and Lucretia May's home. Her lonesome fiancé lobbied with her father for her return to Boston, and the marriage ceremony finally took place in King's Chapel on May 23, 1830. Thirty-year-old Bronson wore a new blue swallowtail coat and fashionable white nankeen trousers pulled taut by straps concealed in his boots. His bell-shaped hat was white beaver; his cane topped with a carved ivory head. Abby's plaid silk walking dress had huge puff sleeves and a hooped hem that stood out a stylish six inches from the floor to reveal white-stockinged feet in black sandals. The twenty-nine-year-old bride's rich chestnut hair (which Louisa would inherit) was bunched in curls over each ear and on top, and her head was crowned by a broad-brimmed black beaver hat with an enormous matching plaid bow a full foot high. After the Reverend Samuel May pronounced bride and groom man and wife, a wedding supper for the few guests followed at Colonel Joseph May's Federal Court residence. Afterward Abby and Bronson walked to Franklin Street to begin married life at Mrs. Newall's boardinghouse.

Abby soon confided to Lucretia May, "I hope we may go through life affected by this lunacy. My husband (hallowed be the name) is all I expected—this is saying a good deal." Abby had married a man with a strong appetite for sex. He would put it in exalted terms a few years later: "Man and woman, united in love, one in members, one in soul." Within the month, Abby was pregnant.

"He is moderate," she had written to Sam. "I am impetuous. He is prudent and humble. I am forward and arbitrary. He is poor, but we are both industrious. Why may we not be happy?"

They were happy, but not with Boston. Attendance at Bronson's school dropped that summer, so when a wealthy Quaker, Reuben Haines, proposed that Bronson and William Russell start a school in Philadelphia, the offer was accepted. By mid-December 1830 the Alcotts had relocated. On March 16, 1831, Anna was born, blue-eyed and fair-haired like her father, and named for his mother.

Bronson Alcott was transfixed by his child. He began recording her every mood and movement with the patience of a scientist: "The subject of the following observations is a female. Respiration and crying, as usual, took place immediately after birth. . . . The power of vision seemed active, the eyelids opening, and the eyes moving. . . . She partook of her natural aliment an hour after birth. The usual indications of health and vital energy followed her introduction to existence." And so it went for a hundred pages, a record of infant development that presaged by a century the work of Arnold Gesell and Frances Ilg in *Infant and Child in the Culture of Today*. The unpublished manuscript is for the most part scientifically detached, but now and then Anna's angelic blonde beauty stirs Bronson to romantic rhapsody: "Behold the babe! It is a flame of light! Behold a halo around its head!"

However over-the-moon its master might be, soon after Anna's birth the Philadelphia school was losing pupils, and the carrying costs were prohibitive, so Bronson and Abby opened a smaller school in the suburb of Germantown and moved into rent-free quarters provided by their patron, Reuben Haines. The sun-filled white cottage, called the Pines, was roomy enough for their little family and ten student boarders. A housekeeper and cook would help with the care of them all. Abby loved most of all the large private grounds, "with a beautiful serpentine walk shaded by pines, firs, cedars, apple, pear, peach, and plum trees." The young couple took pleasure in furnishing the house with a "Pembroke table," the chair and bench covered in "a very beautiful French fabric," bronze busts of Newton and Locke, and a "row of book shelves fitted into a recess and painted white," but their purchases exhausted their small reserve. To make it through the summer they borrowed three hundred dollars from Colonel May, the man who had divested himself of even the rings on his fingers rather than live in debt. It was not his first loan to the Alcotts or his last. Over the next few years Abby applied to her father for funds repeatedly, always casting her husband's impracticality as principle, and their financial setbacks as other people's failures to give Bronson his due. After seeing his loans go to expensive new purchases while back bills went unsettled, and finding no indication that his son-in-law intended either to live within his means or to repay his father-in-law, Colonel May stopped lending money to the Alcotts. He was not ungenerous; at least once he treated his daughter's family to a summer vacation. But to give to the Alcotts was straightforward. To lend to them was to be caught in an endless cycle of evasions, pleas, excuses, accusations, and more pleas for more money.

In the fall of 1831, Bronson's patron, Reuben Haines, suddenly died, leaving no provision for his school. Boarders helped stretch the tiny household budget, but the cost to the Alcotts' privacy was high, the workload overwhelming, and the financial situation dire: "We hardly earn the bread,"

Abby wrote Sam in late August of 1831. "The butter we have to think about."

Before Anna was six months old, Abby became pregnant, but she miscarried. By the following March, she and Bronson had conceived Louisa. Abby's pregnancy with Louisa was "one of those periods of mental depression which women are subject to during pregnancy." She later cited it as the cause of her daughter's unsteady and extreme moods.

In the end, Louisa was born "a fine fat creature," larger and more active than her sister, despite her mother's milk not coming in for five days and the hired wet nurse failing to bathe her for nearly a week. Louisa would describe her struggle as a newborn: "first for a proper quantity of water for my ablutions which was unlawfully withheld from me, then for my rightful food which I was denied till I nearly went out of the world I disliked so much." She was a fitful infant, an affront to her father's conviction that newborn children came from heaven trailing clouds of glory. (Bronson was in a Wordsworthian period.) Louisa was also delightful, in her mother's words, "a sprightly, merry little puss—quirking up her mouth and cooing at every sound."

Bronson began to meticulously record Louisa's moral and physical development. If he found his younger child wanting in tranquillity, he also noted with satisfaction that Louisa was "fit for the scuffle of things." He wrote of her "unusual vivacity, and force of spirit," and called her "active, vivid, energetic." He noted her "power, individuality, and force." Unfortunately, a sprightly baby didn't pay for servants or feed the boarders.

Louisa was five months old in April 1833 when Bronson accepted an offer to open a day school in Philadelphia. The Pembroke table and the other fine furnishings were sold, and the Alcotts went to Mrs. Austie's boardinghouse, in keeping "with the measure of our pockets," Abby said. Louisa's first move was followed just two months later by a second move, to slightly larger rooms overlooking leafy State House Square. Abby began attending Quaker meetings, made friends with the feminist Lucretia Mott, and joined the nascent Female Anti-Slavery Society, where she met Sarah and Angelina Grimké, daughters of a slave-owning South Carolina judge, whose witness of slavery had made them fervent abolitionists. Bronson was teaching his students and himself, puzzling his way through the works of Plato, Aristotle, Bacon, and Kant.

It was a heady and rewarding time intellectually for both Abby and Bronson, but home life with two infants was straining the relationship. At age two, perfect Anna began assaulting her baby sister with kisses one minute and whacks the next. Louisa howled when unhappy, especially after a blow from Anna, and had the unsettling habit of throwing herself on the floor and burying her head between her knees. Abby must have been tempted to do the same when she learned she was pregnant for the fourth time in as many years.

Bronson reacted by withdrawing, announcing that he would stay in Philadelphia to teach and write; Abby and the girls would return to Germantown; he would visit on weekends. For two years he had been absorbed in their lives, eagerly monitoring their progress, lovingly feeding and bathing them, and admiring them at play. The sudden withdrawal of their father from daily contact must have affected the little sisters. Their mother's love was unconditional; their father's, apparently not.

In Philadelphia Bronson's new school venture unraveled as the earlier ones had; parents bewildered by his methods pulled their children out. One former student would recall Bronson Alcott as "the most eccentric man who ever took on himself to train and form the youthful mind."

Absence made the Alcotts' hearts grow fonder; between snatches of Plato's *Republic,* Bronson reflected on how his love for Abby might be revived. Abby longed for her handsome husband on days without her critical, self-absorbed dreamer.

On May 20, alone with the children in Germantown, Abby suffered a miscarriage. Hemorrhaging profusely, she was near death before she could get her addle-brained landlady to call for a doctor. While she recovered, her friend Lydia Maria Child and her sister-in-law Lucretia May shared long stints at Abby's bedside and care of Anna and Louisa. To the children it must have seemed that their father had left them, and that their mother was kept from them by kindly strangers.

Months later, when Abby was finally well enough to travel, the Alcotts packed their things. Bronson had a bright prospect in Boston. The redoubtable and generous Elizabeth Peabody was "*amazed* beyond measure at the composition" of his students' writing. Though on the verge of starting her own school, she threw in her lot—and her prospective pupils—with Bronson. He was "an embodiment of intellectual light," she wrote, "a man destined . . . to make an era in society."

Barely eighteen months old, Louisa had already lived at four different addresses. She would have dozens in her lifetime. Fortunately, she was a born explorer. As the family was boarding the steamer to Boston, she wandered away. After a long, anxious search, she was found in the hot, noisy, and dangerous engine room, playing happily, her white dress covered in soot.

TWO

THE LAW OF MIGHT

The Boston that welcomed the Alcotts in 1834 was no longer the premier city of the nation, or even the best harbor in New England, but it was a cosmopolitan center of trade and manufacturing, pulsing with the radical ideas of a generation that questioned everything their predecessors had held sacred: the nature of God, the meaning of a Christian life, the proper role of women, the treatment of Native Americans, the right to buy and sell other human beings, what the rich owed the poor. The city's post-Revolutionary intelligentsia rejected the Puritan Christianity of their forebears for the European ideals of the Enlightenment and for Romanticism. The friends the Alcotts would soon make had discarded religious authority in favor of their own observation, thought, and instinct as guides to the mysteries of life. Soon they would have a name for their ideas: Transcendentalism.

While most of his freethinking counterparts looked for God in nature, Bronson Alcott searched for the divine in his children's souls. His careful observations of the "Inner Life of their Spirits" resulted in a record of Louisa May Alcott's earliest years. Here is Louisa a month short of two years old, on an ordinary morning, October 27, 1834.

> Louisa shed a few tears while being dressed. She has been less irritable, I understand from her mother. She enjoyed Anna's society with several of the little ones at school for an hour. She took a nap at noon: went to bed,

shedding tears. Her mother deemed it best to discipline her into silence, crying on going to bed being one of her most confirmed habits.

Frustrated by his crying child, Bronson can sound like an unreconstructed Calvinist: "Louisa's deep-seated obstinacy of temper is far from being conquered. Submission is an act . . . she renders doubly painful by her resistance." But Bronson's strategy is not Cotton Mather's; he does not yell. "I find the readier way is to let her rage against herself; . . . the simplest request made in gentlest tone leads to [the desired] reaction." When she is bent on "pursuit of some favorite object, [or] ruffled by disappointment or opposition from her sister . . . the possibility of punishment . . . succeed[s] in controlling her."

~

While the Alcott sisters' quarrels dominated the family, the civic conflict over slavery was threatening to tear Boston apart. A powerful strain of abolitionist sentiment had been building for more than a century since the first antislavery tract, "The Selling of Joseph," by Abby's ancestor Samuel Sewall, was published in New England. Both Abby and Bronson had gone on record in favor of abolition early in their marriage. In November 1830 Bronson formed the Preliminary Anti-Slavery Society of Boston with William Lloyd Garrison, Reverend Samuel May, and Sam and Abby's cousin (another) Sam Sewall. In 1831 Garrison launched the passionate newspaper the *Liberator*. He organized the New England Anti-Slavery Society in 1832 and in 1833 founded the American Anti-Slavery Society, which broke new ground by declaring itself open to women, a de facto recognition that women—Abby among them—were already some of the strongest supporters of the cause.

~

At home, Louisa Alcott was developing the verbal talents that she would use to advance her parents' ideals. On the same day in 1834 that he let her rail unchecked, her father also noted: "In moods of quiet . . . she is most interesting. I had a long interview with her after she had laid herself in bed. Her thoughts come rushing after each other . . . so fast and so evanescent both in idea and expression that it was almost impossible to fasten them in the mind. They were all clear and vivid to her." He delighted in Louisa's "rapid progress in spoken language. She adds new words to her vocabulary daily. I believe she appreciates *all* the relations of expression, using every part of speech." Louisa became deeply involved in books, using them to build towers, or scrawling in the margins. Her tolerant father even let her put her mark on his journal by tracing her small hand on a page of his own handwriting.

Bronson was about to establish a groundbreaking school, thanks to Elizabeth Peabody, one of a generation of independent and mobile women who supplied models for young Louisa to emulate. Peabody had slipped easily into Boston's intellectual inner circle under the wing of Dr. William Ellery Channing, and pursued classical studies under nineteen-year-old Ralph Waldo Emerson, who recognized her as his intellectual equal and spiritual kin.

Emerson contributed an emphasis on self-reliance to the Transcendentalist movement through his influential essay of the same name; Peabody espoused the neglected but important social principle of interdependence. The social principle could be seen in action every day at Mrs. Clarke's boardinghouse, a hotbed of young intellect frequented by Waldo Emerson (he preferred "Waldo" to "Ralph") and Margaret Fuller, where Peabody developed an unrequited love for Horace Mann. Later, she had romantic feelings for her Salem neighbor, Nathaniel Hawthorne. Eventually, she would watch her sister Sophia marry Hawthorne, and her sister Mary marry Horace Mann. No one seemed to deserve more and benefit less from the social principle than Elizabeth Peabody.

She had already ceded to Bronson Alcott the handful of students she had been about to enroll in a school of her own, and now she energetically trolled for additional scholars among the best and most enlightened families of Boston. When Abby confided that Bronson was not qualified to teach Latin, arithmetic, or geography, Elizabeth (so financially strapped that she worked part-time as a governess) volunteered to be Bronson's assistant for two and a half hours a day, on the understanding that he would pay her what he could, when he could.

Bronson rented a pair of rooms on the upper floor of the recently completed Masonic Temple, a dramatic stone Gothic Revival building overlooking the Boston Common; the new institution became known as the Temple School. The grand, high-ceilinged room was flooded with light and furnished with custom-made bookcases and desks. Its walls were decorated with landscapes, portraits, and maps. In a contemporary sketch, a small but unmistakably nude statue of Psyche can be seen on a bookcase at eye level. This representation of the original Greek concept of self, or soul, reveals more about Bronson's thinking at this time than the other icons—Plato, Socrates, and Jesus—in the room.

Louisa's father understood that play was a powerful learning tool. In a charming passage in *Little Men,* she appropriated his method of teaching her to identify letters as patterns her body could form. Bronson would lie on his back and lift his legs to form a *V*; Louisa would copy him. Bronson would say "V," and Louisa would shout "V!" Her father would reach out one leg to join his foot to Louisa's and say "W," and Louisa would shout "W!" Bronson called the letter *I* the "egotist," and taught it to his daughters by having them strut across the room; *S* walked like a goose, hissing "sssssssssssss."

Temple School opening day, September 22, 1834: twenty students, most under age ten, and almost half girls—perhaps a reflection of parents' greater willingness to try the unconventional with girls—sat in a semi-circle around their tall, handsome teacher standing behind his tall, handsome desk. Mr. Alcott asked what they believed the purpose of school to be. "To learn" was the uniform answer, to which the teacher replied, "To learn what?" and continued, using the modified Socratic method he had first employed in Cheshire. "Every face was eager and interested," Elizabeth Peabody wrote. "The conversation naturally led into the necessity of feeling in earnest, of thinking clearly, and of school; Mr. Alcott's duty, and the children's individual duties, and the various means of producing attention, self-control, perseverance, faithfulness." Elizabeth Peabody's detailed notes would become the basis of a book published the following July, *Record of a School.*

Bronson had left the care of Anna and Louisa exclusively to Abby while he got the new school up and running. Exhausted from her last miscarriage and from three uprootings in as many months, Abby was becoming isolated. "Boston," she wrote her brother Sam, begging for a visit, "feels more like a sepulchre than a home to me. There are few here that I care anything about and fewer that care anything about me." She was soon just one step ahead of physical and emotional collapse, locked in combat with a pair of wild imps who vied for her attention day and night. Seeing the distress and chaos, as abruptly as he had bowed out of his children's daily life in Germantown, Bronson reinserted himself. He relieved Abby of her duties when he was home, and by occasionally taking Anna to school with him, shifted the household dynamic. Anna and Louisa's mornings now started with a leisurely soak in a tub filled with aromatic herbs, with plenty of unhurried time to play. At night, their father read them stories or respun familiar fables to incorporate their day's adventures. Having restored the benign domestic order he believed necessary, Bronson proceeded to shape his daughters' moral character using the same Socratic method he employed with his students. In place of external threats, he aimed to internalize conscience in his children by appealing to a child's natural desire to love a parent and be loved in return. With the eager-to-please Anna, Bronson's approach was an easy sell.

"Do you want to be good now?" he asked Anna after punishing her for some infraction. "Yes, I do," she answered.

"Do you think the punishment made you feel as you now feel?"

"Yes; you made me want to be good."

Louisa was a tougher nut to crack. When Anna reported that Louisa had pulled her hair and pinched her, Bronson administered the same treatment to Louisa, calmly.

> She hesitated a moment whether to mind the pain or not. At last she said, "Father, I was naughty to hurt Anna so."
>
> "Yes, Louisa, and what has father been doing to you?"
>
> "Hurting me," said she . . .
>
> "Father hurt Louisa to show her how she hurt Anna. Did you know that you hurt her so when you pulled and pinched?"
>
> She made no answer, but she understood me.

"There is a self-corroding nature," he would write of his younger daughter when she was not yet out of the nursery, "a morbid action of the spirit, induced by indulgence. The *will* has gathered around itself a breastwork of *Inclinations* and bids defiance to every attack."

Though in principle Bronson disapproved of corporal punishment, he quickly succumbed to it in a bout with his recalcitrant two-year-old at the dinner table.

> I told her she must stop crying and sit in the chair, or I should punish her—hurt her—for she "must mind father." "No! No!" she exclaimed with more vehemence than before. I said, "Father must spank Louisa if she does not do what he says. Will she?" "No! No! Sit with mother," she reiterated. I spanked her. She cried the louder. I then told her that she must sit on her little chair by the side of her mother, and be still, or I should punish her more. She was unwilling to give up her purpose, and set up crying again. I repeated the punishment, and did not attain peace and quiet for her, 'till I had repeated it again.

The Temple School, meanwhile, was thriving. It was both a school and a salon, a glittering showcase for Bronson's theories and a magnet for Boston's intellectual elite, who observed the proceedings from the comfortable green velvet visitors' couch under the enormous Gothic window. The eminent Dr. Channing—whose portrait hung on the wall and whose daughter Mary was enrolled in the school—put in an appearance, though he was less generous in his praise than Bronson had hoped. The English social critic Harriet Martineau, on a tour of the United States, also stopped in that first winter, and the not-yet-famous Ralph Waldo Emerson was deeply impressed.

In the spring of 1835, the Alcotts persuaded Elizabeth Peabody to join them at their boardinghouse. Abby, pregnant for the fifth time in four years and starved for adult company, was grateful to have Elizabeth to talk to and occasionally relieve her by reading to the girls. The arrival of a third daughter at sunset on June 24 was unremarkable except that Bronson witnessed the birth. Wild Louisa had been sent away to relatives. When she returned, Anna led her into the room to see her baby sister. "It has a little head and pretty hair, let me take it in my arms" was Louisa's response, as recorded by Bronson in the journal he began within moments of his third daughter's arrival in the world, and would later title "Psyche."

But the appearance of the new baby—whom Bronson regarded from the first as a distinctly celestial being—prompted a fresh wave of Louisa's wildness. In contrast to the virtuous Anna, Louisa behaved like the displaced two-year-old she was. "I don't love little sister, I wish she was dead, I will throw her out the window," her father recorded her saying. Punished for her outburst, she was later found sobbing in bed, proclaiming her badness. "I am very naughty. I feel bad. . . . Father don't love me, mother don't love me, little sister don't love me, God won't love me." Though she repented and received her father's absolution, the refrain that she was bad and consequently unloved would shadow Louisa's self-image for years. In contrast, "little sister" Lizzie would become the family saint, protected and adored by all the family—most fervently by Louisa, who immortalized her as Beth in *Little Women*.

In a tribute either genuinely meant or shrewdly balanced against a debt he knew he was unlikely ever to repay, Bronson had suggested that they call the new baby Elizabeth Peabody Alcott. Abby made no objection, as the name also memorialized Abby's sister Eliza, who had died at twenty-three, probably during or soon after childbirth. The ties between the Alcotts and Peabody were publicly reinforced a month later with the publication of Peabody's *Record of a School,* an immediate success within the small audience of enlightened educators and parents Peabody and Bronson had hoped to win.

The new school term opened with a doubled roster of nearly forty students, the addition of a drawing teacher, and a schedule of lectures on literature by the essayist Richard Henry Dana (whose namesake son would write *Two Years Before the Mast*). Although Elizabeth Peabody had resolved over the summer that she could not afford to work for Bronson without payment much longer (and distanced herself by boarding with her sister Mary), she again took up her teaching duties and her note-taking. The success of *Record of a School* had given Bronson the idea for a sequel, to be called *Conversations with Children on the Gospels*.

That triumphal autumn brought two events that would resonate in Louisa's memory. One was political, alarming, and thrilling; the other was personal and poignant.

In the 1830s Boston was the epicenter of the abolitionist movement, but abolition was a serious threat to economic stability in a city where the fortunes of many prominent citizens were founded upon the slave trade, and new fortunes were being made in the mills supplied by Southern cotton. The Alcotts and their friends were dangerously ahead of popular opinion. In advance of an October 1835 antislavery meeting, Bronson Alcott overheard talk of five-hundred-dollar bounties for the capture and delivery of abolitionists to be tarred and feathered, a horribly painful and sometimes fatal form of vigilante justice. A mob of several thousand gathered, and the British abolitionist George Thompson was targeted. Thompson had been warned and did not appear at a public lecture, but the mob's blood was up. Next door, working in his office, was William Lloyd Garrison, the outspoken editor of the antislavery *Liberator.* The mob stormed the building by a back entrance, seized Garrison, and dragged him through the streets by a rope tied around his neck. Garrison's sympathizers pushed their way through and hustled Garrison to safety. He spent the night under official protection in the Leverett Street jail, before leaving Boston the next morning to make himself scarce for several months.

Afterward the Alcotts' rooms filled with agitated abolitionists gathered to discuss Garrison's and Thompson's near misses. Louisa slipped away to hide under the bed, where the Alcotts had hidden Thompson's portrait, to "comfort the 'good man who helped poor slaves.'" She often said she became an abolitionist at the age of three.

A month later, Louisa shared the center of attention at a party held at the Temple School on the occasion of her third birthday and Bronson's thirty-sixth. As birthday girl she was given the honor of handing out the refreshments—individual plumcakes, sweet pastries the size of cupcakes. When the last few children approached to claim their treats, it was clear even to a three-year-old that that there were not enough to go around. "By some oversight," she recalled, "the cakes fell short, and I saw that if I gave away the last one *I* should have none. As I was queen of the revel, I thought that I ought to have it, and held on to it tightly till my mother said, 'It is always better to give away than to keep nice things; so I know my Louy will not let the little friend go without.' The little friend received that dear plummy cake, and I a kiss and my first lesson in the sweetness of self denial." Bronson, who had been presented with a fine edition of *Paradise Lost*, remarked in his journal that "the whole celebration gave much pleasure." Louisa remarked thirty years later in hers that her birthdays were always dismal.

Feeling flush the following spring, the Alcotts rented a large house and grounds on Front Street, on the south side of the Common. There Anna, just turned five, and Louisa, three and a half, continued their contest for domination. When Anna came down with a cold and a sprained ankle, Louisa seized the upper hand, "Louisa having her sister more under her power from her perfect helplessness," observed Bronson. "Anna seemed to fear her sister's approaches and so alarming has she become to her that some discipline will be needed to reduce Louisa to tameness. She seems practically the law of might.... Anna ... wears the mark of her sister's hand at present on her cheek!"

Little Louisa seems to have conquered her sister by a calculated show of force. "Louisa, from the mere love of action, often assaults her sister and looks on to see what will be the result of her temerity." She seemed ready to take on the entire family. "Her violence is at times alarming," Bronson reported. "Father, mother, sister, objects all are equally defied, and not infrequently the menace ends in blows. . . . Sitting with me today Louisa held my hand in hers, and while enjoying the sense of bodily contact, she seemed to be instinctively tempted to pinch me."

Her father suspected "that Louisa's untamable spirit derives something of its ferocity from the nature of her diet." Louisa liked to eat meat. Bronson became a vegetarian before the word was coined, and although Louisa would publicly declare herself a "vegetable production," she remained a carnivore at heart and served expensive cuts of meat once she had the means and opportunity.

Bronson was probably the first to realize that "Louisa's spirit seems to limit its labors in self-control to short periods," but when she was interested, his daughter was capable of calm concentration. "I found at the book store some very appropriate little books," he noted in 1836. Alcott was distressed at the poor state of children's literature; he would eventually press Louisa to devote her literary gifts to children, because they deserved better—inadvertently making the family fortune. "The cuts [pictures] are better than those usually given in children's books and are *colored*." When he showed his purchase to her, he was "much interested in the intensity and abstraction of thought awakened in Louisa's mind from the inspection of these pictures. Seated in her little chair, she spent a half hour on them."

Although she "seemed rather unwell today—she had a severe fall the other day—she is very lively, however, and thrives beyond all my expectations. She is a perfect image of luxuriant childhood. . . . Hers is the wild exuberance of a powerful nature. . . . Here is a deep and affluent nature." For Anna's relative delicacy, what was needed was "love, kindness, with little vigor of reproof." For Louisa's force, talent, and violence, Bronson prescribed "discipline mingling severity and kindness."

As a father who allowed his children to play naked after their bath, Bronson could not help but note that "Louisa's form discloses itself in beautiful proportions. Her physical being seems modeled on a dignified and imposing type: and the characteristic traits of her spirit . . . partake of a similar boldness and amplitude."

After a tranquil half-year boarding with her sister Mary, Elizabeth Peabody rejoined the Alcotts. Shortly after settling in at Front Street, Elizabeth reported to her brother George on its "neat light parlor" and welcoming atmosphere. She had been given a large front room on the second floor, with a fireplace and a view, which she quickly arranged to suit her orderly habits. "You cannot think what luxury my life is now," she told George, and wrote to Mary, using the customary personal plural, "It was really delightful to find ourselves in a small family by ourselves."

Over the course of the school year, however, Elizabeth Peabody had come to doubt the wisdom of Bronson's approach to teaching. She especially disliked how he invited students to defy him and then punished them by public shunning—making visible what it meant to lose God's love, he maintained. Adding to her unease over Bronson in the schoolroom, and his lordly dismissal of any views but his own, was her distress over Abby's ranting about Harriet Martineau, whom Elizabeth had befriended during the English writer's Boston visit. Perhaps Abby had an inkling that upon her return to England, Martineau would write an unflattering article about the Temple School. Martineau, according to Abby, could not appreciate a moral subject and did not care about the poor. Elizabeth wrote her sister Mary that same night, saying "No pen can do any justice to the impetuosity with which all this was poured out. She went out still speaking—so there was no time to answer it . . . and when she had gone I trembled from head to foot with clear rage—and if this is the style in which she intends to go on—I think it will be more comfortable to live on the top of a whirlwind than to live with her." She was not the first and would not be the only one to liken Abby to a malevolent force of nature. Abby's husband had already, before their marriage, cited a hurricane by comparison.

Peabody's unease continued to grow as she transcribed Alcott's *Conversations with Children on the Gospels*. Bronson was not a churchgoer, did not believe in the divinity of Christ, had even studied Hinduism and flirted with reincarnation, but he believed that the Bible, and especially the Gospels, were worthy texts for the education of young souls.

"We are now going to speak of the Life of Christ," begins the published version of *Conversations*. ". . . You will all try, I hope, to keep [your thoughts] steady. . . . The best thoughts do not lie on the surface of our minds. We have to dive under for them, like pearl fishers."

Dive they did, inexorably, toward the mysteries of life itself by way of the births of John the Baptist and Jesus, with frequent reference to the children's own beginnings. After reading an account of John's birth, Bronson invited the children's comments.

> NATHAN.   I don't see why John came in the night. All other babies come in the day.
>
> MR. ALCOTT.   No, more frequently in the night. God draws a veil over these sacred events, and they ought never to be thought of except with reverence. . . . Men have been brought before the Courts of Justice for saying vulgar things about the birth of Christ; and all birth is as sacred as Jesus Christ's.

Bronson told the children that an angel of love announces to a mother that a child is coming, and vaguely mentioned that she later has other signs. He inquired if they knew the meanings of *quicken* and *conceive*, and asked, "How is the body made?" Precocious six-year-old Josiah Quincy said, "By the naughtiness of people." Another child volunteered, "The mother has something to do with making the body." Alcott said, "A mother suffers when she has her child. . . . She gives up her body to God and he works on it in a mysterious way and brings forth the child's spirit in a little body of its own." (One ten-year-old boy opined, "I think it ought to be the father. He is so much stronger.") Alcott verged on the explicit with remarks like "Love begets love, and is not a baby love made flesh . . . ?" Elizabeth Peabody had little doubt how these suggestive exchanges would be received by the public. She wrote to Mary of her concern for her own reputation, and Mary, who had worked for Bronson briefly, advised her to quit the project if she could not ensure its integrity.

Returning one evening, Elizabeth discovered Bronson and Abby waiting for her. "Mrs. Alcott came into my room & looked over my letters from you & found your last letter to me & carried it to Mr. Alcott," she wrote Mary in disbelief.

"Miss Peabody left me today for Salem," Bronson recorded in his journal for August 1. "She will not resume her connections with the school after the holidays."

Elizabeth Peabody's place at Bronson's side was filled by her delicate, headache-prone younger sister Sophia, who adored all the Alcotts on first acquaintance, reporting that at the breakfast table Louisa broke into a broad smile and said, "I love everybody in dis *whole* world." Later Sophia would say, "[Louisa's] *force* makes me retreat sometimes from an encounter." Sophia was followed at the Temple School by the learned and bold Margaret Fuller. Bronson's stellar quintet of better-educated assistants included Dorothea Dix, who did not take to teaching and afterward suffered a breakdown and went for treatment to England—returning to agitate for the reform of institutions for the mentally ill. Alcott's Temple School was truly a crossroads where the burgeoning transcendentalist philosophers and social activists, male and female, came to be "refreshed with the living waters that flow soft by the oracles of God, and descend in gentle dew and small rain through the eternal azure of Mr. Alcott's spirit," as Sophia Peabody put it. No wonder she would inspire the rapture Nathaniel Hawthorne expressed in his letters to her.

The skies opened when the first volume of *Conversations with Children on the Gospels* was published at the end of 1836 (at Bronson's expense, more than seven hundred dollars). In deference to Elizabeth Peabody's opinion, he made a disastrous compromise and placed all her suggested deletions in an appendix, the better for critics to spot. In his journal Bronson remarked upon the "unusual degree of excitement [that] has pervaded this metropolis" regarding his book. Abby's brother Sam had been right when he wrote that he didn't "expect this book to meet with a very favorable reception."

Boston's reaction to *Conversations* was pitiless. "A more indecent and obscene book (we can say nothing of its absurdity) than any other we ever saw exposed for sale on a bookseller's counter," thundered the *Boston Courier*. "Radically false and mischievous," pronounced the *Daily Advertiser*. The *Courier*'s editor one week said Bronson must be "either insane or half-witted," and the next called him "an ignorant and presuming charla-tan." Andrews Norton, the eminent professor of sacred literature at Har-vard, called the book "one third absurd, one third blasphemous, and one third obscene."

Bronson's fellow Transcendentalists rallied to the defense of the man who was at the center of their nascent movement. Margaret Fuller wrote to one paper to say that Bronson was a philosopher worthy of "the palmy times of ancient Greece," before Socrates was made to drink hemlock for corrupting the Athenian youth. High-minded Elizabeth Peabody rose above their dispute to support her former colleague for attempting to free children from the "imposition of the adult mind upon the young mind." Friends sent Bronson notes expressing their outrage and sympathy. Waldo Emerson was pained for the man he felt to be "wise" and "simple"; "[a man] who grows upon me every time I see him." He wrote to his new friend, "I hate to have all the little dogs barking at you." Among themselves, the members of Alcott's circle marveled at his calm.

Bronson did not fail to notice "the clamor and misapprehension" that ringed around him, "sounding forth even from the children in the street," who called him names and lobbed stones in his direction. Louisa and her sisters could have witnessed such scenes during walks with their father on Boston Common. "At one time the excitement threatened a mob," Bronson reported, but apparently the necessary critical mass was lacking. It was not the last time Bronson Alcott would fall short of martyrdom.

He and Abby remained certain of ultimate vindication. Abby felt that society owed her a debt and would ultimately pay it. Her stance of wounded nobility fueled her for the economic trials to come. Their credi-tors, responding to a deep recession, pounced; despite the success of the school, the Alcotts were one thousand dollars in debt. Between the high tuition, the poor economy, and the "sex education" scandal, Bronson's crucial paying constituency—parents—found reason to withdraw his scholars. By spring, the Temple School was down to ten students, and Bronson was forced to sell his beautiful classroom furnishings and li-brary. Margaret Fuller wrote to plead that the unique collection of chil-dren's literature be spared if at all possible, but it was not. The school moved from the light, airy top floor of the Masonic Temple to a window-less room in the basement. The big house on the Common was surren-dered in favor of smaller quarters in the undesirable South End.

⌒

Louisa, four years old, kept running away. As the successful author of the autobiographical children's story "Poppy's Pranks," she appreciated that "She wasn't a wilfully naughty child . . . but very thoughtless and very curious. She wanted to see everything, do everything, and go everywhere: she feared nothing, and so was continually getting into scrapes." One time, thrilled by new green shoes, she showed them "to the servants, the cat, the doves, and the flowers, and then opened the gate that the people in the street might see," and wandered into the streets of Boston, down to the wharves, where she showed her green shoes to some sailors.

She lost her bearings as night fell. Finally, "a big dog welcomed me so kindly that I fell asleep with my head pillowed on his curly back, and was found there by the town crier. . . . My fun ended next day when I was tied to the arm of the sofa to repent at leisure." Undaunted, on another escapade she shared a grubby picnic with some Irish immigrant children in the ash heaps.

Bronson's characterization of Louisa at this age, though flowery to the modern reader, comes close to his aspiration to reveal his child's "spirit."

> On the impetuous stream of instinct she has set sail and regardless alike of the quicksand and the rock, of the careering winds and winter currents that oppose her course, she looks only toward the objects of her desires and steers proudly, adventurously, and yet without compass or chart save the gale and gleaming stars of her own will, toward the heaven of her hopes. The stronger the opposing gale, the more sullenly and obstinately does she ply her energies and when compelled to yield, she yields but to await the calming of the angry waters that she may ride on again toward her end.

THREE

THE TOPSEY TURVEY GIRL

After the Temple School debacle the family retrenched, and despite the fault line that ran through it—between Abby and Louisa on one side, Bronson and Anna on the other, and Lizzie floating above, not quite of this squabbling world—they tolerated the blows and losses without turning upon each other.

Even in their reduced material and social circumstances Abby Alcott remained proud and fiercely loyal to the man she had married for love. "You have seen how roughly they have handled my husband," she wrote her brother Sam. "He has been a quiet sufferer. . . . I rail; he reasons, and consoles me as if I were the injured one. I do not know a more exemplary hero under trial than this same 'visionary.'" She was the injured one, working like a domestic servant (she knew, because she had grown up with servants), while her husband didn't bring in money enough to provide food.

Of more concern to Abby were their children—specifically, living long enough to see them into adulthood. Approaching thirty-seven, she was pregnant for the sixth time, and it did not require a morbid personality to imagine the worst possible outcome as the end of her pregnancy drew near. Abby had lost three adult sisters in (or soon after) miscarriage or childbirth. She had deep and well-founded fears about her own survival, which Bronson, who had not been there when she had nearly hemorrhaged to death in Germantown, did not comprehend.

It was all too much for Abby. In June of 1837 she stepped back from marriage and motherhood for the first but not the last time, entrusting the children to Bronson and going alone to visit Sam and Lu May in Scituate, a seaside town to the south of Boston. Soon after she got there she miscarried; by the time she was well enough to return home, Bronson was ill.

Hearing that his friend was not well, in late July Waldo Emerson sent money for the pressing bills, along with an invitation for Bronson to stay with him in Concord. "My wife is a capital nurse, and joyfully offers her service." Bronson gladly accepted and spent four leisurely days recuperating in Concord.

Emerson's deep and lifelong attachment to Alcott probably owed something to timing. At their first weekend colloquy, in 1835, they were joined by Emerson's beloved brother Charles. Emerson felt comfortable and expansive with them both. Both men helped Emerson to clarify his thoughts and stimulated him to eloquence as no others could. Charles Emerson died just a few months after that meeting; the grief-stricken Waldo turned to Bronson Alcott in part as a replacement. Alcott's Temple School ordeal, his loss of the beautiful classroom with the green velvet visitors' couch, where Emerson had sat and heard his own truths issue from little children, inspired Emerson to take on the role of protector of Alcott and his family.

Three years after opening in the aerie of the Masonic Temple, Bronson's basement school had only six paying students. "We are as poor as rats," Abby wrote her brother in October 1838. "Dr. Alcott [Bronson's cousin and boyhood partner in study, William] is to take half our house." The family depended on handouts of clothing, food, and the occasional cash gift. To feel justified asking for loans and accepting gifts, Abby needed to believe that the Alcotts were better than other people. Her choice of a husband who did not support his family or pay his debts would mark her as an utter failure unless her husband could claim moral superiority. He lived above the material plane. Despite the shrinkage all around him, Abby could say, "Mr. A is of good comfort" and "Poverty presents no terrors to him." While she did the worrying for them both, her husband was absorbed with the manuscript of "Psyche," his account of the spiritual development of Elizabeth Alcott, now age three. She was Elizabeth *Sewall* Alcott now; Abby had banished "Peabody" from her name and replaced it with her mother's.

Abby miscarried in February 1838, for the second time in eight months. The extended family came forward once more: Dr. Charles Windship, widower of Abby's sister Catherine, kept watch for two weeks while Abby hovered between life and death. After that, she was delirious on and off for weeks, crying out her fears of what might become of her daughters if she died. Lydia Maria Child replaced Windship at Abby's bedside and later wrote that she had never known a more heroic woman. But Abby herself reported to Sam that in her lowest moments she had been ready to surrender. "I care less for this world than ever," she wrote, in a note that began with belated thanks for a sack of potatoes, "and when for 24 hours I balanced into another, I felt a serene satisfaction which I may never know again, and which I could not account for."

Louisa's whereabouts during her mother's illness is unclear. She was sent away, probably to her Grandfather May, the closest nearby relative. While Joseph May's relations with his daughter were strained by his refusals of Abby's requests for money and Abby's dislike of her stepmother, in a family crisis he would take in his five-year-old granddaughter, as difficult as she turned out to be.

"She got so wild that no one could manage her but mamma, and she was ill; so [she] was sent away to grandpa's," Louisa wrote in "Poppy's Pranks." She plied her grandfather, "a very stately old gentleman," with "all manner of impolite questions": why didn't he have hair, why did he snore, why did he turn out his feet when he walked? After a day or two of "respectable" behavior, she was frantic with boredom. She "wanted to run in the street, and longed to see mama," but settled instead for exploring the "rather dull" house. "She found a big empty room on the topmost floor, where she liked to lean out of the window as far as she could, and look at the people in the street, with her head upside down. It was very dangerous, for a fall would have killed her; but the danger was the fun."

When the delirious Abby wailed about what might become of her girls if she died, Louisa was surely the girl she meant. Anna and Lizzie could control themselves; Louisa needed her mother to reel her in from the perilous heights of excitement, and to pull her out of the depths of despair at the other extreme of her careening moods.

It took almost two months for Abby to recover. When Louisa's temperamental twin of a mother could finally resume the running of her household, she did it with a vengeance, as if she needed to demonstrate anew her talents as a mother, and to make plain her indispensability.

Bronson escaped his wife's volcanic displays of practicality with increasingly frequent visits to Concord, occasionally walking the eighteen miles for the pleasure of seeing roses run riot over fences along the route. "I spent three days with Emerson this week," he wrote in late June of 1838. From his big white house overlooking the Lexington Road, Emerson played the twin roles of literary eminence and gracious host. Bronson described his friend's idyllic life: "He gives his days to observations of nature, . . . to use in his lectures. There he also sees his friends, and . . . interviews with these supplies matter, also, for the Diary. Hence the freshness of all his discourses, taken as these are from life and nature."

The contrast between Emerson's comfortable life in Concord and his own grubby struggle for survival in the South End seems never to have troubled the "serene" Bronson Alcott. Once, his income and prominence had equaled Emerson's. Now, with the settlement from his first wife's family, Emerson had an assured income of twelve hundred dollars a year. Since the 1835 publication of *Nature*—an essay that borrowed heavily from Bronson Alcott's journals—he had been in constant demand as a writer and lecturer. Emerson hoped he could use his influence to help his inspiring friend Alcott build a career as a writer. They discussed "Psyche," and Bronson left the manuscript for Emerson to "decide on [its] fitness for publication." A week after his return from Concord, he recorded Emerson's evaluation of "Psyche." Notwithstanding Emerson's earlier encouragement and hopes, he found "Psyche" unpublishable (and so it has remained). "When he sits down to write," Emerson related, "all his genius leaves him; he gives you the shells and throws away the kernel of his thought." Bronson took the rejection with superhuman calm: "I judge the counsel wise, and feel inclined at present to lay [the book] aside . . . for worthier composition at some future day."

Abby was not calm: "It never was so dark with us," she had written her mother-in-law the month before. It would get darker still. The Temple School closed in June of 1838. The receipts for the four years of its existence came to $5,387, but expenditures had exceeded the total by $5,000. Bronson Alcott had begun the school $1,000 in debt; now he owed the astronomical sum of $6,000. Even so, the family again took rooms for the summer in Scituate near Lu and Sam May. To get out of the city in pestilent weather was a necessity. How the lodgings were paid for, or if they were paid for, is unclear; the Alcotts had fallen into a pattern of moving to ever-smaller and shabbier places, leaving accounts unsettled.

While the three Alcott sisters ran carefree with their cousins, probably only Anna was conscious of the family's financial free fall. Abby enjoyed being with her beloved Lu and Sam, and Bronson pieced together a miniature lecture circuit to peddle conversation as he had once peddled thread and tea cozies to Southern planters' wives. At thirty-nine, he was still a commanding figure, tall and graceful, with a high-domed forehead, eyes of sky blue, and a riveting, almost hypnotic manner that owed something to certainty that his was a spiritual mission. The guided discussions he called "Conversations" were especially popular among intellectual women shut out of higher learning. The intelligent sisters, wives, and daughters of Boston's educated men flocked to the new Lyceum to hear talks by Ralph Waldo Emerson and Horace Mann, and packed the sermons of eloquent preachers such as Dr. William Ellery Channing at the Arlington Street Church. Bronson Alcott hoped to find a niche and a living among them. He continued to teach the young in a school at home, with his daughters as the nucleus of his class.

Six-year-old Louisa Alcott moved into her twelfth new home on dusty, noisy Beach Street, a few blocks away from the Common, in the autumn of 1838. Her father talked his old colleague William Russell into moving his family in with the Alcotts, to share the cost. In an ad hoc classroom in the parlor he taught Russell's son Frank along with Anna, Louisa, and Lizzie, and some half dozen other students he had found through advertising.

Louisa's education would take place only rarely in a classroom other than her father's, and during those brief periods she would enjoy school mostly for the opportunity to meet good playmates. She knew her letters (though she couldn't master arithmetic), and now she would learn to focus her mind for the study of words—tools she would use to excavate life's meaning. Bronson taught one word at a time, asking, to use an example recorded by Elizabeth Peabody at the Temple School, "What ideas does the word *blade* bring into your mind?" and then calling for the students' contributions: "A spire of grass, and the part of the knife that cuts, said one. The next added, a gay young man; the next, a sword; the next, a scythe. . . . Mr. Alcott then read [Dr Samuel] Johnson's definition, and spoke of the blades of corn, and quoted the expression in the Bible, 'first the blade, then the ear; then the full corn in the ear.'"

For Louisa, words became as tangible as the letters she had enacted with her father. Words were like actors who could play different roles in many contexts. They could be seized and mastered and made to dance like dolls or march like warriors. Words were Louisa's playthings for the tongue and the page, her nonviolent means to power, her passport to riches. That is, if she could resist being distracted by Frank Russell—the "first . . . boy, to whom I clung . . . with a devotion which I fear he did not appreciate." Getting his attention, then earning his respect was a test of her mettle.

Frank "was something of a tyrant" and tried to make Louisa cry by slapping her hands "with books, hoop-sticks, shoes, anything that came along capable of giving a good stinging blow." She felt rewarded when she heard Frank tell the other boys, "She's a brave little thing, and you can't make her cry." But her show of bravery did not win the tomboy Louisa admission to play football on the Common with the boys. "I revenged myself by driving my hoop all around the mall without stopping, which the boys could *not* do." Girls' pastimes were for individuals or small groups, never for competing teams. Girls who craved athletic combat, camaraderie, and the suspense of choosing sides were out of luck.

As winter closed in, Louisa and her "first well-beloved boy," Frank, explored a piano factory behind the house, the perfect arena for the physical risk-taking she craved. She would describe themselves climbing into the carts used for rolling "heavy loads from room to room, and . . . go thundering down the ramps, regardless of the crash that usually awaited us at the bottom."

Outside the classroom, Bronson's new venture, a series of Conversations on topics such as "Free Will," "Instinct," and the "Theory and Practice of Self-Culture," sometimes sold only half a dozen tickets, sometimes as many as fifty, but too few to turn a profit. Either Bronson didn't notice the poverty crowding in on every side, or the "Hoper"—the nickname Bronson's mother gave him, and Abby adopted—didn't want to upset his mother. He wrote to her at Spindle Hill in an optimistic vein: "[I am] living by talking more than by my school, and shall be able, by and by, I trust to live by this entirely. . . . So you see I am still the same Hoper that I have always been." Then he mentioned that he and Abby expected a baby boy. "His sisters will jump for joy," he predicted.

Abby was not joyful about sharing her parlor with a school and her kitchen with another family, not to mention her womb with another child who might not live to be born. But she usually liked the quiet evenings each week when Bronson would read to her from his journal. (Louisa, too, had happy evenings of puppy love, with Frank Russell. "We snuggled in sofa corners and planned tricks and ate stolen goodies, and sometimes Frank would put his curly head in my lap and let me stroke it when he was tired," Louisa wrote in *My Boys*.) But one journal-reading evening in early February, Abby took umbrage at Bronson's treatment of her in his pages. "She thought some passages, particularly such as had reference to herself, were caricatures," he explained. "I said that I wrote from my convictions, and what seemed to me plain fact." Abby would not let Bronson's record stand. She excised hundreds of offending pages with her sewing shears, and a few days later sent her vegetarian husband to the butcher shop. "Death yawns at me as I walk up and down in this abode of skulls. Murder and blood are written on its stalls. . . . I feel myself dispossessed of the divinity," he said of the experience. Not only was he horrified; he was humiliated when Abby dressed him down for bringing home an overpriced inferior piece of meat. Dispossessing her husband of divinity while she was earthbound and pregnant was just the comeuppance Abby had in mind.

Louisa, too, was disappointed by her man. "I did something very naughty, and when called up for judgment fled to the dining room, locked the door, and from my stronghold defied the whole world." But Frank betrayed her. He "climbed in the window, unlocked the door, and delivered me up to the foe." She never forgave him.

Apparently Louisa had not learned the meaning of the word *blame*. At the Temple School, Elizabeth Peabody recorded that "one little boy said, to blame was to punish; another said it was to scold. . . . A good deal was said of bearing blame meekly."

Louisa did not bear blame at all. Like her mother, she thought that other people wronged her. When Frank brought her to justice for something "very naughty," she handed him a life sentence of shunning. "Peanuts and candy, ginger-snaps and car rides were unavailing; even football could not reunite the broken friendship." He had humiliated her. In a clash of peers she had to be dominant, especially when the peer was a boy. "No boy could be my friend until I beat him in a race," she wrote in "Recollections of Childhood."

Early in April, at full term and following a long and exhausting labor, Abby gave birth. As Bronson had predicted, the baby was a boy. He was "full grown, perfectly formed, but not living," Abby wrote with eerie precision, adding a pathetic wish "for one vital spark of that heavenly flame to rekindle, reanimate its cold and quiet clay." Bronson retrieved his copy of the letter predicting the birth of another Hoper and scribbled a bitter postscript: "My thrill of hope proved a pang of grief—a true son of its mother—a joy in a winding sheet."

After miscarriage, birth, or stillbirth, the nineteenth-century woman emerged weak from loss of blood, with only her immune system and bed rest as her defense against infection. She needed protection from demanding children, and they needed protection from her germs; germs were still an unknown concept, but contagion was all too familiar. So while Abby recovered from the stillbirth, three-year-old Lizzie was sent to stay with her grandfather Colonel May, who might have suggested that wild Louisa was too much for him. Anna, just turned eight, visited her Windship cousins but was home through most of Abby's recovery, being self-controlled and useful. Louisa, six and a half, had to be exiled. She appears to have stayed with friends, not relatives, fifty miles away at a communal farm in Providence, Rhode Island.

She must have felt banished to a strange, faraway land. There were no children to play with, only young adults. One of the young men, called Christy, let Louisa "ride the cows, feed the pigs, bang on the piano, and race all over the spice mill, feasting on cinnamon and cloves . . . but in a week [she] had exhausted every amusement and was desperately homesick." A letter to the Alcotts from a "Miss C" of Providence confirmed that "she has had several spells of feeling sad." Louisa sent home a carefully printed letter saying she was unhappy. Louisa could write now.

In good moods Louisa was supremely charming. "She is a beautiful little girl to look upon, and I love her affectionate manners," Miss C said in a second letter that must have crossed in the mail with Bronson's consoling reply to Louisa. He had used print rather than cursive handwriting—"[so] you can read it all yourself." He acknowledged her homesickness: "You want to see us all I know. And we want to see you very much. Be a good girl and try to do as they tell you."

Out in the world, away from the Alcott and May clans for the first

time, she did try to be good with a spectacular and conspicuous good
deed.

> I collected several poor children in the barn and regaled them on cake
> and figs, helping myself freely to the treasures of the pantry without
> asking. . . . Being discovered before the supplies were entirely exhausted,
> the patience of the long-suffering matron gave out, and I was ordered up
> to the garret. . . . I felt myself an outcast, and bewailed the disgrace I had
> brought upon my family. . . . If the mice were to come and eat me then
> and there . . . it would only be a relief to my friends.

Christy was her salvation. He came to the garret, "full of sympathy
and comfort. . . . I cried tempestuously, and clung to him like a ship-
wrecked little mariner in a storm."

"You shall see us all in a few days," Bronson had written. "You was
[*sic*] never away from home so long before. It has given you some new
feeling." Perhaps the new feeling was grief. "I often wish I had a little
brother," Louisa would write in her journal at the age of eleven, "but as I
have not I shall try to be contented with what I have got (for Mother often
says if we are not contented with what we have got it will be taken away
from us)." If Louisa did not exactly blame herself for her brother's death,
she knew she was not a good girl and deserved rejection and exile. She
vowed to improve.

On a cold Sunday morning a few days after his letter to Louisa, Bronson
and Colonel May went together to watch "this bud of a son, nipt ere it had
bloomed, fall into the ground." Colonel May had buried nine of his twelve
children, and during the winter had lost his second wife, Abby's detested
stepmother. For a few hours the tensions between father and son-in-law
disappeared under the weight of grief.

The two men walked to the Central Burying Ground on Boston Common, past the ten-year-old grave of Gilbert Stuart, who had painted the
first six U.S. presidents and Colonel Joseph May. Within sight of the May
family vault, on a bare-branched winter's day, was the new Public Garden
with its botanical specimens and manmade Frog Pond. The Frog Pond
was the site of a recent accident that had nearly landed Louisa in that
vault. Rolling her hoop in triumph past the boys, she had driven both the

hoop and herself straight into the pond. She felt the water go down her throat and close over her. She couldn't breathe and couldn't find the surface. Then a pair of arms came down, grabbed her neatly, and pulled her out. They belonged to a handsome black boy of about eight, who must have come from the vital African American neighborhood around the Charles Street Meetinghouse a block or two away.

She was soon to know an African American girl about her age. Two months after the birth and death of his son, Bronson accepted a student named Susan Robinson into his small home school. Little is known about Susan Robinson apart from her color, and her first name is known only because Anna Alcott wrote it in her journal.

Bronson was ahead of his time by more than a century; the white parents sent a representative to confront him. "My patrons, through Dr. John Flint," Bronson noted in his journal, "urge the dismissal of the Robinson Child. I decline." Overnight, his paying students disappeared, leaving his daughters, Frank Russell, and Susan Robinson.

Bronson was never employed as a teacher again.

Colonel May, to stand by his principles, rewarded Abby and Bronson for holding to theirs, and paid for the family to escape to Scituate for the summer after a wretched year in city harness. Again the cousins played while the adults discussed reform with Sam and Lu May. But summer is short in New England; the last week of August brought days of crystalline light and nights with a perceptible chill, harbingers of the inevitable reckoning of fall. Back in Boston, with no work apart from an occasional Conversation, Bronson's long walks around the Common grew longer, his visits to the Athenaeum library more protracted. Perhaps trying to find himself, he researched his ancestors. Abby paid attention to her ancestors' descendants and quietly began taking in sewing to support them. The carefree summer had left its usual memento. She was pregnant.

In late November, as winter approached, Bronson and Louisa shared a birthday that was a momentous marker for both; Bronson was forty, by any contemporary count an older man, and Louisa was seven, considered the age of reason in cultures around the world and through history. Father and daughter watched in turn as each opened Abby's carefully wrapped present. Bronson's was a handsome portfolio; Louisa's a pretty doll Abby had made, with a note saying she hoped it would be a quiet playmate for her active daughter. This doll was small enough—around ten inches tall— to be tucked into an apron waistband or a patch pocket. Her old doll had been a sprawling set of limbs; "topsey turvey" Louisa would have called it. The new doll looked more like a little woman than a small child. She had dark hair like Louisa's, arms that stayed close to her sides, and legs not easily set wide apart. The doll went nearly everywhere with Louisa during the next seven years, displacing the one that had been her companion for much of the first seven. She describes that first doll in "Poppy's Pranks": "This dolly had been through a good deal. Her head had been cut off (and put on again); she had been washed, buried, burnt, torn, soiled and banged about till she was a mournful object. . . . She was two feet tall, and had once been very handsome: so her trials only endeared her to her little mamma." Both dolls went by the generic "dolly." Louisa named and renamed them as she gave them roles to play in her countless fantasies. Like the heroines she would create on paper, they were all Louisa.

Her father's present was his usual note in elaborate calligraphy. Louisa, just coming into a magnificent literacy, read it aloud to the family: "You are Seven years old, today. . . . You have learned a great many things since you have lived in a Body, about things going on around you and within you. . . . You feel your Conscience, and have no real pleasure unless you obey it. . . . It is GOD trying in your soul to keep you always GOOD."

Louisa experienced God in nature, a kind God who loved her to feel pleasure. Conscience spoke to her in the voice of Bronson, threatening her with the loss of pleasure and of love if she could not keep herself "always GOOD." In her life so far, pleasure and power had been her objectives. Being good *always* was impossible; trying to be good was like sailing into a relentless stiff wind that took the fun out of the trip and put the destination out of reach.

She had begun to feel responsible for her behavior but was nowhere near controlling it. In Providence, her first time away from home and family, in a world of adults, her attempt to be and do good had been a failure. She suspected herself of being "the worst child ever known." She had not had pleasure or attained power there. Away from her parents she could not even distinguish right from wrong. But they loved her anyway, for some reason; at least her mother did.

For years, Emerson had been urging Bronson to join him in Concord, where he might work the land and spread his ideas in the pleasant green of the country. Now he offered financial help, promising to pay the rent on an acre and a half of land and a small house within walking distance of his own. The Alcotts had no other prospects, and the move would put them out of reach of their creditors.

On March 31, 1840, the day she left Boston with her family to live in Concord, Louisa was a city kid through and through. Her boldness had made her far more familiar with Boston's streets, wharves, crowds, and all kinds of characters than the usual middle-class seven-year-old girl. She knew the neighborhoods where she had lived, the way they were in the morning, at night, and on Sunday. She had gotten lost, been alone with the city's dangers and delights. Boston had been a theater where she was both audience and performer, where she was constantly on the lookout for a good show. Although she became associated forever with Concord after she wrote *Little Women* in 1868, Boston was Louisa Alcott's hometown. Whenever she could escape her parents, she would return.

FOUR

WILD EXUBERANT NATURE

The weather on April first was frigid and the landscape bare, but an early spring ice storm made for a dazzling introduction to Concord. The girls were "in rapture," Abby wrote her father a few days after they arrived. "The trees, encrusted with ice, wore a most fantastic and fairy-like appearance; nothing has escaped their notice and admiration." Dove Cottage, the small and jerrybuilt brown house on Main Street, was a mansion compared to their cramped rooms in Boston.

Anna and Louisa were soon taking lessons at the Emersons' with Mary Russell, wife of the educator William Russell. There they met their father's and Mr. Emerson's friend Henry Thoreau, a twenty-three-year-old schoolteacher who expressed himself in short bursts of conversation punctuated by long silences. He preferred solitude to most people's company, but children were excepted. Louisa and her sisters trailed after the odd young man as he tramped the Concord woods in his gray pants and straw hat, always with notebook, pencil, and flute. Projecting fanciful personalities and stories onto plants and animals, showing her their ingenious processes, Thoreau taught Louisa to see, read, and appreciate nature. In *Little Men*, Louisa portrayed Thoreau at this age as Mr. Hyde, who "could make birds come to him, and rabbits and squirrels didn't mind him any more than if he was a tree. . . . He'd make snakes listen to him while he whistled, and he knew just when certain flowers would blow, and bees wouldn't sting him, and he'd tell the wonderfullest things about fish and flies, and the Indians and the rocks."

⌒

Free bands of unsupervised children roamed the woods of Concord, their only fears the ones they invented. This domain was an arena for fantasies Louisa made so compelling that other children would play them out no matter how weird or destructive. "The Naughty Kitty-Mouse" was provoked by Louisa's fascination with cats. A malevolent deity who spoke through Louisa, the cat-god's high priest was Anna, who "found a fearful pleasure in its service, blindly obeying its most absurd demands." In chapter 8 of *Little Men*, "Pranks and Plays," Louisa describes a sacred rite of the dread Naughty Kitty-Mouse, a sacrificial fire inspired by Bronson's stories of the ancient Greeks. The children submit as offerings treasured lead soldiers, paper dolls, a wooden toy village, and a squeaking lamb toy. In anguish they watch the bonfire swallow their favorite playthings forever, wondering how a storyteller could make them do such a terrible thing.

⌒

Emerson's long campaign to bring Bronson to Concord was part of a larger effort to persuade his friends to resettle within walking distance of his big white house off the Lexington Road. "I think no man in the planet has a circle more noble," Emerson wrote. "Will they separate themselves from me again, or some of them?" Some would, on and off, usually to avoid not Emerson but someone in the circle. Their letters and journals are full of gossip about each other, and their long visits generate more. The brilliant Margaret Fuller, who wore her hair loose and walked with Emerson or was shut up with him in his study at all hours, is given in her letters to hyperbolic enthusiasms and to pleas to Emerson that he tell her if and how much he loves her; the married Emerson keeps asking her to stop asking—and keeps inviting her to visit again. Then there is the case of Henry Thoreau, who lived in Emerson's home for months on end, delighting his son Waldo with stories and music, staying on in Emerson's absence. Among other guests for weeks at a time were Elizabeth Peabody, the theologian Frederic Hedge, the half-mad poet Jones Very, the second-rate poet William Ellery Channing, the exquisite Anna Barker Ward, her wealthy husband, Samuel Ward, and Margaret Fuller's friend, the free-spirited Caroline Sturgis.

Subsidizing his friends to keep them nearby made economic sense to Emerson; it bought their intellects for his benefit and afforded them the freedom to develop theirs. He would give the use of his ancestral home, the Old Manse, to Nathaniel Hawthorne and his bride, Sophia Peabody, give Thoreau the use of his land for a cabin at Walden Pond. But of all his friends, he would shore up and subsidize Bronson Alcott the most, opening doors to influential people, giving him work and regular gifts of money, even cosigning loans and volunteering to hold title to property Alcott lived on when his newly acquired socialist principles prohibited it. To get him to come to Concord, he paid Alcott's fifty-two-dollar annual rent for Dove Cottage as part of a plan for him "to get his living by the help of God and his own spade" as a farmer-philosopher, an "Orpheus at the Plow," as William Ellery Channing put it.

Abby flung herself into the latest incarnation of family life, scrubbing and cleaning and fitting out the house with fresh hope. "Every new experience in the art of living charms me," she wrote Sam early on. "I enjoy the quiet and comparative solitude of the country, and am convinced that the only source of happiness is to bring the spirit in harmony with its lot." Abby's spirit had rarely been in harmony with her lot.

While Abby labored indoors, Bronson worked long days outside, repairing the front steps, whitewashing the fences, planting a vegetable garden, attaching trellises to exterior walls, and transplanting roses closer to the house to climb the trellises. "I place myself in peaceful relations to the soil," he wrote Sam a few days into the adventure. "My garden and Acre are rich in promise; and if I can draw with temperance on the stock of strength that yet remains within these shoulder blades and shackle bones, I see an independence made out to my household. Debts, I will pay in all honor whensoever I may." The repeated qualifications ("*if* I can draw on strength that yet remains," "soil rich in *promise*," "whensoever I *may*") mark the statement as more a fine sentiment than a firm intention. At forty, even a "Hoper" might lack confidence in a plan to live by manual labor.

Edmund Hosmer's children next door were natural playmates for the Alcott girls. Three of the five matched up closely in age with Anna, Louisa, and Lizzie: Anna developed a crush on eight-year-old Henry; Lizzie found a friend in six-year-old Lydia; and seven-year-old Louisa adopted Cyrus, Lydia's twin, as her special friend.

"Cy was a comrade after my own heart," Louisa wrote. ". . . We kept the neighborhood in a ferment by our adventures and hair-breadth escapes." As she had with Frank Russell, Louisa made Cy Hosmer the scapegoat for her misbegotten adventures.

> He did not get into scrapes himself, but possessed a splendid talent for deluding others into them. . . . It was he who incited me to jump off of the highest beam in the barn, to be borne home on a board with a pair of sprained ankles. It was he who dared me to rub my eyes with red peppers, and then sympathizingly led me home blind and roaring with pain. It was he who solemnly assured me that all the little pigs would die in agony if their tails were not cut off, and won me to hold those thirteen little squealers while the operation was performed. Those thirteen innocent pink tails haunt me yet, and the memory of that deed has given me a truly Jewish aversion to pork.

Louisa and Anna conscripted the Hosmers and another neighbor, Priscilla Lane, into their first theatricals, rigging up a stage in the rickety barn behind the house where, in Louisa's account: "We dramatized the fairy tales in great style. Our giant came tumbling off a loft when Jack cut down the squash vine running up a ladder to represent the immortal bean. Cinderella rolled away in a vast pumpkin and a long black pudding was lowered by invisible hands to fasten itself on the nose of the woman who wasted her three wishes."

As an adult, Cyrus's twin Lydia recalled the Alcott children as "always very busy about the house, but never too busy to romp and play. Louisa of course was always the leader in the fun . . . racing down the street, usually with a hoople [hoop] higher than her head."

That first Concord spring of 1840, Bronson's attention was split between his garden and the long-anticipated literary journal the Transcendental group planned to launch in midsummer. Abby Alcott described it to her cousin Hannah Robie, with a hint of sour grapes, as "a new periodical by which we of the sublunary world are to be informed of the time of day in the Transcendental regions." Bronson had suggested the new magazine's name, the *Dial*, as in *sundial*, drawn from an obscure line in his journal, "Dial on time thine own eternity." Emerson wanted Bronson to write a series of maxims, "Orphic Sayings," for the first issue, hoping through them to restore his friend's tattered reputation. Bronson set to work, eventually spinning out fifty maxims of varying length. When Emerson read over his friend's "cold vague generalities," his heart sank. "You will not like them," he wrote coeditor Margaret Fuller. "I do not like them." For Abby the question was not a literary one. "Neither the butcher nor tailor will take pay in aphorisms," she remarked.

Margaret Fuller reassured Emerson that some of Alcott's sayings were "quite grand, though oft times too grandiloquent," having in mind as grand perhaps this almost straightforward call to integrity: "Engage in nothing that cripples or degrades you. Your first duty is self-culture, self-exaltation; you may not violate this high trust. Your self is sacred, profane it not. . . ." In the "grandiloquent" category, she quotes the inscrutable number 43: "The popular genesis is historical. It is written to sense not to the soul. Two principles diverse and alien, interchange the Godhead and sway the world by turns. God is dual. Spirit is derivative. Identity halts in diversity."

When the first issue of the *Dial* landed in the parlors of Boston's resident wits, the knives came out to lance Bronson's inflated "Orphic Sayings." The reaction was not so fierce as the reception of *Conversations with Children on the Gospels*, but it carried a sting of a different kind: ridicule.

The *Boston Transcript* ran a parody of number 43 called "Gastric Sayings." The *Boston Post* compared Alcott's utterances to "a train of 15 railroad cars going by with only one passenger," a jibe that was scribbled down in a hundred journals and letters, Emerson's among them. The poet-minister-artist Christopher Cranch published a satirical drawing and lampoon. The critic James Russell Lowell composed a ditty that rang true even to Bronson's fiercest defenders:

> *While he talks he is great but goes out like a taper*
> *If you shut him up closely with pen, ink, and paper.*

Bronson pasted the clippings into his journal without annotation.

⌒

Abby, approaching forty, was nearing the end of her eighth pregnancy. Louisa was exiled for six weeks to her grandfather's in Boston. At home she made too much noise, required too much attention, and caused too much concern. A typical uproar is this tale of a common childhood misdemeanor from chapter 8 of *Little Men:*

> I had no beans, so I took some little pebbles, and poked several into my nose. I . . . wanted to take them out again very soon, but one would not come, . . . I went for hours with the stone hurting me very much. At last the pain got so bad I had to tell, and when my mother could not get it out the doctor came. . . . He used his ugly little pincers till the stone hopped out. . . . how people laughed at me!

In late June, shortly after Louisa's departure for Grandpa May's, Bronson wrote her a letter rare for its appreciation of his daughter, with only a mild reminder to be good.

> My Dear Louisa,
>   We all miss the noisy little girl who used to make house and garden, barn and field ring with her footsteps, and even the hens and chickens seem to miss her too. . . .
>   I wished you here very much on the mornings when the hen left her nest and came proudly down with six little chickens, every one knowing how to walk, fly, eat, and drink almost as well as its own mother. . . . You would have enjoyed the sight very much. But this and many other pleasures all wait for you when you return. Be good, kind, gentle, while you are away, step lightly, and speak soft about the house; Grandpa loves quiet as well as your sober father, and other grown people.
>   Elisabeth says often, "Oh I wish I could see Louisa, when will she come home, mother?" And another feels so too. Who is it?
>   Your Father.

Abby's last delivery went well. Within two weeks of giving birth to a girl on July 26 she was back on her feet. The baby was called "Baby" for several months before she was given her mother's name. As a teenager, young Abby would first change the spelling of her name to "Abbie," then abandon it altogether in favor of "May," her mother's maiden name, which she considered more sophisticated. Self-assertion came naturally to blue-eyed, golden-haired Abby/May; as last-borns often are, she was indulged. Bronson did not keep a journal of her infant development; he had moved on, along with the other intellectuals, to an interest in the socialist ideas of Charles Fourier and Robert Owen.

Communal living and cooperative labor gave a poetic gloss to farm work. "Tomorrow I enter the meadows with my neighbors," Bronson wrote Sam during mowing season. "Labor is indeed sweet, nor is that a severe, but beneficent decree, which sends a man into the fields to earn his Bread in the sweat of his face."

The social and philosophical movement that Emerson, Alcott, Elizabeth Peabody, and a few others had originated came to be called "the New-ness" in much the same sense that "New Age" did more than a century later. Like the New Age, the Newness was a mixed bag of frivolous and significant, enduring and transitory. Emerson frequently found himself trying to discern the dividing line between transcendentalism and tripe. His aversion to fringe elements (Dunkers, Muggletonians, Come-outers, Groaners) did not lessen the value of the ideas and the people at the core, among them his best friends.

Abby's appreciation of the transcendental heroics was even more limited than Emerson's. Her journal sounds a plaintive, accusing note, clearly aimed at Bronson. "Why so much talk, talk, talk; so little give!" and "Why are men icebergs when beloved by ardent natures and surrounded by love-giving and life-devoted beings."

Reality had reclaimed her. The large garden Bronson had planted would not produce enough to feed them through the winter. She appealed to her father again for money; he refused. She asked Sam to help find Bronson work: "Do bear this in mind and among all your host of acquaintances something might come."

Bronson's list of moral scruples grew longer with every arrangement that did not suit. The protosocialist farmer-philosopher had decided that he would accept donations for his Conversations and cash rewards for his principles, but could not accept wages.

No one will employ him in his way. He cannot work in theirs, if he thereby involve his conscience. He is so resolved in this matter that I believe he will starve and freeze before he will sacrifice principle to comfort. . . . I and my children . . . have less to sustain us in the spirit, and therefore, are more liable to be overcome by the flesh. . . . He has, for a long time gone without everything which he could not produce by labor. . . . No one can in truth reproach him.

It was the tendentious argument of a desperate but loyal woman. Her brother responded by mildly pointing out that he and other men of principle had to work and were not wealthy, and could not be expected to view Bronson as superior to themselves, however much Abby might. Rebuffed, Abby directed her remaining energies toward keeping the family together with their chins up.

Thanksgiving was observed with due ceremony and a turkey-less feast along the new vegetarian principles of Sylvester Graham, inventor of the graham cracker. A few days later, Louisa's eighth birthday was celebrated Alcott-style, with homemade presents and greetings. Bronson's was a delicate miniature card with a decorated border and a pair of engravings cut out and pasted from a magazine. One showed an angel playing a harp representing Love, Music, and Concord; the other an angel clutching an arrow signifying Anger and Discord. Underneath, Bronson had written an admonitory birthday greeting in his powerful calligraphic hand: "Two passions strong divide our life, Meek gentle Love, or Boisterous strife."

That the Alcotts were not like other people was a great part of their fascination for their neighbors, and central to their image of themselves. Yet there was a deepening contrast between the richness of the intellectual company they kept and the material poverty of their daily lives, between Bronson's high-minded pronouncements and expectation of moral perfection, and Abby's unceasing labor to make do with the barest resources.

"I am so weary," Abby wrote Sam at the end of January, "that if anybody should ask me the way to Boston I should say it was in the oven, or if I had read the last *Liberator*, I would reply it wanted darning."

Emerson's concern and regard for the Alcotts led him to offer to shelter them in his own house; his wife, Lidian, was not consulted. Bronson was prepared to accept, but Abby knew she could not be dependent and also on good terms: "I cannot see [myself] in another person's yoke and I know that everybody burns their finger if they touch my pie—not because the pie is too hot but because it is mine."

In February Colonel May died at the age of eighty. When his will was read, Abby wrote, "My father did *not* love me." Though Abby believed her own needs warranted the largest share, her father had divided a legacy of fifteen thousand dollars into seven equal parts, three for his surviving children, and four for the children of his daughters who had died. Abby was enraged. Her portion amounted to a little over two thousand dollars and a handful of treasures from Federal Court, her mother's silver teapot among them. Her father's worst offense in her eyes was the unique limitation he put on Abby's legacy: the money was to be "secured by my Executors to her sole and separate use, without the control of her husband or liability of his debts, in such manner as they judge best." Given that Bronson's Boston creditors—to whom he owed more than six thousand dollars—pounced on the Alcotts upon learning of Colonel May's death, the provision was wise. The money was tied up for years while creditors fought to have the protective provision overruled, and Sam May and her cousin Sam Sewall fought to preserve it for Abby. Abby's response was as defiant as it was off the mark. "If I am despised and rejected by my kindred as a wayward and ungrateful daughter, my life shall prove that there is virtue and power in . . . [being] a faithful wife [and] vigilant fond mother."

Colonel May's will, and Bronson's unwillingness to work for money, inevitably made for tension in her marriage, but not, it seems, a cessation of marital relations. As always, Abby unburdened herself to Sam. "We have in no wise been aliens in affections," she wrote, "but our diversity of opinion has at times led us far and wide of a quiet and contented frame of mind."

As she groped for ways to bring in money, Abby found herself wishing she could be more like other women in her circle—like Elizabeth Peabody, who supported her parents and sisters by running a bookstore, or Lydia Maria Child, who supported herself with her pen. Abby was an excellent writer, as witty and succinct in her expression as Louisa would be, but she had never had the intellectual ambition or the discipline of those women, and as a mother of four children under the age of ten, she had neither the time nor the energy to start a school or run a boardinghouse.

She finally overcame her pride and took the obvious course. She put the word out to friends that she would welcome work as a seamstress, and resolved, "My girls shall have trades." She thought Louisa might trim hats and make decorative items for a living; she had a knack for embellishment. Louisa was showing a knack for writing too. At age eight, she responded to the beauty of a Concord spring with a poem, "To the First Robin." The other "little stranger" to Concord, Louisa would have liked to hear its sentiments directed at herself.

Welcome, welcome, little stranger,
Fear no harm, and fear no danger
We are glad to see you here,
For you sing, "Sweet Spring is Near."

Now the white snow melts away;
Now the flowers blossom gay;
Come dear bird and build your nest.
For we love our robin best.

With the fair weather, Bronson went back on the road to peddle philosophy. He paid a visit to Brook Farm, the new utopian community that would attract Nathaniel Hawthorne and Margaret Fuller, spent two weeks in the Green Mountains in Vermont, and was followed back to Concord by so many straggly fellow discoursers that Abby considered hanging out a hotel shingle.

In May, ten-year-old Anna went to Boston to visit the Sewall cousins. Her father kept her up to date on the family by letter. "I miss you, but baby misses you more, though Louisa's ready arms support her long, within doors and out; in garden and street; to barn and bridge." He had been planting peas, he reported, on a day that the sun had shown its face after long seclusion, "Elisabeth hastes daily to school; Louisa plies her hands nimbly with her Mother, or flies over the garden, and field." Louisa not only "plied" and "fly'd," but as she described in "Poppy's Pranks," on one occasion or another she "slipped into the brook, and was half drowned. She broke a window and her own head, swinging a little flatiron on a string; dropped baby in the coal-hod: buried her doll, and spoilt her; . . . and broke a tooth, trying to turn heels over head on a haycock [haystack]."

No wonder she would later say, "If it were not for the blessed fact that everything has its comic as well as tragic side, I should have lost my wits long ago." The merry tone of her accounts disguises painful experiences.

The Alcotts were slipping out of genteel poverty and into the grueling variety. When Abby's cousin Hannah Robie came at Thanksgiving in 1841, she brought a bundle of old clothes for Abby to use to make dresses for her girls. Abby could rip them apart, turn the pieces inside out, and resew them so the unfaded side of the fabric showed.

During the visit, Abby took Hannah to see an abandoned woman with four children. To help them, the Alcotts had reduced their own meals to two a day. Now the "sweetness of self-denial" was about starvation, not plumcakes. The urgency of the situation became clear: Abby entrusted Hannah with the sale of her silver teapot and spoons. Hannah Robie returned to Boston carrying the tale of Abby's troubles all over town.

Louisa, observing the adults from a corner of the kitchen while stitching a hem or playing with her doll, missed very little. At almost nine, hunger told her how dire things were; as an adult, she would give more of her money to feed children than to any other cause. Her raw hands reminded her that she and Anna performed dirty chores their playmates never thought about; in *Little Women*, she would give the March family a servant, and she herself would have ten when she died.

FIVE

MAN IN A BALLOON

Bronson's outwardly dignified demeanor masked a growing desperation but did not conceal a moodiness and agitation that Abby had never seen before. Since the failure of the Temple School, he had counted on regaining his footing with some grand success, but for years the only endorsement of his views came from a group of admirers in England who had read of his work in Elizabeth Peabody's *Record of a School*. James Pierrepont Greaves, a wealthy iconoclast, had founded an institution on Temple School principles in Surrey, named it "Alcott House," and through an associate, Charles Lane, extended Bronson a standing invitation to visit.

Alcott had been hugely flattered when he'd first learned of Alcott House two years earlier, but he was convinced that his next great work, whatever it proved to be, awaited him in the United States. By 1842, when Lane repeated the invitation, Bronson's sights were on the new utopian communities promoting cooperative living as a philosophical and economic solution to poverty and wage slavery, the very conditions plaguing Bronson, but he found no existing utopian community worthy of the name. Like Emerson, he had rejected Brook Farm for its "party" atmosphere. Besides, it was George Ripley's dream, not Bronson Alcott's.

For almost two years Emerson had sympathized, defended, and encouraged Bronson in the conviction that his misfortunes were less of his own making than a reflection of America's small regard for its most principled citizens. But at times Bronson the man was too much for him.

"Here is a fine person with wonderful gifts but mad as the rest & by reason of his great genius, which he can use as a weapon too, harder to deal with. . . . I am not large man enough to treat him firmly and sympathetically as a patient, and if treated equally & sympathetically as sane, his disease makes him the worst of bores."

That Emerson would rebound from a fit of mean-spiritedness with a compensatory act of charity was characteristic. The illness of his only son made it certain. Late in January, five-year-old Waldo contracted scarlet fever. On the morning of the twenty-seventh, Abby sent Louisa to ask after Waldo. "Child, he is dead," Emerson told her, and turned away. "Then the door closed," Louisa would recall, "and I ran home to tell the sad tidings. I was only eight years old, and that was my first glimpse of a great grief, but I never have forgotten the anguish that made a familiar face so tragical."

Two weeks after Waldo's death, Emerson offered to finance a trip to England for Bronson to meet his followers. He confessed in his journal that he was motivated as much by a wish to be free of the "tedious Archangel" Bronson Alcott as by the hope that his friend would find appreciation there. "You might spend the summer in England and get back to America in the autumn for a sum not exceeding four or five hundred dollars," Emerson suggested. "It will give me great pleasure to be responsible to you for that amount; and to more, if I shall be able, and more is necessary." He wrote letters of introduction to the literary lights he knew in London, among them Thomas Carlyle, the essayist, historian, and purveyor of German romanticism to the English-speaking public. "What shall I say of [Alcott] to the wise Englishman?" he asks himself in his journal of March 1842, then pours out his mixed feelings about his friend of seven years.

> I know no man who speaks such good English. . . . He takes such delight
> in the exercise of this faculty that he will willingly talk . . . for days successively, and if I, who am impatient of much speaking, draw him out to
> walk in the woods or fields, he will stop at the first fence and very soon
> propose either to sit down or to return. He seems to think society exists
> for this function. . . . He never affirms anything today because he has
> affirmed it before. . . . Having left him in the morning with one set of opinions, [you] find him in the evening totally escaped from all recollection

of them. . . . He is quite ready at any moment to abandon his present residence and employment, his country, nay his wife and children, . . . to put any new dream into practice which has bubbled up in the effervescence of discourse.

Emerson's actual letter to Carlyle asked only that he meet Alcott and judge for himself. With him Bronson carried a letter from William Lloyd Garrison commending him to leaders in English reform circles for his "rare moral courage," though cautioning that he did not subscribe to "all his speculations, religious, metaphysical, and social."

Passage on the *Rosalind* was booked for early May, and Abby began assembling Bronson's wardrobe. "I am summoning all the important and agreeable reasons for this absence," she confided to her diary, "and amongst the most weighty is the belief that these trans-Atlantic worthies will be more to him, in this period of doubt, than anything or anybody can be to him here." She echoed Emerson's opinion that "wife, children, and friends are less to him than the great ideas he is seeking to realize." Louisa as an adult would describe her father's relationship to the family in less reverent terms. "A philosopher is a man up in a balloon, with his family and friends holding the ropes, trying to haul him down." Abby saw it in terms of male and female: "how naturally man's sphere seems to be in the region of the head, and the woman's in the head and the heart and affections!"

She wrote to Sam May for money to get them through the summer. Sam sent $150, guaranteeing his sister a rare interlude of financial independence, and Bronson's gentle younger brother Junius Alcott came to live with the family in his absence. Junius was more protected than protector. Bronson knew his younger brother was mentally unstable and prone to despair. He would try to persuade him to join his family over the next ten years. Perhaps Junius was more comfortable with his brother's family in the absence of his brother; this was his sole extended visit.

The morning after Bronson left, provisioned with several loaves of Grahamite bread and a large supply of apples, Abby rose early, "feeling sick and sad. . . . Must we be robbed of our treasure to know its real value?" The longer Bronson was gone, the more he recovered the stature of their courtship days in Abby's eyes. Three weeks after he had sailed, she was still trying to get used to living without him.

Bronson's absence was deeply felt by the children, though Louisa tried hard to be brave and not to cry. More than a year later, overhearing the adults talk about traveling, Louisa's thoughts returned to her "father going off to England, and [she] said this bit of poetry [she] found in Byron's poems: 'When I left thy shores, O Naxos / Not a tear in sorrow fell / Not a sigh or faltered accent / Told my bosom's struggling swell.'"

In late June, a letter from Bronson confirmed that he had made it safely to England. He had found London noisy and its citizens antagonistic; he had managed to make the acquaintance of several of his literary heroes, including Thomas Carlyle.

Alcott and Carlyle got along, Carlyle said, "as ill as it was possible for two honest men kindly affected towards one another." The gruff, combative Scotsman meant to be charitable when he described Bronson to Emerson as a "venerable Don Quixote whom no one can even laugh at without loving." Literary London did not take Emerson's friend to its bosom. The poet Robert Browning ridiculed him as a "crazy or sound asleep—not dreaming—American." Word got back to Bronson, it appears. While Carlyle told Emerson that Alcott was "bent on saving the world with a return to acorns," and that his thinking was "imbecility which cannot be discussed in this busy world," Alcott's retort to Abigail was that Carlyle was slavishly devoted to "Work! Work!" which "is with him both motto and creed . . . instead of devotion to living humanity."

The endless speculations that men exchanged with one another were of no moment to Abigail Alcott. His letter told her that Bronson was safe. She was finally able to relax, and even to write, "I am enjoying this separation from my husband."

By contrast with London, Bronson was received at the school based upon his pedagogical principles, Alcott House, like the Messiah himself. Though he was surprised to learn his correspondent James Greaves had died in March, he was welcomed ceremoniously by Greaves's associates, young Henry Wright and Charles Lane, a man his own age, forty-two. Alcott House, a rambling, gabled country manor ten miles southwest of London, surrounded by towering shade trees, its vegetarian principles proclaimed in perfectly tended gardens, took his breath away, but the moral character of the inmates impressed Bronson most deeply. He especially liked twenty-eight-year-old Henry Wright, the strikingly handsome schoolmaster. In a community of mostly committed celibates, Wright was a wild card: he had taken up with a housemaid, conceived a child, and secretly married. James Greaves had never married. Charles Lane, who supported himself as manager of a London financial paper, had divorced his wife and taken custody of their ten-year-old son. William Oldham, the bookkeeper, had also renounced a wife.

Bronson Alcott was not a solitary man in any respect. He enjoyed the company of women and carried on flirtations with them all his life. The intimate privilege of marriage was for him a necessity, ballast for his balloon. "Wedlock! blessed union of Spirits! Blending of two natures in one! Incarnation of love," he had written in "Psyche." But after a month at Alcott House, he made no objection to the manifesto of his disciples: "If you ask where evil commences, the answer is, in Birth [sexual intercourse]. . . . The most sacred . . . the most solemn, the most reverent, the most godlike, yet possibly the most profane of acts."

Bronson's ambivalence about celibacy would eventually invade the Alcott marriage. He continued, however, to pen fevered love letters to his wife. "Dearest!" he wrote Abby, "this few months Divorce is the sacrement [sic] of our Espousals—this Absence an Invitation of Guests to our Wedding." To his daughters, Bronson wrote: "I think of you all every day, and desire to see you all again. . . . Anna, with her beauty-loving eyes and sweet visions of graceful motions . . . Louisa, with her quick and ready senses, her agile limbs and boundless curiosity, her penetrating mind and tear-shedding heart . . . Elizabeth with her quiet-loving disposition and serene thoughts . . . little Abba [May] with her fast falling footsteps, her sagacious eye and auburn locks." Louisa would appropriate this letter, practically word for word, for the first chapter of *Little Women*.

Bronson's adoration was reciprocated in Concord, where Abby and the girls had made a little shrine, garlanding his miniature portrait with wildflowers and pine branches. For Lizzie's seventh birthday celebration in June, the barn was given the same treatment. Abby composed a poem addressed to her absent husband: "Father dear / We wish you here / To see how gay / On this birthday / We are." May's second birthday was observed with an excursion up the river in Uncle Junius Alcott's rowboat, a happy outing that triggered a somber reflection in Abby's journal. "I seldom omit these occasions for showing my children the joy I feel in their birth and continuance with me on earth. I wish them to feel that we must live for each other." Then her thoughts turned to her anxieties about Louisa's "peculiarities and moods of mind, rather uncommon for a girl her age. United to great firmness of purpose and resolution, there is at times the greatest volatility and wretchedness of spirit—no hope, no heart for anything, sad, solemn, and desponding."

⌒

Across the Atlantic, meanwhile, after Greaves's followers failed to persuade Bronson to stay, Lane and Wright decided to pursue a utopian future with him in the United States. A new Eden was being proposed, Bronson wrote Abby; a grand experiment in communal living in the New World: the founding of a new social model, what he called a "Consociate Family" that in theory included all mankind. Bronson would be its lodestar. The experience would be the defining event of Louisa's childhood.

Bronson and the three newcomers—Henry Wright, Charles Lane, and Lane's ten-year-old son William—arrived in mid-October, the peak of New England's annual blaze of autumn foliage, to a house scrubbed, scoured, and garlanded by an ecstatic Abby and the four overjoyed girls who welcomed them. On a tour of Concord with the visitors, Louisa could not contain her ebullience. "Mother, what makes me so happy?" Abby reports her asking. The question suggests Louisa's wish to understand her wildly variable emotions, not just the joy triggered by her father's return after almost six months.

Bolstered by his disciples, Bronson returned full of enthusiasm for his utopian vision. The first order of business was to find recruits and donations for the venture. It would soon be self-sustaining, they presumed. In the pages of the *Dial*, the grandiloquent Alcott and his right-hand man, Lane, trumpeted their "effort to initiate a Family in harmony with the primitive instincts of man." Those who joined would "access . . . the channels . . . of wisdom and purity" to further "the great work of human regeneration." With "Universal Love" as its credo, the colony was to be a "New Eden" and a model for the world.

⌒

Bronson hoped Emerson would take to his English disciples, but Lane and Emerson were both possessive toward Bronson, and enmity broke out instead. "Mr. Lane," Emerson told friends, "does not confound society with sociableness." Lane pronounced Emerson "no prophet of the future" and decidedly "off the railroad of progress." Emerson dismissed Wright and Lane as "cockerels." He may have been prejudiced by Carlyle, who had written that Bronson had thrown in his lot with a pack of "bottomless imbeciles."

Quite apart from his aversion to Lane was Emerson's antipathy to living anywhere other than where he was. He would not support Bronson's new project with his presence or his fortune. "[For] a founder of a family or an institution," Emerson wrote to a friend, "I would as soon exert myself to collect money for a madman." He was almost as blunt to Bronson's face, urging him to find a way to support the family he had before undertaking to found another. Emerson's vehement rejection of Bronson's scheme may have arisen from his own feelings of rejection. Alcott did not seem to recognize that he was withdrawing from a deliberate community— Emerson's Concord—to found another one around himself.

The utopian proselytizers received a warmer welcome in the salons and symposiums of New England, where their novel proposal and oratorical gifts made for an entertaining evening. Bronson won the audience with his hypnotic eloquence, then Lane delivered the call to action in a voice that one listener thought as beautiful as the sound of a silver bell. Pretty as it was, the bell went unanswered by converts or cash.

There are few testaments to the charms of Charles Lane; his only surviving photograph shows a stern, bony face with thin lips pressed tightly together in eternal disapproval. Abby's friend Lydia Maria Child said of Lane that "His countenance . . . looks as if the washwoman . . . scrubbed it on a washboard . . . [and] there is an expression which would make me slow to put myself in his power." Lane already had the Alcotts in his power. He controlled Bronson through his worshipful regard; no one else could make Bronson feel he might yet be the man of the hour. Abby looked on as Lane and his son appropriated her husband's first-floor study, and Wright settled into one of the two small upstairs bedrooms. Anna, Louisa, Lizzie, and the baby had to sleep in a tiny alcove outside their parents' room.

While autumn lasted, the children could go outdoors to run and make noise, but as cold weather closed in, the house became unbearably crowded. Personalities and needs bumped up against each other. When Louisa sat in her habitual corner drinking in everything going around her, she was unobtrusive, but much of the time she was uncontrollably running and shouting and slamming doors. Her mishaps required a lot of attention. She swung from the garret stairs, fell more than a floor, and

sprained both her ankles again. On Cy Hosmer's dare, she chewed tobacco, and got sick. She picked fights with her older sister, Anna. She was
impatient, critical, and rude.

Abby was just as discontented, if more restrained in expressing it.
Charles Lane was dictating every detail of daily life. Plates would no longer
be used, thereby "saving" Abby and her daughters the trouble of washing
them—never mind that they would sooner need to launder the napkins
on which orphan-sized portions of apple and cold potatoes were served to
them and the three extra mouths. The household's already strict dietary
rules grew ever more stringent, as foods believed to stimulate sensual
desires—including milk, butter, and molasses, their only sweetener—were
embargoed one by one.

Abby had been teaching the girls in Bronson's absence; now Mr. Lane
gave them their lessons. The school day began with spelling, grammar,
arithmetic, and journal writing. Temple School–style dialogues in Lane's
hands became exercises in self-criticism productive of humiliation rather
than insight. And Lane did not limit school to three or four hours a day,
as Bronson had. The afternoon brought more lessons, in geography, geom-
etry, French, Latin, and music, after which Louisa, Anna, and Lizzie were
released to join Abby in her ceaseless rounds of housework and care of
toddler May. Evidently Lane did not concur with Bronson's opinion that
recreation developed the mental and moral capacities of children, judg-
ing from how little of it they had. To Louisa's list of playtime accidents
was a work-related one: chopping wood, she cut off a chunk of flesh from
a finger. Louisa would soon write, in her earliest surviving journal, that
she didn't like "the school part, or Mr. Lane."

Even more painful to Abby than being demoted to cook and cleaning
woman was being replaced as Bronson's primary companion and confidante. On Bronson and Louisa's joint birthday, she set down her misery
in her journal: "Circumstances most cruelly drive me from the enjoyment of my domestic life. I am prone to indulge in occasional hilarity, but
I seem frowned down into stiff quiet and peace-less order. I am almost suffocated in this atmosphere of restriction. . . . All these causes have com-
bined to make me somewhat irritable, or morbidly sensitive."

Abby had scant appreciation for what Lane called the "love community." The "stupidly obtuse" dreamers had engineered "this invasion of
my rights as a woman and a mother," she grumbled. "Give me one day of

practical philosophy. It is worth a century of speculation and discussion."

Lane recognized the need to subdue his opponent. He wrote a friend that "Mrs. A. has passed from the ladylike to the industrious order but her pride is not yet eradicated and her peculiar maternal love blinds her to all else."

The extent of Louisa's resistance to the new regime can be measured by the displeased tone of the letter Bronson wrote on her tenth birthday and his forty-third. He could not bring himself even to decorate his note with his usual sketch or newspaper woodcut. "I sought . . . for some pretty picture to place at the top of this note," he wrote, "but I did not find anything that seemed at all expressive of my interest in your well being, or well-doing, so this note comes to you without any such emblem."

He struggled but failed to keep criticism and blame out of his apparent message of goodwill and desire for her happiness.

> I live, my dear daughter, to be good and do good to all, and especially to you and your mother and sister[s]. Will you not let me? . . . The good Spirit comes into the Breasts of the meek and loveful. . . . Anger, discontent, impatience, evil appetites, greedy wants, complainings, ill-speakings, idlenesses, heedlessness, rude behavior . . . drive it away, [leaving] the poor misguided soul to live in its own obstinate, perverse, proud, discomfort.

It was a familiar lecture, if not always delivered so vehemently or on her birthday, and one Louisa always responded to with tearful discouraged pledges to do, and be, better. What she could not do was change the situation or free herself from it.

Her mother could. "Left Concord to try the influence of a short absence from home," she noted in her journal, and abruptly fled to Boston, taking with her Louisa and, for reasons unknown, William Lane. Perhaps it was a gesture of pity for the son of the household tyrant. There was an element of the wildcat strike to it, and the three truants enjoyed a holiday week of pleasure with Abby's relatives, traipsing from one brilliantly lit parlor to another of the merrymaking Mays, Willises, Windships, and Sewalls. They feasted on forbidden foods, sang carols, attended lectures and concerts, and on Christmas night watched as the candles on a towering fir tree were lighted in Amory Hall. The Christmas scenes Louisa concocted in *Eight Cousins* and many other novels and stories were the May family version, materialistic and pagan by comparison with typical subdued celebrations of the day, graced with overflowing stockings, new skates *and* a sled, halls decked with boughs of bright holly and aromatic cedar, mistletoe-blessed kisses, and indulgent aunts and uncles and cousins sitting down to "bounteous stores" of food on the table.

Louisa and her mother were not the only stir-crazy inmates in Dove Cottage that winter. Henry Wright had never found his footing. He too made forays into Boston and surrounding towns to pitch the idea of the Consociate Family, but in a crowded field of loquacious seers, he failed to make his mark. Trapped in the crowded little house in Concord, forbidden so much as a cup of tea for comfort, he became less interested in the perfection of his character. Then, given his youth (he was not yet thirty), his demonstrated ambivalence about celibacy (viz., the impregnated housemaid of Alcott House and the convenience of having left that wife and child behind in England), he did what came naturally: he fell in love. The woman was a member of Boston's reformist circle. He met her at a favorite kind of Transcendental social event: a picnic. By January, the besotted Wright had forsaken his monk's cell at Dove Cottage for his paramour's house in Lynn, where the infatuated couple signaled their immoral activity to the neighbors by shrouding the parlor windows. Bronson never mentioned Wright again.

Abby's trip was a tonic. "I left home toil-worn and depressed. I returned feeling quickened by a new spirit of confidence" ready "to resume the quiet duties of home and love." She reported herself as "less tenacious" of her rights or opinions. "I do believe that the miracle is about being wrought."

To provide an "opportunity for the children, indeed all of us, to interchange thought and sentiment . . . a pleasant way of healing all differences and discontents," she revived the household post office she had instituted in Bronson's absence. A basket was hung in the entry; Louisa and her sisters took turns playing postmaster.

Lane subverted the letterbox to win Abby over. "You are most certainly mistaken in supposing that in any quarter your excellencies are overlooked," he wrote to her in late January. "To have your approval to whatever is done seems to me highly desireable; nay, should we not do wrong to adopt any important step until we have attained unanimity?" He saluted her devotion to family (which he disparaged to Oldham in England) and shamelessly appealed to her nobility. "Your destiny, your heart binds you to a circle in which you may become a radiation of beneficence, in which you may rise above all annoyances and crosses whatever, and shed a benign luster on husband, children, friends and the world. Upon yourself it alone depends to be this warming and shining light." Lane signed his letter to Abby "thy brother, Charles." It worked like a snake charmer. Abby pasted the note into her journal with the comment: "A truly kind and fraternal note from our friend. . . . This is just what I much need."

In the middle of January there was "a day of some excitement" in Concord, when Bronson, making an all-purpose protest against "the state," refused to pay the town's annual $1.50 poll tax. He was promptly arrested, but by the time he was escorted to the town jail, the tax had been paid by his influential neighbor Judge Samuel Hoar. "Thus were we spared the affliction of his absence," Abby wrote in her journal, "and he the triumph of suffering for his principles." That honor would go to his friend Henry Thoreau, who two years later linked his own refusal to pay tax to a protest against slavery and the Mexican-American War. The eloquent essay Thoreau based on this incident, "On Civil Disobedience," would contribute to the reshaping of entire societies. Bronson may be credited with enacting in a potentially powerful way the conviction that fidelity to morality can require infidelity to the law; his precedent almost certainly inspired his friend Thoreau.

A few days after Bronson's protest, Abby noted that Edmund Hosmer and his children had spent the day visiting. "The gentlemen discussed the overthrow of state government and the errors of all human government." Louisa, exposed to this line of thought nearly every day, would grow up to regard civil law as more in need of reform than enforcement, and as a poor representation of a higher law that held all people equal in status and in rights.

The Hosmers lingered for a "simple dinner which Mr. Alcott had neatly prepared in the morning: an oatmeal pudding, apples, bread, and nuts." Afterward the children went to the schoolroom, where, as Louisa would describe in the autobiographical chapter 8 of Little Men, they had a choice of pastimes, among them "chess, morris [a board game resembling checkers], backgammon, fencing matches, recitations, debates, or dramatic performances of a darkly tragical nature."

While the children played and Lane and Abby mended fences, no actual progress toward the realization of the Consociate Family, that nebulous concept, was being made. "Our purposes, as far as we know them at present," Bronson wrote in a letter to a "Friend" in February, "are briefly these:

> To obtain the free use of a spot of land adequate by our own labor to our support; including, of course, a convenient plain house, and offices, woodlot, garden, and orchard. . . . To live . . . with benignity towards all creatures, human and inferior; with beauty and refinement in all economies, and the purest charity. . . .
>
> Doubtless such a household, with our library, our services and our manner of life, may attract young men and women, possibly also families with children, desirous of access to the channels and fountain of wisdom and purity.

The material world was immaterial to Bronson Alcott; he left it to Abby to scramble to pay off their debts before they left Concord for utopia, whenever and wherever that might be located. "Am greatly beset by men to whom we are owing small sums of money," Abby wrote in her journal in January. "Mr. Alcott feels that nothing can just now be done but let them wait." By March, as plans for the move to some still unknown and unfinanced location were discussed, she again turned to Sam to clear their debts. Instead, he asked why Bronson couldn't support his family without the help of his friends. They had to work—why shouldn't he?

With her brother denying her, Abby turned to her soulmate in the family, ten-year-old Louisa, for consolation. Fearful images of ruin no doubt spinning in her head, in a pathetic letter she enclosed a picture of a sick mother watched over by an attentive daughter: "a picture for you which I always admired very much, for in my imagination I have thought you might be just such an industrious good daughter and that I might be a sick but loving mother, looking to my daughter's labors for my daily bread. Take care of it for my sake and your own because you and I have always liked to be grouped together."

It was an extraordinary acknowledgment of the reality Abby had spent much of her married life denying, and an even more extraordinary claim to make upon a ten-year-old daughter. Bronson never requested or assumed that his daughters would support him. Though there is no doubt that Louisa had a big breach of paternal obligation to step into, her mother also bound her to the family fortunes by guilt and love.

By early spring, Charles Lane realized that no patron would be throwing in his lot with the Consociate Family. "I do not see anyone to act the money part but myself," he wrote in a letter to England. He and Bronson began scouring the countryside for a suitable site to buy in time to plant crops to carry them through the following winter.

Emerson urged Bronson to consider a sixteen-acre property in Concord overlooking the Sudbury River. To Lane it might as well have been a tent in Emerson's backyard, and equally unacceptable. In the town of Harvard, fourteen miles west of Concord, he found an isolated farm of ninety acres. A dilapidated two-story farmhouse and a pair of derelict barns stood in the protective lee of a steep slope with "the prospect from the highest part very sublime." The inscrutable term *Consociate Family* was soon replaced by Bronson's name for the property, *Fruitlands* (no doubt giving rise to the occasional wit's designation of its members as "fruitcakes"). Lane managed to get the price reduced to within reach of his pinched purse, with rent-free use of the house for a year—a bargain, the former editor of the *Mercantile* said, that should "entitle transcendentalism to some respect for its practicality." Before they could buy the land and resettle there, the Alcotts' Concord debts had to be paid off. In a characteristic assertion of entitlement, but not without justification, Abby charged Lane with the cost of his own and his son's room and board and her labor during the months since their arrival. Lane had never anticipated such an obligation; it would leave him short of cash to buy Fruitlands.

An appeal was made to Sam May, who agreed to become a trustee for the purchase of the property in lieu of paying Bronson's debts directly, which he had already rejected on principle. Instead, he signed a promissory note for three hundred dollars of the farm's purchase price, to be paid out over two years' time. Emerson, acting on friendship rather than reason, also signed his name as a guarantor of the property. Bronson, no longer believing in private property, would not have put his name on a deed even if he could have afforded to make the purchase. Lane was then able, barely, to settle the Concord accounts. The Alcotts were free to leave Concord with a clean ledger; after seven months as their guest, it was Lane who now carried a five-hundred-dollar debt to the owner of the farm.

In the end, Lane's willingness to act softened Emerson. "Mr. Lane paid me a long visit," he wrote Thoreau shortly after the Alcotts and Lane left for Harvard, "in which he was more than I had ever known him gentle and open; and it was impossible not to sympathize and honor projects that so often seem without feet or hands."

SIX

TRANSCENDENTAL WILD OATS

On the first day of June 184_ , a large wagon, drawn by a small horse and containing a motley load, went lumbering over certain New England hills, with the pleasing accompaniments of wind, rain, and hail." So begins "Transcendental Wild Oats," Louisa's wry account of her father's experiment in communal living, recalled from the safe distance of thirty years.

Actually, June 1, 1843, was a perfect day, sunny and a little cool. The entire summer of 1843 was generous to New England, arriving early, staying late, bathing the region in hazy sunshine day after long day. In the heady climate of that nineteenth-century summer of love, when Millerites anticipated the end of the world and planted no crops, Brook Farmers held weekly dances and awarded flowers to the best-dressed girl, Mormons indulged in polygamy, and Shakers practiced celibacy, Bronson Alcott and his entourage made their way to a "sequestered dell" in Harvard, Massachusetts, to live out yet another native-born utopian scheme.

Louisa's source for much of "Transcendental Wild Oats" was the journal she kept at Fruitlands. The first surviving fragment begins midsentence with an unpunctuated burst of social news: "and he brought his son James* with him when Lizzy and I came home from our walk we played

---

* Neither father nor son James has been identified.

a little. After supper I played some again and then went to bed, having spent a very pleasant day."

Louisa and Anna recorded many pleasant days that summer in their journals. Louisa's is by turns exuberant and self-critical: "I ran in the wind and played be a horse, and had a lovely time in the woods with Anna and Lizzie. . . . I felt sad because I have been cross to-day and did not mind Mother." Anna's is studied and dutiful: "I felt sad at the thought of leaving Concord and all my little friends . . . but Father and Mother and my dear sisters were going with me, and that would make me happy anywhere."

Both parents read, commented upon, and sometimes commented *on* the pages of the journals. On her eleventh birthday Louisa wrote: "I told mother I liked to have her write in my book. She said she would put in more, and she wrote this to help me—'Dear Louy,—Your handwriting improves very fast. Take pains and do not be in a hurry. I like you to make observations about our conversations and your own thoughts. It helps you to express them and to understand your little self. . . . May it be a record of pure thought and good actions, then you will indeed be the precious child of your loving mother.'"

Louisa mined her Fruitlands diary for material for "Transcendental Wild Oats." Like her mother, she periodically left sympathetic comments in her journals.

> Friday, Nov. 2nd. Anna and I did the work. In the evening Mr. Lane asked us, "What is Man?" These were our answers: A human being, an animal with a mind, a creature, a body, a soul, and a mind. After a long talk we went to bed very tired.
>
> [No wonder, after doing the work, and worrying their little wits with such lessons.—L.M.A.]
>
> Sunday, [Sept.] 24th . . . I was cross today, and I cried when I went to bed. I made good resolutions, and felt better in my heart. If I only kept all I make, I should be the best girl in the world. But I don't, and so am very bad.
>
> [Poor little sinner! She says the same at fifty.—L.M.A.]

Two of Bronson and Lane's handful of recruits were at the red farmhouse when the Alcotts arrived. Twenty-year-old Sam Larned was a Brook Farm dropout in search of greater discipline. Wood Abram, the former Abram Wood, was a young eccentric from Concord, a friend of Thoreau's, "whose peculiar mission was to turn his name hind part before. . . ." Another Fruitlander, "believing that language was of little consequence if the spirit was only right, startled newcomers by blandly greeting them with 'good morning, damn you,' and other remarks of an equally mixed order."

Also on hand were two neighbors. Joseph Palmer was a sympathetic local farmer "persecuted for wearing the beard," as his gravestone still attests. Palmer was jailed for a year for defending his right not to shave. Louisa thought his "idea of reform consisted chiefly in wearing white cotton raiment and shoes of untanned leather. This costume, with a snowy beard, gave him a venerable, and at the same time a somewhat bridal appearance." The other neighbor, Christy Greene, was a young teacher in the nearby Tyngsboro school, who gave lessons to the girls and helped with the farm work that summer.

The two recruits and the two neighbors had made a pass at cleaning up the derelict red farmhouse. They welcomed the travelers with a meal of roasted potatoes, brown bread, and water, served up "in two plates, a tin pan, and one mug" (according to Louisa's 1873 account). "But having cast the forms and vanities of a depraved world behind them, the elders welcomed hardship with the enthusiasm of new pioneers, and the children heartily enjoyed this foretaste of what they believed was to be a sort of perpetual picnic." With their furniture yet to be delivered, the weary pilgrims camped out on the kitchen floor.

The following day, Abby threw herself into bringing the century-old house back to life as she had at Dove Cottage three years before. Anna and Louisa were old enough to help, while Lizzie looked after toddler May. "We are cleaning, white-washing, driving nails here and there, putting up curtain stuff," Abby wrote Hannah Robie, begging her to come see for herself.

The house's greatest treasure was a collection of a thousand volumes of wisdom, books that Bronson had inherited from James Greaves, the founder of Alcott House in England. Emerson described the hoard in the *Dial* as the richest collection of writings in the mystic tradition in the country. Included were tomes on Buddhism and Confucianism, possibly the first of their kind to make their way across the Atlantic. "To this rare library," writes Louisa in "Transcendental Wild Oats," "was devoted the best room in the house."

Sleeping quarters were less than best. At the back of the house, a steep, narrow staircase led to three small bedrooms. Lane and his son shared one, the Alcotts and three-year-old May another. Presumably all the disciples squeezed into the third—where they slept is not recorded. Nearly invisible on the second-floor landing, a small door opened to a second set of stairs leading to the low-ceilinged attic that Anna, twelve, Louisa, ten, seven-year-old Lizzie, and sometimes May would share. It was little more than a crawl space, where even the littlest child would have to climb into bed on all fours. The only light came from small windows at either end of the rafters. It was pitilessly hot in summer, bitingly cold in winter.

Anyone counting heads at bedtime might have wondered where the fervently hoped-for future members of the family would be housed. But Abby was exhilarated. "Walked over our little territory of woodland, vale, meadow, and pasture," she wrote in her journal that first week. "The soul expands in such a region of sights and sounds." To Sam a couple of weeks later she exulted, "The prospect . . . is indescribable—an interminable range of lofty hills 'whose summits pierce the heavens as if with a wedge,'" and added, "We owe *nobody nothing*. It is a comfortable feeling after a perturbation of 10 years." (Actually, they still owed the Boston creditors six thousand dollars.)

If possible, Bronson's open-air exertions outdid his wife's indoor efforts. He worked ten to twelve hours a day, plowing and planting. "Mr. Alcott is as persevering in practice as last year we found him to be in idea," Lane reported. "His hand is everywhere, like his mind." Lane's mind was everywhere but on farming. In "Transcendental Wild Oats," Louisa suggests that he was lazy and bossy.

> "Each member is to perform the work for which experience, strength, and taste best fit him," continued Dictator Lion [Lane]. "Thus drudgery and disorder will be avoided and harmony prevail. . . ."
> "What part of the work do you incline to yourself?" asked Sister Hope [Abby], with a humorous glimmer in her keen eyes.
> "I shall wait till it is made clear to me. Being in preference to doing is the great aim. . . ."
> "I thought so." And Mrs. Lamb [Abby] sighed audibly, for during the year he had spent in her family Brother Timon [Lane] had so faithfully carried out his idea of "being, not doing," that she had found his "divine growth" both an expensive and unsatisfactory process.

They needed help, and they needed to hurry. Already more than a month late in planting, they meant to do it without animal labor. Louisa's Moses White (the bearded Joseph Palmer) inquires of Abel Lamb [Bronson] in "Transcendental Wild Oats" how they will plow the ten-acre lot: "'We shall spade it,' replied Abel [Bronson]," meaning that they would turn over the ten acres of long-fallow earth with shovels, a square foot at a time. Moses said no more, "though he indulged in a shake of the head as he glanced at hands that had held nothing heavier than a pen for years."

Not long after, the communards accepted the loan from the genial Palmer of a mixed team of an ox and a cow. Abby insisted on milk for May, principles be damned. Anna would recall that disciples starving on the apple, bread, and water diet could be found in the barn, secretly drinking the outlawed product of the animal labor of Farmer Palmer's cow.

Cleanliness and frigid water were both fetishes at Fruitlands. Bronson rigged up a large bathing enclosure out of sheets and clothesline, then stood on a ladder and poured wet purity through a sieve onto his shrieking daughters' heads. "I rose at five and had my bath. I love cold water!" Louisa trilled. After showering, Fruitlands' males dressed in tunics and trousers of Bronson's design and manufacture. Female garb consisted of tunics and bloomers, a half century before Amelia Bloomer reinvented the latter for a few daring lady bicyclists. These revolutionary garments were made of linen, so as not to exploit the slave labor that made cotton, or the sheep labor that made wool. Even had they been able to afford it, silk would have been forbidden as "worm-slaughter."

Alcott dressed the most ordinary events of the day in the trappings of ritual. Following the morning's unleavened bread, porridge, and water— each introduced at the table with song—came chores, the children's lessons, and work in the fields. Lunch was accompanied by graham crackers imprinted with mottoes. Louisa recorded them in her diary. "Vegetable diet and sweet repose, Animal food and nightmare" was one truism that the girls swallowed. Another asserted that "without a flesh diet there could be no blood-shedding war." A puzzling and pagan saying was "Apollo eats no flesh and has no beard, his voice is melody itself."

Hours of self-criticism and philosophical questioning were supplemented by Sunday readings of two hours' duration, and impromptu sermonettes from Bronson or Lane aimed at consolidating the consociate ethic.

Alcott birthdays had always been celebrated with sacramental solemnity as well as joy and presents, but the first Fruitlands birthday was a sylvan spectacle as much about the new community as the eight-year-old honoree. "This was Lizzie's birthday," Anna described it in her diary for June 24. "I arose before five o'clock and went with mother, William, and Louisa to the woods, where we fixed a little pine tree in the ground and hung up all the presents on it. I then made a wreath for all of us of oak leaves." After breakfast, the consociates made a procession into the woods, where Lane played his fiddle and the others sang. Bronson read a parable and then an original ode of five stanzas with lines such as "And Father's friends / Whom Briton lends / To noblest human ends." Finally the company heard Bronson's salute to Lizzie: "A rose of Fruitland's quiet dell / A child intent on doing well / Devout secluded from all sin / Fragrance without and fair within / a plant matured in God's device / An Amaranth in paradise."

A stream of curious visitors passed through that summer: Sam May and his family drove over for the day from Lexington, the poet William Ellery Channing came from Concord, Abby's nephew Sam Greele from Boston, George Ripley and his wife from Brook Farm, a Mr. Orris from Oberlin College, and a Mrs. Hays and her son, Jewish friends of the May family, from Philadelphia. They came to see for themselves, and left with a store of amusing anecdotes to carry them through many a social occasion.

When Ralph Waldo Emerson visited the new settlement on Independence Day, he must have been reminded of the fable of the grasshopper and the ants. "The sun and the evening sky do not look calmer . . . than Alcott and his family at Fruitlands," he wrote in his journal. "I think there is as much merit in beautiful manners as in hard work. . . . They look well in July. Let us see how they fare in December."

"The right people, with the right motives, and holy purpose, do not come," Abby wrote in frustration. Samuel Bower, who believed in nudism, may have been one of the wrong ones. He makes a memorable appearance as Brother Pease in "Transcendental Wild Oats": "Occasionally he took his walks abroad, airily attired in an unbleached cotton poncho, which was the nearest approach to the primeval costume he was allowed to indulge in. At midsummer he retired to the wilderness, to try his plan where the woodchucks were without prejudices and huckleberry-bushes were hospitably full. A sunstroke unfortunately spoilt his plan." The following winter Bower forsook cold New England for sunny Florida.

From Vermont came Abraham Everett, a forty-two-year-old cooper (barrel or tub maker). In Lane's view, Everett was "not a spiritual being, at least not consciously and wishfully so." Lane's reasoning can be adduced from the following passage in Louisa's "Transcendental Wild Oats."

> A second irrepressible being held that all the emotions of the soul should be freely expressed, and illustrated his theory by antics that would have sent him to a lunatic asylum, if, as an unregenerate wag said, he had not already been in one. When his spirit soared, he climbed trees and shouted; when doubt assailed him, he lay upon the floor and groaned lamentably; . . . and when a great thought burst upon him in the watches of the night, he crowed like a jocund cockerel, to the great delight of the children and the great annoyance of the elders.

Emerson exploited the humor in Fruitlands long before Louisa did, delivering a satirically edged lecture on the would-be utopias of the "Newness" that was later disseminated in the *Dial*. His ostensible subject was competing communities, but his references all came straight from the tenets of Alcott and Lane.

> They defied each other, like a congress of kings. . . . One apostle thought all men should go to farming; and another, that no man should buy or sell; another, that the mischief was in our diet, that we eat and drink damnation. . . . Others attacked . . . the tyranny of man over brute nature. . . . The ox must be taken from the plough, and the horse from the cart. . . . Even the insect world was to be defended, . . . and a society for the protection of ground-worms, slugs, and mosquitos was to be incorporated without delay.

Perhaps the most spiritual being to grace Fruitlands was Isaac Hecker, who would convert to Catholicism and found the Paulist priesthood in 1858. Tall and blond and in his early twenties, he had clear blue eyes that brightened a broad, pocked face. Hecker had been living at

Brook Farm, but Charles Lane reported that he was "by no means satisfied with [its] schoolboy, dilettante spiritualism," and persuaded him to exchange its well-financed order for Fruitlands' promise of greater purity and deprivation. Hecker recorded some of its nonstop stream of philosophic chat: "This morning after breakfast a conversation was held on Friendship and its laws and conditions. Mr. Alcott places Innocence first; Larned, Thoughtfulness; I, Seriousness; Lane, Fidelity."

Even Lane agreed that the fledgling community needed more women to do women's work. Abby complained that she and the girls were wearing themselves out entertaining ungrateful community members and curiosity seekers. She wrote to her brother that she felt like "a noble horse harnessed in a yoke and made to drag and pull instead of trot and canter." When Lane decided that Abby was not to take part in any discussion apart from so-called carnal matters, that is, food, shelter, and clothing, she refused to eat with the others until Anna begged her to come back.

The only woman to join Fruitlands did not fare well. When Ann Page appeared, Abby at first found her agreeable. She did some housework, and gave the girls music lessons. Louisa was not appreciative: "I had a music lesson with Miss P. I hate her, she is so fussy." She mentions her just once more—with a trenchant "Miss P. is gone." Sharp-eyed Louisa apparently did not observe the lady busying herself with housework, either. Ann Page's portrayal as Jane Gage in "Transcendental Wild Oats" is not flattering:

> Miss Jane Gage was a stout lady of mature years, sentimental, amiable, and lazy. She shirked all duties as clogs upon her spirit's wings. . . .
> When to the question, "Are there any beasts of burden on the place?" Mrs. Lamb [Abby] answered, "Only one woman!" The buxom Jane . . . laughed at the joke, and let the stout-hearted sister tug on alone.
>   Unfortunately, the poor lady hankered after the fleshpots . . . , and on one dire occasion, she partook of fish at a neighbor's table.
>   One of the children reported this sad lapse from virtue, and poor Jane was publicly reprimanded by Timon [Lane].
>   "I only took a little bit of the tail," sobbed the penitent poetess.
>   "Yes, but the whole fish had to be tortured and slain that you might tempt your carnal appetite with that one taste of the tail. Know ye now,

consumers of flesh meat, that ye are nourishing the wolf and tiger in your bosoms?"

At this awful question, and the peal of laughter which arose from some of the younger brethren . . . poor Jane fled from the room to pack her trunk and return to a world where fishes' tails were not forbidden fruit.

There is no independent evidence that Ann Page was banished for the crime of filching a fish tail, but Abby turned against her, as she often did when other people came too close. In midautumn there was a blowup, and Page fled—or was sent packing. Louisa's mention of tattling on and ridicule of Page by the younger brethren suggests that the children might have had something to do with it.

Once the planting had been completed, the overseers of paradise were rarely to be seen in their infant community. Bronson and Lane went trolling for fresh recruits, extolling Fruitlands to local audiences.

After just two weeks Isaac Hecker, their prize catch, announced he was leaving. Pressed by Bronson to explain, Hecker cited five hindrances, among them Bronson's lack of openness, his family, and the fact that Fruitlands had very little fruit.

Many would-be adherents must have been discouraged by the excess of renunciation at Fruitlands, summed up in a letter by Bronson and Lane that appeared in the *Herald of Freedom* in early September, and which Abby clipped out and pasted into her journal.

Shall I sip tea or coffee, the inquiry may be. No. Abstain from *all* ardent, as from alcoholic drinks. Shall I consume pork, beef, or mutton? Not if I value health or life. Shall I stimulate with milk? No. Shall I warm my bathing water? Not if cheerfulness is valuable. . . . Shall I become a hireling, or hire others? Shall I subject cattle? Shall I trade? Shall I claim property in any created thing? Shall I adopt a form of religion? Shall I become a parent?

The answer to all these questions was the same: abstain. In Louisa's diary of August 28, she reported, "We had a dinner of bread and water." The perpetual picnic was over.

A mile from Fruitlands, in the town of Harvard, was a thriving Shaker settlement established fifty years earlier by the group's founder herself, Mother Ann Lee. Based upon the principles of separation from the world, communalism, confession, and celibacy, the Shakers are remembered more now for their industry, their labor-saving technologies— metal pen nibs, the flat broom, the circular saw, seed packaging—and their elegantly simple baskets and furniture. The two hundred Harvard Shakers were unapologetic flesh eaters and milk drinkers who kept cattle, horses, and pigs, and traded freely and pragmatically with the secular world. Their pursuit of spiritual perfection through sexual abstinence was enforced by a strict segregation of the sexes in every phase of community life.

In the Alcotts' day, the Shakers were in the heat of a revival that brought the movement to its peak membership of six thousand men, women, and children living in nineteen villages. After decades of institutionalization when the ecstatic prayer that had given the group its name was abandoned, the Shakers were set in motion again in response to messages from Mother Ann brought back from children's "visits" to the spirit realm. Celibacy was made more intriguing by earthly visitations from heavenly spirits who set young Shaker women dancing, whirling, and speaking in tongues. The "Era of Manifestations" coincided with and no doubt owed something to the "Newness" of the Transcendentalist movement.

Louisa's Fruitlands diary for August 4 recorded the first of several visits by Fruitlands' founders to nearby Harvard: "Father and Mr. Kay and Mr. Lane went to the Shakers and did not return till Evening." The journal for the Shaker community also recorded their presence, called them "Transcendentalest [sic]," and noted, "they seem to be inquiring into our principles."

Lane was enthralled by the purity of the scheme. In talks Abby was not permitted to join (but which were held in her presence), he pounded away at Bronson to impose sexual abstinence on Fruitlands. Perhaps the ultimate renunciation, it was one that only the Alcotts would have to make. Bronson conceded the difficulty of being both a prophet and a family man, but went no further, held back by ties of affection and the impossibility of severing conjugal relations with Abby. He withdrew into a stony silence.

As one by one Bronson's adherents fell away, by late summer the idea of selling Fruitlands and joining the Shakers grew more attractive. Bronson and Lane took Abby to see for herself. "Visited the Shakers," she reported. The rigid way of life held no charms for her, and she found the apparent harmony suspect. "There is a servitude somewhere, I have no doubt. There is a fat sleek comfortable look about the men, and among the women there is a stiff awkward reserve that belongs to neither sublime resignation nor divine hope." Abby saw no equality in separation between the sexes: "Wherever I turn, I see the yoke on woman in some form or another." All that was beside the point. Abby Alcott could never have given the nurture of her children to a group, let alone see them only once a year, under the supervision of an elder, as Shaker parents did.

In mid-September, Bronson and Lane took off on a last-ditch recruiting tour stopping in Boston, Brook Farm, and the utopian communities in Hopedale, Northampton, and Providence before drifting south to New York, where they turned up in their linen regalia in Lydia Maria Child's parlor. When Child asked them what had brought them there, Bronson replied, "I don't know. It seems a miracle we are here." Penniless by the time they headed home, they boarded a steamer for New Haven. Bronson admitted that he and Lane had neither tickets nor money; he paid their way by conducting a Conversation with the passengers and the crew.

With the same blithe indifference, they had left Fruitlands with the freshly cut barley crop lying uncollected on the ground. The next day, Abby watched black clouds speeding in their direction and lightning crackling in the distant sky. Gathering up all the available baskets and sheets, she raced with the three older girls and William Lane to the barley field. They filled the baskets and sheets, carried or dragged them back to the barn, then ran back for more until the storm broke over their heads.

After that, William Lane was in bed for a month with a low fever. Anna had been complaining throughout the summer of fatigue and lightheadedness. The usually unshakable Louisa had a heavy cough, headache, and pain in her side.

After a summer of affection and growing closeness, Louisa and Anna were suddenly as much at odds with each other as when they were toddlers, acting out the growing tensions in the disintegrating household even as they strained to be virtuous. "When I woke up," Louisa wrote the night of October 8, "the first thought I got was, 'It's Mother's birthday: I must be very good.' I ran and wished her a happy birthday and gave her my kiss." The letter that accompanied Louisa's gift of a cross-shaped bookmark made of moss and a piece of poetry included a backhanded confession.

> Dearest Mother
>   I have spent a very pleasant morning and I hardly dare speak to An-
> nie for fear she should speak unkindly and get me angry. O she is so
> very very cross I cannot love her it seems as if she did every thing to
> trouble me but I will try to love her better. I hope you have spent a
> pleasant morning. Please axcept this book mark from your affectionate
> daughter.
>
> > > > > > > > > Louisa

A few days later, Abby made a visit to Boston, taking Lizzie with her, and leaving the other girls with Bronson and Lane. "I shall be very lonely without dear little Betty [Lizzie], and no one will be as good to me as Mother," wrote Louisa. She turned to reading and writing for comfort. "I read in Plutarch. I made a verse about sunset:

> *Softly does the sun descend*
> *To his couch upon the hill*
> *Then, oh then, I love to sit*
> *On mossy banks beside the rill.*

In early November, Abby informed Sam, "It is concluded, I believe, that we are to stay here this winter. I will predict nothing but try to fortify myself for all the storms." The storms would be constant; they would be stranded in the derelict farmhouse during the worst winter in a century, with snowfall totalling a hundred inches. Abby stiffened into a pillar of strength for her children while the men fell apart. "Mr. Lane," she noted, "looks miserably *and acts worse.*"

Bronson acted downright unhinged. Of all his journals, only the year of Fruitlands is lost—left, he claimed, on a train. Bronson later recalled fearing he was losing his sanity during the dark days at Fruitlands. He was probably right. During an episode not long before, Abby had described Bronson's state of mind to Sam May in terms that suggest manic paranoia. She had confided to her brother: "I do not allow myself to despair of his recovery, but oh, Sam that piercing thought flashes through my mind of insanity, and a grave, yawning to receive his precious body, would be to me a consolation compared to that condition of life."

Abby had a plan to rescue her family from Fruitlands. She had already laid the groundwork when, on her way back from Boston, she stopped in Lexington to confer with her brother. Apparently she asked Sam not to honor his written commitment to make a November payment on the loan that had secured Fruitlands. She suggested he make the argument that Fruitlands was not a proper home for his sister, and that the note had been signed on the assurance that it would be. Sam said he would think about it. After her return to Fruitlands, Sam May wrote to Abby that he would renounce the debt. Abby must have been very convincing to succeed in getting her minister brother to welsh on a financial obligation.

"Your letter was duly received and pleased me better than it did the other proprietor of the Estate," Abby replied to Sam in mid-November, referring to Lane. "I do not wish you to put a cent here. I am sifting everything to the bottom. I will know the foundation, centre and circumference. . . . I see no clean healthy safe course here in connexion with Mr. L." Abby's three adjectives, *clean*, *healthy*, and *safe*, before *course* suggest a suspicion of homosexuality. While it seems valid to say that Abby suspected that Lane and Bronson's relationship was homosexual or homoerotic, or both, the truth cannot be known. That there was a love triangle with Bronson at the center is undeniable.

Sam May's decision sent Bronson and Lane scrambling to make alternative arrangements. Bronson talked of using the frame of Mr. Wyman's smaller barn to build a house in the woods. He and Lane considered selling off part of the land to Joseph Palmer's son or to a young farmer from Boxboro who had made them an offer for thirty acres. "Mr. Lane thought of accepting it," Abby wrote Sam, "and letting us go out naked."

But Abby trumped Lane. She announced her plan to leave—and to take the furniture with her. Bronson could go with the rest of the family or stay with Lane. Now it was Lane who accused Abby of leaving him "alone and naked in a new world." In a letter to Oldham in England, Lane reported that "Mrs. Alcott gives notice that she concedes to the wishes of her friends and shall withdraw to a house which they will provide for herself and her four children. . . . You will perceive a separation is possible." Lane is clear that Mrs. Alcott and the children might separate from him, but who was separating from Bronson?

Louisa, almost eleven, was aware of the turmoil in the house and was even drawn into it. "In the evening," she wrote on the twentieth of November, "Father and Mr. L. had a talk, and Father asked us if we saw any reason to separate. Mother wanted to, she is so tired."

Another painful family discussion took place on the tenth of December. "Mr. L. was in Boston and we were glad. In the eve father and mother and Anna and I had a long talk." Louisa was devastated to learn that her father might leave the family for Charles Lane: "I was very unhappy and we all cried. Anna and I cried in bed, and I prayed God to keep us all together." Where any of them would go from Fruitlands was not clear. The Shaker colony was the closest refuge for the homeless. "Winter Shakers" were an annual phenomenon. The tension in the farmhouse built while outside snowdrifts piled up against the doors and a howling wind penetrated the walls.

In early December, Lane set off for Concord to refuse to pay his taxes, as Bronson had done the year before. He too was jailed and released after Judge Hoar denied him glory by paying the tax himself, as he had for Bronson. Lane spent a few days with Emerson before returning to Fruitlands, where he kept to himself (although the house is so small it is hard to tell how). Bronson was the next to bolt, leaving on Christmas Eve to attend a conference in Boston. While Lane sulked and Mr. Lovejoy, their reliable neighbor, twice shoveled a path from the rutted track to their front door, Abby filled her daughters' stockings with bonbons and poems and organized a little party with the neighbors. She led the children in singing in hopes of bringing Christmas cheer to the cold farmhouse in the cheerless landscape. Louisa copied into her diary the poem Abby had written for her.

Christmass Rimes

Christmass is here
Louisa my dear
Then Happy we'll be
Gladsome and free

God with you abide
With love for your guide
In time you'll go right
With heart and with might.

Eleven-year-old Louisa spent hours writing in her journal on Christmas Day, filling page after page with stanzas from *Pilgrim's Progress* that had special meaning for her mother, and now for her. They continued to resonate in later years, as annotations by the adult Louisa suggest.

I am content with what I have,
Little be it or much
And Lord! Contentment still I crave
Because thou savest such.

[Little Lu began early to feel the family cares and peculiar trials.—L.M.A.]

They move me to watch and pray,
To strive to be sincere
To take my cross up day by day,
And serve the Lord with fear.

[The appropriateness of this song at this time was much greater than the child saw. She never forgot this experience, and her little cross began to grow heavier from this hour.—L.M.A.]

"I mean to take my cubs and retreat," Abby had declared, and on January 1 she recorded her decision to follow through: "Concluded to go to Mr. Lovejoy's, until Spring, having dissolved all connection with Fruitlands." There is no mention of whether Bronson would be joining them. On January 6 she noted that Lane and his son had gone to shelter with the Shakers, and that she had sent a "load of goods to Mr. L's." On the seventh, she reported cataloging the library in preparation for the move, and a final exhausted lament: "The arrangements here have never suited me, and I am impatient to leave all behind and work out my way in some more simple mode of life. My duties have been arduous, but my satisfaction small."

Bronson's response was to take to his bed, not speaking, eating, or drinking. Later he would write that these were the worst days of his life; he felt completely desolated and had hallucinations of being tortured by demons. "Very sad, indeed, it was to see this half-god driven to the wall," Emerson wrote of his friend's crisis. Abby left no account of this last excruciating chapter, but Louisa absorbed every detail. She recreated the scene in "Transcendental Wild Oats," abandoning her comic tone for sincere if over-the-top sentiment.

> Silently he lay down upon his bed, turned his face to the wall, and waited with pathetic patience for death. . . . Days and nights went by, and neither food nor water passed his lips. . . . When body was past any pang of hunger and thirst, and soul stood ready to depart, the love that outlives all else refused to die. "My faithful wife, my little girls— they have not forsaken me, they are mine by ties that none can break. . . . This duty remains to me, and I must do it manfully. For their sakes, the world will forgive me in time; for their sakes, God will sustain me now."

The defeated idealist reached for the food his faithful mate had left for him: "In the early dawn, when that sad wife crept fearfully in to see what a change had come to the patient face on the pillow, she found it smiling at her, saw a wasted hand outstretched to her, and heard a feeble voice cry bravely, 'Hope!'"

On January 11 Abby reported her victory to Sam. "Yesterday, having ate our last bit and burnt our last chip we sent for Mr. Lovejoy to come and get us out. . . . All Mr. Lane's efforts have been to disunite us. But Mr. Alcott's conjugal and paternal instincts were too strong for him. He comes away convinced that Mr. Lane and he were never truly united." The marital balance of power had shifted away from Bronson. He would never again exert sole control over the family's movements.

Louisa took it all in—the near-collapse of the family, her father's breakdown, and her mother's taking up of the reins—and was inspired to think of her own future. She was bursting with pent-up desire: for power, for freedom, and for the material and sensory gratification she was not supposed to want, but did want very much.

On October 8, her mother's birthday, Louisa poured out her life's desires in a sentence: "I wish I was rich, I was good, and we were all a happy family this day." If she were good, she would be loved. If she were rich, they could be happy. She wanted especially for her mother to be happy. The bit of poetry she enclosed with the moss-covered bookmark was probably "To Mother," written that year. It revealed the dream Louisa would strive to make real. The poem became a touchstone; Louisa would repeat phrases from it far into her future.

To Mother

I hope that soon, dear mother,
You and I may be
In the quiet room my fancy
Has so often made for thee,—

The pleasant, sunny chamber,
The cushioned easy-chair
The book laid for your reading,
The vase of flowers fair;

The desk beside the window
Where the sun shines warm and bright;
And there in ease and quiet
The promised book you write;

While I sit close beside you,
Content at last to see
That you can rest, dear mother,
And I can cherish thee.

The last paragraph of Louisa's Fruitlands diary demonstrated where her happiness lay: not in riches and fame, but in the exhilaration of movement, the sensations of nature, and the enchantment of good books.

I wrote in my Imagination Book, and enjoyed it very much. Life is pleasanter than it used to be, and I don't care about dying any more. Had a splendid run, and got a box of cones to burn. Sat and heard the pines sing a long time. Read Miss Bremer's "Home" in the eve. Had good dreams, and woke now and then to think, and watch the moon. I had a pleasant time in my mind, for it was happy.

"Moods began early—L M A," reads Louisa's comment thirty years later.

SEVEN

THE HAPPIEST YEARS
OF MY LIFE

A sled ride down the rutted track from Fruitlands, the Alcotts had the use of the kitchen and three rooms in the Lovejoy farmhouse for fifty cents a week, "quite comfortable for winter quarters," a relieved Abby wrote in her journal, but hardly a permanent solution.

In the spring they relocated to Still River, the nearest village, to rent half of a house called "Brick Ends" because its sides were faced in brick. The Alcotts had five rooms, a kitchen, and permission to build an outdoor shower room to serve the unusual Alcott bathing practices. "Our home is humble," Abby recorded in her diary on April 24, the day of the move, "but we have much comfort and few responsibilities—Mr. Alcott laboring unremittingly in his garden, producing neat regular beds and borders, verdure presenting itself and food promising for us. What a calling is the husbandman's! How intimately he relates himself to God!" Abby's ecstasy may have sprung from relief that Bronson was finally up and at work.

In Still River, Louisa, Lizzie, and Anna had the rare experience of attending a town school. The sisters were thrilled to find friends their own age. "As sure as the sun shone and the skies were blue, just so sure was the afternoon gathering on the grass plot in front of the 'Brick Ends,' and all of us enjoyed jumping rope, tossing ball, and rolling hoop," Annie Clark, one of their playmates, remembered. "Mrs. Alcott was like the guardian angel of the merry company." Abby was a beloved presence to her children's friends, "smiling benignly upon our gay pranks."

In Clark's recollection, Louisa was the foremost of the sisters, and the ringleader of the group. Besides Annie Clark and others there were three Gardners, Polly, Sophia, and Walter. Louisa "married" Walter Gardner in the Brick Ends woodshed sometime that giddy spring, wearing an apron on her head for a veil and "jumping the broom" slave-style to tie the knot. The "brief and tragical experience," as Louisa laughingly referred to it some two decades later, came to a violent end with a slap to the groom from the bride.

Clark recalled that Louisa often "got mad . . . she *could* be severe." At eleven, Louisa still sometimes expressed herself in violence. She even took out her anger on inanimate objects. "One day the neighbors were astonished to see a chair suspended from one of the Brick Ends windows. It appeared that Louisa, while cleaning house with great energy, had 'bumped' herself against a chair, whereupon that devoted article of furniture was arraigned, found guilty, and immediately hanged!" There are various versions (including one from Still River) of another "scrape," as Louisa dubbed her escapades, involving lamp oil. Louisa's own version, in "Poppy's Pranks," begins on a familiar note, with the naughty child locked in a room for punishment. Bored and angry, she breaks a lamp, spills the oil, then uses it to shine up everything in the room, including her hair, which makes it beautifully glossy, but "how it did smell! If she had been a young whale, it couldn't have been worse."

Clark recounted a performance Louisa put together for Lizzie's birthday that June. She concocted a satisfying bill of fare out of dubious romantic legends—vaguely Gaelic, Germanic, and Native American—that appealed to her yearning to take part in stirring events on a stage larger than the kitchen, against backdrops more exotic than the usual Alcott boughs of evergreen. Louisa stole the show as Alfarata, an Indian girl who like Louisa was "swift as an antelope through the forest going, / loose were her jetty locks in waving tresses flowing, / Strong and true my arrows are in my painted quiver, / Swift goes my light canoe adown the rapid river." Louisa's costume was made of feathers from local poultry and the duster. Abby stained her skin with the dark red sap of the plant locally called Indian paintbrush (bloodroot). It would take days to fade away; not many mothers would have gone along with the idea.

Louisa's explosive exuberance bewitched fourteen-year-old Frederick

Lllewellyn Willis, an orphan raised by his grandmother, who was boarding in Still River for the summer. The Alcotts soon realized he was a cousin of their own Willis cousins. Within a week of meeting the Alcotts, Fred Willis persuaded his grandmother to let him move in with them, inaugurating a long period of intimacy. Fred, Anna, and Louisa spent much of that adolescent summer at a nearby swimming hole called Bare Hill Pond, blissfully unsupervised and untroubled. "We christened a favorite nook, a beautiful rocky glen carpeted with moss and adorned with ferns opening upon the water's edge, 'Spiderland,'" Willis wrote. "I was the King of the realm, Anna was the Queen, and Louisa the Princess Royal." Louisa loved spiders as she loved all animals. When eight-legged residents of Spiderland died, she enjoyed her duty as Princess Royal to give them ritual burials, complete with monuments and epitaphs.

Willis was deeply devoted to Abby, who confided her worries and trusted her tears to him. "No matter how weary she might be with the washing and ironing, the baking and cleaning," he remembered, "it was all hidden from the group of girls with whom she was always ready to enter into fun and frolic, as if she never had a care." Her daughters were not so protected within the privacy of the family.

Willis was also greatly taken with Bronson and described him as a man "strangely out of place in the midst of the practical utilitarianism of the 19th century," but whose gift for teaching never left him. "Mr. Alcott's table talks were constantly delightful. . . . I have seen him take an apple upon his fork, and while preparing it for eating, give a fascinating little lecture as to its growth and development from germ to matured fruit, his language quaintly beautiful and charmingly practical." This was the kind of disquisition Louisa enjoyed too. An apple tasty enough to eat raw would have been a novelty as well as a marvel. The introduction of hybrid varieties unknown in Bronson's youth might have added to his appreciation of the apple's Edenic charms.

While the children and her husband thrived on fine weather and fresh produce, Abby orchestrated their survival with regular appeals to Sam May and other relatives. They were living in Still River on borrowed time and money, but where to go from there was not clear. Emerson urged a return to Concord. Abby had little desire to go back to a town she thought was boring and stupid, and had already raised with Sam the possibility of a move close to his family in Lexington. But she recognized the value of Emerson's influence on Bronson. "Emerson will nurture a wiser, [more] rational view than Mr. A's celestial cogitations. . . . I dread his falling into that solitary life he led last winter." So although Abby could have exercised her newfound power in the family, she quietly abandoned the idea of Lexington. "Mr. A's inclinations are all for Concord," she wrote Sam. In early October, the Alcotts loaded up their earthly goods, boarded a stagecoach, and said good-bye to Still River.

This move was wrenching to Louisa, as the one from Fruitlands had not been, and her memories of Still River were as bright as those of Fruitlands were dark. She would hanker for her friend Sophia Gardner to the point of walking from Concord, some fifteen miles each way, to visit her. Not until a year after the departure from Still River was Louisa ready to render it in comic terms, writing to Sophia, "My dear Fire, as Abby [May] still calls you. [Her name was pronounced "So-FY-a," hence "Fire" to four-year-old May.] Oh, if you had only been with us when we came home!—a stage[coach] full of bawling babies and nervous marms to take care of the little dears. I had to be perched on top, and pitched up and down like butter-in-a-churn." Midway, they transferred to the new Fitchburg Railroad. Louisa's first train ride was a smooth run to Concord at twenty miles per hour, twice the speed of the stagecoach.

Sam May, trustee for Abby of their father's small estate, had a plan to help the Alcotts while honoring Bronson's inconvenient ideals. He wrote to Emerson, who yet again had offered to help and had located a house and land near his own.

> It is very important that . . . my sister and her family might have a shelter . . . without implicating [Mr. Alcott] in the sin of living upon soil appropriated to his exclusive use. . . . Mr. Sewall and myself, as trustees of the little property which has been saved for Mrs. Alcott—$1350—will expend $1000 in the purchase of the house and a portion of the land . . . leaving the rest to be held by yourself or any one you please to appoint. . . . Let Mr. Alcott's wishes, that all feel welcome there, as to a common inheritance, be considered. . . . Not that I think that plan practicable. . . . But he is so sincere, so devout, so full of faith, that I long to have him try his experiment to his own entire satisfaction.

Louisa said her three years at Hillside, their new home, "were the happiest years" of her life, and based most of the incidents of *Little Women* on them. The house, situated on a crescent of land between the busy road and a sloping ridge, was already old at the time of the Revolution, had been added to haphazardly, and was much in need of repair inside and out. Horatio Cogswell, the most recent owner, had kept pigs in the front yard. Across the road were eight acres of meadow for an orchard and garden that Bronson, ever the "Hoper," thought would sustain them for all but a few months of the year.

Bronson embarked upon renovations enthusiastically. He took pride in his do-it-yourself improvements, curious as some of them were. A cottage on the property he sliced in two, and placed one half on either side of the main house. He dug a new well and installed a pump so that water was brought through a trapdoor directly into the kitchen, a tremendous and novel convenience. He tore down the rotting fence and made a new one. The garden was impressive—all the more so for being created just as horticulture was beginning to be considered an art. Ralph Waldo Emerson was one of the champions of that idea. "Mr. Emerson . . . brings everybody to see it," Abby proudly wrote Sam in early June, adding that "Louisa is enjoying the season—weeds with her father like a Trojan. Anna sticks to her books. Elizabeth [Lizzie] is smiling on everything as if love was as cheap as dirt."

A steady stream of the curious made their way up the Lexington Road to visit the bohemian Alcotts; their antic family life made for entertaining anecdotes. "[Bronson] had been a citizen of the town long enough to acquire a reputation of being a fanatic in belief and habit," recalled Clara Gowing, a contemporary of Louisa. A few Alcott practices were so far ahead of the times they could only be seen as bizarre. "On the opposite side of the road their land extended to a brook where Mr. Alcott built a rustic bathhouse with a thatched roof, which they used daily in warm weather; the girls scampering across the road and field, plunging into the brook and back again," Gowing recalled in 1909, still sounding a little scandalized.

⌒

Some Concordians regarded Bronson Alcott as a mainstay of the Transcendentalist community; many more thought him pompous and criminally impractical. Thoreau saw his friend as a prophet without honor. "Though comparatively disregarded now, when his day comes, laws unsuspected by most will take effect, and masters of families and rulers will come to him for advice," he wrote. Thoreau came to talk with Alcott nearly every day. He borrowed Bronson's ax to chop timbers for his cabin on Emerson's land at Walden Pond; Bronson helped him frame the structure. Thoreau described his frequent visitor in *Walden*: "he was pledged to no institution. . . . Whichever way we turned, it seemed that the heavens and the earth had met together, since he enhanced the beauty of the landscape. A blue-robed man, whose fittest roof is the overarching sky which reflects his serenity. I do not see how he can ever die; Nature cannot spare him." Louisa was surrounded by the best, the brightest, and the friendliest intellectuals of the day. At thirteen, she could understand her father's talks with Thoreau now as she could not two years before; when Margaret Fuller came to visit, she could picture herself a grown woman like Fuller, independent, romantic, and literary.

Abby, ever on the lookout for ways to bring in money, thought they could cover living expenses by running a small school. She fixed up two bedrooms for boarders—one of them Frederick Willis—and invited as teacher Sophia Ford, a naturalist. The group got on famously. Louisa described the kind of wild excursion that made these years her happiest in her letter to Sophia Gardner in Still River.

> [At Sandy] Pond . . . we found lots of grapes and some lovely flowers, and now, if you won't laugh, I'll tell you something—if you will believe it, Miss F.—and all of us waded across it, a great big pond a mile long and half a mile wide, we went splashing along making the fishes run like mad before our big claws, when we got to the other side we had a hard time getting on our shoes and unmentionables, and we came tumbling home all wet and muddy; but we were happy enough, for we came through the woods bawling and singing like crazy folks.

The little school failed to attract students. The schoolmaster was still controversial. Instead of studying at home with their father, Anna and Louisa briefly attended the local school and made friends with other Concord children. Clara Gowing, who was one of them, reported that the sisters were inseparable, that Louisa was the dominant one, and that she "often shocked her sensitive sister by some daring speech or deed." Once she took Gowing joyriding in a horse and sleigh hijacked from a neighbor.

At school Louisa found romance. She described Augustus, whose surname is not known, in a letter to her sister and in "My Boys," her auto-biographical short story: "Augustus! Oh, my Augustus! my first little lover, and the most romantic . . . with large blue eyes, a noble brow, and a beautiful straight nose. How innocent and soft-hearted and full of splendid dreams he was, and what deliciously romantic times we had floating on the pond . . . as he tried to say unutterable things with his honest blue eyes." He took her to a berry-picking party and then home, "when he languished on the gate, and said he thought chestnut hair the loveliest in the world." Augustus soon went away to boarding school but called on Louisa when he returned, shocking her with his maturity, "so big and handsome and generally imposing that I could not recover myself for several minutes." When she did, she "blushingly" agreed to go "boating and berrying and all the rest of it again." Sadly "I never went, and never saw my little lover any more, for in a few weeks he was dead of a fever . . . and so ended the sad history." Louisa's teen romance would provide material for her early sentimental tales for "story papers" such as the *Boston Saturday Gazette*.

To keep in touch with their many new friends over the long summer vacation, Louisa made a post office, as Abby had and as Jo March in *Little Women* would do, using a hollowed-out tree stump on a hill between the Alcotts' house and the Gowings'. "It was visited almost daily or oftener, and cruelly abused did we feel if on going there we did not find something for ourselves," Clara Gowing remembered. "Louisa's letters especially were refreshing, witty and warm-hearted and earnest, indignant at wrongs, sympathetic, full of energy and shy daring, much as Louisa was herself."

Louisa's mother was daring, too. On winter evenings she let the teenagers play the card game whist, at a time when card playing, especially by children, was frowned upon in many quarters. But as Clara Gowing explained, Mrs. Alcott thought "a game of cards much more enjoyable and less harmful than the kissing games usually resorted to among the young. At one time a boy in some game ventured to kiss Anna [then fourteen or fifteen], much to the indignation of all, and Louisa especially stormed about it. He was ever after known in the family as 'Mr. Smack.' "

Louisa vigorously opposed any romantic attachment that might part her from her older sister. After she had prevailed over Anna when she was barely more than a toddler, Louisa possessed her conquest with the protective jealousy of an older brother. The dramas that the girls (mostly Louisa) wrote and performed together first as teenagers at Hillside drew some of their power from that personal tie. *Norna, or The Witch's Curse,* the melodrama Louisa used to comic effect in *Little Women*, was written in dead earnest. The name of Louisa's character was Louis, the masculine version of her own; Anna was Theresa, possibly for the charismatic saint.

"Ah, Louis, why art thou here?" says Anna-as-Theresa when Louis appears in her heavily fortified chamber. "Some danger must have brought thee; tell me, dear brother."

"Sister dearest, . . . I came to say farewell," says Louisa-as-Louis, who has been banished from the kingdom because he "charged [Theresa's] husband [the king] with neglect and cruelty." Louis must depart immediately. "But I shall return," he promises, to "free thee from his power!" Could Louisa have been charging King Bronson with neglect, and vowing to rescue her mother from *his* power?

Anna Alcott admired and enjoyed Louisa, and does not seem to have been jealous of her sister's talent and drive. "Louisa is so interesting and funny that other girls seem commonplace. I think she'll write something great one of these days," she wrote in her journal. Louisa considered *The Witch's Curse* to be the masterpiece of her childhood plays, Anna revealed in an 1893 introduction to *Comic Tragedies*, an anthology of the Alcott household theatricals. In the essay Anna called herself "Meg" and Louisa "Jo," so identified had the Alcott sisters become with the March sisters of *Little Women* twenty-five years after its publication:

> Jo [Louisa] and Meg [Anna] usually acted the whole play, each often assuming five or six characters, and with rapid change of dress becoming, in one scene, a witch, a soldier, a beauteous lady, and a haughty noble . . . who vanish and reappear at most inopportune moments, and in a great variety of costume. . . . Great skill was required to preserve the illusion, and astonish the audience by these wonderful transformations.
>
> As the fame of the performances spread abroad, contributions were made, . . . and the girls became the proud possessors of a velvet robe, a plumed hat adorned with silver, long yellow boots, . . . mock pearls and tinsel ornaments.

The Witch's Curse, Anna explained, gave Louisa a "chance to stalk haughtily upon the stage in the magnificent boots. . . . It cost hours of thought and labor: for to construct a dungeon, a haunted chamber, a cavern, and a lonely forest taxed to the uttermost the ingenuity of the actors. . . . But inspired by the desire to outshine themselves, the children accomplished a play full of revenge, jealousy, murder, and sorcery, of all which indeed they knew nothing but the name."

The Alcott home was overflowing with outsiders again. No sooner had Fred Willis and Sophia Ford settled at Hillside than Charles Lane turned up. He had left the Shakers after a year and a half—and left his son William with them. Abby was merciful to her old enemy, reporting to Sam that he was "very quiet and gentle seeming saddened by something. The reunion between him and Mr. Alcott was quite affecting." Lane was eager to return to England. He was also penniless and in need of a place to stay. Louisa grumbled about the family hospitality in her diary: "I wish we could be together and no one else." The turbulent girl recorded her irritation, high spirits, disappointments, remorse, and despair in rapid succession: "I am so cross I wish I had never been born," she wrote on a Wednesday. By Thursday things were looking up: "Read *The Heart of Mid-Lothian* and had a very happy day." This novel by Sir Walter Scott had his first female and also his first working-class protagonist. Based on the historic incident of a young woman who walked from Edinburgh to London to get a pardon for a sister unjustly accused of infanticide, the book must have struck a chord for Louisa, who also walked long distances and was all too familiar with some of childbirth's tragic aftermaths.

Wherever else it might ramble, Louisa's journal always returned to her inner turmoil. Her mother was her salvation; even surrounded by strangers and overburdened with responsibilities, Abby could be counted upon to notice, sympathize, and care.

I found this note from Dear mother in my journal:
MY DEAREST LOUY, I often peep into your diary hoping to see some record of more happy days. "Hope and keep busy," dear daughter, and in all perplexity or trouble come freely to your

MOTHER

DEAR MOTHER, You shall see more happy days, and I will come to you with my worries, for you are the best woman in the world.

L.M.A.

Another note from Abby respects Louisa's difficulties: "Your temperament is a peculiar one, and there are few who can really help you." She advises Louisa to "set about the formation of character ... believe me, you are capable of ranking among the best."

Her father had his doubts about that. A "Socratic dialogue," set out in Louisa's journal, sounds like an excruciating catechism.

BRONSON: How can you get what you need?
LOUISA: By trying.
BRONSON: How do you try?
LOUISA: By resolution and perseverance.
BRONSON: How gain love?
LOUISA: By gentleness.
BRONSON: What is gentleness?
LOUISA: Kindness, patience, and care for other people's feelings.
BRONSON: Who has it?
LOUISA: Father and Anna.
BRONSON: Who means to have it?
LOUISA: Louisa, if she can.
[She never got it. L.M.A.]

One evening, after Bronson made Louisa take her dinner alone as punishment for neglecting her journal—Anna and Lizzie had been writing "very faithfully," Bronson noted, while "Louisa was unfaithful"—Abby attempted to soften the blow with another tender note of encouragement: "My Louy, I was grieved at your selfish behavior this morning, but also greatly pleased to find you bore so meekly your father's reproof. . . . It is not to be expected that children should always do right; but oh, how lovely it is to see a child penitent and patient when the passion is over."

Knowing how Louisa struggled to keep her temper, Abby advised her to pick up her pen or go for a walk when she got angry, and at all costs, to hold her tongue. "I encourage her writing," Abby wrote Sam. "It is a safety valve to her smothered sorrow, which might otherwise consume her young and tender heart."

"I was very dismal and then I went to walk and made a poem," Louisa wrote. She had taken Abby's advice.

Despondency

Silent and sad,
When all are glad,

And the earth is dressed in flowers.
When the gay birds sing
Till the forests ring,
As they rest in woodland bowers.

Oh, why these tears,
And these idle fears,
For what may come to-morrow?
The birds find food
From God so good
And the flowers know no sorrow.

If He clothes these
And the leafy trees,
Will He not cherish thee?
Why doubt His care;
It is everywhere,
Though the way we may not see.

Then why be sad
When all are glad,
And the world is full of flowers?
With the gay birds sing,
Make life all Spring,
And smile through the darkest hours.

The upbeat ending ("smile through the darkest hours") seems tacked on for Abby's benefit. It comes across as orthodoxy, not belief.

Possibly seeking to make himself useful while boarding with the Alcotts, Charles Lane resumed teaching the Alcott daughters on occasion.

A Sample of our Lessons
"What virtues do you wish more of?" asks Mr. L.
I answer—
Patience, Love, Silence,
Obedience, Generosity, Perseverance,
Industry, Respect, Self-Denial.

"What vices less of?"
Idleness, Willfulness, Vanity,
Impatience, Impudence, Pride,
Selfishness, Activity, Love of Cats.

Louisa was better armored against Lane at Hillside than at Fruitlands, even ridiculing him by slyly including "Love of Cats" as a vice.

⌒

"I have been thinking about my little room, which I suppose I never shall have. I should want to be there about all the time, and I should go there and sing and think," Louisa confided in a letter to her mother just before the move to Hillside in 1845. In March of 1846, with Sophia Ford resettled at the Emersons and Charles Lane returned to England, Abby reclaimed one of the downstairs bedrooms for thirteen-year-old Louisa's exclusive use. "I have at last got the little room I have wanted so long," Louisa exulted. "It does me good to be alone and Mother has made it very pretty and neat for me. My work basket and desk are by the window and my closet is full of dried herbs that smell very nice. The door that opens into the garden will be very pretty in summer and I can run off to the woods when I like." Having the sanctuary she had desired for so long spurred a resolution to reform on a higher order of seriousness than before.

> I have made a plan for my life, as I am in my teens, and no more a child. I am old for my age, and don't care much for girls' things. People think I'm wild and queer, but Mother understands and helps me. I have not told anyone about my plan, but I'm going to *be* good. I've made so many resolutions, and written sad notes, and cried over my sins, and it doesn't seem to do any good! Now I'm going to *work really*, for I feel a true desire to improve. And be a help and comfort, not a care and sorrow, to my dear mother.

For years she had written variations on her pledges to be good. At thirteen, she channeled her adolescent prayer for self-mastery into a poem of such skill and sincerity that it was later set to music and sung as a hymn.

My Kingdom

A little kingdom I possess,
Where thoughts and feelings dwell;
And very hard I find the task
Of governing it well.
For passion tempts and troubles me,
A wayward will misleads,
selfishness its shadow casts
On all my will and deeds.

How can I learn to rule myself,
To be the child I should,
Honest and brave, nor ever tire
Of trying to be good!
How can I keep a sunny soul
To shine along life's way
How can I tune my little heart
To sweetly sing all day.

Dear father, help me with the love
That cast-eth out my fear!
Teach me to lean on thee, and feel
That thou art very near:
That no temptation is unseen,
No childish grief too small,
Since thou, with patience infinite,
Dost soothe and comfort all.

I do not ask for any crown
But that which all may win;
Nor try to conquer any world
Except the one within.
Be thou my guide until I find,
Led by a tender band,
Thy happy kingdom in myself,
And dare to take command.

The contrast between wild Louisa's tumultuous adolescence and placid Anna's orderly transition to womanhood led their father to admit that his theory that children were blank slates was inadequate to explain his own.

> I once thought all minds in childhood much the same, and that in education lay the power of calling these forth into something of a common accomplishment. But now I see that character is more of a nature than of acquirement, and that the most you can do by culture is to adorn and give external polish to natural gifts.

Bronson paid homage to Louisa's "natural gifts" on her fourteenth birthday, presenting her a book of her poems in his elegant calligraphic script. Abby also recognized her talents with a gift of a pen and a poem.

> *Oh! may this Pen your muse inspire*
> *When wrapt in pure poetic fire*
> *To write some sweet, some thrilling verse*
> *A song of love or sorrow's lay*
> *Or Duty's clear but tedious way.*

Long after adolescence Abigail Alcott found Duty's way clear but tedious, and as Marmee would tell Jo in *Little Women*, she was angry every day. The fictional Mrs. March had conquered her temper under the wise tutelage of Mr. March, but Mrs. Alcott's black moods and rages were almost as frequent as Louisa's. Mother and daughter remained closely linked in Bronson's mind. He reverted to a Calvinist view when he wrote in his journal, "Two devils, as yet, I am not quite divine enough to vanquish— the mother fiend and her daughter."

Adolescence brought not only turmoil but what Louisa would call her "sentimental" phase. Thoreau had been a trusted older brother or uncle figure, her first tutor in nature, a gentle companion on long walks through the woods. In his Walden phase, which overlapped her early teenage years, he took on the heroic aura of a potential lover. In her 1864 novel *Moods*, she would cast herself as Sylvia and conjure Thoreau as the manly Adam Warwick.

In *Moods*, Louisa positions Sylvia at the center of a love triangle. She marries a kind and gentle man, Geoffrey Moor, a figure clearly modeled on Emerson, but is in love with his best friend, Adam Warwick, based on Thoreau. Thoreau also appears in *Little Men*, as a tutor, and on paper in *Rose in Bloom*, as the romantic hero's favorite writer; he and the heroine come together through their shared appreciation of Thoreau's work. But Thoreau's biggest role is in the adult autobiographical novel *Work*, as a sterling character named David Sterling.

Like Thoreau (and like Warwick of Moods), David is "broad-shouldered, brown-bearded, with an old hat and coat, [and] trousers tucked into his boots. Like Thoreau, Sterling is good, modest, opinionated, and loyal, a man who keeps his distance from society and feels more at home with things of the earth. The Louisa character, Christie Devon, falls in love with him, and through him, with nature. On long walks, he teaches her "not dry facts, but the delicate traits, curious habits, and poetical romances of the sweet things the speaker knew and loved as friends." Misunderstandings and a wealthy suitor keep the two apart, but they marry and live happily until tragedy separates them forever.

In Thoreau, Louisa found an outlet for her romantic imagination, while Emerson appealed to her adolescent sense of what made a man great. A well-educated man (as Louisa's father was not), Emerson became her literary mentor, even allowing her to interrupt him in his library. "I used to venture into Mr. Emerson's library and ask what I should read, never conscious of my audacity, so genial was my welcome. I recall the sweet patience with which he led me around the book-lined room. . . . His kind hand opened to me the riches of Shakespeare, Dante, and Carlyle," she wrote several years after his death.

Louisa's infatuation with Emerson was inspired as much by a literary model as by the great man himself. "Browsing over Mr. Emerson's library I found *Goethe's Correspondence With a Child*" (Bettine von Arnim's fictionalized account of her feverish and largely one-sided flirtation with the great German writer), and at the time wrote in her diary, "She calls herself a child, and writes about the lovely things she saw and heard, and felt and did. I liked it very much." Von Arnim was believed by readers to be an innocent thirteen-year-old girl; actually she was a twenty-three-year-old woman of uncertain virtue. In the novel, Goethe's aged mother acts as a courier between Bettine and her idol until their melodramatic first encounter: "The door opened and there *he* stood solemnly, grave and looked with fixed eyes upon me. I stretched my hands towards him—I believe, I soon lost all consciousness.—Goethe caught me quickly to his heart.'" In sexually charged language Bettine reports a half-dozen breathless meetings.

> *He* entered, enveloped to the chin in his cloak, and shut the door softly after him, and looked round about, to see where he might find me: I lay in a corner of the sofa rolled up in darkness, and was silent. Then he took off his hat, and as I saw the glancing forehead and searching look, and as the lips asked: "Now, where art thou?" I uttered a low cry of amazement at my own bliss, and then—he had found me.

Louisa's parents admired *Goethe's Correspondence with a Child*, as did Emerson himself. The effect of the book on Louisa (and many other young girls) was galvanizing: "[I was] at once fired with the desire to be a second Bettine, making my father's friend my Goethe. So I wrote letters to him, but was wise enough never to send them, left wild flowers on the doorsteps of my 'Master,' sung Mignon's song in very bad German under his window, and was fond of wandering by moonlight, or sitting in a cherry tree at midnight till the owls scared me to bed."

That the older man–younger woman attraction is a recurring motif in Louisa's romances, in her thrillers, and in her works of domestic realism such as *Little Women* is not surprising. She had been locked in a power struggle with her father since infancy, straining to satisfy his idea of her while holding on to her own. Her insistence on privacy and her campaign for a room of her own were essential to her psychic integrity. In her writing she created romantic alternatives, father figures more in line with her own longings, basing them not only on her father's closest friends Thoreau and Emerson, but also on Goethe, borrowed for the German professor who marries Jo March. Bronson appeared, watered down and offstage, as her benevolent father in *Little Women*. But he was also the tyrannical villain in "A Marble Woman," a sculptor whose flesh-and-blood victim turns to opium to endure his campaign to bend her to his will. In *A Modern Mephistopheles* Bronson can be found in Jasper Helwyze ("Hell-wise"), an embodiment of the devil, serving up hashish to the heroine from a tortoiseshell candy dish. Louisa's strongest tales featured battles for power between the sexes. Given the trials and deprivations Bronson Alcott put his family through, it was natural sometimes to cast him as the villain of the piece.

"I don't see who is to clothe and feed us, when we are so poor now," Louisa confided to her diary. Much as he might labor in the Hillside garden that she had helped him to prepare, she knew by now that Bronson Alcott would not rescue them. That the usual Alcott meal was a piece of bread, an apple, and water, with frequent stretches of only bread and water, did not seem a problem to him. "Providence will provide," he would pronounce calmly, surveying his growing children. Louisa, like her parents and her sisters, was tall and growing taller. (One source says she grew to be just under six feet; another gives her a statuesque five feet nine inches, and Louisa at one point calls herself five feet six inches tall, which could be true—still tall for her time—or could have been revised downward to be not quite so outlandish.) During her early teen years at Hillside she was skinny, undernourished, and usually hungry. Year by year the Alcotts had descended to the level of hand-me-down rags and baskets of food left discreetly on the doorstep. By the fall of 1847, the Alcotts' credit in Concord was exhausted. Abby looked around for a way to survive, and her faithful cousin Hannah Robie found her one. "The happiest years" of Louisa's life were soon to come to an end.

Just a few weeks before her fifteenth birthday, the household took in a girl boarder almost exactly Louisa's age. Eliza Stearns was "in a state of sad mental imbecility," as Abby described it to Sam, but apparently not insane or dangerous. Her father was advised by doctors to board her with a family, and Abby told Hannah Robie she would try it out for a month. "I found nothing in the girl . . . but what with Mr. A's gentle reserve and discipline I could manage," Abby reported to Sam, and "have engaged the care of her for one year—for 4 doll[ar]s per week. . . . I shall have less time for reading with my girls, but if by faithful care of this bewildered child we can make her path more sunny and straightforward, I shall be well repaid for the sacrifice of personal comfort. I know of no so righteous way of adding to our income and paying our debts." Abby's choices of respectable employment were limited. She already took in sewing, the hallmark of genteel poverty.

An invitation unexpectedly arrived for Anna to go to Walpole, New Hampshire, for the winter to open a school there; her cousin Elizabeth Wells had no doubt heard of the Alcotts' plight and come forward with the offer. Sixteen-year-old Anna was willing. Teaching was not for Louisa,

Abby told Sam; Louisa required "retirement, agreeable occupation, and protective provident care about her. She has most decided views of life and duty. And nothing can exceed the strength of her attachments, particularly for her mother. She reads a great deal. Her memory is quite peculiar and remarkably tenacious." Inexplicably, for a mother who knew her daughter so well, the "agreeable occupation" she came up with for her physically and intellectually restless daughter was decorating small boxes and other articles to be sold in "the fancy stores." It was true that Louisa enjoyed and had a gift for ornamentation; at thirteen she had set up as a dressmaker to dolls, specializing in turbans trimmed with turkey feathers snatched from the tails of the neighborhood birds. Desperation was clearly getting the better of Abby's judgment, but Bronson's implacable calm was unshaken by the prospect of having his home sold out from under him, or watching his children go hungry. "Make no arrangements for them," he counseled Abby. "The place or work will come when they are prepared. Anna no sooner was ready than the niche she could best fit was provided without any effort at all." Abby dismissed her husband's faith in Providence.

In the spring of 1848, Abby accepted a three-month trial of a job, for five hundred dollars a year, as matron of a water cure spa in Waterford, Maine. She set off with Eliza Stearns, who she hoped would benefit from the water cure, and seven-year-old May, whom she thought too young to be left in her sisters' care. At forty-seven, Abby now had three major responsibilities: as keeper of Eliza Stearns, mother of May, and matron of the spa.

In Concord, Louisa was working too, down the road in the Emerson barn. There she established a summer school for twenty of the neighborhood children, holding their attention with fairy tales heavily influenced by the stories of plants and animals that Henry Thoreau had told her in the Concord woods. Ellen Emerson loved Louisa's versions so much that Louisa wrote them down for her. A favorite began, "Three little fairies sat in the fields eating their breakfast; . . . 'Ah, me,' sighed Primrose, throwing herself languidly back, 'how warm the sun grows! . . . Tell me, dear Violet, why are you all so sad?'" Ellen's father Ralph Waldo Emerson observed that Louisa was "a natural source of stories. . . . She is, and is to be," he said, "the poet of children. She knows their angels."

Early reports from Abby at the spa in Maine were cheerful, despite her enormous workload, but she confessed to doubts. "I begin to wonder more at myself how I ever came to this decision to leave you. It seems a great experiment in the heart and the life of a family to sever it occasionally; make it bleed at every pore, re-unite, heal and live again." She dreamed of them—Elizabeth crying over her music, and "Louisa in the lane running with her hair flying, trying to catch somebody. I called to her. She screamed, 'Mother, mother, is it you?' and in a moment I had her close grip around my neck. And then the tears tumbled all around and I waked, . . . drenched in tears."

Abby was also concerned about May, and in early July sent for Louisa to take her back to Concord. Now the oldest of the three sisters at home, Louisa kept spirits up with energetic productions of plays and pantomimes. When Anna returned from Walpole later in the month, the productions became even more elaborate.

By early August, with a few days yet to go on her contract, Abby packed up Eliza Stearns and returned to Concord. The great experiment had not ended well, but after years of anxiety and resentful helplessness, Abby had proved she could earn her family's bread. She put out the word to her friends, and within a short period, Hannah Robie and the wife of her uncle Samuel May had persuaded a group of wealthy Bostonians to find, or create, some acceptable employment for her.

A fund was pieced together to set Abby up in Boston as a "missionary to the poor." A tenant was found for Hillside, and a basement apartment located in Boston's dreary South End. As usual, the arrangements were made on short notice, and the departure made in haste. For all his difficulties with Bronson over the years, Emerson felt the move to Boston as a great personal loss. "My friends begin to value each other, now that A[lcott] is to go," he wrote in his journal. "Henry [Thoreau] says, 'He is the best natured man I ever met. The rats and mice make their nests in him.'"

On a Saturday morning in late November, five of the six Alcotts piled into a Fitchburg Railroad car for the one-hour trip to Boston. The missing Alcott was observing her sixteenth birthday on a visit to family friends, for once not sharing it with her father's—his forty-ninth. Bronson sent Louisa a birthday note, signing it "Your affectionate Father," and enclosing a circular for the Conversations he meant to resume as soon as they were settled. Among the guests were Ralph Waldo Emerson, Theodore

Parker, Margaret Fuller, William Ellery Channing, and Elizabeth Peabody, Boston and the nation's leading intellectual lights.

⌒

Almost forty years later, Louisa recalled the strain of the family's decision to leave Concord. "It was an anxious council," she wrote of one of the family's final talks before leaving, "and always preferring action to discussion, I took a brisk run over the hill and then settled down for a good 'think' in my favorite retreat."

> It was an old cart wheel, half hidden in grass under the locusts where I used to sit to wrestle with my sums, and usually forget them scribbling verses or fairy tales on my slate instead. Perched on the hub, I surveyed the prospect and found it rather gloomy, with leafless trees, sere grass, leaden sky and frosty air, but the hopeful heart of fifteen beat warmly under the old red shawl, visions of success gave the gray clouds a silver lining, and I said defiantly, as I shook my fist at a fate embodied in a crow cawing dismally on the fence nearby,—
>
> "I will do something, by and by. Don't care what, teach, sew, act, write, anything to help the family; and I'll be rich and famous and happy before I die, see if I won't!"

 ⌒～⌒

EIGHT

HEAVEN'S SO FAR AWAY

The Alcotts had lived in Concord for nearly four years, most of the time in a home they owned. When Louisa called them "the happiest years" of her life, she described the troops of young friends and riotous excursions like the one across Sandy Pond, but the foundation of her happiness was the unity and stability of the Alcott family. After they left Concord in the month of Louisa's sixteenth birthday, November 1848, the Alcotts were in perpetual motion for the next decade. From the time of her birth until her midtwenties, Louisa's family moved some *thirty* times. Life in Boston was nearly as unsettled as the Alcotts: one in three households moved every year. The sudden move relocated Louisa to four rooms in a basement in Boston's crowded South End.

"Since coming to the city I don't seem to have thought much," Louisa told her journal, "for the bustle and dirt and change send all lovely images and restful feelings away. Among my hills and woods, I had fine free times alone, and . . . they helped to keep me happy and good. . . . I know God is always ready to hear, but heaven's so far away in the city, and I so heavy I can't fly up to find him."

Louisa was left at home to keep house. "[I felt] like a caged seagull as I washed dishes and cooked in the basement kitchen where my prospect was limited to a procession of muddy boots," she recalled in later years. Every morning, her parents and sisters went out into the world: Abby to her all-absorbing poor; Bronson to the seminars he called "Conversations" on respectable West Street; Lizzie and Abby to public school; and Anna to her first job, as a governess in nearby Roxbury.

Boston had become both strikingly richer and strikingly poorer in the eight years since the Alcotts had fled from their debts. When Louisa fell in the Frog Pond at four or five years old, Boston's population was 95 percent native-born. The city had a settled provincial air, modest neighborhoods, and farms on the outskirts. Now its center was ringed with areas like the South End, where Louisa lived alongside factories and businesses. Immigrants made up half of Boston's population. Many were Irish, the dazed survivors of "coffin ships," penniless and unskilled. At the wharfs where a runaway toddler Louisa had once mingled in her new green shoes with sailors and dockworkers, there was now a dirty, noisy throng of the miserable unemployed living in shanties.

Stephen Foster's song captured the 1850s for the poor: "Hard Times." Hundreds of people shared single toilets and reversed the progress of sanitation; incidents of tuberculosis and smallpox went back up. Contagion used the poor as its vehicle; when cholera hit American port cities in the summer of 1849, two-thirds of its Boston victims were Irish immigrants. Only the wealthy had indoor plumbing. The Alcotts got along with indoor chamberpots and outdoor latrines.

Juxtaposed with the Boston of squalor and poverty was another, newer Boston, one of luxury. The merchant class of Abby's childhood had been marked by an egalitarian distaste for display born of the ideals of the Revolution. Their midcentury counterparts built mansions on Beacon Hill and bought fine carriages that jostled each other along Washington Street. There Louisa could look into the windows of grand emporia and sumptuous shops stocked with extravagant goods for the elegant Boston woman. In *Godey's Lady's Book*, the *Vogue* of its day, she could read lavish descriptions of dresses fit for the ladies of a European royal court. "Walking-dress and mantilla, of heavy green silk"; "Dress of claret-colored brocade silk, made plain and full. A sacque of velvet, the same shade, with satin cording and buttons"; "Black-spotted tulle over a pink silk slip. Double skirt, and a triple berthe cape. The hair is arranged very simply, with a wreath of pansies and drooping green foliage. A tasteful and simple costume."

Seventeen-year-old Louisa, in hand-me-downs from Hannah Robie, was tormented by the riches around her. "In the street," she lamented, "I try not to covet fine things. My quick tongue is always getting me into trouble, and my moodiness makes it hard to be cheerful when I think how poor we are, how much worry it is to live, and how many things I long to do I never can." She fulfilled her material needs by imagining them, furnishing her first novel—*The Inheritance*—with the fine things she coveted. Her book imitated the kind she devoured like plumcakes— sentimental novels and gothic romances that carried her far from the South End to a fantasy Europe, the "chick lit" of the day.

The heroine of *The Inheritance* is Edith Adelon, a penniless young Italian orphan, loyal governess, and talented pianist, Louisa's own Jane Eyre. "Lord Hamilton's stately home, half castle, and half mansion," where she lives, is picturesque and improbable. Louisa had never seen either a castle or a mansion, but loved them equally in books, so she gave them both to Edith and reveled in describing them. "Here and there rose an old gray tower or ivy-covered arch" (the tower seemingly detached from a structure, the arch apparently not holding anything up), "while the blooming gardens that lay around it and the light balconies added grace and beauty to the old, decaying castle," wrote the teenager stranded in the basement dump.

Edith demonstrates her noble nature when her companion slips off a ledge and Edith risks her life to save her. Louisa rewards her bravery with proof that she is the real heir to the half-castle-half-mansion. True, she is an orphan; the author of this Cinderella tale has replaced her hapless parents with a wealthy, glamorous, and dead twosome incapable of asking anything of her.

Edith (foolishly, but not to the author) leaves the fortune unclaimed and wins the love of Lord Percy, who has a large fortune, a fine character, and a superior physique.

Louisa never attempted to publish *The Inheritance*. She had written it only for practice, and as an exercise it is impressive.

Like her heroine Edith, Louisa spent much of her time with better-off friends, relatives, and benefactors. Sometimes she and Anna were welcomed as peers and guests; at other times the same people disdained or exploited them as governesses or teachers. Even harder to bear were the sideways looks and loaded remarks, what Abby called "the cold neglect, the crude inferences, the silent reproach of those who profess to love us and desire to help us."

At the same time, the family continued to keep the fanciest intellectual company in the young nation. Emerson, Thoreau, the Lowells, the senior Henry James, Theodore Parker, and William Lloyd Garrison were all guests in their shabby quarters on Dedham Street. They also attended the more upscale West Street rooms where Bronson hosted meetings of the Town and Country Club, a select gentlemen's discussion group.

Abby Alcott's work took her far from the genteel precincts her husband frequented. Her profession was so new it had no name: she was one of the first social workers in America. Her employment was engineered by Hannah Robie and a Mrs. Savage (probably a childhood friend of Abby's), who called the job *missionary to the poor*, a term with a connotation significantly different from Abby's choice, the more egalitarian *sister of charity*. She plunged into her work with the fevered enthusiasm she brought to every new venture, walking poor neighborhoods to distribute food and clothing along with advice on diet and hygiene. Within weeks Abby had identified the gap between the enormous needs of the poor and her inadequate resources to meet them, and was filled with righteous indignation on behalf of her clients, with enough to spare for herself.

She complained to her backers, dunning them for bigger piles of clothes and cash, scolding when they wanted praise and gratitude. She informed the Ladies Bountiful of correct attitudes toward have-nots when they were confident of their own goodness. The poor are "treated with too much severity," Abby told them. "We induce them to deceive us, for they feel we do not love them. Let us infuse more love into our gifts, and it will be doubly blest."

The thirty dollars a month from the ad hoc group Hannah Robie rounded up was half the blessing Abby thought she deserved, so she took up another offer of fifty dollars a month to open a relief room on Washington Street, where clients who had no place to live or concealed their plight could come for help.

Among the needy of the streets were young girls with no protection from "the sharks of lust that wait to devour [their] last remnant of innocence." If the innocence of Mary Ann Moore, a girl Louisa's age, had been replaced with a pregnancy, Abby still would have taken her into the Alcott home until she found her one. Relatives cautioned Abby against exposing her daughters to such horrors, but Abby needed her girls to console her for the family's every indignity and crisis. Louisa became one of the poor who tried to conceal her distress, at least from Abby. She confided to her diary, "I can't talk to anyone but mother about my troubles, and she has so many to bear now I try not to add any more."

The poor were always with them. Word of Abby's kindness got out, and the desperate found their way to the Alcotts' door. Usually Louisa was the only one there to receive them. She and Anna went with Abby to distribute monthly food baskets, and gave evening classes in literacy to immigrant and black women, teaching them enough to read and write up bills and count their pay.

Like the young Charles Dickens, who tumbled down from the middle class and wrote his way back up, Louisa was snatched from pastoral Concord and relocated in the grimiest corners of urban life. Unfortunate as they were, both Dickens and Alcott were versatile and resilient people, and for them the ordeals of childhood were transmuted into rich literary endowments. Louisa drew from her wide store of experience for the autobiographical novel *Work,* a pilgrim's progress through women's lives. Dickens transformed his misfortunes into his favorite and probably his best novel, *David Copperfield.*

Dickens in poverty was a solitary outcast, but Louisa belonged to a close family and was cousin to half of Boston's wealthiest circle. Under the capacious roofs of relatives she sat in airy rooms and ate good food. She went to their parties and with them to theaters, wearing their hand-me-down clothes. But they had no idea of how she lived, or of what it was like to have no money. She thought they should, and from her platform as an author she would let them know, more artfully, what Abby had tried to tell her sponsors in social work. An incident in *An Old-Fashioned Girl* fulfills her earnest teenage vows to show the world who she is and what she knows: her poor country heroine takes her wealthy city cousin to meet her friends, an assortment of resourceful, talented girls and women struggling to survive. The cousin emerges from the visit a humbled and better person, full of respect for the plight and the pluck of the Louisa Alcotts of the world. The episode would be pure treacle were it not for the appearance of Kate King, a successful author and benefactor, worn down from work, but wise, witty, and fun to be with, like Louisa Alcott.

Thanks to wealthy friends and relatives, the Alcotts were regularly catapulted from squalor to higher ground. In June of 1849, sixteen-year-old Louisa and nine-year-old May were sent to Leicester for a country holiday with some of their cousins. The rest of the family settled into generous Mrs. Savage's handsome house across from the Common, vacated by the owners for the healthier air of the country. When they rejoined the family, Louisa launched a family newspaper called the *Olive*

Leaf—named for the *Olive Branch*, a popular weekly the family liked—a rainy-day diversion that Louisa would adapt for chapter 10 of *Little Women*. She calls the March family paper the *Pickwick Portfolio*, "which was filled with original tales, poetry, local news, funny advertisements, and hints, in which they good naturedly reminded each other of their faults and shortcomings."

The *Olive Leaf*'s lively inaugural issue overflows with odes to felines by its four contributors, beginning with one titled "To Pat Paws" by Louisa, who a few years before had flaunted her "love of cats" in the list of her vices assigned as homework for Charles Lane.

Oh my kitty Oh my darling
Purring softly on my knee
While your sleepy little eyes dear
Look so fondly up at me

Dearest of all earthly pussies
I will shrine you in my heart
Where no dogs can ever reach you
Oh my precious little guwart [?]

May the biggest fattest mouses
Be your never failing portion
Softest crumbs in heaps around you
And of drops a boundless ocean.

The issue also contains an essay on botany by "Tracy Tupman" (Lizzie), a family "report card" of inexcusable deportment: "Annie, bad; Louisa, bad; Elizabeth, bad; Abba, bad," and a serial about a poor wood-cutter, called *Little Trot*, by Louisa.

Midway through his fiftieth year that summer of 1849, while living at Mrs. Savage's house on Temple Place, Bronson slipped into a prolonged, sometimes hallucinatory state of reverie and began writing a rambling and incoherent philosophical tract filled with diagrams, drawings, and quotations from his mystical and philosophical heroes. While Bronson's sometimes obsessive preoccupations and behavior, by his own and others' reports, point to incapacitating mental illness, public opinion—then and now—paints him as merely selfish and uncaring. Bronson knew of his vulnerability to episodes of madness and described them in his journals and in poetry as prolonged attacks by demon torturers so relentless that he was driven to the brink of suicide. In their grip his only defense was to reach for what he called "the brimming fount of family."

While Abby and his daughters were Bronson's sanctuary, he knew that his wife and daughter Louisa were subject to the same debilitating despair. His relentless criticism of Louisa as a child was not only reflexive annoyance, but also an attempt to guide her to the safety of self-control. His intense involvement in her education and conduct was a form of vigilant protection—also self-protection. His own journal-keeping, like the daughter's writing, was both a compulsion and a means of keeping the kingdom of his mind in order. The tactic did not always work. The denial that buttressed his apparent serenity during periods when he could function crumbled and collapsed.

Bronson's relationship with his brother, Junius, twenty years younger than Bronson and like him something of a mystic, was a less fraught version of his relationship with Louisa. He recognized in Junius his own mental instability, knew Junius had considered suicide, and more than once, he believed, had talked him out of it. The invitation Bronson extended to Junius to stay with Abby and the children while he was in England was an offering of the same safe harbor he found his family to be. Yet Junius detached himself from Bronson afterward, ignoring a stream of letters pleading with him to join them. He lived for a while in Oriskany, New York, near their sister Betsy, married a woman named Mary Jane Pritchard, then returned to Connecticut to operate a factory with his and Bronson's brother Ambrose. Like Bronson, Junius had a talent for design and construction; he built much of the factory's machinery. One day in 1852, thirty-two-year-old Junius, by then the father of four, kissed his mother good-bye, telling her he was going on a trip. Then he went to the factory, and before Ambrose could stop him, hurled himself into the wheel of his own machine, dying almost instantly. His mother noted the death and her anguish once in her journal. Bronson never mentioned his brother Junius again. Of her gentle uncle Junius Louisa leaves no word on the record, but one chapter of *Work* is about the suicide of a woman from a family cursed by hereditary insanity.

That summer of 1849, seeing her husband again stranded in the workings of his mind, Abby came to the rescue. She packed him off to Concord, where he spent long hours in discussion with Thoreau and Emerson. She and the girls sent care packages, and he thanked them in upbeat letters about his evening swims with Henry Thoreau and visits to old Concord haunts, while in Boston a chorus of voices was being raised over Bronson's failure to contribute to his family's support.

After a year and a half, Abby's enthusiasm for patrolling the streets to distribute pittances to the deserving poor was spent. She delivered her final report, a stinging litany of complaint, to a sparsely attended meeting of the Ladies of the South End Friendly Society. Some household roles were redistributed: Lizzie left school to take up the housekeeping, a huge relief for Louisa. Nineteen-year-old Anna became the sole source of Alcott family income. That autumn she had opened a small school on Canton Street and eventually had twenty pupils. Louisa sometimes went along to help, though she found it hard to set an example of gentle manners.

The underpaid, full-time abolitionist Sam May had to rescue Bronson's family again. He drafted two of the family's other Sams, cousin Sam Sewall and Sam Greele, to shore up the Alcotts' finances. Abby's brother pledged thirty dollars to the local grocer—he would no longer give cash to the Alcotts. A fourth Sam, their uncle Samuel May, who had made a fortune in shipping, lent his mansion a few tree-lined streets from the Common as a residence for the summer, while his family went to their country seat in Leicester.

Abby remained inconsolable. "Quite dejected, feeble, weeps from anxiety . . . cannot be comforted," wrote Bronson, vaguely acknowledging her woes: "no income, no earnings, etc., etc."

He had been shoring up his own deteriorating ego with a return to better days via new inquiries into Alcott family genealogy, perhaps also trying to trace the strain of madness he believed to be there. Later that summer he passed many happy early mornings walking in the Common with one of his disciples, twenty-four-year-old Ednah Littlehale, who had a swan neck, black eyes, and long curly locks to match. She would be the first known, and most tempting, object of a lifelong series of flirtations with maidens among the mostly female attendees of his Conversations. Intellectual women shut out of institutions of higher learning had to educate themselves, as Bronson had. Tall, elegant Mr. Alcott did not condescend to them, and they liked his approach to discussion of a topic, which was to seek common ground and explore it gently rather than dispute competing claims. Inevitably the common ground was in his neck of the woods.

Abby was still looking for a way to earn a living. She even considered going West to join the gold rush! Sam May convinced her that the plan was wildly impractical. Eventually he helped her reach a decision to open an employment office and had a flyer made up.

Best American and Foreign Help. Families provided, at the shortest notice, with accomplished COOKS, good PARLOR and CHAMBER GIRLS, NURSERY MAIDS, SEAMSTRESSES, TOILET WOMEN, and DRESS MAKERS. Any person paying the subscription of $1 shall be furnished with a ticket, entitling her to a choice of help for six months from Mrs. Alcott's rooms.

"It was not fit work for her, but it paid," Louisa noted realistically.

A job offer for Anna soon arrived from Lenox, across the state in the Berkshires, where Sophia Peabody Hawthorne was living with her husband, Nathaniel Hawthorne, and their two small children on the estate of a wealthy young friend, William Tappan.* His wife, Caroline Sturgis Tappan, had need of a young nursemaid for their new baby, Sophia Hawthorne wrote. A note from Mrs. Tappan soon followed: "Anna would find much to enjoy in Lenox, and would not, with me, have any work too hard for her." She would "give a nursery girl six dollars a month, & cannot very well afford to give Anna more." Abby could not afford to let Anna turn down the offer.

The plan hit a snag when the entire family got sick. "We had small pox," Louisa noted in a footnote to her journal entry for the year, "caught from some poor immigrants whom mother took into the garden and fed one day." (Earlier Abby had cut her children's rations in half to feed the poor; the smallpox episode would not deter her from exposing them to contagious disease again.) Abby and the girls suffered a mild form of smallpox, but Bronson was hit hard by the variety that killed several thousand in the nation that year, among them the former president James

---

* Tappan, the son of Lewis Tappan, a financial mainstay of the antislavery movement, had married the poet Caroline Sturgis, whose poem "Life"—"Greatly to be / Is enough for me / Is enough for thee"—had been published in the *Dial* when she was nineteen, winning her a place in the Transcendental inner circle.

Polk, out of office only a few months. After the family recovered—without medical help, not that medicine had much to offer—Anna went to Lenox, and Louisa took over her sister's teaching.

The children liked Louisa and learned quickly, but her impatience made it "very hard." She also missed Anna—"so much I needed to cry over my dinner."

Anna was having problems at work, too. After four weeks Mrs. Tappan sent her home. The letter she wrote to Abby afterward hints at a cause. While she expresses concern, it is not for Anna but for herself. "Her unhappiness was such a weight upon my thoughts and spirits from the first hour she came—indeed it affected everyone in the house. I saw it was useless to attempt to make her happy because I could not change the circumstances." The well-mannered nineteen-year-old made a dramatic and insulting parting gesture, leaving her pay for the full two months behind in a sewing basket. No one seems to have recorded whether Caroline Sturgis Tappan enclosed the much-needed twelve dollars in her letter.

With Anna's return to run the school, and Louisa recast as assistant, Louisa decided that she disliked teaching. "School is hard work. . . . I get very little time to write or think, for my working days have begun." Spending those days giving lessons to small children was not the future she had planned.

Life upon the wicked stage was more in her line. "Anna wants to be an actress, and so do I. We could make plenty of money, perhaps, and it is a very gay life. Mother says we are too young, and must wait. . . . I like tragic plays, and shall be a Siddons if I can." Sarah Siddons was a member of a celebrated British acting family, known for her portrayals of Lady Macbeth and Hamlet.* Louisa yearned not only to *play* Lady Macbeth and Hamlet but to *be* them. Her taste was for the "lurid," for everything dangerous, unconventional, and extreme. The thrilling option of taking to the stage, in defiance of respectable opinion, contained the promise of escape and the risk of ruin that she craved. Other than writing, acting was the only career for which Louisa had any enthusiasm.

The year before, she had tried another route to self-support and independence: she took a job in the home of James Richardson. Her relations were horrified—which she quite enjoyed—and though being a servant

---

* The reputation-making role of Hamlet was performed by several ambitious actresses in the nineteenth century.

was lowly, it was work that had served as a launching pad to bigger things for many a young girl in the stories she read.

Richardson had been a classmate of Thoreau's at Harvard and was part of Bronson's wide circle of young admirers. Louisa was at her mother's employment office when he called to hire a companion for his sister. Though at eighteen she was impressed when she met him—he was thirty-five, tall, and well built—her description from a retrospective view is cynical.

> He possessed an impressive nose, a fine flow of language, and a pair of large hands, encased in black kid gloves. With much waving of these somber members, Mr. R. set forth the delights awaiting the happy soul who . . . "will be one of the family in all respects, and only required to help about the lighter work." . . . When my mother turned to me, and asked if I could suggest anyone, I became as red as a poppy and said abruptly: "Only myself."

Mr. Richardson became the Reverend Josephus, the employer in "How I Went Out to Service," one of Alcott's most autobiographical and satirical stories. The experience it relates was a demoralizing demonstration of how little power Louisa had as an impoverished female in the wide world. Like Louisa, her nameless heroine thinks she is stepping into the pages of a sentimental romance when she is setting herself up to be humiliated by a creepy psychological predator. The "stately old mansion" that the fictional Reverend Josephus advertises as a paradise of "books, pictures, flowers, a piano and the best of society" turns out to be a dilapidated old pile; the sister in need of a companion is a "timid mouse" of forty wrapped in shawls; an ancient father is tucked away out of sight. Only one room is luxurious, "full of the warm glow of firelight, the balmy breath of hyacinths and roses, the white glimmer of piano keys and tempting rows of books along the walls"—her employer's parlor. What the Reverend Josephus seeks, it turns out, is a companion not for his sister but for himself, an attractive maidenly presence to be with him through long fireside evenings (and, it is implied, smoldering bedchamber nights).

The fraternal invitation to both Louisa and her heroine was not to read or rest, but to listen, to be "a passive bucket, into which he was to pour all manner of philosophic, metaphysical and sentimental rubbish."

Louisa could read all manner of philosophic, metaphysical and sentimental rubbish at home, so she took refuge in household tasks; when
asked by her employer (in her fictionalized account) if she actually prefers
scrubbing the hearth to sitting in his "charming room" while he reads
Hegel to her, she replies, "Infinitely." Louisa refused to play adoring audi-
tor, and Richardson retaliated by making her a galley slave. "The roughest
work was . . . my share. I dug paths in the snow, brought water from the
well, split kindlings, made fires, and sifted ashes, like a true Cinderella."
Although much of what Louisa wrote in "How I Went Out to Service" has
the charm of self-mockery, her degradation while a prisoner to an ostensibly righteous man was a lasting injury, according to Louisa's friend
Maria Porter. "This experience of going out to service at eighteen made so
painful an impression upon her that she rarely referred to it, and when
she did so it was with heightened color and tearful eyes." Apparently
Louisa was given easily to tears far into adulthood.

After seven weeks she quit. Like Anna in Lenox, she could not stick it
out for a second month. Her employer's frail sister slipped a cheap purse
into Louisa's pocket, and she set off on foot behind the wheelbarrow that
carried her shabby belongings to the Boston stagecoach. In the pocket "I
fondly hoped was, if not a liberal, at least an honest return for seven
weeks of the hardest work I ever did. Unable to resist . . . I opened the
purse and beheld *four dollars.*" As a nursery maid, Anna was underpaid
at six dollars a month; Louisa was paid four dollars for nearly two months
of very hard labor.

In "How I Went Out to Service," her heroine's family indignantly
sends the paltry four dollars back; in actuality Louisa could not afford the
gesture. Life was still an uphill struggle of governessing, teaching, and
sewing, with no relief in sight.

At least she could improve herself, Louisa thought, and resolved to
read fewer novels, listing high-minded books by authors she admired and
Emerson had recommended: Carlyle, Goethe, Plutarch, Schiller, Madame
de Staël, Charlotte Brontë, and Harriet Beecher Stowe, whose *Uncle Tom's
Cabin* had sold three hundred thousand copies that year.

While Louisa presumably was steeped in the passionate rigor of Madame de Staël, the most exalted literary woman of her time, her own first
published story, "The Rival Painters," came out in the *Olive Branch.* Another auspicious event of 1852 was Nathaniel Hawthorne's unexpected
offer to buy Hillside, four years after the Alcotts had put it on the market.

For the seven previous years the Hawthorne family of five, like the Alcotts, had scrambled for lodging from Salem to Lynn to the little red cottage on the Tappan estate in Lenox. Finally Hawthorne's literary ship came in with the publication of *The Scarlet Letter* in 1850, *The House of Seven Gables* in 1851, and *The Blithedale Romance* in 1852. At forty-eight, Hawthorne was not a rich man, but he could make an offer of $1,500 for Hillside. Bronson quickly accepted.

The Alcotts suddenly had liquid assets and immediately overextended themselves to move up to Beacon Hill, home to several of their May relatives. They rented a four-story brick house on Pinckney Street, a narrow cobblestone lane of shuttered townhouses and quiet respectable neighbors. Abby advertised for boarders to help pay expenses. They were quartered in a pleasant neighborhood, but at the Christmas of 1852 the Alcotts were still struggling to get by, as Louisa's forthright acknowledgment of the "great bundle of goodies"—hand-me-downs—sent by her cousin Charlotte, Sam's daughter, over the holidays makes plain. "Mother broke down entirely over your letter, and *we* like dutiful children followed her example for we felt somewhat forlorn and forgotten among the giving and receiving of presents all around us, and it was so cheering to find that . . . someone had remembered the existence of the 'Pathetic Family.'" To the author of "Christmas won't be Christmas without any presents," the holiday was a measure of the family's fortunes and her personal happiness. A festive Christmas was synonymous with prosperity, affection, and the brilliant, happy side of life. At low points, a lack of Christmas presents was proof of how little she counted in the world.

Louisa's "How It All Happened" is a Christmas story that takes her past and repairs it in a homely, Dickensian way. Two impoverished young sisters, lamenting their miserable Christmas prospects, are overheard by a neighbor in their boardinghouse. "Don't you wish there really was a Santa Claus, who knew what we really wanted, and would come and put silver dollars in our stockings, so we could go and see Puss and Boots at the Museum tomorrow afternoon?" one of them, who can only be Louisa, asks. The other, evidently Lizzie, declares that when she is rich, as she imagines her boardinghouse neighbors to be, she will "go round each Christmas with a big basket of goodies, and give *all* the poor children some." Though her neighbors are in fact modest working people, Miss

Kent, a simple milliner, and Mr. Chrome, a self-absorbed artist, rise to the occasion, join forces to produce an unforgettable Christmas for the children, and fall in love along the way.

The joyless holiday over, early in January Anna went to New Hampshire, to help out with her cousin Eliza Wells's two children. Probably at her parents' urging, Louisa opened a little school for about a dozen children in the Pinckney Street parlor. Abby noted that Louisa's pupils loved her—like her father, she was gifted with children. Her mother was satisfied for the time being, but Louisa was not. As soon as her school closed for the summer, she embarked on her own plan. She would return to the Leicester country house of Abby's wealthy uncle Samuel May; she had visited the household twice for a few weeks and liked the surroundings very much. Now she would relocate as a "second girl," a low-ranking servant, but she didn't care; all honest work was dignified in her egalitarian view. Plus she would get out from under the family roof, try her wings, live her own life. She knew the people and the place as she had not in the disastrous debacle at wintry Dedham. "I needed the change, could do the wash, and was glad to earn my $2 a week"; this was Louisa as pure Jo March, pragmatic, brave, and bold. No matter that working as a laundress put her at the very bottom of the servant class. Her indifference could not have extended to the actual performance of the job: carrying large tubs of water, making fire enough to boil it, stirring the heavy, wet load over the scalding steam, scrubbing heavily soiled items on washboards with rough soap that left her hands raw, wringing the laundry, hanging it outdoors to dry, taking it down, folding it up, carrying heavy baskets of it indoors.

While Louisa was working as second girl in Leicester, Abby was visiting her brother Sam in Syracuse, Anna was continuing as nursemaid to relatives in Walpole, New Hampshire, May was making long visits to assorted Mays and Willises, and Lizzie kept house for her father at home. There the eighteen-year-old received notes from her mother in Syracuse that almost seem intended to alarm: "My home-child, my patient little housekeeper . . . I wish every day you were here, this sweet place might be enjoyed by us all—but where is our employment or means of livelihood? . . . Our lives seem very stupid and unsatisfactory." Abigail May Alcott gave her children unreserved love; she never varnished the truth, either.

Autumn brought another reshuffling of Alcotts. Abby, Louisa, Lizzie, and May came together on Pinckney Street. Bronson set out for the West (now called the Midwest) on his first speaking tour, and Anna went to Syracuse for a second year of teaching and living with Sam May's family. She wrote home complaining of headaches. "Put on your bonnet and cloak and walk 100 times across the piazza," Abby advised her. "Oh my daughter, get firm health. I see so many sickly mortals to whom life is a burden and a daily sorrow that I dread chronic evils being harnessed upon you." In a time before vaccines could prevent debilitating illnesses, or antibiotics could cure them before they did lasting damage, almost everybody had "chronic evils" that no known medicine or painkiller could control or alleviate.

Something was also wrong with Lizzie. "It seems as if there had been some collapse of the brain," Abby wrote to Bronson in Cincinnati in mid-November. "At times she seems immoveable—almost senseless. Louisa and I both relieve her of all the work. . . . There is a great struggle going on in her mind about something." A brief comment in Louisa's yearly summary suggested the "something" might have been heartbreak: "Betty . . . had a little romance with C."

The third Alcott daughter is impossible to pin down. She appears never to have asked anything of anybody or of life itself. Her only image, a photograph made in her late teens, does not reward scrutiny. It shows a soft round face set off by dark hair, with delicate features and a hint of a smile unique in Alcott sister portraiture. Abby's characterizations of her third daughter's mental state as a "collapse of the brain" and "a great struggle . . . about something" indicate that Lizzie was as opaque to her insightful, articulate mother as she is to us. "Immoveable—almost sense-less" sounds like a description of someone in a deep depression bordering on catatonia and requiring hospitalization. "A little romance with C," who-ever "C" was, seems insufficient as a cause and was probably a wrong guess. Louisa knew that it was by the time she wrote the incident's fic-tional counterpart in *Little Women*, when Jo thinks that Beth has fallen for her admirer Laurie and goes to New York to leave Beth a clear field. But Jo is mistaken; Beth suffers no passion for Laurie.

Whether any of the Alcott girls had suitors or marriage proposals is almost as hard to pin down as Lizzie's smile. Birth into a prosperous family and marriage to an income-producing husband were a woman's only routes to economic security. Neither had worked out for their mother, the sisters were well aware. For an independent woman to earn enough for even subsistence-level food, clothing, and shelter was practically impossible. Yet none of the Alcott daughters entered into matrimony at the age their peers did, in their late teens and early twenties. Their constant moves, ambiguous social standing, and pitiful wardrobes may have stood in the way. Nonetheless, in *Little Women* and her later domestic novels Louisa conveyed a convincing familiarity with the parties, outings, and flirtations of girls their age, and in "My Boys" she described a roster of admirers and crushes not mentioned in her journals or letters—probably Louisa expunged them. The answer Anna wrote to the favorite question of *Little Women* fans—was there a real-life Laurie?—implies that Louisa had a lively social life: "There was once a beautiful Polish boy, whom she [Louisa] met abroad . . . whose good looks and 'wheedlesome' ways first suggested to her the idea of putting him into a book," Anna explained. "She has therefore put upon him the lovemaking and behavior of various adorers of her youthful days."

Around the time of Lizzie's puzzling sorrow, Abby alluded to Anna in a letter written to Bronson, suggesting it was her oldest daughter who had suffered an unrequited love. "I think she feels better about the heart pang. . . . It was severe while it lasted—but the inevitable soon quiets inflammation—perhaps it is as well."

The unhappiness of two of her daughters did not spring solely from the heart, Abby perceived. The empty pocketbook also hurt. "I think Anna and Lizzie are a good deal oppressed with this [economic] uncertainty." They were not as well equipped to endure or cure it as Louisa was. "Louisa feels stronger and braver—to meet or to bear whatever destiny may have in store for us. . . . The other girls are not so firm in health and there is more dependent feeling on their parents."

While Abby did not recognize how oppressed Louisa felt by poverty—Louisa deliberately hid it from her—she was right. Louisa loved but did not feel dependent on her parents; in fact, she dreamed of earning enough to support them financially while she led her own life. And while Abby's second daughter was a dreamer, she was also practical and realistic. Not only did she see and accept reality; she also defied it by finding and making *fun*. She knew how to entertain herself and other people, to create diversions—her plays, her Hillside mailbox, her newspaper—to wrest attention from poverty for days at a time. "Louisa is to give a Masquerade Ball tonight in fancy costume," Abby wrote Bronson on his fifty-fourth birthday, and Louisa's twenty-first. "You can predict its brilliancy and success." Louisa was brave, as her mother said, to take a job far from home, and daring, to try to get her writing published. Her material resources were limited, but the intense force of her imagination coupled with the energy of her capabilities were equivalent to possessing an enormous fortune.

Bronson's first tour of the West was a tonic for his battered ego. Transcendentalism was now twenty years old, and word of it had reached the provinces, where Bronson was billed as a great thinker from the storied East. The culture-hungry came to see him in the flesh, handsome Bronson Alcott, a man who knew Emerson, whose transparent blue eyes were mesmerizing. They felt what Emerson said he felt in Bronson's presence: an atmosphere that brought out his best thinking. They came away feeling they had participated in American culture, and that they understood the ideas of the great thinkers of their nation. They might not recall the thoughts or the ideas the next day, but they would remember being lifted off the quotidian plane.

Louisa's journal account of her father's return from his first "Conversations" tour in the winter of 1854 reads like a draft of a story. "Mother flew down, crying 'My husband!' We rushed after, and five white figures embraced the half-frozen wanderer." Bronson "came in hungry, tired, cold, and disappointed, but smiling bravely and as serene as ever," and then, as in a parable, the youngest child, May, asked the question they all want answered: "'Well, did people pay you?' . . . With a queer look, he opened his pocketbook and showed one dollar, saying with a smile that made our eyes fill, 'Only that!'" His overcoat had been stolen, his travel expenses had been great, promises of large audiences or generous payment were not kept. "I shall never forget how beautifully Mother answered. . . . With a beaming face she kissed him saying, 'I call that doing very well. Since you are safely home, dear, we don't ask anything more.' It was half tragic and comic, for Father was very dirty and sleepy, and Mother in a big nightcap and funny old jacket." Long after, reviewing her journals, Louisa wrote below this entry, "I began to see the strong contrasts and the fun and follies in every-day life about this time."

Bronson's trip was not as pitiful as Louisa painted it. True, his audiences were small, and he spent many days waiting for more to be arranged, but early on he sent Abby a check for $150. Later he sent her twenty-five dollars, with small, thoughtful Christmas presents for all of them, and assurances that he would take care of all debts upon his return. But whether he came home with just a dollar or somewhat more, Bronson's tour didn't change the family's fortunes one bit.

Louisa had five dollars for the family coffers when she sold a story to the *Saturday Evening Gazette.* "The Rival Prima Donnas" was as fluent and dramatic as her first published tale, "The Rival Painters," was stiff and forced. Set in Italy, a favorite locale for intrigue and romance, it takes us onstage with Beatrice, a reigning opera star about to relinquish her position to Theresa, a rising young singer, for the love of a painter, Claude. All three characters are ruined, but in the most violent and glamorous way. "The Rival Prima Donnas" was published in the November 11, 1854, *Gazette* under the pseudonym "Flora Fairfield."

That same season Louisa published a short book that she could claim in her own name. *Flower Fables* was a small collection of fairy tales, fanciful interpretations of nature patterned on the stories she had heard from Henry Thoreau. Louisa first told her flower fables the summer she was almost sixteen, to the Concord children in Emerson's barn. Afterward she wrote them down for Ellen Emerson, who loved the stories and worshipped Louisa. With Lidian Emerson's encouragement, and a payment of three hundred dollars as a guarantee against losses (by a rich acquaintance of the Emersons aptly named Wealthy Stevens), *Flower Fables* came out in time for the Christmas market of 1854.

Louisa made Abby a gift of the first copy, with a note that mixed pride and gratitude. "Whatever beauty is to be found in my little book is owing to your interest in and encouragement of my efforts from the first to last," she wrote. "I hope to pass in time from fairies and fables to men and realities." Ellen Emerson was thrilled with Louisa's dedication to her. *Flower Fables* was well reviewed in the *Transcript* and the *Saturday Evening Gazette,* and the book turned a profit.

"The principal event of the winter is the appearance of my first book *Flower Fables,*" reads Louisa's first journal entry of 1855. "An edition of sixteen hundred. It has sold very well, and people seem to like it. I feel very proud that the little tales I wrote for Ellen E. when I was sixteen should now bring money and fame. I will put in some of the notices. . . . Mothers are always foolish over their first-born."

Louisa had published her first book at the age of twenty-one. Three decades later, she compared the receipts for *Flower Fables* to her earnings in the previous six months, and wrote a note in the margin of her original entry: "I was prouder over the $32 than the $8000."

NINE

THE INDEPENDENT FEELING

People began to feel that topsey turvey Louisa would amount to something after all. Perhaps she may," Louisa wrote after publishing her first book. Now, in the spring of 1855, she began to make her mark as an actress and playwright as well. Her Boston stage debut was a benefit performance for the Federal Street Church (where her uncle Sam Greele was deacon), in which her ridiculously named character "Oronthy Bluggage" delivered a pseudo-lecture on "Woman, and Her Position." The foremost comedian in the nation, William Warren, attended the benefit and afterward invited Louisa to repeat her performance at the Howard Athenaeum, this time for money. Capitalizing on the new connection, Louisa wrote a farce, *Nat Bachelor's Pleasure Trip*, and asked Warren to assess its prospects.

Louisa was getting around town, thanks in part to a flock of cousins: Charles Windship, Hamilton Willis, and Willis's wife, Louisa Windship Willis, who was Louisa's cousin twice over. Ham and Lu Willis became Louisa's first intimate adult friends and included her in their privileged Boston life. Windship and the Willises were fervent theatergoers who found the charm of Louisa's company well worth the price of an extra ticket.

Ham Willis was a regular contributor to the "Alcott Sinking Fund," telling Abby as he slipped her a hundred dollars that his pleasure was to earn enough money to subsidize his friends. As financial editor of the

Saturday Evening Gazette, Ham had given Louisa's career a big boost by introducing her to the editor William Clapp and acting as her go-between with the paper. The *Gazette* was Louisa's foot in the door of the market for the sentimental fiction that women craved. For the first five years of her career, Louisa published most frequently in the *Gazette*, but also in *Peterson's Magazine*, the *Olive Branch*, and *Dodge's Literary Museum*, tailoring her escapist stories for each readership from shopgirls to ladies of leisure.

Just as Boston began to favor Louisa, the Alcotts' Pinckney Street landlord decided he wanted his house back, and gave them three months to find another. As they considered wildly disparate options, Louisa observed that the Alcotts were like the feckless Micawbers of *David Copperfield*, always counting on something to turn up. The "something" turned up first for Louisa: an invitation from Lu and Ham Willis to spend the summer with them in Walpole, New Hampshire, a fashionable resort whose year-round population of 1,500 swelled each summer with wealthy families from Boston and New York. (Walpole was where sixteen-year-old Anna had briefly taught school.) Set high among the hills of southern New Hampshire, Walpole was a paradise of pinewoods and fresh air, with a lively cultural life that gave a sophisticated tone to the rustic setting. The Shakespeare Club drew the high-minded, and the new Walpole Amateur Dramatic Company reflected the growth of regional theater.

Louisa set to work refurbishing her hand-me-down dresses with trimmings bought with her winter's wages and had enough cash left over to outfit her sisters too. She liked being the family benefactress and liked even more being independent, but no sooner were her own plans made than the "something" that turned up for the rest of the Alcotts was a house, also in Walpole, rent-free, indefinitely. Abby was glad to escape. On a walk to Federal Court, where she had lived as a child, she had told Louisa that Boston was no longer the city she had known and that she was exhausted by the effort to survive financially. Abby, chronically yearning for a place to call home, threw her hopes and energy into every new place, and in the end was always bitterly disappointed.

The first to leave Boston for Walpole was Louisa, traveling by train and stagecoach, enjoying her own company. After years of city life she found the country town invigorating. Every day she rose at five to take a run in the ravine "seeing the woods wake," spent the morning writing, the afternoon helping Lu tend her large garden, savoring "the smell of the fresh earth and the touch of green leaves." Evenings were for fun. The rest of the family entered into this unaccustomed life of pleasure a month later. Bronson prepared a garden, Abby luxuriated in leisure, and Louisa and Anna threw themselves into Walpole's first theater season.

The driving force behind the Walpole Amateur Dramatic Company was the summer resident Dr. Henry Whitney Bellows, descendant of the founder of Walpole and the town's leading light. Pastor of the First Congregational [Unitarian] Church in New York, forty-one-year-old Bellows made the Alcotts his pet project. He so liked shy twenty-year-old Lizzie Alcott that he presented her with a piano. Louisa called Bellows "the gayest of the gay" and incorporated his generous act into *Little Women*, as Mr. Laurence's gift of a piano to Beth. Bellows gave starring roles to Anna and Louisa all that summer, and the Alcott sisters became indispensable to the Walpole Amateur Dramatic Company's nine-play season. Anna played the ingenues, while Louisa tore through juicy character parts. Louisa's Mrs. Malaprop, the hilarious mangler of English in Sheridan's *The Rivals*, must have been rich. In J. R. Planché's *The Jacobite*, Anna was the saucy daughter Patty to Louisa's Cockney hell-on-wheels Widow Pottle. The sisters would reprise those roles for charity performances so often in years to come that they sometimes switched for the sake of variety.

Among their contemporaries Anna was thought the better dramatic actress of the two sisters, and Louisa the superior comedienne. Frank Preston Stearns, who had acted with the Alcott sisters in Concord, recalled them both as exceptional performers, "always in demand when private theatricals were on foot and yet—[Louisa's] acting had this peculiarity, that she seemed always to be herself and the character she was representing at the same time." Stearns was describing what directors and critics mean by *star quality*, the talent of actors whose own personalities are expressed through the characters they play. Louisa's star quality owed something to self-consciousness as well as to her intriguing personality. Outside her family—and much of the time within it—she was "on," engaging people with a bravado that guarded her vulnerable emotional core and covered up what she described as shyness. Anna was the kind of actress who could disappear into a role; she was more vivid onstage than off.

The company played to audiences of one hundred or more over the three-week season, received favorable notices in the Boston papers (one singled out Louisa for "superior histrionic ability"), and raised an impressive sum for charity, although the Alcott sisters could have used salaries themselves.

The theater season ended, the town emptied of summer visitors, and the Walpole idyll was over as abruptly as it had begun. Louisa set to work on her new book of stories, *Christmas Elves*. She judged it better than *Flower Fables* and asked fifteen-year-old May to draw the illustrations. Anna returned to Syracuse for a third year, this time to a teaching job at "the great idiot asylum" (actually for its day a progressive mental hospital), where she struggled dutifully and miserably into the next spring. Her only bright spot was starring in a local production of *Scenes from Dickens*, a staple of the amateur theater of the day. Louisa struck out for Boston in dull November, a good time to leave the New England provinces, but as her father had warned, too late in the year to sell a book about Christmas elves. Hoping to stay in the city, she looked for teaching and sewing jobs. The roof over her head was provided by her Aunt Bond, Louisa Greenwood Bond, an orphan adopted by Colonel May late in life.

Louisa found independence in Boston exhilarating. On the brink of her twenty-third birthday and Bronson's fifty-sixth, she sent her father a letter that celebrated their differences:

> I think it is but right & proper that a thanksgiving feast should be held in the states where we both are to celebrate the joyful day on which two such blessings as you & I dawned upon the world & I please myself with imagining how differently we looked & acted on making our debut upon the stage where we have been acting our parts so well ever since.
>
> I know *you* were a serene & placid baby . . . looking philosophically out of your cradle at the big world about you. . . . *I* was a crass crying baby, bawling at the disagreeable old world. . . . I scrambled up into childhood, . . . fell with a crash into girlhood & continued falling over fences, out of trees, uphill & down stairs tumbling from one year to another till strengthened by such violent exercise, the topsey turvey girl shot up into a topsey turvey woman who now twenty-three years after sits big brown & brave, crying not because she has come into the world but because she must go out of it before she has done half she wants to, & because it's such hard work to keep sunshiney and cheerful when life looks gloomy and full of troubles, but as the big brown baby fought through its small trials so the brown woman will fight thro her big ones & come out queen of herself tho not of the world.

She was going to the theater at least twice a week, responding to performances with a new discernment born of her own first season on stage:
now she was unimpressed by energetic scenery-chewing. Seeing Edwin
Forrest, the nation's preeminent Shakespearean actor, she scoffed, "I can
make up a better Macbeth & Hamlet for myself than Forrest with his
gaspings & shoutings." While Louisa's taste in acting was becoming more
refined, her enthusiasm for a career as a professional actress was cooling,
at least while closing a birthday letter to a parent who might have trepida-
tions about his daughter venturing into dangerous territory completely
unknown to him: "After being on the stage & seeing more nearly the tinsel & brass of actor life (much as I should love to be a great star *if* I could),
I have come to the conclusion that its not worth trying for at the expense
of health & peace of mind."

For Christie Devon, the Louisa-like heroine of *Work*, acting would be
"only one of many experiences which were to show her her own weakness
and strength." She was "no dramatic genius . . . had no talent except that
which may be developed in any girl possessing [a] lively fancy, sympathetic nature, and ambitious spirit." Mr. Kent, the comic actor based
upon Louisa's Boston mentor, William Warren, predicted that in time
Christie Devon "would make a clever actress, never a great one."

Louisa was learning her limitations and considered her face to be one
of them. An intriguing glimpse into Louisa's opinion of her own looks
is mirrored in Christie Devon's.

> "If I had beauty I should stand a better chance," sighed Christie, survey-
> ing herself with great disfavor, quite unconscious that to a cultivated eye
> the soul of beauty was often visible in that face of hers, with its intelli-
> gent eyes, sensitive mouth, and fine lines about the forehead, making it
> a far more significant and attractive countenance than that of her friend,
> possessing only piquant prettiness.

Ingenue looks would have held her back, Louisa thought, especially
when she played Dickens's grotesque comedic characters. But because
like Christie Devon she believed "she had little beauty to sacrifice," Louisa
played those roles "with a spirit and ease that surprised those who had
considered her a dignified and rather dull young person."

"The Sisters' Trial," a precursor to *Little Women* published in 1856,
came to the "tinsel and brass" conclusion about acting, although it began

with one character's fervent wish to play on the professional stage. The schematic plot laid out the fates of four sisters, who roughly corresponded to the Alcott girls. As in the first book of *Little Women,* the story took place within a single year, and like its successor all four sisters were also Louisa weighing her alternatives and considering what she could or ought to be. The story has two scenes: In the first, the orphaned, homeless, and penniless sisters announce their various plans. They agree to meet after a year to evaluate their choices. The second scene is their reunion.

One of the sisters, Agnes, has become an actress but has quit the stage. She has had some theatrical success, but the man she loves will not consider marrying an actress—not even a former actress. Agnes is homeless and penniless, as she had been the year before.

Sister Ella—Lizzie Alcott crossed with Cinderella—has been governess to the three children of a widowed Southern slaveholder. She has fallen in love with her charges and with their parent and will soon marry, happily trading freedom for a secure subordinate position in an immoral social structure. Amy—May Alcott, the same self-centered, lucky Amy whom Louisa would depict in *Little Women*—has traveled through Europe as companion to a wealthy friend and patron of her art studies, and returned confident of her prospects as a painter. Nora, who has been supporting herself by sewing and teaching while writing a novel, has sold her book and can now offer a home to any of her sisters who wants it; the failed actress Agnes will certainly need it.

Despite her literary success, Nora seems mysteriously sad, and the reason is soon made clear: she also has had a romantic disappointment. Her lover was a wealthy cousin who submitted to his father's wish that he marry a woman of his own rank. As Nora finishes telling her story, the cousin appears, disowned and impoverished but devoted and loyal, to present himself to the woman he loves in hopes she will accept him as her husband.

There were almost too many clues to Louisa's life-planning in "The Sisters' Trial." Agnes's acting career was a failure that won her neither success nor love—too great a risk for Louisa. The character's rejection of the stage makes us wonder if Louisa might have turned away from professional acting because it would have jeopardized her chance for a happy marriage. Amy's good fortune might have been a possibility for a pampered youngest child, a girl who had talent and determination but no concern for the rest of her family—but was not a possibility for a girl like

Louisa, highly educated in hard knocks. Ella's path was the surest road to financial security, but Louisa shunned the idea of compromising herself or her principles for marriage. Nora's outcome was the only one Louisa could imagine for herself: Nora worked hard and suffered deeply, but won money and love in the end. With enough financial power to maintain her independence within a romantic relationship, Louisa might support the right man with her pen.

Was there a man in Louisa's life who could have been the model for the wealthy cousin Nora loves? Her cousin Samuel Sewall Greele might have filled the bill. Sam Greele was the son of Abby's sister Louisa May Greele, for whom Louisa was named, and was among the Sams who contributed to the rescue of the Alcotts in 1850. Sam Greele's father was the deacon of the church for whose benefit Louisa had recently performed Oronthy Bluggage's comic monologue. The deacon may not have thought his raffish niece a suitable match for his son, a graduate of Groton, Harvard, and the Rensselaer Polytechnic Institute, and Louisa may have known it; she didn't much like the deacon either. In 1853 Sam Greele left Boston for Chicago to work as a surveyor. A few months later Louisa wrote to her cousin Charlotte, Uncle Sam May's daughter, commenting, "I suppose you see cousin Sam's letters. If you *don't*, allow me to remark they are perfectly beautiful and it is a matter of great astonishment to us that such lovely thoughts can come from a descendant of a certain *corpulent Deacon.*"

Sam Greele married Annie Morris Larned of Providence, Rhode Island, in 1855, the same year he was elected Chicago city surveyor. They had four children. Louisa reported the death of Annie Greele in her journal for January of 1864, and again in her notes and memoranda at the end of that year, suggesting that the event had significance for her throughout the year. In September of 1866 Greele returned to Boston and married his and Louisa's wealthy first cousin Eliza May Wells. In her journal Louisa wrote that "E. Wells married S. Greele, a foolish match. Went to the wedding and had a dull time." There seems to have been some bad blood between Eliza Wells and Louisa—could it have been over Sam Greele? In her 1858 letter on the subject of Lizzie Alcott's death, Louisa had alluded to a misunderstanding or grievance, closing with "Dear Eliza, perhaps if I ask you now you may be able to forgive & forget whatever unk[ind]ness you believe me guilty of, & I hope you may sometime learn to know me as I really am, *& have been,* your grateful and loving cousin."

William Clapp at the *Saturday Evening Gazette* paid six dollars for "The Sisters' Trial," a raise of a dollar. The story ran in the January 1856 issue under the transparent pseudonym "M.L.A." By March, L.M.A. could report that her prices had gone up again. People liked her stories and asked for more. She was paid ten dollars for "Bertha" and saw "great yellow placards announcing it." Louisa felt famous—even though she was identified only as "the author of 'The Rival Prima Donnas.'" Her sisters went to see the placard that windy afternoon, and seeing it was torn, boldly made away with the evidence of Louisa's success and flourished it in triumph at home.*

Her farce, *Nat Bachelor's Pleasure Trip,* was going to be produced in Mobile, Alabama, and she had in the works another *Flower Fables* sort of book called *Beach Bubbles,* intended for summer publication. But most of Louisa's income came from the poorly paid drudgery of sewing jobs like the ones she described in her journal in 1856: "Sewed a great deal and got very tired; one job for Mr. G. of a dozen pillow-cases, one dozen sheets, six fine cambric neckties, and two dozen handkerchiefs, at which I had to work all one night to get them done. I got only $4." Needlework offered one great advantage over teaching: "Sewing won't make my fortune, but I can plan my stories while I work, and then scribble 'em down on Sundays."

Beach Bubbles was rejected, and the prospective producer of her farce dropped dead, but Louisa was enjoying her independence too much to think of giving it up. Anna, however, was sick of her own independence, and in May she came to Boston from Syracuse for a visit of indeterminate length. Abby wrote her brother Sam, Anna's host in Syracuse, that she thought it would be Anna's "last effort to leave home—at least to be separated from Louisa for whom she has a passionate attachment." Abby sympathized. She knew of "no young woman whose life-history has been more checkered by duties." Both parents begged Anna to come home to Walpole, but she made no move to leave Louisa. Bronson appealed to Louisa to return with Anna, but while Anna did eventually return to Walpole, Louisa stayed put in Boston until June. Her preferred plan was to spend only the warm months with her family; most years she did not get her preference.

---

* The torn "Bertha" placard is in the collection at Orchard House. Once the home of the Alcotts, it is now a museum.

Louisa arrived in Walpole to find Lizzie very ill with scarlet fever "caught from some poor children Mother nursed when they fell sick, living over a cellar where pigs had been kept." Sixteen-year-old May had also been infected but recovered quickly; twenty-two-year-old Lizzie languished all summer. Louisa took turns with Abby at her bedside, helped Anna with housework, and wrote stories, while her father and Dr. Bellows offered Conversations to the summer visitors. There was no Walpole theater season for the Alcott girls. It was "an anxious time," as Louisa noted in her journal.

Even with a daughter critically ill, Abby had not lost sight of the troubles in the wider world. She was deeply involved in support of antislavery settlers in "bleeding Kansas," where fighting broke out after a fiercely contested election over whether to enter the union as a free or slave state. Appeals for help for the embattled settlers went out in New England's antislavery newspapers, and Abby was soon organizing clothing drives. The chance to lose herself in a good cause was a rescue of sorts for Abby. Even before Lizzie's illness, she had been lonely and restless, with her older daughters and Bronson in distant cities. Increasingly impatient with her neighbors—she called Walpole "a dark valley of selfish propriety"—she begged Bronson to find them a haven in a more sympathetic region.

Louisa was even more desperate than her mother to escape a winter in Walpole. In October of 1856 she plotted her return to Boston. Rather than be chaperoned by Aunt Bond, she struck out on her own, taking a room in Mrs. Reed's boardinghouse, a focal point for Boston's best and brightest youth. Her literary market now included the *Olive Branch* and the *Ladies Enterprise*. The *Gazette* and the *Sunday News* paid poorly, and "as money is the principle [*sic*] object of my life just now I want to add another string or two to my bow." She asked William Clapp to contract with her for a story a month for six months at fifteen or twenty dollars each, depending on how long or good they were. Clapp came back with an offer of ten dollars a story, which Louisa viewed in a rosy light. Willis and Sewall cousins would give her sewing work, and so would Mrs. Reed, whose attic room, firewood, and food would cost her three dollars a week. If she could get part-time work as governess to little Alice Lovering, she could swing it, she figured. Louisa was training herself as a business-woman as well as a fast, versatile pen for hire.

"I took my little talent in my hand and forced the world again, braver than before and wiser for my failures," she wrote of her descent upon Boston. Upon later reading this journal entry, she would insert, in brackets: [Jo in N.Y.—L.M.A.] In *Little Women*, Jo March addresses her epistles from a New York boardinghouse to Beth and Marmee; Louisa Alcott's correspondent was Anna, her "beloved lass." She wrote her older sister about living on her own: "[I have] a queer pie shaped room, but nicely carpeted, with two bureaus, (for which I give praise), a dormer window with a table & a rocking chair for my private benefit." She reported to her that their cousin Lu Willis's husband, Ham Willis, was so glad to have someone escort Lu that he would give them tickets to anything they wanted to see; "(hear oh my people!) he is [also] going to get a 'Pass' from Barry so that I can go in to the Theatre with them when I like & for nothing." Lu had given her a scarlet crepe shawl of such fine quality that she felt "illuminated" when she wore it. She was invited to a state house reception for her "idol" Charles Sumner.* She reveled in the city.

> Boston is nicer & noisier than ever. Cars go rumbling about, the sidewalks are perfect rainbows in point of color, Fremont† flags are flapping like birds of prey over a lady's head & crowds of people are swarming up & down in a state of bustle very agreeable to behold after the still life of Walpole.

She called her Boston venture her "experiment to be independent of everyone but my own two hands & busy head." At the same time she wanted more help: "It seems rather queer sometimes to be in a city full of very rich relations & yet feel as if I dared not ask them for any help even to find work, for when I do they are so busy about their own affairs that my concerns seem a bother & I go away thinking I will never ask again." Lu

---

* Sumner had been brutally beaten on the floor of the Senate after giving an inflammatory antislavery speech.
† General John Frémont was the Republican Party's first presidential nominee, in 1856. His antislavery platform provoked threats of secession from Southern states in the event of his election. He lost to James Buchanan.

and Ham and the Sewalls were exempt from complaint "for they give me something better than work or money, in their good will & sympathy." But as her mother's daughter, she resented the indifference of wealthy relatives and was so on guard that sometimes she must have imagined it.

Louisa had a second set of rich relatives in Boston, an intellectual circle where being an Alcott meant as much as or more than being a May. Encouraged by her parents, she began attending the charismatic preacher Theodore Parker's Sunday evening salon, the gathering place for the leaders of the legions of reform. She looked on as the Harvard-educated Wendell Phillips, who advocated the expulsion of the South, discussed the fraying state of the Union with the antislavery giant William Garrison, a son of immigrants who began in journalism as a typesetter; met the future lyricist of the "Battle Hymn of the Republic," Julia Ward Howe ("a straw colored supercilious lady with pale eyes & a green gown in which she looked like a faded lettuce"); took refreshments with Sumner; and chatted with her father's disciple Frank Sanborn, who "bowed like a well-sweep & talked about books as usual" (and was soon to join "the secret six" to plot John Brown's raid on Harpers Ferry). Her sedate behavior among distinguished elders was replaced by Jo March–like antics at Sumner's parade, when she joined the cheering throng; "[I] pitched about like a madwoman, shouted, waved, hung onto fences, rushed thro crowds & swarmed about in a state [of] rapterous [sic] insanity til it was all over & then I went home hoarse and worn out."

Between bouts of self-doubt and the occasional rejection slip, she was having the time of her life. One memorable day she was whisked off by Ham Willis to meet Mr. Barry of the Boston Theatre, who actually wanted to be introduced to the author of *The Rival Prima Donnas*, a melodramatic adaptation of her story. Barry had passed along Louisa's play to an associate, and if he approved, it would be staged. In a letter to Anna she described waiting behind the curtain, roaming the immense stage, and investigating the equipment that made rain and thunder effects. She poked into dressing rooms and the scenery shops. She eyed actors up close, and eavesdropped on a lot of beautifully voiced swearing, chattering, and scolding during an opera rehearsal. When Barry appeared, he regaled Louisa and Ham Willis with tales of young people who needed to be cured of sick longing for a life in the theater, a job at which he claimed to be an expert. He had the opposite effect on Louisa, who was stage-struck all the more for meeting the impressario. Louisa left with Barry's promise that she could attend any production and bring a friend. She hoped Anna would come to Boston to take advantage of the offer with her.

Twenty-five-year-old Anna did not have Louisa's initiative, or even sixteen-year-old May's: a week later May turned up in Boston to stay with Aunt Bond and study drawing at the new art school. Aunt Bond was paying May's tuition and asking in return none of the sewing, or sitting, or reading to invalid relatives Louisa had done the year before. Louisa "dared not ask" her relatives "for any help even to find work," but May could inspire outright gifts.*

May already had what Louisa would bestow upon Amy at sixteen in *Little Women*: "the air and bearing of a full-grown woman—not beautiful, but possessed of that indescribable charm called grace . . . in the lines of her figure, the make and motion of her hands, the flow of her dress, the droop of her hair—unconscious, yet harmonious, and as attractive to many as beauty itself." Though Louisa had better features and a vivid, rosy olive complexion, May had the fair skin, blue eyes, and golden curls that were more widely prized. May was tall, beautifully built, and had the smooth grace of a Venus. Louisa was tall and graceful, too, but hers was the long-limbed athletic movement of a Diana.

Abby may have guessed that Aunt Bond's generosity to May was leaving Louisa feeling undervalued. Knowing that she liked to be nicely dressed, Abby had Bronson buy a cloak pin for Louisa's birthday at a fancy store in New York, where he was giving a series of Conversations arranged by his Walpole patron, Dr. Bellows.

Louisa's letter thanking Bronson was prefaced by a stinging remark: "I think I shall come out all right," she told her impecunious parent, "and prove that though an *Alcott* I can support myself. I like the independent feeling, and though not an easy life, it is a free one, and I enjoy it." Her brains were her capital: "I will make a battering ram of my head and make a way through this rough and tumble world," she wrote. The

---

* In her mild exploitation of Louisa and generosity toward May Alcott, Aunt Bond bears a suspicious resemblance to Aunt March of *Little Women*. Although Louisa revealed the models for her other characters, she denied flatly that Aunt March was based on anyone, probably because she was fond of Aunt Bond.

suggestion of anger toward her father at the beginning of this letter is unique in the surviving Alcott letters. That the complete record would include a good deal more anger toward Bronson seems reasonable to assume, and many Louisa supporters then and now hope it did. On the other hand, Louisa may have realized as early on as at Fruitlands that her father was incapable of any labor for hire except as a teacher.

For the first time Louisa spent Christmas away from her sisters and parents. She prepared for the holiday enthusiastically, buying presents, accompanying Lu Willis on a "shopping excursion" to G. W. Warren & Co. on Washington Street, then teaching Alice Lovering for two hours to pay for it all before heading back to Mrs. Reed's to find a package from home:

> I clutched it, swept upstairs, & startled the family by dancing a hornpipe with it in my arms, then like a young whirlwind swarmed to my garret, ripped it open and plunged in, laughing crying, munching the gingerbread, putting on the flannel cap, flapping the yellow butterfly holder & sprinkling salt water over letters & presents in a perfectly rapterous & imbecile manner. You dear good souls, to think of me in the middle of your hustle!

Louisa was a master of the thank-you note. She could make a gift of gingerbread and a flannel cap sound better than a sapphire necklace.

Christmas was a glamorous round of parties, tree trimmings, and more presents than Louisa had ever received. Most memorable was her gift from Lu: "a handsome silk gown the first I ever had," she reported to Anna, "one stripe bronze & black and one of silvery grey." She went to Christmas dinner at the Windships. More gifts (laces, gloves, perfume, a pretty handkerchief) were followed by tea and another party. May "arrived with the Bonds looking very pale & lofty in her meek gown & as I sat in a corner I enjoyed the remarks her relations made about her for they seemed astonished that an Alcott should dance & talk like other people."

Full of optimism, she promised Anna—as miserably stranded in Walpole as Abby, who had taken to calling it "Mount Blank"—to find them a new home, an extraordinary pledge from a twenty-four-year-old who had "eight cents in the bank at present, $10 owing [her], & a fortune in prospect." But her scrupulous accounting for 1856 confirmed that she had nearly doubled her income, and earned nearly half of it from writing. Regarding her job as a governess to the Lovering children, she wrote, "[It is] hard work but I can do it, and am glad to sit in a large fine room part of each day, after my skyparlor, which has nothing pretty in it and only the gray tower and blue sky outside as I sit at the window writing. I love luxury, but freedom and independence better."

In February Louisa surprised Anna and Abby with a visit to Walpole, announcing herself as a valentine for her mother. Abby had been complaining to Bronson by letter about the neighbors. "They seem specifically sent into life to take care of their house, horses, and money. . . . Culture of Soul and Self is no part of the programme." They were oblivious to the needs of others, with no use for the creative likes of the Alcotts until someone was needed to mount a production or organize a charity. Louisa was "a glad surprise to us and a joy in this region of Snows and Snubs. She is quite intent on getting us nearer Boston." Louisa returned to Boston for the rest of the happy winter to look into schemes to get the family out of Walpole and bring them closer together. They had been scattered for years. In the spring, May returned to Walpole triumphant with the progress of her art. Louisa followed soon after, equally pleased by her winter's work. "I have done what I planned,—supported myself, written eight stories, taught four months, earned a hundred dollars and sent money home."

Grown family members often lament that they see each other only at weddings and funerals. The Alcotts would finally be reunited for both. Both profoundly affected Louisa's future.

The decline and death of twenty-three-year-old Lizzie Alcott were immortalized in *Little Women* as the passing of sixteen-year-old Beth March. Louisa took many details for the book from the nearly two-year period of her sister's illness. She used a poem she wrote at the time, whose second and third stanzas read:

Oh, my sister, passing from me,
out of human care and strife,
Leave me, as a gift, those virtues
which have beautified your life.
Dear, bequeath me that great patience
which has power to sustain
a cheerful, uncomplaining spirit
in its prison-house of pain.

Give me, for I need it sorely,
of that courage, wise and sweet,
Which has made the path of duty
green beneath your willing feet.
Give me that unselfish nature,
that, with charity divine,
can pardon wrong for love's dear sake—
meek heart, forgive me mine!

In *Little Women* Louisa cataloged the sweet parting gifts Lizzie made before the needle became "too heavy," but omitted the gruesome truth— that "she looked like a woman of forty, all her pretty hair gone." And she rearranged the course of events so that Beth March could attend Meg's wedding. In life, Lizzie's funeral came first.

The family described Lizzie's failure to recover after her bout with scarlet fever as a retreat from adult life. She had never been interested in the world outside the family. Unable to understand her weight loss, weakness, stomach pains, nausea, vomiting, sweating, hair loss, depression, irritability, drowsiness, and restlessness, Abby ventured an inadequate explanation that "perhaps want of more cheerful society may have caused this sad wrench of her frame." There is little doubt that Lizzie was suffering from the effects of scarlet fever, which triggered rheumatic fever and led to congestive heart failure. Without the benefit of medical knowledge, the family's interpretations of her disease leaned toward self-blame, for causing it, and for failing to cure it.

Her sisters did their best to make life seem normal that summer of 1857. They rejoined the Walpole Amateur Dramatic Company to amuse Lizzie with tales of their adventures. Bronson's mother made an extended visit and charmed Louisa with her sweetness. She was much in demand among her many far-flung children and grandchildren.

Doctors consulted in desperation by the Alcotts, who believed in homeopathic medicine or none, made confident misdiagnoses of Lizzie's disease. In seaside Swampscott, salt water and sunshine did not restore Lizzie. The local medical man whispered "tuberculosis" and suggested only rest, home, and family comfort. Aunt Bond sent the family authority, Dr. Charles Windship, to Swampscott to examine Lizzie. He concluded that she was *not* suffering from tuberculosis. "It seems to me that the system of medicine is a prolonged *Guess*," Abby wrote in helpless confusion. Bronson came to Swampscott to consult a Dr. Newell, with Abby and Lizzie. Newell had nothing better to suggest than a bland diet, rest, and Tincture of Time. Bronson admitted that "the case is a critical one, and there is . . . a dark side to the prospect."

The only clear—if irrelevant—course of action was for the family to return from exile in Walpole. Bronson took charge, orchestrating his scattered family's movements and economic welfare with a rare competence brought into being by emergency and paternal love. Sympathetic friends made or renewed offers of houses or land. The Alcotts scouted Roxbury and Brookline to satisfy Louisa; she was clinging to a hope of resuming her independence in nearby Boston. But as Louisa knew he would, Bronson chose Concord; "he is never happy far from Emerson, the one true friend who loves and understands and helps him."

By late September, with a four-hundred-dollar deposit from Emerson, the Moore house and ten acres of orchard next to Hillside on the Lexington Road were theirs. For her unforeseen return to Concord or for the new house Louisa had little enthusiasm: "The people are kind and friendly, and the old place looks pleasant enough, though I never want to live in it." Until Bronson could make the rattletrap old house livable, they would rent one of the Hosmer cottages.

As the autumn leaves reached the blazing intensity of their colors just before they fell from the trees, the Alcotts were reunited in Concord to attend their household saint. Named at birth Elizabeth Peabody Alcott, revised as Elizabeth Sewall Alcott during the destruction of the Temple School two years later, she was "Lizzie," the humblest of the multitude of diminutives for "Elizabeth"—Eliza, Betsy, Libby, Elsbeth, and on and on. "Lizzie" was a nickname associated so strongly with Irish housemaids that it was generic, used by insensitive employers to call any female person serving in a position too lowly to acknowledge by name. Louisa, deliberately or unconsciously, began to refer to her younger sister as "Betty" when she was writing about her illness. "Find Betty a shadow, but sweet and patient always," Louisa wrote when she rejoined the family in Concord. "Betty" was a short step to "Beth," a nickname that comes from the Hebrew word meaning "belonging to the house." The name Louisa chose to give to the immortal form of her sister Elizabeth Alcott would become so universally known and definitive that a Hebrew-English dictionary gives "Beth March, a fictional character in Louisa May Alcott's *Little Women*" under one of the meanings of *beth* in English.

Once together in Concord, the whole family made a room pleasant for their invalid and centered family life there. To provide the happy bustle that Lizzie so enjoyed when plays were put on, her sisters organized the Concord Dramatic Union with some students of Franklin Sanborn, the schoolmaster and radical abolitionist. Louisa and fifteen-year-old Alfred Whitman distinguished themselves as the comic couple Sophia and Dolphus, from Dickens's tale *The Haunted Man*, and began a comfortable and lasting friendship. Anna was cast opposite John Pratt, a handsome man in his midtwenties, in productions including the romantic drama *The Loan of a Lover;* offstage they starred in their own romance. A recent resident at Brook Farm, John Pratt would appear in *Little Women* as John Brooke, the man Meg March loves and marries.

Alf Whitman and John Pratt were often at the Alcotts' during the long days of Lizzie's last illness. By the time Whitman wrote his account of those days, the sisters were so well known from *Little Women* that he furnished their characters' names as well as their own: "No written words can convey an adequate idea of the love and care which Louisa ('Jo') lavished upon Elizabeth ('Beth')," he wrote. "Louisa would be backwards and forwards from the upstairs room, making everybody feel happy and cheerful, yet at all times ready to answer a call from Lizzie." At her sister's bedside Louisa would slip into another Dickens comic role, the Cockney nurse Sairy Gamp of *Martin Chuzzlewit.*

Louisa produced the high spirits of the theater and nursed her sister in character with all the acting skill she possessed. Alfred Whitman had a glimpse of her undisguised feelings when he dropped by after church on a Sunday: "I entered the house without knocking, and as I opened the door of the little sitting-room, found Louisa there alone. She had turned her back to the door as she heard me come in. Before I could speak, she threw down the white garment upon which she was sewing . . . burst into tears, and with the words, 'It is Lizzie's shroud,' hurried out of the room."

There was no pretense that the vigil was anything but a death watch, made as loving and painless as possible, but death from congestive heart failure is painful. Louisa described the final scenes upstairs: "For two days, she suffered much, begging for ether though its effect was gone. Tuesday she . . . called us all round, . . . held our hands and kissed us tenderly. Saturday . . . at midnight [she] became unconscious, then, with one last look of the beautiful eyes, she was gone." Louisa and Abby washed and dressed Lizzie's body for burial. The family held a private service and sang her favorite hymn. Then Ralph Waldo Emerson, Henry David Thoreau, Franklin Sanborn, and John Pratt took Lizzie to Sleepy Hollow Cemetery, a new burial ground landscaped to appear as natural and native as possible, in keeping with Transcendentalist values. The style would be perfected by Frederick Law Olmsted in New York's Central Park.

Afterward Louisa described a strange experience that had taken place at the end of the long death vigil: "A few moments after the last breath came, as Mother and I sat silently watching the shadow fall on the dear little face, I saw a light mist rise from the body, and float up and vanish in the air. Mother's eyes followed mine, and when I said, 'What did you see?' she described the same light mist." Louisa might have thought the incident too strange and unsettling to use in *Little Women*.

Bronson had asked Lizzie if she knew she might not recover. Yes, she replied, adding that of his four daughters, she was the one who could best be spared. Many women today would agree. Lizzie (as well as her fictional counterpart Beth) was so lacking in blood, spirit, and *will* that they find her alternately pathetic and infuriating; hers was a nineteenth-century personality type that has not worn well. The modern reader cries less for Beth than for Jo March, whose powerful love and wrenching grief are expressed so delicately.

"She is well at last," Louisa said of Lizzie's passing, as Jo says it of Beth's. The sentiment is unconvincing, especially as consolation for the sister left behind. Louisa had to carry on without the sister who stayed home and kept house. If Lizzie knew the gap she was leaving, and she must have, she saw it as a loss to her parents rather than a burden to her sister. In *Little Women* Beth March tells Jo that she must learn not to be Jo, but to be Beth. Lizzie Alcott probably made a speech to Louisa something like this one from *Little Women*, part 2, chapter 17, "The Valley of the Shadow."

> "You must take my place, Jo, and be everything to father and mother when I'm gone. They will turn to you—don't fail them; and if it's hard to work alone, remember that I don't forget you, and that you'll be happier in doing that, than writing splendid books, or seeing all the world, for

love is the only thing that we can carry with us when we go, and it
makes the end so easy."

"I'll try, Beth"; and then and there Jo renounced her old ambition.

In her journal Louisa wrote, "So the first break comes, and I know
what death means—a liberator for her, a teacher for us." The lesson was
a cruel one.

TEN

NATURE MUST HAVE A VENT

Just three weeks after Lizzie's death Anna announced her engagement. Only the timing came as a shock to the Alcotts; John had been a household regular during their long winter vigil, his place in the family confirmed when he joined Emerson, Thoreau, and Sanborn as pallbearers for Lizzie. Though Pratt's prospects hinted at none of the riches twenty-seven-year-old Anna had dreamed of since childhood, at this point in her life a safe harbor in the hand was worth two castles in the air. Anna had never had Louisa's ambition or confidence; her fantasies had always been predicated on Louisa's. She and John were both shy, virtuous children of Transcendentalists, both fond of acting, both bolder onstage than playing their own timid selves.

For Louisa, Anna's decision to marry was a huge blow. On top of the loss of Lizzie, her only real confidante was defecting, leaving her alone to shoulder the family's financial and household burdens—May had returned to Boston and another open-handed sponsor. With a decade of toil behind her, Louisa's future unrolled before her as one of endless labor as her parents' breadwinner, housekeeper, and sole devoted daughter.

Suspended in the emergency of Lizzie's death was the move to the house on the Lexington Road, next door to Hillside. Only the pre-Revolutionary building's dilapidated condition stood in the way of making it their permanent home; Bronson already saw it in his mind's eye as Orchard House, while Louisa was calling it "Apple Slump," after a thrown-together dessert. The Nathaniel Hawthornes, who had bought Hillside from the Alcotts, were living abroad and offered the use of it while Bronson made repairs at Orchard House.

Settling into her childhood home with her parents—Anna was staying at the Pratt family farm—was a throwback to adolescence for a twenty-five-year-old who had treasured "the independent feeling" of her life in Boston. She had been happy in Concord, but now she was bereft of the sister—the three sisters—who had made her so. The Hawthornes had changed the name of the house from Hillside to Wayside and embellished the plain jerry-built structure with gothic arches and a tower where Mr. Hawthorne hid away to write. Yet the house held powerful memories. A decade earlier Louisa had come of age here, when Concord represented the greatest stability she had ever known, and her own room her first taste of privacy. Ten years later she had solitude and deep loneliness. Her parents were absorbed in the new house, which didn't interest her. She no longer cared to roam the woods, much as she appreciated Concord's natural setting. In Boston she was a writer and an actress. Concord offered just one role: spinster family caretaker.

When Anna and May returned home, Louisa rushed to Boston at her first opportunity to visit Ham and Lu. She saw the celebrated actress Charlotte Cushman through a two-week run that included her renowned portrayal in the male role of Hamlet, and was stagestruck all over again. When Charles Windship persuaded Thomas Barry to cast Louisa in the *Jacobite* at the Boston Theatre, she was game to try.

> I was to do Widow Pottle, as the dress was a good disguise, and I knew the part well. It was all a secret, and I had hopes of trying a new life, the old one being so changed now. I felt as if I must find interest in something absorbing. But Mr B. broke his leg, so I had to give it up; and when it was known, the dear respectable relations were horrified at the idea. I'll try again by and by, and see if I have the gift. Perhaps it is acting, not writing, I'm meant for. Nature must have a vent somehow.

She worked off her stage fever by writing a story and got twenty-five dollars, funds enough to refurbish the four Alcott women's summer clothes and purchase new hats. She figured that the inside of her head could earn enough to cover the outside at least. Given the alternatives of acting and writing, Louisa would follow the money.

By July she was back in Concord with Anna and May, helping her parents settle into the refurbished Orchard House, and feeling less deserted. Their new/old house was warmed by a flood of visitors eager to see what the clever Alcotts had made of their latest ruin. Bronson's hand showed in the Saxon-arched alcoves that defined bookshelves and cupboards, in an ingenious drying rack in the kitchen that swung out from its resting place against the wall to benefit from the heat of the adjacent fireplace, and in beautifully laid out walkways and vegetable gardens. His daughters handled the interior decoration, painting and papering upstairs and down. May adorned "all the nooks and corners with panels on which she had painted birds, or flowers," recalled a delighted Lydia Maria Child, "and over the open fireplaces, mottoes in ancient English characters. Owls blink at you and faces peep from the most unexpected places."

"All seem to be glad that the wandering family is anchored at last," Louisa wrote. "We won't move again for twenty years if I can help it."

But in October Louisa headed for Boston—"on my usual hunt for employment, as [I] seem to be the only breadwinner just now." She painted herself something of a martyr, but she probably left Concord with relief, expecting to resume her independent Boston life.

She moved in with her Sewall cousins on Chestnut Street in Beacon Hill and made the neighborhood rounds of old contacts. She called at the Loverings to ask for a job as Alice's governess, only to find Mrs. Lovering out. She "tore across the Common" to Mrs. Reed, the boardinghouse keeper, who had no sewing work but promised to keep her in mind. John Sargent, a distant antislavery movement acquaintance of her parents, had nothing and suggested nothing for her. She hated having to beg work from a comparative stranger—and get turned down on top of it. She began to panic and after an anxious night went to Theodore Parker, said she was desperate, and asked for help. She was willing to take any kind of honest work.

Hannah Stevenson, the Parkers' associate in the work of social improvement, knew of a job sewing ten hours a day at a reform school for girls in Winchester, far from Boston's theaters and social life and also distant from the family in Concord. At the thought of that miserable existence Louisa began to despair. In October's waning light, as she approached her twenty-sixth birthday without a single pleasurable prospect in sight, her sister Lizzie's release from worldly troubles began to seem not only beautiful but enviable.

"Last week was a busy and anxious time, & my courage most gave out," she wrote the family, "for everyone was so busy, & cared so little whether I got work or jumped into the river that I thought seriously of doing the latter. In fact did go over to the Mill Dam* & look at the water."

The brief account in Louisa's letter did not reveal much of her state of mind and her thoughts, but an episode in *Work* gives a good idea of what they were. In the novel Christie Devon, exhausted by a succession of failed careers, unfairly accused of theft, and in desperate need of a job, approaches the Mill Dam after catching a glimpse of a wedding party, with "a bonny bride, standing with her father's arm about her, while her mother gave some last loving touch to her array. . . . The sharpness of the contrast between the other woman's fate and her own . . . made her wring her hands together and cry out bitterly, 'Oh, it isn't fair, it isn't right that she should have so much and I so little. What have I ever done to be so desolate and miserable, and never to find any happiness, however hard I try to do what seems to be my duty?'" Christie looks down into the swirling waters.

> Something white swept by below—only a broken oar—but she began to wonder how a human body would look floating through the night. It was an awesome fancy, but it took possession of her, and, as it grew, her eyes dilated, her breath came fast, and her lips fell apart, for she seemed to see the phantom she had conjured up, and it wore the likeness of herself. . . . So plainly did she see it, so peaceful was the white face, so full of rest the folded hands, so strangely like, and yet unlike, herself, that she seemed to lose her identity, and wondered which was the real and which the imaginary Christie. Lower and lower she bent; looser and looser grew her hold upon the pillar; faster and faster beat the pulses in her temples, and the rush of some blind impulse was swiftly coming on, when a hand seized and caught her back.

In real life Louisa saved herself but minimized the event and her own anguish. There is a provocative blank in the journal after she looks down at the water, followed by a show of character: "My fit of despair was soon over,

---

* Mill Dam was a fifty-foot dam that ran for a mile and a half from Beacon Hill to present-day Kenmore Square. Built to harness waterpower, by 1858 it was used primarily to link Boston to Brookline.

for it seemed so cowardly to run away before the battle was over I couldn't do it. So I said firmly, 'There *is* work for me, and I'll have it,' and went home resolved to take Fate by the throat and shake a living out of her.'"

She went to a sermon by Theodore Parker on the subject of "Laborious Young Women," probably inspired by and directed at her, then decided she should take the sewing job in the Winchester reform school and packed her bag. The evening before she was to leave, "came a note from Mrs. L.[overing] offering the old salary and the old place." Louisa "sang for joy and next day early posted off to Miss S"—Hannah Stevenson—to tell her she wouldn't need the sewing job after all. "She was glad and shook hands, saying 'It was a test, my dear, and you stood it.'" Stevenson, the Parkers, the Sewalls, the Loverings, and many more people Louisa had not yet approached made Louisa a strong safety net. But she saw only the holes and not the web.

Encouraged by her parents, who were worried by her Mill Dam letter, she went home to Concord for a few days, then returned to the city to work four hours a day at the Loverings instead of ten a day in a reform school. Bronson paid her a surprise visit, ostensibly to help her find lodging away from the Sewalls, but more likely to check on her state of mind. They took long walks, attended lectures and conversations, and talked as equals about her writing and her prospects in Boston. Bronson wrote to Abby after a second such visit that Louisa "bore herself proudly and gave [him] great pleasure," and that he had taken one of her stories to William Clapp at the *American Union* before leaving town.

Shortly after her twenty-sixth birthday, she took stock of her mood and her prospects. "This past year has brought us the first death and betrothal—two events that change my life. I can see these experiences have taken a deep hold, and changed or developed me." Louisa judged herself stronger and more mature for her ordeals, and more confident of her powers. "I feel as if I could write better now—more truly of things I have felt and therefore *know*. I hope I shall yet do my great book, for that seems to be my work, and I am growing up to it. I even think of trying the *Atlantic*. There's ambition for you . . . ! If Mr. L. takes the one Father carried to him, I shall think I can do something."

"Mr. L." was James Russell Lowell, poet, satirist, and the first editor of the *Atlantic Monthly*, the publication dreamed up in a leisurely powwow at the Parker House Hotel the previous April by literary eminences including Emerson, Longfellow, and Oliver Wendell Holmes Sr. Within two years the magazine was the country's premier literary journal and had a paid circulation of thirty thousand. Lowell had skewered Bronson's "Orphic Sayings" in the *Dial* twenty years earlier, but the two men had since settled into affability at the lecture halls of Boston and the Town and Country Club. Bronson had stopped in at the *Atlantic* office to urge Lowell to consider Louisa's story "Love and Self-Love," which made use of an attempted suicide as a turning point. Louisa drew from the Mill Dam episode but in a completely different context and tone than she would later in *Work*.

"Love and Self-Love" is the story of a May-December marriage, a union made not for love but for the protection of a penniless sixteen-year-old orphan, Effie Home. Effie's guardian and husband, the self-absorbed Basil Ventnor, regards her as a child and ignores her love for him. When the married woman Ventnor truly loves returns to him a widow, Effie attempts to sacrifice herself by drowning, but her husband rescues her. The near-death experience transforms Effie from child to woman; her husband, impressed by her selfless attempt to free him from their loveless marriage, begins to respect her. But Effie no longer cares for him and goes away to nurse her dying grandfather, who leaves Effie his fortune; in the meantime Basil Ventnor loses most of his.

Ventnor arranges to provide for Effie with what little money he has left, then retreats to his "solitary hearth" a broken man. Learning of his reversals, Effie returns to keep her wedding vow to stand by her husband through thick and thin. Touched by her constancy, Ventnor finally addresses Effie as his wife, the barriers come down, the past is forgotten, and Effie reveals that she brings him her fortune. "Take it, Basil," she says. "And give me a little love."

To cast "Love and Self-Love" as a two-character play with Louisa in the role of Love and Bronson as Self-Love makes a certain sense. Like Ventnor, Bronson had been cold and distant from Louisa's love, criticizing her and preferring Anna. Only after Louisa showed Bronson her desperation by nearly leaping from the Mill Dam did Bronson come down from his superior position to respect Louisa for who she was, as Effie's near-drowning caused Ventnor to do. Bronson gave Louisa acknowledgment and care, and showed her his affection after the Mill Dam incident, coming to Boston to see and to help her. "I take pride in your enterprise and courage," Bronson wrote her from Chicago just before Christmas. "Much joy and love in you." Louisa must have been gratified by that message from her father; it put them almost on the footing Louisa felt necessary for marriage. In "The Sisters' Trial," the wealthy cousin has to submit to being supported by Nora before a union can take place. In "Love and Self-Love," only after Effie rights the inequality of age and fortune can she accept her husband's love. Louisa's solution to the problem of marriage recalls her childhood requirement for a bond of affection: "no boy could be my friend until I beat him in a race." Louisa and Bronson would become genuinely companionable only after she began to support him financially.

While Louisa grappled in private with questions of love and attachment, she showed her family a face that was funny and practical. To Anna she listed what she intended to do with the "grand sum of $35," her earnings for the fall. "I shall get a second-hand carpet for the little parlor, a bonnet for you, and some shoes and stockings for myself [as] the prejudices of society demand that my feet be covered in the houses of the rich and great. . . . If any of my fortune is left, will invest it in the Alcott Sinking Fund."

With Alf Whitman, Louisa played the wise older sister in the cheering letters she sent him in faraway Kansas,* and gave the homesick boy a shoulder to lean on. In a reply to a forlorn letter, she offered sympathy ("I have been through all that sorrowful loneliness") and advice to keep his chin up ("If we take it patiently & bear it bravely it will make us better & stronger"). She could also play the older brother with Whitman. After all, she told him, "I was born with a boy's nature" and "have fought my fight for nearly fifteen [years] with a boy's spirit . . . and a boy's wrath."

Alf's adventurous correspondent is perpetually hatching schemes: "Lets you and I go as sailors & work our passage over," Louisa suggests. On the other side of the Atlantic they'll take jobs "all over Europe having a nice time—Will you go?" Like Fred Willis before him, Alf was a foil for the adventurous male alter ego Louisa had to suppress. Once past girlhood she had few acceptable outlets for her enormous nervous energy, both physical and psychic. "Walked from Concord to Boston one day, twenty miles in five hours," she noted happily in May, "and went to a party in the evening. . . . Well done for a vegetable production!" ("Vegetable production" referred to her meatless childhood.) Her journals are full of references to running, "kilting" her long skirts, tying them aside

---

* The Whitmans were among the abolitionist settlers attempting to vote Kansas into the Union as a free state.

for freedom of movement. In *Little Women*, Meg (the character based on Anna) admonishes Jo, saying, "You've been running, Jo. When will you stop such romping ways?" Jo replies, "Never till I'm sick and old and have to use a crutch." Until her last weeks of life Louisa's journals would refer to taking a "run." It might have been a walk at that point, but it was made for the sake of exercise, which she insisted on having and later urged upon her young female readers in defiance of the practice and beliefs of the day.

Concord offered a glimpse of the violent Civil War years to come when the antislavery warrior John Brown, an Alcott family hero, made a one-day visit as the guest of Frank Sanborn. Bronson, Abby, Emerson, and Thoreau—all of whom had also spoken out against slavery and the failure of the federal government to enforce laws against it in the territories—were among the large crowd that filled Town Hall to hear Brown speak about the bloody events in Kansas and his readiness to take the antislavery campaign to the deep South. Thirty years of largely futile protest—almost Louisa's entire lifetime—had tried the patience of New England's most staunch abolitionists. Although it was unlikely that Concord's peace-loving eminences could have raised swords or drawn guns against slavery's defenders, they had come to believe that violence against slavery's violence was justifiable and necessary.

Five months later, on October 16, 1859, Brown made his nighttime assault on the federal arsenal at Harpers Ferry, Virginia, with a band of twenty-one followers, including three of his four sons. The raid was a debacle. Ten of Brown's force were killed, and Brown, his sons, and three others were taken prisoner, putting an end to the most serious assault on slavery the South had seen since the Nat Turner rebellion of 1831. The raid at Harpers Ferry was the first breaking news story to be transmitted nationally by telegraph wire, and the impact was immediate. "We are boiling over with excitement here," Louisa wrote to Alf Whitman a few weeks after the raid, "for many of our people (Anti Slavery, I mean) are concerned in it. We have a daily stampede for papers, & a nightly indignation meeting over the wickedness of our country & the cowardice of the human race. I'm afraid mother will die of spontaneous combustion if things are not set right soon."

They could not be set right. The trial of John Brown was short and the verdict of death by hanging a foregone conclusion. Frank Sanborn, one of the "Secret Six" who helped fund and plan the raid, met with coconspirators Theodore Parker, Thomas Higginson, and Samuel Gridley Howe (editor of the antislavery *Boston Daily Commonwealth*)* daily to discuss what might be done to save Brown from hanging. They considered organizing a physical rescue. Sanborn himself escaped an attempted arrest and kept out of town for a while. Thoreau wrote an eloquent, 8,500-word defense of the raid and delivered it before audiences in Concord and Boston, the most public act of his life. Sanborn suggested that Bronson travel to Virginia—to visit Brown if he could, and to appeal to Governor Henry Wise of Virginia for mercy. By the end of November, Concord was making plans for a solemn observance on December 2, 1859, the day of execution. No speeches would be made, it was agreed. Bronson was chosen to read the "Martyr Service," Emerson to read from Brown's writings, Thoreau and Bronson to read passages from the Bible and Plato. At the end, all joined in to sing a dirge composed by Frank Sanborn. "The execution of Saint John the Just took place on the second," Louisa wrote in her journal. "A meeting at the hall, and all Concord was there . . . full of reverence and admiration for the martyr." Following the service, Louisa returned to Orchard House and "made some verses on it," sending the result off to the *Liberator*, which published "With a Rose, That Bloomed on the Day of John Brown's Martyrdom" in the January 20, 1860, issue. It read in part:

> *There blossomed forth a grander flower in the wilderness of wrong,*
> *Untouched by Slavery's bitter frost, A soul devout and strong . . .*
>
> *No monument of quarried stone, No eloquence of speech,*
> *Can 'grave the lessons on the land His martyrdom will teach . . .*

The acceptance of the John Brown poem came on the heels of an acceptance from the *Atlantic*. Lowell had been sitting on "Love and Self-Love" for over a year before pronouncing it "fine" and asking "if it was not a translation from the German, it was so unlike most tales." Mixed with doubt that Louisa could produce an original story was his era's admiration for all things German, but she chose to take the remark as a compliment.

"I felt much set up," she wrote in her journal, "and my fifty dollars will be very happy money. People seem to think it is a great thing to get into the *Atlantic*," she added, "but I've not been pegging away all these years in

---

* The *Commonwealth* had been founded in 1851 by a group of abolitionists that included Julia Ward Howe and her husband, Samuel Gridley Howe.

vain, and may yet have books and publishers and a fortune of my own. Success has gone to my head, and I wander a little. Twenty-seven years old, and very happy." Her spirits were barely dampened by a rejection two months later. "Mr.—— won't have 'M.L.' as it is antislavery, and the dear South must not be offended." The antislavery *Boston Common-wealth* bought the story—a daring tale of interracial marriage between a young white woman and a handsome, brilliant musician, formerly en-slaved and passing as a "Spaniard"—and ran it in two installments in January and February.

In April Louisa sent off "A Modern Cinderella," "with Nan [Louisa's nickname for Anna] as the heroine and John for the hero." Like "Love and Self-Love" an exploration of marriage, it has a completely different tone—wry, affectionate, comic, and filled with the kind of sisterly banter she would perfect in *Little Women*. Lowell snapped it up and ran it in the October issue. By then the real-life Anna and John had been married for four months and were settled in a cottage in Chelsea, across the Charles River from Boston. They had been engaged for more than two years, as the bride's parents had been, and probably for the same reasons—perceived family obligation on the part of the bride, and the shaky financial status of the groom.

"The dear girl was married on the 23rd," Louisa wrote in her journal at the end of May of 1860, "the same day as Mother's wedding [thirty years before]. A lovely day, the house full of sunshine, flowers, friends and happiness." The ceremony was performed by the bride's uncle, the Rever-end Samuel May, in the front parlor "with no fuss, but much love, and we all stood round her." A small feast followed, and a German folk dance played by Henry Thoreau on his flute had the "old folks" encircling the bridal pair on the front lawn, "under our Revolutionary elm." But for all her pleasure in her sister's happiness, Louisa could not be happy for herself. She said of the gray dresses she and May wore to complement An-na's silver-gray silk, "Sackcloth I called it and ashes of roses, for I mourn the loss of my Nan, and am not comforted." The farewell kiss Emerson bestowed on the bride earned a sly remark: "I thought that honor would make even matrimony endurable." Abby reported that before the wed-ding she "found Louisa putting a small wreath of wood violets around a picture of Lizzie that hung in the parlor." When she approached her, Louisa looked up with tears in her eyes and said, "I am trying to keep Lizzie's memory inviolate [in violet]." In a letter to the newly married

Anna a few days after the wedding, Louisa wrote of the "bereaved family" solacing "their woe by washing dishes for two hours and bolting the remains of the funeral baked meats."

The other big event of that week was the afternoon reception the Alcotts hosted for John Brown's widow and her widowed daughter-in-law. A handful of friends and supporters had been invited, but when word got out that the two widows (along with the younger woman's baby) were to be there, Orchard House was overrun. Louisa spent much of the afternoon ferrying platters of sandwiches and pitchers of tea from the kitchen to the parlor, but she did not fail to notice that Brown's widow "had a natural dignity that showed she was better than a 'lady,' though she did drink out of her saucer and used the plainest speech." Louisa also managed to find a spot near the young mother, where she and Carrie Pratt, John's sister, "went and worshipped in our own way at the shrine of John Brown's grandson, kissing him as if he were a little saint, and feeling highly honored when he sucked our fingers, or walked on us with his honest little red shoes."

Nearly lost amid the deluge of social and political notes that busy spring was a rare reference to a suitor, "a funny lover who met me in the cars, and said he lost his heart at once." He was handsome, by Louisa's own report, about forty, and a Southerner, and he presented himself at Orchard House in hope of paying court. Louisa had her family scare him off (whether because he was a Southerner or odd is unclear), but he persisted, writing letters and "haunt[ing] the road with his hat off, while the girls laughed and had great fun over Jo's* lover. He went at last, and peace reigned. My adorers are all queer," she commented.

Also queer, presumably, was a Mr. Condit, who asked Louisa to marry him. He was probably Sears Byram Condit (1831–1916), a prosperous manufacturer of silk hats Louisa's age who lived in nearby Somerville. Louisa's first biographer, Ednah Cheney, says that Louisa considered the proposal. "She consulted her mother, telling her that she did not care for the lover very much. The wise mother saved her from the impulse to self-sacrifice, which might have led her to accept a position which would have given help to the family." The marriage proposal was answered with a succinct but telling note: "I have decided it be best for me not to accept

---

* Ednah Dow Cheney, who transcribed some of Louisa's journals, may have made a slip of the pen referring to Louisa as "Jo." The journals subsequently disappeared, so whether she did cannot be known.

your proposal, In haste, L.M. Alcott." A month or so later, after visiting Anna's nest—"where she and her mate live like a pair of turtle doves," she decided that marriage was not for her at all. "I'd rather be a free spinster and paddle my own canoe," she said.

July of 1860 saw the return of the Hawthorne family to Concord, which gave the Alcotts "new neighbors and something to talk about besides [the radical abolitionists] Parker, Sumner and Sanborn," Louisa wrote her cousin Adeline May. The Hawthorne family had been absent from Concord since 1853, when Nathaniel's college friend Franklin Pierce, elected president in 1852, appointed him consul in Liverpool. They had spent the previous three years wandering Europe, and when they came back to a Concord preoccupied with slavery and rumors of war, they seemed as exotic as peacocks. Nathaniel Hawthorne was notoriously reclusive. "Mr. H is as queer as ever," Louisa reported, "a mysterious looking man in a big hat and red slippers darting over the hills or skimming by as if he expected the house of Alcott were about to rush out and clutch him. Mrs. H is as sentimental and muffing [clumsy] as of old, wears crimson silk jackets, a rosary from Jerusalem, fire-flies in her hair, and dirty white skirts with the sacred mud of London still extant thereon." Her account of the eldest of the three Hawthorne children, Una, was as catty as it was deft: "A stout English looking sixteen year older with the most ardent hair and eyebrows, Monte Bene airs . . . and no accomplishments but riding which was put an end to this morning by a somerset [somersault] from her horse here in the grand square of this vast town." Louisa's ridicule of the neighbors' European airs probably had its source in envy. The Hawthornes had seen and lived in places Louisa longed to go herself.

In August, Louisa was as hard to spot out of doors as her famous neighbor. She was writing *Moods*, her long-planned novel. "Genius burned so fiercely that for four weeks I wrote all day and planned nearly all night, being quite possessed by my work. I was perfectly happy and seemed to have no wants. Finished the book, or a rough draft of it, and put it away to settle. Mr. Emerson offered to read it when Mother told him it was 'Moods' and had one of his sayings for motto."* When she emerged from

---

* The motto (epigraph) of *Moods* comes from Emerson's essay "Experience": "Life is a train of moods like a string of beads, and as we pass through them they prove to be

the "vortex," as she called these fevered spells of inspiration, she felt released, exhausted, and satisfied. "Daresay nothing will come of it," she
wrote in her journal, "but it *had* to be done." A month or so later she read
her new novel to Anna, who said it was good. Encouraged, she made a
vow: "[I] will touch it up when duty no longer orders me to make a burnt
offering of myself."

In the meantime, she turned her talents to material uses. "This must
be a frivolous and dressy letter," she wrote Anna in late August, "because
you always want to know about our clothes, and we have been at it lately.
May's bonnet is a sight for gods and men," she went on, warming to her
subject, "with a great cockade boiling over the front to meet a red ditto
surging from the interior, where a red rainbow darts across the bow, and
a surf of white lace foams up on each side. I expect to hear that you and
John fell flat in the dust with horror on beholding it." With evidently
mixed feelings she reported that Lu Willis was urging her to race up to
New Hampshire for a visit—"very aggravating to a young woman with
one dollar, no bonnet, half a gown, and a discontented mind." She complained that nothing was stirring in Concord but the wind.

The town would soon look "as if a gale had set in." Dio Lewis's "New
Gymnastics" struck Concord during hurricane season, setting young
and old to swinging Indian clubs, reminding Louisa of "perambulating
windmill[s] with all four sails going." The "city fathers approve of it," she
wrote her Aunt Bond, "& the city sons and daughters intend to show that
Concord has as much muscle as brain, & be ready for another fight if
Louis Napoleon sees fit to covet the famous land of Emerson Hawthorne
Thoreau Alcott & Co."

Despite selling almost everything she wrote that year—the *Atlantic*
bought "Debby's Debut," making her three for four with the best literary
magazine in the country—at twenty-eight, Louisa felt old, shabby, and
left behind. Invited to an anniversary observance for John Brown a year
after his execution, she had no "good gown" to wear, and sent instead a
poem she judged inadequate: "I'm a better patriot than a poet, and couldn't
say what I felt." A strong current of dissatisfaction underlay her entertaining letters to Anna, Alf, and Aunt Bond. Mundane housework was
consuming her energy; tedious visitors were wasting her time. In October,

---

many colored lenses, which paint the word their own hue, and each shows us only what
lies in its own focus."

with Abby away on an extended visit to Sam in Syracuse, the writer who had just torn off a draft of a novel in a month's time and deposited a seventy-five-dollar check for her latest story was in Concord. While Louisa replaced her mother as cook, adding to her toil as family breadwinner and housekeeper, May was in clover: Hannah Robie had given her thirty dollars for more art lessons. "She is one of the fortunate ones, and gets what she wants easily. I have to grub for my help or go without it. Good for me, doubtless, or it wouldn't be so; so cheer up Louisa, and grind away!" Louisa wrote in November. In December it was "more luck for May" when a job teaching art opened up at the asylum in Syracuse. The nineteen-year-old left the family nest unencumbered by guilt or blame, leaving Louisa alone again with her parents. "What shall I do without her?" she wrote Anna. "Her room is so empty, the house so old & still without our lively girl." Her epitaph for 1860 was a mix of sadness and resignation: "A quiet Christmas, no presents but apples and flowers: No merry-making, for Nan and May were gone, and Betty under the snow. But we are used to hard times, and, as Mother says, 'while there is famine in Kansas we mustn't ask for sugar plums.'"

～∽

ELEVEN

I'VE OFTEN LONGED
TO SEE A WAR

Louisa's cheerless Christmas was followed by a shower of New Year's gifts. "A most uncommon fit of generosity seemed to seize people on my behalf," she noted with the amazement she always expressed when her expectation of being neglected was not met. "I was blessed with all manner of nice things, from a gold and ivory pen to a mince pie and a bonnet." Louisa did not name the donors. Undistracted by her loot, she retreated to her second-floor bedroom and threw herself and her pen into *Success,* the autobiographical novel she would eventually publish as *Work.* She had barely warmed up when Abby's second midwinter collapse in three years forced her to "cork up" her inkstand and turn nurse. Abby recovered quickly, but when Louisa returned to her desk, it was not the dropped thread of *Success* she picked up but *Moods*, into whose whirling depths she disappeared as completely as she had the previous August.

> From the 2d [of February, 1861] to the 25th, I sat writing, with a run at dusk; could not sleep, and for three days was so full of it I could not stop to get up. Mother made me a green silk cap with a red bow, to match the old green and red party wrap, which I wore as a "glory cloak." Thus arrayed, I sat in groves of manuscripts, "living for immortality," as May said. Mother wandered in and out with cordial cups of tea, worried because I couldn't eat. Father thought it fine, and brought his reddest apples and hardest cider for my Pegasus to feed upon. All sorts of fun was going

on, but I didn't care if the world returned to chaos if I and my inkstand only "lit" in the same place.

She pronounced the writing fit "very pleasant and queer while it lasted, but after three weeks of it I found that my mind was too rampant for my body, as my head was dizzy, legs shaky, and no sleep would come. So I dropped the pen, and took long walks, cold baths, and had Nan up to frolic with me." In the throes of creation she was no longer comic Louisa, moody Louisa, or Louisa the drudge, but the unquestioned genius of the family, fussed over by her mother, applauded by her father, indulged by the older sister, and glorified by the younger. In *Little Women* she bestows the same gift of literary ecstasy on her alter ego.

> Every few weeks she would shut herself up in her room, put on her scrib-bling suit, and "fall into a vortex," as she expressed it, writing away at her novel with all her heart and soul, for till that was finished she could find no peace. . . . She gave herself to it with entire abandon, and led a blissful life, unconscious of want, care, or bad weather, while she sat safe and happy in an imaginary world, full of friends almost as dear to her as any in the flesh. . . . The divine afflatus usually lasted a week or two, and then she emerged from her "vortex," hungry, sleepy, cross or despondent.

When Louisa emerged from her second bout with *Moods*, she read the complete manuscript to the family. "Mother pronounced it wonderful, and Anna laughed and cried as she always does over my works, saying, 'My dear, I'm proud of you.'" Her father hit the note most likely to please her. "Emerson must see this," he said, and asked in apparent seriousness, "Where did you get your metaphysics?" As his daughter, she could hardly have avoided them.

"Even if it never comes to anything, it was worth something to have my three dearest sit up till midnight listening with wide-open eyes to Lu's first novel."

As literature, *Moods* has aged poorly. The heroine's behavior, meant to be charmingly childish, feels forced and silly. Overheated trappings weigh down a clumsy plot. To a modern reader, the book seems little more than a nineteenth-century Harlequin romance, a fantasy about a young woman with a choice of two attractive suitors. But Louisa's tale of the volatile young Sylvia Yule was written in all seriousness and meant to be taken at face value, and for no one did it have more value than for Louisa, who wrote, published, and rewrote it over a period of more than twenty years.

As a representation of Louisa Alcott's milieu and her response to it, *Moods* is still of interest. Sylvia Yule is Louisa's conception of herself at sixteen; her two admirers are the fictionalized love objects of Louisa's adolescence, Henry David Thoreau and Ralph Waldo Emerson. Henry Thoreau, cast as Adam Warwick, is "the manliest man [she] had ever seen, living out his aspirations and beliefs at any cost, with grey eyes that seemed to pierce through all disguises." Waldo Emerson, cast as Warwick's older friend Geoffrey Moor, betrays "in every gesture the unconscious grace of the gentleman born, a sweet, strong nature, and inward tranquility." Photographs of Thoreau and Emerson reflect perfectly Louisa's descriptions of Warwick and Moor; Warwick is reminiscent of Heathcliff, Emily Brontë's untamed romantic of *Wuthering Heights*, while Moor is cut from the same cloth as Mr. Knightley, the aristocratic older neighbor of Jane Austen's *Emma*.

Moods' Sylvia Yule respects kind, protective Geoffrey Moor but is sexually attracted to the man of action, Adam Warwick. During Warwick's long absence she marries Moor. When Warwick returns he becomes a frequent guest at Moor's home, and Sylvia finds that she loves her husband's best friend—and he loves her. She realizes that she cannot love her husband as he deserves.

The audience for Louisa's *Saturday Evening Gazette* stories would have expected the author to resolve Sylvia's dilemma by killing Moor off—without attaching any blame to the tormented lovers—and thrusting Sylvia into Warwick's powerful arms. But the ambition and imagination of Louisa the neophyte novelist was no small thing. She produced instead an intriguing character, Faith Dane, to guide Sylvia through the morass she has created by her youthful indiscretion. *Moods*, however overwrought, should be credited to Louisa as an attempt to deal seriously with a woman's struggle for self-knowledge, the hypocrisy of society, and the limits of love. Even so, the modern reader may appreciate *Moods* less as an earnest narrative of ethical choice than as a rich roman à clef of the romantic intrigue of the Transcendental inner circle. Not only does Louisa provide Emerson and Thoreau in heroic guise; she also (in Faith Dane) gives us the group's boldest personality, Margaret Fuller, a woman Louisa had admired and emulated from childhood.

Margaret Fuller, Emerson's brilliant coeditor of the *Dial* and author of the seminal feminist work *Woman in the Nineteenth Century*, conforms well to Louisa's description of Faith Dane as "past thirty, shapely and tall, with . . . a face never beautiful, but always singularly attractive from its mild and earnest character . . . a right womanly woman, gentle, just, and true; possessed of a well-balanced mind, a self-reliant soul, and that fine gift which is so rare, the power of acting as a touchstone to all who approached, forcing them to rise or fall to their true level."

With Margaret Fuller in the mix, *Moods* is revealed as being not only about an unmarried girl's fickle behavior but also about the romantic longings that continue after marriage. Observant Louisa, watching from her corner, cannot fail to have noticed her own father's mooning after the young Ednah Littlehale (now Mrs. Cheney); before that, from another corner, she had seen her father's loyalty waver at Fruitlands. But in *Moods* she focused more on a different marital situation, the one at Emerson's house; Louisa herself hinted as much. Concord gossip to this day holds that Lidian Emerson was deeply in love with Henry Thoreau, who lived alongside Lidian in the Emerson home for months while Emerson traveled in Europe in 1847—apparently in pursuit of Margaret Fuller, who the year before had been sent overseas as a journalist by Horace Greeley of the *New York Tribune*. Whatever did or did not actually transpire between Fuller and Emerson, Emerson returned home to Lidian, Henry Thoreau returned to his mother's house—and no marriages or friendships were ruptured. Fuller's newspaper work took her to Rome in 1848, on the eve of the nationalist uprising that some two decades later ended in the unification of Italy. Thirty-eight-year-old Margaret became deeply involved in the movement—and with twenty-six-year-old Count Giovanni Ossoli, a handsome revolutionary. The two had a child late in 1848 (whether they ever married is unclear), and after the brief Roman Republic failed, the little family resettled in Florence. In 1850 Fuller, Ossoli, and their twenty-month-old son, Angelo, sailed for the United States, against advice that the couple's unconventional relationship would not be accepted. They were never to find out: their ship was wrecked in a hurricane off Long Island, and Fuller, Count Ossoli, and their son drowned in full view of would-be rescuers on shore. Emerson sent Thoreau to search the wreckage for their bodies or for the manuscript of Fuller's book about the history of the Roman Republic. Nothing was ever found.

Fuller's dramatic life and tragic death made a deep impression upon

Louisa. She appeared as Faith Dane not only in *Moods* but also in a later tale about warring loyalties, "My Contraband, or The Brothers." In both *Moods* and "The Brothers" Faith Dane had no role in the action of the story; she was more an enlightened spirit, even a ghost, than a human being.

After consulting *Moods*'s Faith Dane and her conscience, Sylvia decides to live alone, since she cannot be Moor's true wife and cannot leave this good man to become the wife of his best friend. Like Margaret Fuller, and like their Concord neighbor Hawthorne's adulteress Hester Prynne, Sylvia has become a woman with no place in conventional society. Louisa makes Sylvia's social death literal in *Moods*: she sickens and expires.

The nation was not standing still while Louisa pondered the question of marriage—far from it. The seed of abolitionism that Louisa's parents had helped to plant in the early 1830s was about to come to violent fruition in the Civil War. Through the Garrison riots, "Bleeding Kansas," John Brown's raid on Harpers Ferry, and the repugnant Fugitive Slave Act, the Alcotts had aided and abetted the cause. While living at Hillside in Concord in February of 1847, the Alcotts, working with the Underground Railroad, harbored for a week a fugitive they knew only as John. He was "scarce thirty years of age, athletic, dextrous [sic], sagacious, and self-relying [with] many elements of the hero," Bronson recorded in his journal. Over meals with the Alcotts, John's presence gave an "image and a name to the dire entity of slavery" and "was an impressive lesson to [Bronson's] children, bringing before them the wrongs of the black man and his tale of woes." Louisa wrote, "Fugitive slaves were sheltered under our roof," so presumably John was not the only one. She mentioned teaching one man to "write on the hearth with charcoal, his big fingers finding pen and pencil unmanageable."

The Alcotts were living in Boston in 1850 when the passage of the Fugitive Slave Act made failure to turn over an escapee from slavery to authorities a criminal offense. In February of the following year, one captive, Shadrach Minkins, was rescued from a local courtroom by a group of free blacks, and with the help of the Underground Railroad was smuggled to safety in Canada. Two months later, seventeen-year-old fugitive Thomas Simms was captured and committed for trial. This time the courthouse, Bronson noted in his journal, was "surrounded with chains and armed police," and the city was in an uproar. Louisa could hardly contain her outrage at the fate of this boy her own age. She went with Bronson to a rally at the Tremont Temple, where they heard the orator Wendell Phillips, the theologian William Ellery Channing, and others they knew decry the leaders who allowed their government to collude in slavery. Bronson noted that "the State has opened its Court of Justice (so called) not to protect and free, but to convict and remand the fugitive, who sought its protection and sympathy." Louisa said, "I shall be horribly ashamed of my country if this thing happens and the slave is sent back."

After the rally Bronson joined a group that attempted to storm the courthouse. When gunshots were heard within, and word of a fatal scuffle got out, only sixty-year-old Bronson Alcott stepped forward to pursue the effort, and the rescue was abandoned. He joined a hastily assembled Vigilance Committee that patrolled the streets to try to prevent any further arrests of fugitives, but barred from patrolling with her father, Louisa could only dream up plots to free Simms. Despite her lawyer cousin Samuel Sewall's vigorous defense, the Massachusetts court sent Thomas Simms back to Georgia, where he was publicly whipped and nearly died from the punishment.

After decades of this type of dangerous, piecemeal resistance to slavery, the outbreak of war on April 12, 1861, came as a relief. Bronson thought it was abolition's greatest day. After years of violent skirmishes, the issue would be decided on the battlefield. Louisa welcomed the advent of the righteous crusade against slavery, not least because of the excitement. "I've often longed to see a war," she confessed, "and now I have my wish."

Concord was "a sight to behold," she reported to Alf Whitman, "Everyone wears cockades wherever one can be stuck, flags flap over head like parti colored birds of prey." Boys and young men were drilling on the Common, and sixteen-year-old Edward Emerson organized a company of cadets "who poke each others eyes out, bang their heads & blow themselves up with gunpowder most valiantly." The Concord Artillery (some forty members of the Massachusetts Volunteer Militia) mustered in response to President Abraham Lincoln's order for seventy-five thousand troops to report immediately. In a week the town raised $4,400 for travel expenses, and at midday on April 19, the anniversary of the Battles of Lexington and Concord, the company assembled to the ringing of church bells and their neighbors' "huzzahs." Emerson, Alcott, and Judge Hoar spoke, a prayer was sent up, and the men marched to the Boston train. "A sad day seeing them off," Louisa wrote, "for in a little town like this we all seem like one family in times like these."

For all the excitement in her journals and letters to Whitman, Louisa was distressed at being left behind. "Are you going to have a dab at the saucy Southerners?" she teased Alf. She studied up on gunshot wounds and plotted to get appointed as a nurse. "I long to be a man," she confided to her journal, "but as I can't fight, I will content myself with working for those who can." With three hundred Concord mothers, daughters, and sisters she took part in a two-day marathon in Town Hall, "sewing violently on patriotic blue shirts." She joined an afternoon sail from Cambridge to the forts in Boston Harbor. "I felt very martial and Joan-of-Arc-y as I stood on the walls with the flag flying over me and cannon all about," she said.

Stuck at Orchard House, Louisa watched autumn go by at a crawl. "Wrote, read, sewed and wanted something to do" was her valedictory for 1861. The "something to do" that turned up was not what she wanted. Elizabeth Peabody, who, unlike Abby, was not one to hold a grudge, enlisted Louisa to run a kindergarten at the Warren Street Chapel in Boston, and low on cash, Louisa agreed. The unwelcome advice of James T. Fields, Lowell's replacement as publisher at the *Atlantic*, may have swayed her. He turned down her story "How I Went Out to Service" and advised, "Stick to your teaching; you can't write." Fields reinforced his message by making Louisa an unsolicited loan of forty dollars to set up her schoolroom.

Annie Fields, James Fields's beautiful young second wife and Louisa's distant cousin, invited her to board with the family to save on expenses. Though she enjoyed the elite literary company at the Fieldses' Greek Revival mansion overlooking the Charles River—meeting "Mrs. Stowe, Fanny Kemble, Holmes, Longfellow & all the fine folks"—she resented being treated as the court jester. "Hate to visit people who ask me to help amuse others," she scribbled. "I never knew before what insolent things a hostess can do, nor what false positions poverty can push one into." The contrast between her own circumstances and those of her cousin Annie—a bright, pretty, celebrated, and influential hostess just a year older than Louisa—must have been difficult to bear, though probably less difficult than bearing her lack of power as a guest and dependent. On top of that, running the school was not just disagreeable; she was also losing money.

By the end of March Louisa was commuting the thirty miles between Concord and Boston rather than endure the salon life at the Fieldses' until the last month of school, when she persuaded May to take her place. She used the time to turn out a story for the fledgling *Concord Monitor* for thirty dollars, more than her earnings in four months of teaching, but not enough to pay Fields back. "A wasted winter and a debt of $40," she summed up, "to be paid if I sell my hair to do it." Still infuriated by Fields's remark that she couldn't write, Louisa vowed, "I won't teach. I can write, and I'll prove it."

Henry Thoreau, suffering from a lingering case of bronchitis, had ignored medical advice to recuperate in the West Indies, went instead to Minnesota (with Horace Mann Jr.), and returned weaker still. He had been failing since the winter. Bronson visited him at the family home on Main Street on May 4 and found his friend with "not many days of mortality to give us." Louisa was in Concord when her beloved mentor died, on May 6. The funeral three days later was a public burial from church at Emerson's request, Louisa wrote to her old teacher Sophia Ford, who had asked her to pass along news of Thoreau.* It was a service "Henry would not have liked but Emerson said his sorrow was so great he wanted all the world to mourn with him." William Ellery Channing composed a hymn for the occasion, the church bells tolled forty-four times to mark Henry's years, and Bronson read selections from Henry's books. Louisa approved of the service, "for many people said he was an infidel, [but] if ever a man was a real Christian it was Henry." She enclosed in her letter to Ford a sprig of andromeda, his favorite plant, snipped from a wreath the Alcotts had placed on his coffin.

Not long after, Louisa went to a reception for Rebecca Harding Davis, the wealthy author of the muckraking *Life in the Iron Mills*, whose first novel, *Margret Howth*, "has made a stir, and is very good." Davis's recollection captured both Louisa's social vulnerability in her late twenties, and her sense of herself as tragically forlorn.†

---

* Ford (also spelled Foord), an amateur naturalist, had been in love with Thoreau and proposed to him, to Thoreau's horror. "I sent back a distinct No, as I have learned to pronounce after considerable practice," he wrote Emerson, "and I trust this No succeeded. Indeed I wished that it might burst like hollow shot after it had struck and buried itself, and make itself felt there." (*Familiar Letters of Henry David Thoreau*, ed. F. B. Sanborn [Boston, 1894], 14 November 1847.)

† Davis also derides the Transcendentalists, especially Bronson, for their naive view of

I saw . . . a tall, thin young woman standing alone in a corner. She was plainly dressed, and had that watchful defiant air with which the woman whose youth is slipping away is apt to face the world which has offered no place to her. Presently she came up to me.

"These people may say pleasant things to you," she said abruptly; "but not one of them would have gone to Concord and back to see you, as I did today. I went for this gown. It's the only decent one I have. I'm very poor"; and in the next breath she contrived to tell me that she had once taken a place as "second girl." "My name," she added, "is Louisa Alcott."

Louisa's journal account was briefer and more collegial, with no mention of racing home to retrieve the "claret colored merino" she described in an earlier entry, and which Davis identified as the dress she wore that night. Davis, Louisa wrote, said "she never had any troubles, though she writes about woes. I told her I had had lots of troubles, so I write jolly tales, and we wondered why we each did so."

Louisa's next three stories were not the least bit jolly, but they were entertaining. As she wrote Alf Whitman in Kansas in late June, "They are easy to 'compoze' & are better paid than moral & elaborate works of Shakespeare, so don't be shocked if I send you a paper containing a picture of Indians, pirates, wolves, bears & distressed damsels in a grand tableau over a title like this 'The Maniac Bride' or 'The Bath of Blood. A thrilling tale of passion,' & c." Two of the tales were for *Frank Leslie's Illustrated Newspaper*, a popular weekly specializing in the lurid. Frank Leslie, an Englishman, was the Rupert Murdoch of his day, controlling a small empire of American publications that included the *Gazette of Fashion,* the *New York Journal,* the *Boy's and Girl's Weekly*, and the *Budget of Fun.*

Leslie's publications paid better than the *Atlantic*, and a lot better than the *Concord Monitor*, but money was not Louisa's sole motivation for writing pulp fiction. These psychologically complex tales of lust, betrayal, revenge, and violence satisfied Louisa's thirst for adventure as nothing else in her life could. Her daring tales of scheming heroines and villainous suitors allowed her to explore incest, sadism, murder, suicide, swindling, transvestism, revolution, espionage, unwed motherhood, and above all power struggles between the sexes. Her own violent, passionate, even

---

the war as a glorious crusade against slavery, and reports Hawthorne's facetious and correct prediction that Alcott would deliver an encomium to pears.

homicidal thoughts drew her to the darker side of human nature embodied in sinners who, despite her claims, often have no good in them at all. In Frank Leslie, who praised her stories for their dramatic action and intriguing plots, she had a ready buyer for as many fantasies as she could spin. In a decade of becoming a professional writer, she had published fairy tales, poetry, literary fiction, and several kinds of popular fiction for a wide array of markets. She had taught herself a trade that few practiced successfully enough to support themselves—even highly regarded writers such as Hawthorne.

By 1862, at almost thirty, Louisa had passed the marriageable age of most women of her time, although both Abby and Anna had been twenty-nine at the time of their marriages. "At twenty-five," Louisa wrote in *Little Women*, "girls begin to talk about being old maids, but secretly resolve they never will; at thirty, they say nothing about it, but quietly accept the fact." Louisa called herself a spinster long before that, cheating gossips of the privilege, but as she approached her birthday she was restless, and hungry for adventure before it was too late. "Decided to go to Washington as a nurse if I could find a place," she wrote in her journal for November. "I love nursing and *must* let out my pent-up energy in some new way."

Thirty was the minimum age for being an army nurse. Dorothea Dix, the superintendent of the Union army nursing corps, had also stipulated that volunteers be "plain looking" and married. But under the pressure of casualties from the Battle of Bull Run in the summer of 1862, Dix had to revise her rules to take any respectable woman willing to risk her life in the hellhole of an army hospital. An applicant still needed to come recommended, but as Dorothea Dix had been one of Bronson's assistants at the Temple School, acceptance for Louisa could be assumed. She sent in her name through Hannah Stevenson, the friend who had found her the grim sewing job at the reform school.

While she awaited her call to duty, Louisa wrote tales and letters. To her friends Edward Bartlett and Wilkie James* serving on the front lines she sent Concord nuts and apples, news of her own imminent service,

---

* Bartlett was a member of the Forty-fourth Regiment of the Massachusetts Volunteers; James, younger brother of Henry and William, was an officer in the famed Massachusetts Fifty-fourth Colored Infantry Regiment.

and advice: "If you intend to be smashed in any way just put it off till I get to Washington to mend you up." She sorted papers, prepared her clothes, and laid out the most spartan items in her wardrobe, saying, "Nurses don't need nice things, thank Heaven!" She found time to enter a writing contest for *Frank Leslie's Illustrated Newspaper*; if she won, the one-hundred-dollar prize would be her biggest payday yet. The story, "Pauline's Passion and Punishment," featured a dark, amoral Cuban as villainess-heroine, and a melodramatic plot that raced to a cliff-hanging, poetically just conclusion that left Pauline with nothing to cling to but remorse.

Louisa's orders came on December 11; she was to leave for Washington the next morning, to report to the Union Hotel Hospital in Georgetown. Abby, Anna, May, and their next-door neighbor Sophia Hawthorne frantically helped Louisa pack in time for the afternoon train to Boston; Louisa took her journal, Dickens to read to the convalescing soldiers, paper for transcribing their letters and writing her own, and enough sandwiches, gingerbread, and apples to eat all the way to the capital. She choked on a last cup of tea that had been stirred with salt instead of sugar in the excitement, and suddenly it was time to go. "We had all been full of courage till the last moment came; then we all broke down. I realized that I had taken my life in my hand, and might never see them all again. I said, 'Shall I stay, Mother?' as I hugged her close. 'No, go! And the Lord be with you.'" Abby waved her wet handkerchief from the door. "So I set forth in the December twilight, with May and Julian Hawthorne as escort, feeling as if I was the son of the house going to war."

She spent the night with her cousin Lizzie Wells. The next day she had a tooth filled, bought a veil, and accepted warm clothes from a friend and cash from the Sewalls. She chased down the ticket she'd been promised as a volunteer, determined to have it though she had "to face the president of the railroad to accomplish it." After an early dinner with Anna and John and another tearful leave-taking at the station, she started on her long journey "full of hope and sorrow, courage and plans."

In New London, Connecticut, she transferred to the *City of Boston*, the steamship that would ferry her south to New Jersey, and spent most of the night in a perfect storm of displaced anxiety. "The boat is new, but if it ever intends to blow up, spring a leak, catch fire, or be run into, it will do the deed tonight," she wrote home, "because I'm here to fulfill my destiny." She woke in time to watch the sun come up over Long Island Sound, with "mist wreaths furling off, and a pale pink sky above us," and to catch the train to Washington. By seven in the morning it had passed through Philadelphia, her native city, an "old place, full of Dutch women," and on to Baltimore, a "big, dirty, shippy, shiftless sort of place." As they passed the site where the Sixth Massachusetts Regiment had been fired on by a Confederate mob in April of 1861, she felt as if she "should enjoy throwing a stone at somebody, hard." Her car came uncoupled and then got hit from behind by its unshackled mate, sending passengers, hats, and water jars flying like circus clowns. Louisa was satisfied, "for no journey in America would be complete without [an accident]."

As the train slowed in its approach to the capital, the novice traveler glimpsed a strange, long-imagined world. "We often passed colored people, looking as if they had come out of a picture book, or off the stage . . . not at all the sort of people I'd been accustomed to see at the North." Encampments along the route "made the fields and lanes gay with blue coats and the glitter of buttons. Military washes flapped and fluttered in the open air . . . and everywhere the boys threw up their arms and cut capers as we passed." Arriving at nightfall, Louisa was cast into the chaos of the wartime city. A stranger corralled a carriage and jumped in with her, pointing out the unfinished dome of the Capitol and the brilliantly lit White House, where "carriages were rolling in and out of the great gate." Louisa could just make out the East Room and wished she could peek in. Journey's end was a formidable building with guards at the door "and a very trying quantity of men lounging about. My heart beat rather faster than usual, and it struck me that I was very far from home."

The Union Hotel had been hastily converted to a hospital. It was badly lit, crowded, and poorly ventilated. The windows were nailed shut, and smashed panes had been draped with curtains to keep out the cold. Many of the rooms still bore their former designations, "some not so inappropriate," Louisa thought, "for [her] ward was in truth a *ball-room*, if gunshot wounds could christen it." She had barely mastered the route to her upstairs room when she was put in charge of a ward of forty soldiers sick with rheumatism or fever, and wondered when her real war duty would begin. Three days later it did: she was awakened "in the grey dawn" by a loud knock and a cry of "They've come, they've come! Hurry up ladies— you're wanted." For a minute she thought the rebels were coming, but in fact the first wounded were coming from Fredericksburg, where a bloody battle was raging. In five days, thirteen thousand Union soldiers had been killed, captured, or wounded.

"Having a taste for 'ghastliness,' I had rather longed for the wounded to arrive, but when I peeped into the dusky street lined with what I had innocently called market carts, now unloading their sad freight at our door . . . my ardor experienced a sudden chill, and I indulged in a most unpatriotic wish that I was safe at home again." Forty carts discharged their injured cargo bound for eighty beds in the once-elegant ballroom. Some were carried in on stretchers, others staggered in on crutches, and the few who could stay on their feet helped the many who couldn't. "All was hurry and confusion; the hall was full of these wrecks of humanity, for the most exhausted could not reach a bed until duly ticketed, and registered; the walls were lined with rows of such as could sit, the floor covered with the more disabled." From behind a stack of folded linens, Louisa stared transfixed at a group of men gathered around the stove, "ragged, gaunt and pale, mud to the knees, with bloody bandages untouched since put on days before; many bundled up in blankets, coats being lost or useless; and all wearing that disheartened look which proclaimed defeat." She could not move from fear until the matron, Hannah Ropes, thrust a washbasin, a sponge, and a block of brown soap into her hands and told her to begin washing patients as fast as she could. "If she had requested me to shave them all, or dance a hornpipe on the stove funnel, I should have been less staggered; but to scrub some dozen lords of creation at a moment's notice, was really—really—."

She did it anyway. For an unmarried woman of thirty, who may have never seen a naked man except perhaps her father, or boys at a swimming hole, or the Fruitlands nudist Samuel Bower by moonlight, it was a turning point. She had not only to see the men's bodies, but to touch them intimately and with assurance. She clutched her block of brown soap "manfully" and made a "dab at the first dirty specimen" she saw, an "old withered Irishman" so delighted to have a well-meaning woman sponge him clean that he blessed her on the spot, which made her laugh. The worst was not over, but the fear of it was. For the next twelve hours she moved from bed to bed, washing putrid gaping wounds, mopping foreheads, bringing water to those who could drink and food to those who could eat, and stifling tears at the sight of young boys with stumps for legs or holes blown through their peach-fuzzed cheeks as she tried to ease their misery. Her gentle touch was usually the only, and the best, offering she could make to them. After she spoon-fed a New Hampshire man, she accepted a pair of earrings intended for the wife of his dead mate because, he said, she looked so much like the man's new widow. A soldier shot in the stomach asked for a glass of water; she returned with it minutes later to find him dead.

The next day she assisted at amputations, where "the merciful magic of ether" was judged unnecessary, and "the poor souls had to bear their pains as best they might." After the sawing, the hacking, and the trimming, she learned how to dress wounds from a surgeon who "seemed to regard a dilapidated body very much as [she] should have regarded a damaged garment . . . cutting, sawing, patching and piecing with the enthusiasm of an accomplished surgical seamstress."

It was a harrowing initiation, but it made of her an instant veteran, confident and useful. Like her father's friend, the poet Walt Whitman, who also served as a nurse, she understood that the battlefield was not necessarily where the essence of the war was to be found. "The expression of American personality through this war is not to be looked for in the great campaign, & the battle-fights. It is to be looked for . . . in the hospitals, among the wounded," Whitman had written. In moments of calm on the ward, Louisa sat with her American personalities as they struggled to write letters home, letters that began with vivid descriptions of battle and ended with "a somewhat sudden plunge from patriotism to provender, desiring 'Marm,' 'Mary Ann,' or 'Aunt Peters' to send along some pies, pickles, sweet stuff, and apples, to 'yourn in haste.'"

She wrote a poem with the rhythm of a march and called it "Beds."

> *Beds to the front of them, Beds to the right of them,*
> *Beds to the left of them, Nobody blundered.*
> *Beamed at by hungry souls, Screamed at with brimming bowls,*
> *Steamed at by army rolls, Buttered and sundered.*
> *With coffee not cannon plied, Each must be satisfied,*
> *Whether they lived or died; All the men wondered.*

"I never began the year in a stranger place than this," Louisa wrote on the first day of 1863, "five hundred miles from home, alone among strangers, doing painful duties all day long, & leading a life of constant excitement in this great house surrounded by 3 or 4 hundred men in all stages of suffering, disease & death. Though often homesick, heart sick & worn out, I like it." The night before she had celebrated the Emancipation Proclamation by leaping from her bed at midnight and racing to the window to add her own cheer to the hollering and singing in the streets of the embattled nation's capital. She waved her handkerchief to a crowd of black men gathered below, and returned to bed to savor the bursts of firecrackers and choruses of "Glory, Hallelujah" that sounded all night.

A few weeks into the routine, she paused to outline a typical day. She was up by six, dressed quickly by gaslight, and then hurried to her ward to fling open the windows to air out the room. It made the men "grumble & shiver," but Louisa (trained under a fierce fresh-air enthusiast) knew it was the only cure for air "bad enough to breed a pestilence." She gave the fire a poke and went off to a quick breakfast with her colleagues. She found the women silly, the men self-important. At midday, she helped the wounded soldiers down big portions of soup, meat, potatoes, and bread, marveling that their appetites exceeded the supply of food, no matter how much was available. Newspapers, conversation, and doctors' final rounds followed supper at five, the gaslight was dimmed at nine, and the day nurses' shift was done.

Dr. John Winslow, a surgeon slow at his work though kind to the men, began to take an interest in Louisa and turned up at her room bearing books in lieu of flowers. She declined to visit his room but accepted his invitations to go walking. They went together to the Capitol to hear a dull sermon by William Henry Channing,* then had a duller dinner at a German restaurant. "Quotes Browning copiously, is given to confidences in the twilight, & altogether is amiably amusing, & exceedingly *young*" was Louisa's assessment of Dr. Winslow. Perhaps to avoid him, she volunteered for the night shift, which also freed her to take long runs in the mornings. From the top of a steep hill on her route, Louisa watched army wagons trundle off to replenish the troops, and saw the bursts of smoke from cannon fire.

Louisa liked being part of what she called the "night side" of life, to be up "owling" when "sleep & death have the house to themselves." The hospital matron, Mrs. Ropes, admired Louisa and gave her the responsibility of assigning the patients in her three-room ward to the appropriate quarters, according to their condition: the "duty room" held the newly wounded;

---

* William Henry Channing (1810–84) was then chaplain of the United States House of Representatives. He should not be confused with his Unitarian theologian uncle, William Ellery Channing (1780–1842), or his cousin (William) Ellery Channing (1818–1901), a Transcendentalist poet and mentor to Thoreau, who lived in Concord.

the "pleasure room" was for recovering soldiers, whom Louisa entertained with games, gossip, and probably the Sairy Gamp imitation that
had been Lizzie's sickbed delight. The "pathetic room" of hopeless cases
was a place to bring "teapots, lullabies, consolation, and, sometimes, a
shroud."

The sleeping men often broke the night silence of the ward talking,
crying, making all kinds of noise. The gruff and reticent soldier by day
became mild and chatty in sleep at night; the stiff facades of control de-
volved into groans and frank cries of pain; a drummer boy sang sweetly.
Sometimes Louisa looked out the window at the moonlit church spire across
the way, at the passersby on the street, at a boat gliding down the Potomac
River. All that river water could not wash out the bloodstains on the land,
she thought, but what *had* been washed away was Louisa's naïveté about
the excitement and glory of fighting a righteous battle.

One night she found herself alone at the bedside of a New Jersey man
reliving the recent horrors of battle. He cheered on or cried out to fallen
comrades, ducked incoming shots, and grabbed Louisa's arm roughly, to
pull her away from imaginary bursting shells. The man's ravings were
pitiful to hear and impossible to restrain. In the meantime, a fever-racked
one-legged soldier propelled himself through the ward like a ghost, telling Louisa that he was dancing home, crashing into beds, and threatening harm to himself and everybody else. With no orderly there, Louisa
was helpless to contain two sadly unhinged men, and the situation dete-
riorated even more when sobbing broke out from the twelve-year-old
drummer boy in the corner bed. The boy's loud lament was for the death
of the wounded soldier who had carried him to safety.

Nursing tempered Louisa, matured her, replaced her book knowledge
of behavior under duress with real-life experience. For all their liberality,
her parents' notions of human character were just that—notions. They
were idealists (especially her father but also her mother) who didn't see
people for who they were so much as for how far they fell short of what
they should be. Louisa wanted to know life in all its true variety, and she
was getting the chance.

John Suhre was a Virginia blacksmith, a big strong man of thirty, her
own age, with a small but indisputably fatal wound in his back that he
could not see and had to lie on in order to breathe. He sat propped up in a
bed that had been extended to accommodate his outsize frame, looking
around with serenity, never making a request or a complaint. When he

slept—and Louisa spent several nights watching him sleep—a tender smile played around his mouth, like a woman's, she thought.

When he was awake, Louisa was a little afraid of the man. Unsure how to respond to his manly strength and dignity, she hung back, thinking she wasn't needed or wanted. From her admiring description in *Hospital Sketches*, the book Louisa created from her letters home, it is obvious that she loved John Suhre, but whether with a worshipper's awe, a woman's desire, or a mother's devotion is hard to discern. "A most attractive face he had," she says, "thoughtful and often beautifully mild while watching the afflictions of others, as if entirely forgetful of his own." She describes his eyes as "child's eyes . . . with a clear, straightforward glance." He "seemed to cling to life, as if it were rich in duties and delights, and he had learned the secret of content."

She asked the doctor which man in her ward suffered the most, and was shocked to hear him name John. Because he was so strong, the doctor predicted a long and painful death. "There's not the slightest hope for him; and you'd better tell him so before long," he instructed. "Women have a way of doing such things comfortably, so I leave it to you." Charged with this awesome responsibility, Louisa stayed close by as the doctor carelessly dressed the terrible wound. For the first time she saw tears slipping down John's cheeks, his silent endurance of pain, and his terrible loneliness: "Straightway my fear vanished, my heart opened wide and took him in, as, gathering the bent head in my arms, as freely as if he had been a little child, I said, 'Let me help you bear it, John.' Never, on any human countenance, have I seen so swift and beautiful a look of gratitude, surprise and comfort, as that which answered me more eloquently than the whispered—'Thank you, ma'am, this is right good! This is what I wanted!'"

The next time his wounds were dressed, Louisa held John, and he squeezed her hand to relieve his pain. When the ordeal was done, she eased him back against the pillows, cleansed his face, smoothed his brown hair, and spent a full hour by his bedside. When she stood to arrange his tray and his sheets, she felt his hand graze her skirt. Another day she put a sprig of heath and heliotrope on his pillow. Finally he said,

> "This is my first battle; do they think it's going to be my last?"
>
> "I'm afraid they do, John." It was the hardest question I had ever been called upon to answer; doubly hard with those clear eyes fixed on mine,

forcing a truthful answer by their own truth. . . . To the end [he] held my hand close, so close that when he was asleep at last, I could not draw it away. Dan [the orderly] helped me, warning me as he did so that it was unsafe for dead and living flesh to lie so long together; . . . my hand was strangely cold and stiff, and four white marks remained across its back, even when warmth and color had returned elsewhere.

She helped prepare John's body for burial, removing the wedding ring his widowed mother had given him to wear in battle and cutting a few locks of his hair to enclose when she sent the ring home to Virginia. A last letter from his family arrived at the hospital an hour before John's death, but was not brought until an hour after it. Louisa placed the unread letter in the blacksmith's calloused hand to bury with him as a signifier of loved ones at his bedside. Farewells were essential to a good nineteenth-century death.

Louisa had always considered herself immune to illness. When she developed a bad cough, she continued her daily runs in the dead of winter, despite colleagues warning her that she risked pneumonia. After three weeks of nonstop rounds, bad food, fetid air, and constant exposure to infection, Louisa's fierce physical defenses gave way to typhoid pneumonia. A staff doctor found her on a staircase, too dizzy to stand, coughing uncontrollably, her forehead so hot she was trying to cool it on the iron banister. When the doctor ordered her to bed, she didn't argue. "Sharp pain in the side, cough, fever & dizziness. A pleasant prospect for a lonely soul five hundred miles from home," she commented before she succumbed, expecting neglect. But nurses ascended to her room to lavish Louisa with the same tenderness they showed their patients. Male attendants she knew from long nights on the ward kept her woodbox full, and a succession of doctors dosed her with calomel, the mercury compound that was used to treat just about everything; she revised her opinion of them sharply upward. Louisa understood their concern. The matron, Mrs. Ropes, had also been diagnosed with typhoid pneumonia and was not expected to survive.

Amid bouts of feverish delusion and constant pain, Louisa tried to "keep merry" by sewing for the soldiers and writing letters home, but felt worse every day. "Hours began to get confused; people looked odd; queer faces haunted the room, and the nights were one long fight with weariness and pain." Though at times she was incoherent, even in sleep she never lost sight of the peril she was in. "Dream awfully, & awake unrefreshed, think of home & wonder if I am to die here as Mrs. Ropes . . . is likely to do." Before collapsing, Mrs. Ropes wondered the same thing about her. She sent the Alcotts an urgent telegram asking that someone come immediately to take Louisa home. She had served for six weeks.

Bronson left Concord that same day on the noon train to Boston and traveled straight through to Washington to arrive on January 16. Louisa, determined to serve out her three-month stint, had rejected every suggestion that she go home. Her father's appearance made real her grave condition and the impact on her family if she were to die.

The room was swarming with people making recommendations. One of them was Dorothea Dix, who wanted Louisa taken to her own quarters for personal care. Louisa wanted to stay where she was. Bronson doubted that his daughter could regain either "strength or spirits" in Washington, but her doctors felt she was not strong enough to travel. Restless and anxious, but forbidden to stay at his daughter's bedside, Bronson made the rounds of Louisa's patients and was disabused of any romantic ideas about the struggle. "Horrid war," he wrote in his journal, "and one sees its horrors in hospitals if anywhere." On the nineteenth, he visited the Senate, and finding a seat near President Lincoln, studied his face at close range and found him "comelier than the papers and portraits have shown him," and his manner impressive. "I wished to have had an interview, but am too anxious about Louisa, and without time to seek it or he to give."

On the twentieth of January, Mrs. Ropes died. The next day Louisa agreed to let her father take her home.

TWELVE

WHERE GLORY WAITED

It was most fortunate for her that I went," Bronson wrote Anna as soon as he and Louisa reached Concord. "Everything was against her at the hospital." At the Concord depot Louisa suddenly recognized the gravity of her condition by seeing its reflection in May's and Abby's faces. She recalled being taken to her bed "in the firm belief that the house was roofless." Her thinking didn't clear for three weeks, and the illness took eight weeks to run its course. The family kept constant watch while neighbors stood by to help, among them Sophia Hawthorne, who extended an open invitation to meals, and Lidian Emerson, who reassigned a servant to Orchard House so Abby could be free to nurse Louisa.

Bronson wrote daily to Anna, who was seven months pregnant and eighteen miles away in Chelsea. He kept his bulletins upbeat: "I beg you will not be alarmed. . . . The Drs. all say there is nothing against [Louisa] getting well." In private, Louisa's parents regretted blessing her mission. "Poor Louy left us a brave handsome woman . . . and returned almost a wreck of body and mind," Abby wrote to her brother Sam. Bronson confided to his mother that had the family known the real danger to Louisa, "[their] contribution to the war . . . should not have been made willingly."

The family at her bedside watched helplessly when Louisa's fever spiked and her brain spun delusions so fascinating she later wrote them down. "The most vivid & enduring was a conviction that I had married a stout, handsome Spaniard dressed in black velvet with very soft hands &

a voice that was continually saying 'Lie still, my dear.' This was mother, I suspect." Abby, in the form of the Spanish spouse, was "always coming after me, appearing out of closets, in at windows, or t[h]reatening me dreadfully all night long." Perhaps Louisa experienced her mother's presence not only as a comfort but also as a nuisance. A person whose body is thrashing uncontrollably while her mind runs riot might resent hearing her mother "continually saying 'Lie still, my dear.'" The "Spanish" characterization of the spouse may have owed something to her mother's coloring and temperament, but also was very likely Louisa's subconscious representation of an African American. "Spanish" was a widely used code word for biracial; in Louisa's story of an interracial romance and marriage, "M. L." (1861), Paul, the talented musician and escapee from slavery, lets people believe he is of Spanish extraction.

Some of Louisa's delusions suggested a sense that she had transgressed. Her adolescent anguish over failed efforts to be good was resurrected in delirium when she asked forgiveness for her sins: "I appealed to the Pope & really got up & made a touching plea in something meant for Latin they tell me." Several of Louisa's hallucinations cast her as a victim of persecution, an evildoer, or both at once. She conjured up "a mob at Baltimore breaking down the door to get me, being hung for a witch, burned, stoned & otherwise maltreated." In one hellish fever-provoked vision Louisa was "tempted to join . . . Dr. Winslow & two of the nurses in worshipping the devil." In another she visited heaven, which was "very busy and dismal and ordinary. Miss Dix,* W.H. Channing & other people were there." She said, "[I] wished I hadn't come," so unappealing were heaven's denizens. The most frightening of Louisa's delusions took her back to the Union Hotel Hospital as a nurse, "tending to millions of sick men who never died or got well." The vision was so upsetting—literally—that she flung herself out of bed and crashed to the floor. May had probably left the room for only a minute, and when she rushed back in, Louisa, still hallucinating, excoriated her sister for leaving her alone in a room full of sick men.

Early in February Louisa came to her senses with powers of mind

---

* Dix seems to have been a tortured idealist. As superintendent of Union army nurses, she was deemed difficult and ineffectual, but was respected for her equal treatment of Confederate wounded.

intact. Of her three-week spell of delusions she said that she enjoyed them. She found them interesting and worthwhile, despite side effects that included a backache so piercing she couldn't walk, and a throat so sore she could barely swallow.

She looked into a mirror and was startled by "a queer, thin, big-eyed face" staring back. Gone, by doctors' orders, was her luxuriant hair. At "1½ yards" it had reached almost to her feet. "Felt badly about losing my one beauty," she confessed. Louisa's chestnut mane was her treasured companion, always available to admire, hold, stroke, brush, braid, toss carelessly or dramatically, and, if necessary, sell. From time to time she talked about cashing in her asset but never found the will to do it. Now she had lost it anyway, without compensation. She "went into caps like a grandma," substituting a silly white cotton bonnet for hair. She was stoic in public but mourned her crowning glory and had to lecture herself: "Never mind. It might have been my head & a wig outside is better than a loss of wits inside." She couldn't know then whether her hair would return to its former abundance—but it eventually did, as a late photograph attests.

Louisa finally managed to profit from this loss, as any reader of *Little Women* knows. In one of the book's best-loved scenes Jo sells her hair, like Louisa's her "one beauty," to raise train fare for her mother to go to Washington, where her father is seriously ill in a Union army hospital. Like making patchwork as Abby had taught her in childhood, Louisa went through her scrap bag of feelings, observations, and experiences, then selected and reorganized them to make stories.

~

By March, she could sit up and eat again. She sorted her papers, organized her actual scrap bag, and dusted her books as prelude to reading "no end of rubbish with a few good things as ballast." Once winter was behind her, Louisa's recuperation accelerated, and on the first day of spring she left her room at last.

A week later Louisa, May, and Abby were in the parlor reading novels when Bronson rushed in, beaming, shouting, " 'Good news! Anna has a fine boy!' Mother began to cry, May to laugh, & I to say 'There, I knew it wouldn't be a girl.'" Their parents, Louisa reported to Anna, were over the moon. Bronson was intoxicated with the maleness of his grandchild, Frederick. Abby punctuated floods of joyful tears with declarations: "I must go right down & see that baby." Louisa signed herself "Ever your admiring Rack a bones Lu," a joking reference to what was left of her after typhoid pneumonia. Louisa was soon strong enough to venture a walk down the Lexington Road in her granny cap, to find everything "beautiful & new," and to reflect, "To go very near to death teaches one to value life, & this winter will always be a very memorable one to me."

Looking out their windows, Concordians saw a dramatically changed Louisa Alcott. Three months earlier next-door neighbor Julian Hawthorne had gone to the station to see off "a big, loveable, tender-hearted, generous girl, with black [sic] hair, thick and long, and flashing humorous eyes." She came back, he said, a "white, tragic mask of what she had been." She regained her cheer and animation, the lesser Hawthorne noted, "but there were occasional tones in her voice and expressions of eyes and mouth that indicated depths of which she could not speak." Louisa had been reborn a different woman, with less girl inside.

She was no longer a peddler of stories working Boston's Publishers Row but an up-and-coming professional writer. Moncure Conway and Frank Sanborn, the editors of the antislavery weekly the *Commonwealth*, wanted Miss Alcott to make a series from her letters home from the Union Hotel Hospital. "They thought them witty & [sym]pathetic," Louisa wrote. "I didn't, but I wanted money."

Hospital Sketches is presented as reportage but in fact is slightly fictionalized. Louisa changed the names of real people (giving herself the Dickensian "Nurse Tribulation Periwinkle") and omitted the woman who inveigled dying soldiers into writing wills leaving her their worldly goods, and the nurses who picked the pockets of the dead. Otherwise it was a truthful rendition of her hospital days, rich with anecdote and full of feeling. The first installment came out in May 1863, just weeks after the chaotic rout of Union forces at Chancellorsville, Virginia. People were hungry for knowledge of the war, and little had been written about the hospitals. All New England was waiting for Louisa's second weekly installment, the touching account of the death of John Suhre.

The *Boston Evening Transcript* pronounced *Hospital Sketches* "fluent and sparkling, with touches of quiet humor and lively wit" and cited its "singular power and effectiveness." The *Waterbury American* said, "The reader is alternately moved to laughter and tears." The *Roxbury Journal* called Louisa "one of the raciest and most delightful of our young female authors," and the book "a new variety of literature . . . fresh and deeply interesting."

Louisa was baffled by the popularity of *Hospital Sketches*. "I cannot see why people like a few extracts from topsey turvey letters written on inverted tea kettles, waiting for gruel to warm or poultices to cool, [or] for boys to wake and be tormented," she said. (By 1879 she understood that realism and truth gave the book its power: "[*Hospital Sketches*] showed me my 'style,' & taking the hint I went where glory waited me.")

Louisa was on night duty at the bedside of a "one-legged lad dying of wound fever" when she wrote "Thoreau's Flute," finally able to express her feelings about Henry Thoreau for the first time since his death the past May. Bronson found the poetic tribute among Louisa's belongings and "read it like a partial parent as he is, to neighbor Hawthorne." Sophia Peabody Hawthorne sent it to Annie Fields, wife of the editor of the *Atlantic* and Louisa's onetime hostess, with a note: "[It is] altogether superior to anything I have ever seen of her—so sweet, majestic and calm and serious." With a few changes suggested by Mr. and Mrs. Fields, it was accepted.

Thoreau's Flute

We sighing said, "Our Pan is dead;
His pipe hangs mute beside the river
Around it wistful sunbeams quiver,
But Music's airy voice is fled.
Spring mourns as for untimely frost;
The bluebird chants a requiem;
The willow-blossom waits for him;
The Genius of the wood is lost."

Then from the flute, untouched by hands,
There came a low, harmonious breath:
"For such as he there is no death;
His life the eternal life commands;
Above man's aims his nature rose.
The wisdom of a just content
Made one small spot a continent
And turned to poetry life's prose.

"Haunting the hills, the stream, the wild,
Swallow and aster, lake and pine,

To him grew human or divine,
Fit mates for this large-hearted child.
Such homage Nature ne'er forgets,
And yearly on the coverlid
'Neath which her darling lieth hid
Will write his name in violets.

"To him no vain regrets belong
Whose soul, that finer instrument,
Gave to the world no poor lament,
But wood-notes ever sweet and strong.
O lonely friend! he still will be
A potent presence, though unseen,
Steadfast, sagacious, and serene;
Seek not for him—he is with thee."

"Thoreau's Flute" appeared in the September 1863 *Atlantic* anonymously, as was customary. When soon afterward Bronson Alcott called upon Henry Wadsworth Longfellow, America's most famous writer of verse praised the poem, and attributed it to Emerson. Bronson had the joy of claiming it for an Alcott.

Louisa never made any claims for her poetry or "Thoreau's Flute" in particular. "It was printed, copied, praised & glorified also paid for, & being a mercenary creature, I liked the $10 nearly as well as the honor of being 'a new star' & 'a literary celebrity,'" she commented matter-of-factly. On that basis, she must have liked ten times more the one-hundred-dollar first prize she won in Frank Leslie's contest for "Pauline's Passion and Punishment" arrived soon after. With it she retired some family debts and spent the rest on a set of furniture for her room, including a dresser and a sleigh bed. The purchase indicates a decision, never recorded or explained, to live full-time at Orchard House. Was she worn out after her wartime experience or sharing the longing for home that swept a nation of grieving families? For whatever reason, Louisa lived at "Home Sweet Home" (a hit song of the day) through the rest of the war. In a photograph from the period, tiny Alcott figures stand in the foreground outside Orchard House, the real subject of the picture. Bronson and Abigail are unmistakable, Anna can be identified standing behind a baby carriage, May is missing, and Louisa can only be found with the help of a magnifying glass and a guess. She sits cross-legged, chin in hand, on the ground, an unconventional woman in a very unlikely pose for the time and place. Perhaps she got tired of standing while the photographer set up his camera, plunked down on the crabgrass, and declined to pose any other way.

After the publication of *Hospital Sketches*, Louisa did think seriously about leaving home for distant Port Royal, South Carolina, to be a volunteer teacher of "contrabands," people who had fled from slavery to the protection of the Union army. James Fields sent word through Bronson that the *Atlantic* would willingly publish any letters Louisa might write. Before war had broken out, Fields had rejected Louisa's story of racial intermarriage, "M.L.," so as not to offend the South; now he snatched up "My Contraband," Louisa's tragic tale of brothers—one a master and the other an enslaved servant—but published it under the less conspicuous title "The Brothers." He had evidently decided that Louisa could write after all.

Louisa was denied Port Royal for want of a male escort or chaperone, but she did undertake another series, this one based upon letters she had sent from her 1861 summer vacation in New Hampshire as guest of her cousins and theatergoing pals Hamilton and Lu Willis. She renamed the pair Will and Laura, and advanced the date of the trip to the present tense so they seemed to be dispatches from the road. As herself, a "brown spinster" and also something of a cutup, she found everything animal, vegetable, or geologic in her surroundings to be alive, strange, and sublime—except for the other tourists, who were frivolous, oblivious, and unintentionally hilarious. She did not exempt herself from mockery; she confessed to lending her green garter to mend a wagon, and to a belief in reincarnation, stating that in a former life she had been a horse or a cat, and wishing that in her next she'd be a college freshman, of which sex she did not say.*

"All my dreams are getting fulfilled in a most amazing way. . . . A year ago I had no publisher & went begging with my wares; now three have asked me for something," Louisa wrote in her journal of October 1863.

---

* Louisa May Willis had died the previous November in a New York hotel, a suicide. Her obituary in the *Liberator* of 5 December 1862 refers to her recurrent "attacks" of the "disease" that eventually claimed her. Louisa Alcott's "Letters from the Mountains" was a resurrection of their madcap times, but it is unsurprising that she abandoned it in the middle. Louisa may also have made use of her cousin's suicide in *Work*.

"There is a sudden hoist for a meek & lowly scribbler who was told to 'stick to her teaching,' & never had a literary friend to lend a hand." It defies credulity that Louisa could believe she "never had a literary friend to lend a hand" in a year when her friends the Nathaniel Hawthornes had sent her poem to her friend James Fields, the editor of the *Atlantic*, and her contacts in the innermost antislavery circles had *invited* her to adapt her letters as *Hospital Sketches*. Ralph Waldo Emerson had selected her reading from his own library. Henry David Thoreau had fostered her deep appreciation of nature. She owed the publication of her first book, *Flower Fables*, to the Emersons' personally locating a backer.

Louisa's Civil War continued on the domestic front she would depict so vividly in *Little Women*, one of the first books to be set during the war. She did her part especially for the Fifty-fourth Massachusetts Regiment, of the USCT, the "U.S. Colored Troops." She made bed sacks (sleeping bags), towels, and uniforms, and donated books to the literacy classes held by Miss Willy Swett at the USCT barracks in Readville. Louisa visited the camp as well, no doubt intensely curious to see the troops in training, and went to Boston to cheer them as they marched off in May of 1863, to be slaughtered at Fort Wagner, South Carolina, in July. She and May volunteered to run refreshment tables at the subsequent "Fair for Colored Orphans" organized by Mary Peabody Mann, widow of the educator Horace Mann and sister of Sophia and Elizabeth. Louisa's table brought in seventy-five dollars, May's eighty dollars.

Louisa's advocacy of complete racial equality necessarily included the right to literacy, still legally denied to enslaved people. To refute the widespread idea among whites—abolitionists included—that African descent conferred mental deficiency, she collected and published (in the antislavery *Commonwealth*) "Colored Soldiers's Letters" sent to Miss Swett by her former pupils at the Readville barracks. The radicalism of Louisa's views is evidenced in "An Hour," a story that offers moral justification for slaves committing violence against their "owners." With much authorial huffing and puffing, she twisted the plot to avert any actual bloodshed. A self-confessed "fanatic" in the cause of abolition—many of whose adherents believed that when emancipation came, former slaves should be segregated or expatriated to Africa—Louisa believed in complete racial integration or *amalgamation,* a term that later evolved into the pejorative *miscegenation.*

Actual blood *was* shed in a brutal and chaotic encounter between Grant's and Lee's forces, including that of the young Alcott cousin Henry Bond, son of Louisa Greenwood Bond, the aunt who had sheltered Louisa and May for months at a time during their early independent years in Boston. The death of a Civil War soldier was awful to contemplate, because the unknown fate of his body gave rise to the worst kind of speculation: the horrible fact was that many corpses were robbed and sometimes mutilated, and left unburied for days on end. Many of the slain lay in mass graves whose whereabouts their families would never learn.

Concord was soon stunned by an unexpected death of a different kind. Nathaniel Hawthorne, one of the town's most distinguished residents, went on a walking tour in New Hampshire with his college friend Franklin Pierce, the former president of the United States. On a perfect morning for hiking, Pierce found Hawthorne dead in his bed. The great writer had been observed to be very ill, but never spoke of it. Compounding the unsettling circumstance of the death of a well-known person away from home and with no farewell, the family chose neither to view nor to display Hawthorne's body: Louisa found it remarkable that "he was not brought home at all as his family did not wish to see him." She helped decorate the church for his funeral, "which was a very peculiar one throughout." Pallbearers who carried his coffin to burial in Sleepy Hollow "in a pomp of sunshine and verdure and gentle winds" included Henry Wadsworth Longfellow, Oliver Wendell Holmes, Louis Agassiz, James Fields, and Bronson Alcott. All fellow members of the Atlantic Club, none felt he had truly known Hawthorne. "I thought there was a tragic element in the event," wrote Emerson, "in the painful solitude of the man." Louisa remembered Hawthorne best on the hill behind Orchard House and Wayside, where on moonlit midnight wanderings as a lovesick teenager she would cross paths with her neighbor, and by unspoken mutual consent neither would acknowledge the other. She revisited the hill to gather violets and had them delivered to his widow. Sophia was touched and wrote a note in return, although it did not heal the mysterious rift that had grown between the families, the choice of Bronson as a pallbearer notwithstanding. Had any of Louisa's mockery of her European affectations reached Sophia Hawthorne's ears?

Louisa had no standing among the writers in Concord, and not only because she was of a younger generation and female. She had trained herself to succeed in genres of writing that had commercial markets—the children's tale, the poem, the short story, the longer serial fiction, and nonfiction—but had yet to command the novel, the form that she and the readers she respected loved most. Louisa had put away *Moods,* her romantic novel of ideas, swearing never to take it out again, and turned to the gritty autobiographical book she was calling *Success. Moods* was still on her mind, but every Boston publisher, most recently A. K. Loring, insisted it be shortened.

One sleepless night a scheme to cut *Moods* suddenly came to her. "I slept no more that night but worked as busily as if mind & body had nothing to do with one another. . . . The fit was on, & for a fortnight, I hardly ate slept or stirred but wrote, wrote like a thinking machine in full operation." When Louisa emerged from this latest vortex, she had cut ten chapters, sacrificing many of her favorite parts, but she was confident she had strengthened and sharpened as well as shortened the story. Loring agreed and promised to bring out the book right away. "Of course we all had a rapture," Louisa reported.

But soon doubts set in. She read *Emily Chester,* a controversial new novel by Ann Moncure Crane that was "just enough like *Moods* in a few things* to make me sorry that it came out now." When the page proofs arrived, she had more misgivings. What was left of the novel seemed "small, stupid & no more my own," she wrote. Initial reaction, however, was encouraging; Louisa "saw, heard & talked *Moods*" everywhere. The edition sold out in days. Henry James Sr. hailed Bronson on the street with the cheerful news that his whole family was enthralled by Louisa's novel— though he misremembered the title and called it *Dumps.* He invited Louisa to a family dinner, where she was treated "like the Queen of Sheba." Henry Jr. had written a review of *Moods,* not yet published, "& was very friendly, being a literary youth."

Friendly and flattering letters were delivered daily to Orchard House, but the critical reception of *Moods* was mixed. On the positive side Miss Alcott was praised for her "quick fancy, lively wit, and clear observation." The reviewer for the *Commonwealth* said the book's plot was "not unlike

---

* Mark Twain thought *Moods* was so much like *Emily Chester* that he accused Louisa of plagiarism in the *Springfield Republican* in 1891. Twain also said Louisa had denounced *Huckleberry Finn* as obscene and unsuitable for children—and thanked her for boosting his sales. (*Louisa May Alcott: The Contemporary Reviews,* Beverly Lyon Clark, ed. [Cambridge: Cambridge University Press, 2004], 45.)

Goëthe's *Elective Affinities*," though it suffered from a "want of consistency and definite outline," implying that she had attempted a novel of ideas but had not pulled it off. Reports came from readers who couldn't grasp her meaning—or could, and disapproved. "Some fear it isn't moral because it speaks freely of marriage," Louisa noted. The *Boston Evening Transcript* judged *Moods* "inferior" to *Emily Chester.* "The grand mistake of both books," the reviewer argued, "is in supposing . . . that attractions and repulsions cannot be conquered. . . . Any woman with a proper sense of duty, . . . recognizing the noblest qualities in her husband, can always conquer." Some readers, picking up the book's false notes, complained that Louisa's characters were not realistic. Others ranked her among "maiden reformers . . . who knew nothing of marriage by experience."

And that was not all. Louisa's misreading of Henry James Jr. as "friendly" was worthy of one of the short stories he would go on to write. The twenty-one-year-old budding literary éminence grise treated her with acid condescension. Warwick (the male protagonist modeled on Thoreau) was "the inevitable *cavaliere servente* of the precocious little girl. . . . Do not all novel-readers remember a figure, a hundred figures, analogous to this?" He dismissed Louisa's authority as a writer: "The two most striking facts with regard to 'Moods' are the author's ignorance of human nature, and her self-confidence in spite of this ignorance."*

Louisa did not excuse her novel's flaws in print but admitted them to friends. "*Moods* is not what I meant to have it," she wrote Moncure Conway, her friend and the editor of the *Commonwealth.*

> Perhaps I was over bold to try . . . treating an old theme [marriage] in a new way. . . . Yet half the misery of the world seems to come from unmated pairs trying to live their lie decorously to the end. . . . My next book shall have no ideas . . . & the people shall be as ordinary as possible, then the critics will say its all right.

Lowering her literary sights, she returned to the easy money and satisfying release of pulp fiction. For *Flag of Our Union* she produced "A Marble Woman," an eerie tale of wifely submission. (She gave her heroine

---

* James's remark is perplexing in light of what comes before: "With the exception of two or three celebrated names, we know not, indeed, to whom, in the country, unless to Miss Alcott, we are to look for a novel above the average."

an opium habit and took her to the brink of father-daughter incest.)
Howard Ticknor wanted a story along the lines of *Hospital Sketches,* and
she supplied it to order at the length he needed. Frank Leslie wanted
Louisa as a regular contributor to his new paper, *Chimney Corner,* and he
agreed to her stipulation that payment be in advance, at fifty dollars per
story. "Alcott brains seem in demand" was Louisa's satisfied comment.
She had aimed her arrow at prosperity and hit the target, if not yet the
bulls-eye.

While Louisa was toiling at her tiny desk in Orchard House that
spring of 1865, the Civil War was coming to a close. After the fall of Rich-
mond, Virginia, the seat of Confederate power and the source of Confederate arms, Louisa rushed to Boston to join the "grand jollification." She
had just been there to see the great actor Edwin Booth as Hamlet and
rated him "finer than ever." Two weeks later Booth's brother, John Wilkes
Booth, assassinated President Lincoln, and jollification turned to mourn-
ing everywhere in the North. Louisa watched the somber Boston procession held in Lincoln's honor by the reunified nation's most ardent
abolitionists. She saw a black mourner and a white mourner arm in arm
and thought it was cause to allow jubilation to trump sorrow. She was
proud of her own sacrifices in the sacred causes of freedom and equality.

Joy was mixed with grief remembered when Anna gave birth to a second son on the twenty-fourth of June, the day that should have been
Lizzie Alcott's thirtieth birthday. The baby was named John, after his
father.* Louisa assessed him as others would all his life, as "a fine little lad
who took to life kindly & seemed to find the world all right."

---

* Anna Alcott Pratt's attending doctor was her cousin Lucy Sewall, one of the first
women in America to get a medical degree and open a practice.

THIRTEEN

A LITTLE ROMANCE

Just when she least expected it, while helping Anna with the new baby, the Grand Tour of Louisa's dreams fell into her lap. Hearing that Louisa had nursing experience and wanted to travel, one of Boston's richest merchants, William Fletcher Weld, asked if she would accompany his daughter Anna—a so-called invalid—and his son George to Europe for a year as a lady's companion. The occupation had the status of a governess, the function of a chaperone, and duties to be performed under the pretense of being a helpful friend of equal social rank but lesser wealth. Louisa had never met the Welds and hesitated briefly, but "everyone said 'Go,'" and after a week of organizing and packing she did. Only as the *China* steamed out of Boston harbor did the enormity of a year away hit her— "[I] might not see all the dear home faces when I came back," she reported thinking.

The companions got off to a shaky start. Louisa spent much of the nine-day voyage seasick in the Ladies' salon, while her charge was as comfortable with the ship's steady rolling as she was with the dull company she found for games of backgammon and gossip over elaborate meals in the first-class dining room. At twenty-nine Louisa's junior by three years, Anna Weld was the petted youngest of six children of her father's first wife; her twenty-five-year-old half brother was the petted only child of William Weld's second marriage. A popular bachelor about town, George Weld was a former member of the Harvard Rowing Club and the future donor of the Weld Boathouse on the Charles River. No love was lost between young Weld and Louisa; he thought seasickness cowardly and she was nothing but. Wherever they went, George shed his sister and her companion at the first opportunity.

The *China* docked at Liverpool, and after a two-night stopover and a cursory drive about the dirty city—filled with more desperate-looking beggars than Louisa had ever seen—the travelers boarded the train for London. The ride through the English countryside did not disappoint. Louisa's first letter home showed her curiosity excited by everything new: the elegant fittings of their carpeted railroad carriage, the "burly guard with badges all over him looking like a horse in a silverplated harness," the "pretty sceneries [that] May would have been wild to stop and sketch," and the calm order of the English landscape. She also liked the pace of life: "Nothing was abrupt, nobody in a hurry, and nowhere did you see the desperately go ahead style of life that we have." Once in London, George took off, Anna took to bed, and for four days Louisa wandered the city alone and amused, observing everything and keeping notes. She thought English weather was horrible, but braved the dank drizzle of London summer days to cross the great green expanses of the parks, shelter in dark Westminster Abbey, and prowl the famous streets feeling as if she'd "got into a novel." At the end of the week, the travelers boarded a Dover steamer bound for Ostend, and from Ostend moved on to Brussels and Cologne, there to board a steamboat up the Rhine. Primed by her beloved Goethe's account of his 1774 Rhine journey, she would turn her own journey into a travel sketch, "Up the Rhine," for the *Independent*, a New York weekly, and get paid a cool hundred dollars for it.

Louisa's fellow tourists made for rich comic material. "The English sat bolt upright," she observed, "as if they had made up their minds to be surprised at nothing." French passengers " 'bon-jour'-ed every mortal who approached," German men "tended their meerschaums," and Americans "stared and asked questions."

Much as she loved nature, as feelingly as she could evoke it as setting or dramatic foil in stories, she was quite unequal to reporting scenic beauty per se. "There is no use in trying to describe the Rhine beyond saying that it is not wonderful or magnificent like Niagara, the Mississippi, or Mount Washington," she admitted. "It is exquisitely beautiful . . . like sailing through a gallery of ever-new, ever-lovely landscapes, painted with a skill no human artist can attain."

Their destination was Schwalbach, a popular spa in the mountains near Wiesbaden, where Anna consulted Dr. Adolph Genth, world-famous author of *The Iron Waters of Schwalbach,* and George disappeared to enjoy himself elsewhere. That left Louisa to amuse Anna—with scant success, though she tried her best to "suit & serve." She comforted herself with the thought that "many would have done still worse . . . for hers is a hard case to manage & needs the patience & wisdom of an angel." Anna Weld's illness was never specified but seems best understood as the neurasthenia that afflicted so many wealthy nineteenth-century women, strangled by corsets and weighed down by pounds of intricate clothing, with little to do but visit each other. As a war veteran whose illness left her arguably more an invalid than her demanding employer, Louisa had limited sympathy for her charge. (Anna Weld eventually married, bore a child, and lived to the age of eighty-nine.)

After weeks of water-sipping and the odd ride or walk with her tiresome companion, Louisa became anxious for mail. She feared that she was not missed at home. A reassuring letter found her late in September: "My absence seems to have left so large a gap that I begin to realize how much I am to them in spite of all my faults." Finally George returned to escort his sister and her companion to Vevey in the Swiss Alps, via Wiesbaden and Frankfurt, birthplace of Goethe, that Transcendentalist patron saint. Louisa longed to go inside Goethe's house, but the Weld siblings had other priorities. Unable to change their plans, a frustrated Louisa recorded their philistine remark: "Who was Goethe to fuss about?" The stopover in Freiburg improved her mood. They spent the night in a grand hotel overlooking a vast picturesque valley, the "most romantic place we have been in," she reported. All that was missing was good company to share it.

George Weld's plan was to spend autumn in Paris after he dropped his female baggage at a resort town on Lake Geneva. The incompatible threesome made the last leg of their summer tour under sail from Lausanne to picturesque Vevey, a happy scene of bustling activity set against the backdrop of the "white Alps of Savoy, shining in the sun like some celestial country seen in dreams." George entrusted his charges to the solicitous Englishwoman who ran the Pension Victoria. Louisa would describe the establishment as "pleasant, well kept, and as full as a beehive with a motley collection of lodgers from all quarters of the world." The members of this diverse temporary society mingled in the salon overlooking Lake Leman, lulled by the sound of water lapping gently against the stone wall of the terrace below. On leisurely strolls in fine weather the guests' every breath was perfumed by the late-blooming rosebushes on the slope behind the hotel, by the herbs in the kitchen gardens of cottages, by the flowers hanging from window boxes and standing in pots on the balconies of cafés, where a stop for tea or a glass of wine could be the mission of an afternoon. Vevey made a perfect stage for a light romance.

Anna Weld and Louisa had been at the Pension Victoria for a month when, in November of 1865, Ladislas Wisniewski turned up.* Louisa was at the breakfast table on the chilly morning when the tall stranger "with a thin, intelligent face and the charmingly polite manners of a foreigner" came downstairs to join her and a few other guests. He was shivering, she said, and "he cast wistful glances toward the warm corner by the stove." As she was in that corner, the glances could as easily have been directed at Louisa as at the stove, but she insisted he take her place, saying that "the heat often oppressed" her.

At dinner the stranger quietly lifted his glass to Louisa's health in the most polite foreign way. Later she saw him pass through the salon, looking handsome in a military-style blue-and-white suit (she confessed "a weakness for brave boys in blue") and also looking ill—tubercular—and in need of a nurse. Young Wisniewski had fought in the recent Polish rebellion, she learned. He brought to mind the wounded soldiers of the Union army to whom she had so freely given her love and care; her heart "warmed to him at once."

The intelligent young man didn't miss the kindling of affection in the American lady. He coaxed the spark with flattering attentions, and perhaps for the only time in her life, Louisa responded to the charms of a man. How could she not? He was vulnerable, a hero, and enough her junior that she could tell herself she loved him like a mother—although he acted nothing like a son. "It was impossible for anyone to long resist his pleading eyes," Louisa explained.

Like Frédéric Chopin, the most popular composer of the day, Ladislas Wisniewski was a talented pianist and a Polish nationalist in exile. He was a recent university student and probably no older than twenty-one. Louisa called him "Laddie" not to simplify his name but the way she used "Lass" or "Lassie" for her sister Anna, as a folksy term of endearment

---

* Louisa described her encounter with Wisniewski in her journals; in two short memoirs, "My Boys" and "My Polish Boy;" and in a sketch, "Life in a Pension."

imported from the pages of Sir Walter Scott. Wisniewski was not the first younger man she had called "Laddie," but as the "best and dearest of all" he was the ultimate. She did Laddie the even greater honor of immortalizing him in *Little Women* as Laurie, Jo March's enthusiastic male playmate and would-be lover. Louisa would eventually allow Alf Whitman and Julian Hawthorne to believe they were, in part, models for Laurie, but at the outset she stated quite clearly that Laurie was Laddie. Laurie appeared in the sequels to *Little Women* (*Little Men* and *Jo's Boys*), but as a character he never developed or became mature. Like Louisa's memory of Laddie, Laurie was eternally youthful.

Once the friendship with Laddie was struck, Louisa said, "the barrier of an unknown language did not long stand between us." In the evenings at the Pension Victoria, while the older people chatted and gambled at cards, Louisa and Laddie gamely tried to teach each other their native tongues. Wisniewski knew four or five languages already and astounded Louisa with his progress, "though he often slapped his forehead with the despairing exclamation, 'I never can will shall to have learn this beast of English!'" Louisa would write that among the guests "romances, like the roses, blossomed far into December. Sometimes grammars and dictionaries were thrown by, and games, gymnastics, or dancing went on in the big *salle à manger*. Cigarettes were allowed there, and as much laughing and as many pranks as we chose." As the girl who once chewed tobacco on a dare, Louisa would have had a puff or two on a cigarette in public, and enjoyed the daring display if not necessarily the cigarette.

"My Polish Boy" describes Laddie and Louisa's long walks and engaging talks about their "splendid plans for the future." Every night at dinner Laddie presented Louisa with a rose, and afterward the two exchanged confidences in a corner of the salon. Five years later, Louisa still had "a pile of merry little notes which I used to find tucked under my door. He called them chapters of a great history we were to write together." She did not leave the history to the inquisitive eyes of posterity.

Louisa described her intimacy with Laddie as familial, like the warm atmosphere of the pension itself. Wisniewski called her "little mamma" and asked Louisa to call him "Varjo" as his mother did. The evening presentation of the rose and the notes slipped under her chamber door, however, suggest a campaign of seduction or at least a "wheedlesome" (as she characterized it) flirtation. He told Louisa that *drogha* meant "friend" in Polish; she took to calling him "ma drogha" and claimed to have discovered only later that she had been calling him her darling, "in the tenderest manner." In Laddie something can be seen of Henry James's opportunistic European playing upon the guileless American. His tuberculosis, for instance, if it was that, may have been exaggerated to disarm sympathetic Louisa with the belief he had not long to live. Eventually his illness miraculously disappeared.

On her birthday, Laddie played Louisa "his sweetest airs as a present" and wished her "all good & happiness on earth & a high place in Heaven" as her reward. The wild and windy day, she wrote in her journal, was "very like me in its fitful changes of sunshine & shade. Usually I am sad on my birthday, but not this time." On the thirtieth anniversary of her formative misadventure with the plumcakes, she was finally having her cake and eating it too. "[I feel] rather old with my 33 years, but have much to keep me young, & hope I shall not grow older in heart as the time goes on."

Laddie was still at the pension when Anna decided to relocate to warmer, more fashionable Nice. In "My Boys," Louisa said of the parting of the ways: "[Although] we jokingly agreed to meet in Paris the next May . . . I felt sure I would soon be forgotten. As he kissed my hand, there were tears in my boy's eyes, and a choke in the voice that tried to be cheerful, said 'bon voyage, dear and good little mama. I do not say adieu, but *au revoir*.'" Until we meet again. "My Polish Boy" gave much the same account. Anna Weld was excised from the picture in both.

After Laddie's departure, the journal entries diverge from the memoirs. The entry for December seems scrambled, as if Louisa did not quite know how, or how much, to describe her relationship to Laddie, or Anna Weld's to Laddie. She recorded there that Wisniewski followed them as far as Lausanne, "& went back to V[evey] disconsolate." Not a significant difference except that Anna is present. But the sentence that followed is puzzling: "Sad times for A. and I but we journeyed away to Nice and tried to forget our troubles."

Louisa and the lackluster Anna shared troubles? This contradicted everything Louisa wrote of her relationship with her employer, before or afterward. To read on in the journal entry is to find Louisa's usually straightforward prose growing gnarled and impenetrable: "Anna troubled about Laddie who was in a despairing state of mind. I could not advise them to be happy as they desired, so everything went wrong and both worried." Later Louisa crossed out "them" and wrote *"him,"* making the sentence read as "I could not advise *him* to be happy as they desired, so everything went wrong and both worried." Who worried? Both Anna and Laddie? Both Anna and Louisa? Both Louisa and Laddie? At a still later date, Louisa reconsidered again and crossed out the whole passage, but not so completely as to make it illegible.

It seems unlikely that Anna Weld, who was full of "whim, selfishness, and folly" and had barely heard of Goethe, was in love with Laddie, or that Laddie was more comfortable with a whining heiress than with the witty, tender woman that Louisa was with him. What happened later makes it even more unlikely—but the journal is there, if only to throw us off the scent.

After a few weeks in Nice, Louisa wrote in her journal that she was "tired of doing nothing pleasant or interesting," and later added that she had "a dull Christmas within doors though a lovely day without. Windows open, roses blooming, air mild & city gay. With friends, health & a little money how jolly one might be in this perpetual summer." Anna was hors de combat in bed, so Louisa had to stay inside too. When she did get out, she soon "tired of the fashionable Promenade for every one was on exhibition. Sometimes before or after the fashionable hour I walked there and enjoyed the sea and sky." Perhaps Louisa's lowly social status had soured her on the social scene; her wardrobe cannot have been much to exhibit either. It must have been galling to be a descendant of distinguished Bostonians, the author of *Flower Fables*, *Hospital Sketches*, and *Moods*, a contributor of stories and poetry to the internationally known *Atlantic*, and be seen at the beck and call of the rich but inconsequential Miss Weld, who as time went on may not have been very nice to her. Later Louisa commented that Anna Weld was not a lady, perhaps meaning that her manners were not the same to all, and that as her paid companion Louisa saw just how much they were not.

By February of 1866 the lady's companion was fed up with her lot; she announced that she had decided to go home in May. Her journal explanation went only so far as to say that she was "tired of it and as [Anna] is not going to travel my time is too valuable to be spent fussing over cushions and carrying shawls."

There were months of shawl-carrying yet to go in Nice, however. An apparent suitor from the numerous Hosmer clan, a "young Germanized American, came much to see us," Louisa recorded, then crossed it out. She got Anna to leave her bed and take a few rides around the countryside. But March, she wrote, was "a tedious month which might have been quite the reverse had I been able to enjoy it my own way." Hosmer came "a good deal, full of German philosophy. Conceited but better than no one." Later she added "queer times with him." At least Hosmer read books, and gave Louisa a break from the fretful Anna. There is nothing quite as hard on the nerves as a travel companion gone sour, and usually the feeling is mutual. Louisa could not always have been able to conceal her bad mood from her employer. The bill payer must have wished the companion to be more pleasant. Louisa would not always have been able to restrain herself from lashing out at Anna with the caustic wit that spoke her mind before her better judgment could control her tongue.

Back in Concord, Bronson and Abby were distressed to learn that with the Welds Louisa was enjoying Europe so little that she preferred to come home early. She may have written that she was looking for a way to stay on in May, or not. In any case, Bronson wrote that he had four hundred dollars from his tour in the West, and her uncle Sam May would add to it another hundred dollars to guarantee Bronson's deserving daughter time to have fun. Bronson had his friend Fred Sanborn write to Moncure Conway (Sanborn's coeditor on the *Commonwealth*, who had relocated to London), so that "every facility will be opened to you for seeing what you desire in England." But England was not where Louisa intended to go, at least not immediately.

At long last the calendar page turned to May. Hosmer trailed along to see Louisa off at the station when, she wrote, "on the first day of the month [I] left Anna and Nice and started alone for Paris feeling as happy as a freed bird," to spend two weeks at Madame Dyne's pension. At the station in Paris she found Laddie; "[he was] waiting for me . . . to take me to my room."

It is unclear whether Bronson and Abby knew of those two weeks, but even if they did, for an unmarried woman to spend an unchaperoned fortnight in the constant company of a man was a bold move. The journals offered no defense or denial of the circumstances, but in the memoirs Louisa maintained, "My twelve years' seniority made our adventures quite proper." For insulation against criticism, in "My Polish Boy" Louisa even said that Laddie's appearance at the station was a surprise, and that he had two student friends in tow, and was staying in shabby digs, with the breadth of the Seine River between their beds. The students and the Left Bank digs were plausible enough, but neither the journals nor the first "My Boys" mentioned a surprise, and to explain how Wisniewski could have ferreted out Louisa's plans down to the arrival time of the train is a challenge. It is almost impossible for the modern imagination to picture the meeting as other than a glorious tryst, and perhaps it was not. Whether it was or wasn't, Louisa noted, she saw "only all that I wished to see in a very pleasant way." In fact, it was "the pleasantest fortnight in all my year of travel."

Putting first things first in the capital of fashion, the fancy-free companions went shopping, with Laddie managing the delicate negotiations "in the best of French," while Louisa looked on, laughingly vetoing "when he proposed gorgeous *chapeaus* full of flowers and feathers" and agreeing to what he presented as "this modest, pearl-colored one with a crape rose. . . . Most elegant for the Sunday promenade." They had "a charming trip about the enchanted city, a gay lunch at a café, and a first brief glimpse of the Louvre." Day after day "I fearlessly went anywhere on the arm of my big son. Not to theatres or balls, but pleasant trips out of the city in the bright spring weather, quiet strolls in the gardens, moonlight concerts in the Champs Elysées; or, best of all, long talks with music in the little red salon [at Madame Dyne's pension], with the gas turned low, and the ever changing scenes of the Rue de Rivoli under the balcony."

In Louisa's journal there is nothing about the parting of the happy pair, but Louisa described a poignant moment in "My Boys."

> At his gift of cologne, [I] responded "you have been so kind to me; I wish I had something beautiful to give you, Laddie," feeling that it would be hard to get on without my boy.
>
> "This time it is for always; so as a parting souvenir, give to me the sweet English good-by."
>
> As he said this, with a despairing sort of look, . . . my heart was quite rent within me, and, regardless of several prim English ladies, I drew down his tall head and kissed him tenderly, feeling as if in this world there were no more meetings for us. Then I ran away and buried myself in an empty railway carriage, hugging the little cologne bottle he had given me.

Julian Hawthorne, son of Nathaniel Hawthorne, speculated about Louisa many years after her death: "Did she ever have a love affair? We never knew; yet how could such a nature so imaginative, romantic, and passionate escape it?" We will never know if she had a love affair, but we do know that Louisa's connection with Ladislas Wisniewski continued through a sporadic correspondence. He married and had children. He settled in Paris, and visited New York. After *Little Women* was published, Louisa acknowledged him as the model for Laurie, always referring to him as "Laddie" and joking that two hiccups and a cough would produce his last name. She was asked about her Polish boy so often that his image in her mind must have become worn and obscure. Louisa had no photograph of Ladislas. None is known to exist.

After the November 1865 journal entry that begins "A little romance with Laddie," there was something else written in Louisa's journal. She later scratched it out so forcibly that she tore the paper—the only such instance in all her journal manuscripts. Over the tattered area she wrote "couldn't be." The entry for May 1866 says, "on the 17th reluctantly left for London."

If Louisa pined for Paris and Laddie, she seems to have kept it to herself, and spent the next seven weeks in England in the best of spirits. She forsook the "dusty" beaten track of the Murray's guidebook, so sacred to the Welds and their ilk, instead trying "the penny boats going up and down the Thames all day . . . [to] get fine views" of the city, dashing off to Tunbridge Wells or Dorking for the pleasure of viewing the country from the top of mail delivery coaches. She joined the locals riding the new underground trains, "the intricacies of which it takes great grasp of mind to fathom," and visiting "the Zoo to hunt up the wombat and see if he really were 'hairy and obtuse,' as Christina Rossetti says." Because there was a camel at the zoo to ride, Louisa rode on a camel. Without the family and with her time her own, Louisa could be herself. And after months away from her own circle, she was again a well-connected Alcott: she met Gladstone, Disraeli, and John Stuart Mill, and felt at home encountering the most outstanding people of her day.

Her first two weeks were spent with a couple her own age, Ellen and Moncure Conway, in Wimbledon Common. Moncure Conway was a remarkable man whose English friends included Dickens, Browning, Carlyle, and Darwin. In Boston, as the founding editor of the antislavery *Commonwealth,* Conway had published Louisa's interracial romance, "M.L." Conway was also instrumental to the success of *Hospital Sketches*: he solicited her letters from the Union Hotel Hospital for the *Commonwealth* and suggested she publish them in book form after their success in his publication.

The tall, handsome son of a wealthy Virginia slaveholder, Moncure Conway became—under Emerson's influence—a Transcendentalist, then went on to become a radical abolitionist and feminist. His like-minded wife, Ellen Dana, so offended his parents by hugging and kissing a young black slave girl that they didn't speak to their son for seventeen years. Conway was a man not only of conviction but also of personal courage. After the Civil War broke out he went to Washington, where some twenty of the people his family held in slavery had fled, to escort them through the slave state of Maryland to safety in Ohio. Later in the conflict, the Southerner's diplomatic overtures to the Confederacy made him persona non grata even to his supporters, and he left for London to continue his distinguished career in religious and social reform until his death in 1907. At the time of Louisa's London visit, Conway was the Unitarian minister of the South Place Chapel in London. (In letters to friends Louisa reported hearing the handsome Mr. Conway speak and having to pry him loose from clusters of admiring women.)

In June Louisa moved to Kensington to stay with an equally fascinating English couple, Peter Taylor, a Unitarian and radical MP, and his wife, Clementia, a prominent figure in the woman suffrage movement. Moncure Conway's memoir evokes the rarified atmosphere Louisa lived in as houseguest.

> Peter Taylor and his wife, Mentia, a lady of finest culture and literary taste, made their beautiful mansion, Aubrey House, a centre of liberal thinkers, writers, artists—a veritable *salon*. Peter Taylor freely gave money to the . . . antislavery cause in America, and to those of the "liberators" of Poland and Italy . . . the Italian agitators especially, and Mazzini* passed nearly every evening of his sojourn in London at Aubrey House.

It was through Mazzini, during one of his periods of exile in London in the mid-1840s, that Margaret Fuller learned of the revolutionary movement in Italy and with his advice made her plans to go there.

While staying with the Taylors, Louisa went to several dinner parties and half a dozen concerts and lectures, paid a visit to the House of Com-

---

* Giuseppe Mazzini (1805–72) was an advocate of Italian unification during the period when the great nation-states of Europe were founded.

mons (as her father had done a quarter century before), and went to hear Dickens read. It seems doubtful that as a child of ten she had seen Dickens on his American tour, but she described her 1866 experience as if she were comparing it with the past: "The youth and comeliness were gone, but the foppishness remained, and the red haired man, with false teeth, and the voice of a worn-out actor, had his scanty hair curled," an image that left his devoted acolyte so disillusioned that when he died she said, "I don't care a pin." She paid a visit to the publisher George Routledge, who gave her twenty-five pounds for the rights to the English edition of *Moods*, and wrote to Mrs. Conway, "As Paradise Lost went for £10 I ought to be satisfied with five pounds for my *great* work. Oh, the vanity of authors!"

In mid-June Louisa left the Taylors and took an inexpensive room near Kensington Gardens. She spent a "very free & jolly" three weeks roaming London on her own, "dining late & resting, chatting, music or fun in the eve." The fun was sometimes in the company of an American, "C——," another of Louisa's bright younger men; this one she referred to as her "grandson." He was a "youth of an inquiring turn, an adventurous soul, a persuasive tongue." He made "a capital guide, guard, comrade, and friend." With this young man she embarked on a daylong expedition in search of the Maypole Inn of Dickens's *Barnaby Rudge*, for Louisa loved to feel transported into the pages of a novel. They traveled by underground to a surface train; then "[we] struck into a pretty country road winding along between hawthorn hedges, pink and white with bloom, the pathways making pleasant walking, with the dust well laid and the grassy banks all starred with flowers. . . . After a good stretch to rest our limbs and fill our lungs, admiring all creation most enthusiastically as we went, it occurred to us that we might as well find out if we were going right or wrong." They were going wrong and would go wrong again. At last they reached the Maypole Inn, "footsore now, but in the best of spirits, after a walk of fourteen miles." There they rested and conjured up the characters and scenes of *Barnaby Rudge*, and returned at dark after walking another four miles to the nearest train station. This was life as Louisa wished to live it.

Louisa's last London excursion of note was a "midsummer's night's dream," a moonlight tour of the London bridges, again in the company of the delightful C——: "On the evening of the Fourth of July . . . I was suddenly seized with a desire to do something revolutionary and independent. So. . . . I rose up, and pointing vaguely to the horizon in general, I said 'Let us go somewhere.'" She and C—— toured the Embankment, London Bridge, and Blackfriars Bridge, where they stood in one of the niches to take in a long view down the Thames. In another niche they noticed a crouching woman who seemed in need of aid. Louisa moved forward to help but was pulled away by a cautious C——, who suspected a trap. The image of the older woman in despair haunted her all night.

Louisa and her young friend next went to the Waterloo Bridge—a sad place, she said, "for the poor who are in earnest pay a halfpenny toll and, thus escaping the idlers so thick on the free bridges, drown themselves as privately as possible." The guard shone his lantern into Louisa's face, possibly, she thought, because her "solemn expression raised a doubt in his mind as to [her] intentions." When Louisa thought of taking desperate measures, drowning was the means. Mixed with her enjoyment of this moment was the memory of her darkest hour, when she contemplated suicide at the Mill Dam, "but there never was less reason for anxiety; for life was wonderfully attractive to me that lovely night, and there were few happier mortals than I, when a little later I sat in a light boat and we went swiftly with the tide along that line of moonshine which always seems like a silvery path to heaven."

Early on the morning of July 7, Louisa took the train to Liverpool and boarded the *Africa* for home. She spent most of the next fourteen days on the rolling waves feeling seasick, isolated, and bored. While she anticipated seeing her family, she dreaded learning the worst about the health of both her mother and the Alcott finances. Louisa was going back to do the duty that was nearest.

FOURTEEN

WE REALLY LIVED MOST OF IT

Louisa returned to find the status quo ante, if anything more so: Concord still dull; her father placid; Anna unwell; May full of plans; and her mother aged, tired, and sick. Abigail Alcott was sixty-six, in nineteenth-century terms elderly. Her deterioration shocked Louisa after a year away, but she carried her mother in a mental miniature that dated back two decades, when four Alcott sisters sheltered under her powerful love. She feared that her mother would not live to enjoy the pleasant, restful chamber that she had promised in her girlhood poem. That ambition still drove her writing. To turn a phrase around, Mother was the necessity of invention.

Louisa didn't need to be told that her family had fallen "behind hand when the money-maker was away." Orchard House was no doubt home to a large pile of unpaid bills. On top of their usual indigence, Louisa was unpleasantly surprised to discover that her parents had lied about the five hundred dollars that had underwritten her eight weeks' independent exploration of Europe. She should have known there was no four-hundred-dollar windfall from Bronson's speaking tour; actually there was a three-hundred-dollar loan he was unlikely to pay back without her help. Within the week she was churning out stories to patch the hole in the family coffers.

Hating "debt more than the devil," at a speed perhaps only Trollope would match, Louisa turned out two stories for Frank Leslie at one hundred dollars per, and supplied James Elliott of the *Flag of Our Union* with a novella and one of her best thrillers. "Behind a Mask *or* A Woman's Power" was a subversive variation on *Jane Eyre*, the familiar tale of the young governess who finds herself the heir to a fortune and/or the bride of one. Louisa had borrowed the story line before, for her first novel, *The Inheritance*, at the age of seventeen. At twice that, in "Behind a Mask" she replaced the self-sacrificing teenage heroine with her opposite, Jean Muir, an over-the-hill actress, "a woman of thirty at least." With the aid of a wig of golden curls, pearly false teeth, and a nightly dose of alcoholic courage, Miss Muir can pass as a nineteen-year-old governess, a role she assumes with the object of seducing into marriage one of several wealthy bachelors in the Coventry family. Only in her room can she shed the persona of the demure victim of unfortunate circumstances to be herself, "if actresses ever are themselves." She takes a hefty swig from a silver flask and swears to the unmasked self in the mirror, "I'll not fail, if there's power in a woman's wit and will!"

Louisa can almost be heard whistling between the lines of this nice piece of literary mischief. Through a thicket of clever plot twists the reader roots for the imposter to triumph over her lazy, complacent employers, and cheers when she does. While Jean Muir bears the same initials as Jo March of *Little Women*, she hasn't a shred of decency. She must have been a breath of fresh air to women compelled to subscribe to the orthodoxy that women always and only gained love and success via the path of goodness and self-denial.

Louisa kept up a phenomenal pace for six months, writing up to fourteen hours a day. When Abby fell ill in September, she hired a household servant and took care of her mother full-time. Once Abby was asleep, she stayed up to write stories and pay bills.

Her mother was not Louisa's only concern. Anna and John Pratt were repeating Abby and Bronson's old pattern of moving from one untenable living situation to the next while John Pratt tried to gain a foothold in business. John's Transcendental childhood at Brook Farm could not have been the best foundation for a career in commerce, or fostered connections or mentors. Between households of their own, the boys and Anna squeezed into Orchard House or the Pratt farm for months at a time while John boarded near his current job and joined them on weekends, just as Bronson once had done. Anna, three-year-old Fred, and toddler John were living in Orchard House when Louisa returned from Europe in the summer of 1866.

Bronson, so patient and gifted with children, devoted himself to his grandsons, outfitting a tiny room with a salesman's miniature sample sofa, board games, and homemade toys. But by November, as cold weather drove the boys indoors and Bronson out on the road for a Western lecture tour, Louisa was finding it all too much and may have made it known. Anna and the boys moved to rooms in Boston that John Pratt already shared with a friend. Louisa was "sorry yet glad to have them go. Shall miss the dear babies but must have quiet for mother & writing."

The year wound down to a depressing end. Bronson returned from his tour "thin, sad, hungry & dirty." Their only Christmas presents were from Anna. "No one else thought of us. Seldom do." With Bronson home, Louisa had more time to write but little energy. "Had a fire in my room & fell to work, but the climate is so different here from where I was last year," she wrote, remembering Vevey and Laddie, no doubt, "that I had heavy colds all the time." She paid bills, "but never expect to see the end of em," so she cranked out two long stories and two sketches for four different magazines. When she totaled her yearly earnings, she found they had never been higher. But they were no match for years of accumulated debt. Her parents seemed to think debts dating back more than a decade— the six thousand dollars they owed when they left Boston in 1839, for instance—were long forgotten. They had forgotten them. But the family history of dependence upon handouts, hand-me-downs, food baskets, and borrowed funds, even borrowed homes, haunted Louisa.

"At Nice till May when . . . I went alone to Paris. 'Laddie' there, & we had a fine time for a fortnight," began Louisa's summation of 1866. "Wrote 12 tales in three months besides much care and company" was its conclusion.

~

After months of manic activity, Louisa's mood plummeted in January of 1867. Frank Sanborn reported that "Louisa Alcott has been alarmingly ill—not that her life was in danger but her writing organs—her head overworked and taking revenge by neuralgia." Louisa concurred: "Sick from too hard work. Did nothing all month but sit in a dark room & ache. Head and eyes full of neuralgia" was her journal entry in its entirety that month. "Ditto ditto" began February's two-sentence entry. March: "Ditto ditto. Got a little better at one time but tried to work & down I went again worse than ever." In April she could write "slowly mending. Nan came to pass the summer at the Pratts," but that was all. In May, the anniversary of her fortnight in Paris, Louisa was "still gaining, but all feeble." Sunny June finally brought to an end the six-month depression that had arrived with the new year. Perhaps more than her "writing organs" taking revenge, Louisa's unconscious may have trumped her conscience and declared a time-out for the Alcott family writing manufacturer, nurse, maid, and bill payer. She had always been up and down in bursts, but as she got older her swift childhood mood swings grew up to become longer and deeper alternating periods of energy and exhaustion. By July Louisa's engine was running again at full steam ahead. Visitors called, assignments poured in, and she took to the stage for charity in John Townsend Trowbridge's popular *Coupon Bonds*.

After the Civil War, the nationwide linking of railroads, the availability of cheap paper, and the efficient flatbed press made possible the expansion of a new mass culture. Smaller families replaced the huge broods of Bronson and Abby's generation. The Romantic and Victorian-era views of childhood as a unique period of life gave rise to a new literary market for children that became quite profitable. Eager to recover income lost to her long slump, Louisa started in on a series of Christmas fables for the publisher Horace Fuller—her first foray into the children's market since the publication of *Flower Fables* twelve years earlier. Halfway through, Uncle Sam May gave Louisa and May each fifty dollars to take a summer trip with friends to Clark's Island, off Plymouth, south of Boston. Louisa put half of her fifty dollars toward bills, justified the holiday for reasons of health, and felt the "harem scarem fortnight" did her some good. She was soon back at her desk to finish up the dozen fables to be called *Morning-Glories, and Other Stories*, so she could move on to the next project, "for bills accumulate & worry me."

The fall of 1867 brought a pair of offers of the kind she could only have fantasized in the old days. "[Thomas] Niles, partner of Roberts, asked me to write a girls book," she noted in her journal. "Said I'd try." The second offer, from Horace Fuller, was the job of editor at *Merry's Museum*, an illustrated children's magazine. She agreed to try that, too, and threw herself into both projects. Finding she had little appetite for writing children's literature other than fanciful fables, she let the novel slide and held on to *Merry's Museum* and Fuller's annual salary of five hundred dollars—which held out the holy grail of solvency. To edit the magazine and write one story and an editorial for each issue would leave enough time to write hundred-dollar stories for Frank Leslie and the pulp fiction market.

The editing job gave Louisa a rationale and means to break free of Concord. On the eve of her thirty-fifth birthday, five years after her last solo foray to Boston and eleven years after her first, Louisa packed up her books, her bed, and her laptop writing desk, and moved. Riding to Boston, possessions piled high on a wagon and Anna's five-year-old Freddie for company, was like "going to camp out in a new country." She hoped it would prove "hospitable & healthy."

The new arrangement turned out to suit everybody. May, commuting from Concord to teach drawing, came often to the top floor room on Hayward Place that Louisa called "Gamp's Garrett" after Sairy Gamp. Bronson spent the night there—whether on the floor or elsewhere in the building is unclear—after lectures or meetings of the Radical Club. Happiest of all was Louisa, who picked up where she had left off, going to cultural events, performing for charity, eating at whatever hour she was hungry, and scribbling late into the night.

"I am in my little room," she wrote in her journal at the advent of 1868, "spending busy, happy days, because I have quiet, freedom, work enough, and strength to do it. . . . My way seems clear for the year if I can only keep well." Since recovering from her six-month illness she had earned almost a thousand dollars. "Keep all the money I send, pay up every bill, get comforts, & enjoy yourselves," she wrote her mother. "Let's be merry while we may. And lay up a bit for a rainy day." In a postscript she asked after her father, using her flattering nickname for him: "Plato." "Don't he want new socks? Are his clothes getting shiney?" When the first potted hyacinth bloomed "white and sweet" in her room, she saw it as "a good omen—a little flag of truce perhaps, from the enemies we have been fighting all these years. Perhaps we are to win after all, and conquer poverty, neglect, pain, and debt and march on with flags flying." Louisa's mood was at high tide again.

The winter passed in frenzied activity. In January she acted the lead in a farce called *Naval Engagements*, was rewarded with flowers and applause, and stayed up half the night talking with a young friend in need of "older-sisterly advice." She went to bed to dream she was an opera dancer and "woke up prancing." A week later she knocked out two stories for Fuller, then raced to the Music Hall to hear Fanny Kemble read from *The Merchant of Venice*. She was invited to a private supper in Kemble's honor afterward, and as one of the "nobodies" (as the author of *Hospital Sketches* called herself) she watched the "lioness feed" from a distance, and bumped into her father's friend, the poet Dr. Oliver Wendell Holmes Sr. As she stared down on "the top of his illustrious head," he peered up at her and asked how many Alcott girls there were. "Four, sir," she answered (counting either Lizzie or her mother). "He seemed to catch my naughty thought, and asked, with a twinkle in his eye, looking up as if I were a steeple. 'And all as tall as you?'"

Apart from the fact that Fuller seemed to expect her to write the entire monthly *Merry's Museum* magazine, she happily turned out wholesome tales for his audience and lurid fiction for Frank Leslie's.

"Perilous Play," one of Louisa Alcott's most daring and personally revealing stories, was the last thriller she wrote. For a decade she had published as many as seven or eight "blood and thunder" tales a year, mostly anonymously but sometimes under a pseudonym. Eventually she commanded prices high enough to make a modest living by writing, no small feat then or now.

Few people outside the family knew that Louisa was the author of racy stories. Respectable young women were presumed not to be personally acquainted with the kinds of activities that transpired in pulp novels and stories—Louisa certainly was not. To write her thrillers she worked out a plot based on her reading, and adapted her own observation and experience to fill it with character and incident. She saw her accomplishment as financial, nothing to boast of in the literary line; members of the high-minded Alcott circle would never even have admitted familiarity with the lowbrow magazines Louisa devoured (along with the works of Shakespeare and Goethe), although some of them were probably not above reading the pulps surreptitiously. After *Little Women* made her name as a purveyor of wholesome reading for children, Louisa had even greater motive to conceal her scandalous past.

After she died, the thrillers were forgotten. Not until 1942, when Dr. Leona Rostenberg traced the pseudonym A. M. Barnard to Louisa Alcott, was her secret writing life exposed.*

---

* The rare book dealer Dr. Leona Rostenberg described the moment when she found the key to the missing stories in Houghton Library at Harvard University while accompanying Madeleine B. Stern on a research trip for Stern's 1950 biography of Alcott. Surveying the contents of a box of letters to Alcott, "[I] espied a small clutch of letters that seemed to belong together. As I picked up one of them, I immediately felt hot and cold and strangely faint." When she realized she knew the pseudonym, A. M. Barnard, and the publisher, James R. Elliot, she said, "my wild warwhoop shattered the

Since then, an astounding thirty or more thrillers by Louisa May Alcott have surfaced and been restored to print or published for the first time. One of these, a novella called *A Long Fatal Love Chase*, made the *New York Times* best-seller list for four weeks in the mid-1990s, over a century after the author's death.* At least a dozen more Alcott stories exist only as tantalizing titles in Louisa's journals. They may yet be located in attics or libraries, as the others were.†

Louisa achieved mastery of the relatively lucrative genre of the thriller by trial and error, teaching herself to tailor her gaudy fictional goods to a variety of markets. For each publication's readers—servants, shopgirls, or fine ladies—she tricked out her tales with suitable heroines (languid and glamorous or pert and spunky), with villains (lithe and leering or elegant and murderous), and with an assortment of heroes, relatives, pets, household trappings, and pitfall-laden landscapes as the stories required. For *Frank Leslie's Lady's Magazine* Louisa furnished high-end dresses specified down to yardage and the depth and number of tiers of ruffles. As deftly as she could retool her own worn wardrobe for a new season, Louisa could invent a disguise to conceal a character's identity or gender for dozens of pages while revolution was fomented, fraud plotted, or any number of variations played out.‡

By the time Louisa wrote "Perilous Play" at the end of the 1860s, she was so at home in the thriller genre that she cast aside her usual props

---

dignified silence of the manuscript room of Houghton Library." She and Stern went outside for "an intermission of congratulation, hilarity, and several cigarettes," then returned to their seats, where Rostenberg "meticulously copied every word." (Leona Rostenberg and Madeleine Stern, *Old Books, Rare Friends: Two Literary Sleuths and Their Shared Passion* [New York: Doubleday, 1997], 123.)

* *A Long Fatal Love Chase* was one of the long stories Alcott wrote during the winter of 1867.

† Missing titles include "King Goldenrod," "Hope's Treasures," "Painter's Dream," "Otilla's Oath," "Steel Bracelet," "A Phantom Face," "Laird of Leigh," "Faith's Tryst," "Monk's Island," "Agatha's Confession," "Our Sunbeam," and "Pea Blossoms."

‡ In "Enigmas" a woman disguises herself as a man and wins the love of a beautiful woman; in "My Mysterious Mademoiselle" the cross-dresser is a man. Alcott thrillers dealt with Mind Cure, Hindu Thuggism, and mesmerism. In stories for fashion magazines, "Betrayed by a Buckle" and "Fate in a Fan," Louisa has her characters use accessories for nefarious purposes. (*The Louisa May Alcott Encyclopedia*, ed. Gregory Eiselein and Anne K. Phillips [Westport, CT: Greenwood, 2001], 110–11.)

and costumes to produce a fresh, modern entertainment for the story-hungry readers of *Frank Leslie's Chimney Corner*.

The characters in "Perilous Play" were attractive but ordinary versions of May Alcott's friends, with nary a title in the bunch, not even Professor, or Doctor, or Bank Officer. The tale was set on plain old Clark's Island off Plymouth, where Louisa and May had vacationed with the group the summer before. (After "Behind a Mask," written upon her return from Europe, Louisa never again felt any need to use England or Europe as a dressy locale for fiction.) No family curses or secret chambers figured in "Perilous Play," only young adults picnicking on the banks of a harbor island on a sunny summer afternoon that turned stormy. The events in the story were the consequence of thoughtless play rather than nefarious deeds. The thrilling moments took place in the hearts of the story's lovers during a common mishap. No locked door, vertical cliff, or disparate social ranking kept the two apart—only the heroine's reluctance to disclose her feelings.

Like Louisa, Rose St. Just has her mother's dark looks and her father's proud bearing. An exotic and gorgeous version of the author, she sits apart from the rest of the group, reading the legend of *The Lotus Eaters*. The lotus is a narcotic; its users forget home and family and feel only a contented lassitude. For Louisa, to forget home and family was prerequisite to indulging in pleasure, at least sensual pleasure, something she might have come to understand under the influence of the opiates she used (legally) for headache, insomnia, "nerves"—also, probably, relaxation and, possibly, recreation.

The "play" of "Perilous Play" is the picnicking group's experiment with hashish-laced candies, offered around by a medical student. Rose takes a little, so discreetly that even Mark Done, whose eyes have strayed in Rose's direction all afternoon, doesn't realize it.

The drug will free Rose to admit her attraction to her admirer, but it takes the "peril" of the title to drag it out of her. Even alone together under sail trying to locate a stray member of the group, not until a sudden storm endangers their own lives does Rose respond—"surrender"—to Mark's aggressive entreaties that she confess her love. Finally she lets go her defenses and returns his kiss. Mark is an ordinary man, and under the sway of his larger dose of hashish his strength of character soon is no match for the lure of unconsciousness. It falls to Rose to keep Mark awake and the boat from getting swept from the harbor out to sea. After their rescue by a lighthouse keeper, while sailing back the next morning, Rose begs Mark not to let anyone know that she took the hashish. He will keep her secret, he says, if she will tell him why she did. "I hoped it would make me soft and lovable, like other women," she admits. "I'm tired of being a lonely statue."

The words could be taken as much for Louisa's own secret cri de coeur as her character's. She had chosen spinsterhood, fearing what she had seen of marriage: bad choices, love outlived, wives without rights, straying spouses, misery till death. When in fiction she envisioned a marriage that could succeed for a heroine like herself, the husband—Basil Ventnor in "Love and Self-Love," Geoffrey Moor in *Moods*, Cousin Walter in "The Sisters' Trial"—was usually disadvantaged in some way. Louisa was at ease only with men who were older like Emerson, younger like Laddic, or weak and in need of her comfort like John Suhre. In life Louisa may have been too proud to accept a younger lover (like Laddie) or an attractive lover of less substance (like a Mark Done), but she could dream up circumstances—playful and perilous—that allowed Rose St. Just to escape her and Louisa's own stony dignity.

"Rose, we have been near death together," says Mark. "Let us share life together, and neither of us be any more lonely or afraid." She extends her hand "with a look of tender submission," and he takes it, saying ardently, "Heaven bless hashish if its dreams end like this!"

To write a wish-fulfilling story like "Perilous Play" and get one hundred dollars for it gave Louisa a good deal of satisfaction, yet a visit to Anna and her two young boys reminded her of what she lacked. "We brooded over Johnny as if he were a heavenly sort of fire to warm and comfort us with his sunny little face and loving ways. She is a happy woman! I *sell* my children, and though they feed me, they don't love me as hers do."

Yet "Happy Women," a contribution to a column called "Advice to Young Women" written for the *New York Ledger* soon after the visit, made Louisa's case for the single life. The editor had enclosed with his request a hundred-dollar bill for inspiration. With the bill propped in front of her, Louisa described "the busy, useful, independent spinsters" she knew—"for liberty is a better husband than love to many of us." The short piece was the distillation of Louisa's thoughts not so much about spinsterhood but about the alternative. Pity for women who didn't marry was misplaced, she thought, and was better redirected to the legions of unhappily wedlocked. "The fear of being an old maid," she wrote, made "young girls rush into matrimony with a recklessness that astonishes."

Too late they realize that "the loss of love, happiness, and self respect is poorly repaid by the barren honor of being called 'Mrs.'"

The fulfilled single women Louisa went on to describe seemed like supportive roommates together defeating the loneliness of the independent life. At least three of them knew each other well: "L., a rich man's daughter," was Louisa's cousin and friend since childhood, Lucy Sewall. Having "tried fashionable life and found that it did not satisfy," L. studied medicine in Paris and London, and now, engaged in "truly womanly work," she "finds no time for ennui, unhappiness, or the vague longing for something to fill heart and life." M., Louisa's sister May Alcott, is "a brilliant, talented girl, full of energy, ambitions, and noble aspirations." Poor but attractive, M. had refused an offer of marriage from a wealthy man she liked but could not love, and says "people tell me I am foolish not to accept this good fortune, that it is my duty to accept it; that I shall get on very well without love and talk as if it were a business transaction . . . but I dare not sell my liberty." Instead, "with her one talent in her hand she faced poverty, cheerfully teaching music, year after year [May was teaching art] . . . and finding herself a happier woman for that act." The next happy woman was S., a city missionary as Abigail Alcott had been, who reaped her reward in the grateful smiles of the forlorn and looked forward to even greater treasures in heaven, as Lizzie Alcott had. "A.," of course, was Louisa Alcott herself,

> a woman of a strongly individual type, who in the course of an unusually varied experience has seen so much of what a wise man has called the "tragedy of modern married life," that she is afraid to try it. Knowing that for one of such a peculiar nature like herself such an experiment would be doubly hazardous, she has obeyed instinct and become a chronic old maid. Filial and fraternal love must satisfy her, and grateful that such ties are possible, she lives for them and is content.

Louisa went to bed a happy spinster and a hundred dollars richer—"to dream of flannel petticoats for my blessed Mother, paper for Father, a new dress for May, and sleds for my boys." If there was something for herself on her list, she didn't admit it in her journal. For Louisa, spending on the people she loved was not only satisfying but a means of control, however benevolent, a way to keep the people she loved bound to her more closely.

Bronson, who accepted Louisa's support without guilt or thank-you notes, turned up in Boston that late February of 1868 to attend an evening meeting of the Radical Club and to keep a morning appointment with the publisher Thomas Niles of Roberts Brothers to discuss his philosophical book *Tablets*. He had been laboring (some wit must have said "belaboring") over it for six years and felt it ready to be shared. Bronson saw Niles and from there returned to Concord, reporting the upshot of the meeting in a letter. Not only had Niles agreed to publish *Tablets*, the excited Bronson related, but Niles was counting on Louisa for the girls' story she had said she'd try (but had given up), and hoped to bring it out in September. Niles was banking on the author of *Flower Fables* and editor of *Merry's Museum* to do for Roberts Brothers what the hugely successful "Oliver Optic" series of boys' books had done for Lee & Shepard, two doors down on Washington Street, and what Mary Mapes Dodge's *Hans Brinker: or, The Silver Skates* and Horatio Alger's *Ragged Dick* were doing for their publishers.

Niles's marketing sense meshed with Bronson's long-held conviction that the story of the Alcott sisters would be great material for the kind of literature children needed, books about actual children rather than paragons. Together they pressured Louisa, who must also have known about authors hitting jackpots with appealing children's books. "They want a book of 200 pages or more," Bronson wrote, assuring Louisa of Niles's high estimate of her ability, growing reputation, and bright future. "He obviously wishes to become *your* publisher and *mine*. Now . . . come home soon and write your story." His trip seemed to have opened "a brighter page for us personally and pecuniarily," he said at the close of the letter that resigned Louisa to writing *Little Women* and making her fortune.* Bronson had avoided saying outright that Louisa should tell the family story out of a mercenary motive, but he recognized an opportunity when he saw it.

Abby's decline and pressure from Bronson succeeded in drawing Louisa to Concord ten days later. Spring weather would make Orchard House pleasant to live in, Concord was preferable to summer in the city, and she

---

* This letter has been characterized as proof that Bronson made publication of *Tablets* a condition of publishing Louisa's book for girls. By 1868 Bronson was an established popularizer of Transcendentalism. *Tablets* and his later books had respectable sales. The letter speaks for itself; no other evidence exists to support or refute the charge.

could save on rent. Once home, Louisa devoted herself to her mother and to the stories that had been promised, one for Fuller and two for *A Youth's Companion*. She put off the clamoring pulp fiction editors, reserving her imagination for the children's market. She was probably plotting *Little Women* in her head and was ready to tackle it when she received yet another nudge from Niles and Bronson. In early May she began to write *Little Women*, working at the tiny half-moon desk her father had built between the windows of her room that looked out over the Lexington Road.

Louisa had prepared the ground for *Little Women* in "The Sisters' Trial," the unpublished sketch "Two Scenes in a Family," and "A Modern Cinderella," a treatment of Anna and John Pratt's romance and marriage that had appeared in the *Atlantic*. She was willing, but not completely ready, to serve up her childhood in long form. She would have to live with it for weeks, delete the painful memories, repair others, and upgrade the poverty from grueling to genteel. The rest of the family was gung-ho: "Marmee [Abby], Anna, and May all approve of my plan," she wrote, "so I plod away, though I don't enjoy this sort of thing. Never liked girls or knew many, except my sisters, but our queer plays and experiences may prove interesting, though I doubt it."

What Louisa meant specifically about "this sort of thing" is unclear, but some fundamental choices went into it. She would use the realistic style of *Hospital Sketches*, not the fervid prose of the thrillers that she enjoyed writing more. As a result, *Little Women* was deemed an early work of "domestic realism" in the canon of American literature. An antidote to the fables and sentimental fiction of the pre–Civil War era, the realistic style was better suited to a country whose rose-colored glasses had been hurled to the ground and smashed to pieces. Louisa made another important—and risky—choice in her setting. Rather than put her childhood in the context of the romantic (and oddball) Transcendental era of her own childhood, she enhanced the tone of struggle inherent in the realistic style by setting it in the middle of the Civil War—not on the battlefield but on the home front. She took the risk of offending the South, but shrewdly limited it by never using the word *slavery*, and by using the word *battle* just once, metaphorically. The war was "where the fighting was," a vague danger far away.

Little Women was one of the first American novels to be set in the

Civil War period. Like the Vietnam War, the Civil War gave rise to works of art only several years after its close, when the immediate shock of it had been absorbed. Louisa sent Mr. March to war in the nonmilitary capacity of minister, as hers had been as a nurse; she also had the character of Marmee, based on Abby but with the edges smoothed, go to an army hospital to nurse Mr. March when he fell ill.

Many critics suggest that Louisa sent Mr. March away from home in *Little Women* because Bronson was such an eccentric model for a father, and his relationship with Louisa so freighted, that she preferred to exile him rather than depict him in her book. A better reason for Louisa's authorial choice was to set up the coming-of-age aspect of the story: with their father gone, the women of the family have to shoulder responsibility and mature, as military families did and continue to do. When their mother leaves to nurse their father, they are completely on their own. Having a patriarch would be, fictionally speaking, unworkable.

Little Women is modeled on a tale of pilgrimage, specifically John Bunyan's *Pilgrim's Progress*, the allegory so beloved of Bronson Alcott. The sisters have burdens to carry: their poverty, their inexperience, and their unique character flaws. They encounter shared obstacles and individual difficulties, and eventually find what they wished for at the outset, a happy Christmas and the best present of all, a reunited family.

Louisa chose to have the March family live in Orchard House rather than Hillside, where most of the "queer plays and experiences" she would adapt for the book had actually taken place. Wherever she went in the house in the infrequent moments she was not at her desk, she must have seen her sisters in their fictional versions, especially Lizzie—Beth in the book. In June she sent twelve chapters to Niles with a note agreeing to his suggestion of *Little Women* as the title of the first book. (She had used a working title, *The Pathetic Family*—meaning "worthy of sympathy," not "inadequate.") She suggested "'*Young Women*,' or something of that sort for No. 2, *if* there is a No. 2."

Niles "thought it *dull*," Louisa wrote in her journal of his response to the first twelve chapters; so did she, but by then the book had taken hold. She plowed ahead in a fever of invention unmatched since *Moods*, dressing her sisters' characters from her scrap bag of memories and imagination.

While the March* sisters of *Little Women* are in a sense all avatars of

---

* The name March is a play on Abby's maiden name, May.

Louisa, they are four distinct people. Each vivid personality has her own trajectory, set in motion from the tableau Alcott presents in the first paragraph.

> "Christmas won't be Christmas without any presents," grumbled Jo, lying on the rug.
>
> "It's so dreadful to be poor!" sighed Meg, looking down at her old dress.
>
> "I don't think it's fair for some girls to have plenty of pretty things, and other girls nothing at all," added little Amy, with an injured sniff.
>
> "We've got father and mother and each other," said Beth contentedly, from her corner.

Always conscious of her market, Louisa gave her plain, long-faced older sister a makeover, explaining to Anna that someone had to be beautiful. Someone had to be the heroine too. After years of trying to curb her pride, control her impulses, rein in her wild side (or sublimate it in fiction not meant for young eyes), Louisa finally gave herself approval in the sublime creation of Jo March. In the character of Laurie, the boy next door, she gave herself the brother she had always wanted.

On July 15, Louisa sent the ten remaining chapters of *Little Women* to Niles, along with the corrected page proofs of the first twelve. She had written 402 pages in ten weeks. Exhausted, she left with May for a two-week vacation in Gloucester with a clear conscience and the hope that *Little Women* would sell. Louisa had taken Niles's advice to retain the copyright, a new and unusual arrangement at the time, and the best business decision she ever made. When she received the final page proofs, she was surprised at how well the book read. "Not a bit sensational, but simple and true, for we really lived most of it; and if it succeeds, that will be the reason." Niles liked the finished book, too, and reported that several girls given early copies thought it splendid. Louisa knew that theirs was the best endorsement.

As a marketing move, Roberts Brothers published the work of both father and daughter, as Bronson had hoped, in September of 1868. Thirty-two years after *Conversations with Children on the Gospels* ruined Bronson's career, an edition of eight hundred regular and two hundred "deluxe" copies of *Tablets* came out to generous notices. Louisa's *Little Women* had materialized as a small red cloth-bound volume with the title and "L.M.

Alcott" inscribed in gold in an oval ring of Greek key design; inside were four illustrations by May Alcott. May Alcott's drawings received a critical drubbing, and viewed in retrospect they fare no better—and possibly worse—than they did in 1868. Her work would improve steadily with study and practice.

Little Women's future as a lasting world cultural phenomenon could not have been immediately apparent, but reviews, the first signs, were promising. The *Boston Daily Evening Transcript* hailed "Bronson Alcott's daughter, Louisa M. Alcott [as] unquestionably one of the best writers for the young that New England has produced for many years." The *Springfield Daily Republican* recognized that she had captured "the restless and confused period which divides the child from the woman" (a concept so new the word *adolescence* had not come into common use), which was "represented under four aspects with the four sisters." The *National Anti-Slavery Standard* took the March sisters seriously, as young women so rarely were taken, calling them "natural, human children, with good and evil impulses struggling . . . for mastery." The characters were so natural that they used slang "like real *American* girls who use frequently the word 'guess' as a substitute for 'think' or 'suppose.'"

The Sunday school library was a major source of reading material for many children of the era. "Capital," said the *Ladies' Repository*, "our Sabbath Schools will all want it." But while the *Ladies' Repository* reviewer allowed as how "the story is vivaciously told . . . it is not a Christian book." Church observance does not figure in *Little Women*; "Don't put [it] in the Sunday school library," warned the *Zion's Herald*. The reviewer for the *Eclectic Magazine* laid it on the line: "the majority of children's books consist of puling, do-me-good copy-book morality, calculated to turn the stomach of any sensible child. . . . Miss Allcott [*sic*] is too appreciative of the truly beautiful in childhood to attempt to preach them into stiff-backed, spiritless propriety."

By late October Louisa had escaped Concord and family for Boston and privacy. The first run of two thousand copies of *Little Women* was sold out and a second edition ordered; Roberts Brothers printed another four thousand five hundred copies before the end of the year. Sampson and Low of London had bought rights for an English edition due out in December—and could Louisa write the second volume for a spring release?

In her quiet room in Brookline Street she began the next day, buoyed by the flood of "pleasant notices and letters" that expressed affection for her little women. "[They] seem to find friends by their truth to life," she wrote, and stated her plan for writing Book 2. She set her goal as "a chapter a day, and in a month, I mean to be done." She came close to accomplishing the feat. *Little Women*'s "little success is so inspiring," she said, "that I now find my 'Marches' sober nice people, and as I can launch into the future, my fancy has more play." She picked up the girls three years after the end of Book 1, in peacetime and at marriageable ages, which made for a different kind of story. Louisa may not have realized what she had let herself in for by setting up Jo and Laurie as an inseparable pair in the first book: her readers (and her publisher) expected them to march to the altar in the second. "Girls write to ask who the little women marry," she complained, "as if that was the only end and aim of a woman's life. I *won't* marry Jo to Laurie to please anyone." Publishers took the readers' side.

> Publishers . . . insist on having people married off in a wholesale manner which much afflicts me. "Jo" should have remained a literary spinster but so many enthusiastic ladies wrote to me clamorously demanding that she should marry Laurie, or somebody, that I didn't dare to refuse, and out of perversity went & made a funny match for her. I expect vials of wrath to be poured out upon my head but rather enjoy the prospect.

The "funny match," Professor Bhaer, was not exactly a man after a teenage girl's heart, unless the girl was Louisa Alcott. He was learned and German like Goethe; older and wiser like Emerson; short, hirsute, and clever with his hands like Thoreau; and in his moral certainty, poverty, and dreamy scholarship he was pure Bronson.

Ultimately Louisa capitulated to the female mob and the publisher. She married off three of the sisters, perhaps out of spite, or for financial advantage, and gave Book 2 the title *Good Wives* (as it is still known in England, where it is frequently published in a separate volume). Her income was rising, but how much and for how long were uncertain. She had parents still in debt and plenty of earmarks for however much money she could get.

Louisa went at Book 2 like the winner of a marathon. Thinking she should try to pace herself, after two weeks she took a day off to go with her father to the Radical Club, where the minister John Weiss read a paper on woman suffrage. She had lunch with four writer friends, spent the afternoon at the Women's Club, and was back at work the next morning. By evening she felt as if she had had no break at all, and gave up the idea, admitting, "I am so full of my work I can't stop to eat or sleep, or for anything but a daily run."

Twelve days later she marked November 29 with a sober notation: "My birthday; thirty-six. Spent alone, writing hard. No present but Father's 'Tablets.' I never seem to have many presents, as some do, though I give a good many. That is best perhaps, and makes a gift very precious when it does come." Variants of the same lament over too few presents, followed by pious affirmations of acceptance, are found in Louisa's journals on all but the few gift-receiving occasions on which she takes tremendous delight in a windfall. As she asserts, a gift *is* genuinely precious to her when it comes. Still, in the sad words and brave rejoinder of thirty-six-year-old Louisa is the wounded three-year-old Louy made to trade her cake for her mother's kiss. Although it's not known when she wrote "Valley of the Shadow," the chapter about Beth's death (among the most affecting scenes in all fiction), it's probable that on her giftless birthday she would have been just past that point in the book—writing at her desk by lamplight as the days grew shorter and the shadows longer.

After Beth's death and its immediate aftermath, Louisa advanced the story by several years while maintaining its mood. Now Jo March is twenty-five and in her own lonely shadowed valley, with Meg absorbed in two children and Amy traveling in Europe with indulgent patrons. On a rainy afternoon Jo finds herself worshipping at a household shrine "up in the garret, where . . . stood four little wooden chests in a row, each marked with its owner's name, and each filled with relics of the childhood and girlhood ended now for all. Jo glanced into them, and when she came to her own, leaned her chin on the edge, and stared absently at the chaotic collection." In a poem that appears later in the book, she describes its contents.

"Jo" on the next lid, scratched and worn,
and within a motley store
Of headless dolls, of school-books torn,
birds and beasts that speak no more;
Spoils brought home from the fairy ground
only trod by youthful feet,

Dreams of a future never found,
memories of a past still sweet;
Half-writ poems, stories wild,
April letters, warm and cold,
Diaries of a willful child,
hints of a woman early old;
A woman in a lonely home,
hearing, like a sad refrain,
"Be worthy love, and love will come,"
In the falling summer rain.

Then, Louisa writes, "Jo laid her head down on a comfortable rag-bag" and cried "as if in opposition to the rain pattering on the roof. Was it all self-pity, loneliness, or low spirits? . . . Who shall say?"

She broke off writing in early December when, with Abby installed at Anna's and Bronson headed west, she closed up Orchard House. She was glad to be past the cold weather and hard work, and to leave Concord. Back in Boston she would bunk with May, who was in town studying and teaching art.

May did not share Louisa's taste for quiet corners. Taking advantage of her sister's largesse and fondness for indulging her, May talked Louisa into booking a "sky-parlor"—a penthouse—at the Bellevue Hotel on Beacon Hill opposite the Athenaeum. Eight stories high, the Bellevue was named for its spectacular vantage point overlooking the gold dome of the State House and the miles beyond. It was a temperance hotel and spa, with "the finest Turkish baths in the country" and "the second passenger elevator built in Boston." While Louisa loved having her younger sister for company, the surroundings didn't agree with her: "Had a queer time whisking up and down in the elevator, eating in a marble café, and sleeping on a sofa bed, that we might be genteel. It did not suit me at all. A great gale nearly blew the roof off. Steam pipes exploded, and we were hungry. I was very tired with my hard summer, with no rest for the brains that earn the money."

It was a strange place to write the ending of *Little Women*, but neither exhaustion nor exploding steam pipes could slow Louisa's pen. She rescues Jo from loneliness, marries her to Professor Bhaer, and kills off her rich Aunt March—who bequeaths her mansion to Jo. Jo and her husband found a successful school for boys based on Bronson's benevolent principles of education and equality. The Temple School flourishes in Louisa's pages under the name of Plumfield; Louisa provides a bountiful orchard as Providence had not at Fruitlands: "There were slow boys and bashful boys; feeble boys and riotous boys; boys that lisped and boys that stuttered . . . and a merry little quadroon . . . though some people predicted that his admission would ruin the school."

In fiction, integration (albeit the token variety) did not have to be the ruin of the school, even in the era of Reconstruction. At the end of the book Plumfield holds a party for Marmee's sixtieth birthday, the most lavish and successful Alcott-style party ever. After the presents are given, the boys disappear quietly: "The Professor suddenly began to sing. Then, from above him, voice after voice took up the words, and from tree to tree echoed . . . the little song Jo had written . . . from tall Franz and Emil to the little quadroon, who had the sweetest voice of all."

⌒

On the first of January, 1869, Louisa delivered *Little Women*, book 2, to Roberts Brothers and with May fled the Bellevue for a boardinghouse on Chauncy Street, on the unfashionable side of the Common. She was soon juggling demands for stories from Horace Fuller of *Merry's Museum* and Daniel Ford of the *Youth's Companion*, though "headaches, cough, and weariness" kept her from working as she once could, "fourteen hours a day."

In a gossipy letter sent in February to Ellen Conway (who with her husband, Moncure, had hosted Louisa in London), the beleaguered tone of the broken workhorse is replaced by the witty voice of the lighthearted Louisa who made her way in London society. She reports a late-night adventure with Theodore Tilton,* the editor of the Washington-based *Independent*, "who don't seem to be grown up yet." Tilton "came strolling in one rainy slippery Sunday evening . . . saying he was home sick, hungry &

---

* Talkative Tilton ignited the juiciest scandal of the day six years later when he exposed the affair of his wife with his friend, the prominent clergyman Henry Ward Beecher, younger brother of Harriet Beecher Stowe and father of ten. Tilton's titillating lawsuit was the best show in town for months in New York civil court and ended in a hung jury.

blue, would I come out for a walk and then take supper at the Parker House?" It struck Louisa as odd, and a bit daring, so she went. Over a "friendly dish o tea," Tilton proceeded to bend her ear for two hours "about everything under the sun—Muller Madonnas,* beer, religion, prize-fighters, his children and eternal damnation. It was as good as a play & I enjoyed it all the more because John Dwight & Henry Denny at their tables were evidently wondering—'What the deuce Louisa Alcott was doing drinking wine with a gay young party in a public house at ten o'clock on a Sunday night.'"

Duty called her back to Concord to reopen Orchard House in March. Her mother wanted to leave Anna's place, and her father wanted to be in his study. It was cold and dull there, and finding she could not write, she lavished attention on her mother and paid old debts. After more than a decade, the doctor's bill from Lizzie Alcott's last illness was finally paid; "every penny that money can pay,—and now I feel as if I could die in peace." Meeting the demand for her writing, however, left her no peace, and by April she described herself in her journal as doing "very poorly": "[I] feel quite used up. Don't care much for myself, as rest is heavenly even with pain, but the family seem so panic-stricken and helpless when I break down that I try to keep the mill going." And so she did. Despite the generous reserve in her bank account that allowed her to send two hundred dollars to Sam Sewall to invest, she continued to scribble for small sums, turning out two more tales for Leslie, and another two for Ford, while keeping up her *Merry's Museum* commitment. Roberts was pressing her for another book as well, but she put the publisher off. "Afraid to get into a vortex lest I fall ill," she wrote.

Book 2 of *Little Women* appeared on April 14, and the floodgates opened. Four thousand copies of the second volume had been preordered by bookstores; within two weeks, thirteen thousand copies had been sold (more than twice what Book 1 had sold in six months) as readers rejoiced at Meg's wedding, wept over Beth's death, and cried foul at Louisa's "perverse" choice of a mate for Jo. Louisa was famous. "People begin to come and stare at the Alcotts," she wrote. "Reporters haunt the place to look at the authoress, who dodges into the woods a la Hawthorne." In those early days of mass culture and literary celebrity, admirers thought

---

* The French painter Charles Louis Muller; later May Alcott studied with him in Paris.

nothing of knocking on the door expecting an audience with Miss Alcott. Residents of Concord brought every visiting relative to meet her and be welcomed. Letters from gushing "Jo-worshippers," complaints about Jo's refusal of Laurie, and requests for autographed photos piled up at the Concord Post Office.

To Louisa the avalanche of approval was junk mail to be sifted for checks from Roberts Brothers' account desk. No longer did she worry about the price of a silk dress or a straw hat, but the financial windfall from *Little Women* made barely a dent in her work schedule. Eager to capitalize on the book's success, Niles pressed her for another book, which Louisa provided by way of a serial for *Merry's Museum* (eventually to be issued in book form) called *An Old-Fashioned Girl*.

The book drew upon Louisa's working years in Boston as an impoverished relative of fashionable people. The heroine, fourteen-year-old Polly, is Louisa as a country cousin from a warm, picturesque farm family, the Mintons—the Alcotts with a settled residence. Polly's relatives, the wealthy Shaws, are headed by a good but preoccupied businessman father and an Anna Weld–ish mother who wants something every five minutes. Polly's older cousin Fanny runs with a materialistic crowd obsessed with appearance and matrimony; Fanny's brother Tom teases Polly mercilessly. But for all their faults Fanny, Tom, and their younger sister Maud are likable. Polly's challenge is to find her way to maturity while holding on to her own family's simpler habits and stronger values in the face of condescension and rejection. She eventually finds a respected place in the household, gains Tom's friendship, and teaches Fanny the value of work in giving purpose to life.

Louisa wrote the first installment of *An Old-Fashioned Girl* so afflicted by rheumatic symptoms that she had to work with her left hand in a sling and her right foot elevated on a chair. She lost her voice to laryngitis and suffered headaches so severe she could find relief only by taking laudanum, a tincture of opium that was the sole effective painkiller in the medical arsenal of the time. When critics complained of poor grammar in *An Old-Fashioned Girl*, Louisa said, "If people knew how O.F.G. was written, in what hurry and pain and woe, they would wonder that there was any grammar at all."

Six years pass between the two parts of the story. Twenty-year-old Polly now lives independently in the city. She teaches music and has a large female social circle—a sisterhood—reminiscent of Louisa's "Happy

Women." Polly takes her languishing cousin Fanny to meet the group, among them "Kate King, the authoress . . . a shabby young woman." Kate is a snapshot of Louisa Alcott in the wake of the success of *Little Women*: "Kate had written a successful book by accident, and happened to be the fashion, just then." She tells the others to "beware of popularity; . . . it is apt to be capricious," leaving the intoxicated possessor of it "gasping, like a fish out of water." Kate mugs as she delivers her speech; like Louisa in entertainer mode, she leaves everyone in stitches. But "Fanny took a good look at her, wondering if the time would ever come when women could earn a little money and success, without paying such a heavy price for them; for Kate looked sick, tired, and too early old."

Louisa had put together the second part of *An Old-Fashioned Girl* in her usual way, drawing from her reading, her experience, and everything she had observed. Tom Shaw, like reckless young men in so many novels of the time, has been expelled from college and is in debt. Mr. Shaw has been keeping secret his financial reverses and has to declare bankruptcy. Like Abby's father, Colonel Joseph May, the good man will pay back every penny he owes, selling everything he owns to do it, and begin again. Tom Shaw's fortune-hunting fiancée, another character familiar in contemporary fiction, ditches Tom. But he and his sisters Fanny and Maud equip themselves for the trials of poverty through the example and advice of Polly, who, among other things, goes through Fanny's closet to show her how she can rework old clothes into an entire spring wardrobe. Eventually Tom follows the path of Louisa's cousin Samuel Greele, going west to make money with Polly's brother Ned. And despite Louisa's making the case for the moral and social value of woman's work, in *An Old-Fashioned Girl* Polly is rewarded by Tom's love and proposal of marriage, and Fanny is restored to wealth and the man she has always loved. Louisa, like Kate King, was addicted to popularity, and knew better than to flout convention too much. She did, however, make little sister Maud a "happy woman" as an independent spinster.

Roberts had capitalized on the phenomenal success of *Little Women* by rushing another Alcott volume into bookstores: a reprint of *Hospital Sketches* bundled together with other stories under the title *Hospital Sketches and Camp and Fireside Stories*. It sold three thousand copies by the end of the year. Louisa gave Sam Sewall another one thousand dollars to invest, noting with satisfaction that she had twelve hundred dollars put away for a "rainy day, and no debts. With that thought [she could] bear neuralgia gayly."

Louisa turned the six installments of *An Old-Fashioned Girl* into a book in time for Roberts to publish it in spring. As always, she totaled her earnings as the year came to a close. They had reached an all-time high of $2,864; $2,154 of the total was from *Little Women*. Thirty-eight thousand copies had been sold.

FIFTEEN

HAPPY BEFORE I DIE

Gentlemen: Many thanks for the check for 2,500 dollars, which made my Christmas an unusually merry one," Louisa wrote. By early 1870, when *An Old-Fashioned Girl* was published to acclaim nearly equal to that for *Little Women*, the way was clear for Louisa to fulfill the last of the three vows she'd made at fifteen, when she shook her fist at a flock of crows and announced, "I'll be rich, and famous, and happy before I die, see if I won't!"

At thirty-seven she was rich and famous; now an appealing opportunity to pursue happiness presented itself. Alice Bartlett, an independently wealthy young friend of May Alcott, invited May to accompany her on an extended trip to Europe. May loyally asserted she would go only if Louisa could join them, and Louisa jumped at the chance. Five years earlier she'd had barely a week to prepare for a trip to Europe made possible by the thankless job of catering to a dull invalid. This time she had both the pleasure of anticipation and the luxury of long preparation. She would be traveling first-class, on her own terms, with charming companions.

On the eve of their departure for New York to meet Alice, their boardinghouse mates on Pinckney Street gave a party for the two sisters. There were dozens of presents, dancing, a big cake—and a second fuss the next day at the station, where "half a dozen devoted beings" turned up to see them off. Her parents had made a farewell visit to Pinckney Street before the festivities had begun. Bronson perspicaciously presented Louisa, the moneymaker, with a pocketbook, and May, the lover of beauty and self, with a hand mirror. Abigail waved her handkerchief gaily as she and Bronson were walking away, but at the corner Louisa saw her wiping tears with it. Both of them knew she might never see her two daughters again.

That she might permanently escape to the freer air of Europe seems to have been a wild hope in the back of Louisa's mind. Her father could do perfectly well without her. Appreciative lecture sponsors feted Bronson all over the West; as a peddler of shiny new ideas he had forged his path and developed his connections over many years. At home, his platonic admirers always included an intelligent young woman. His current favorite in the parade of distinguished female intellects that began with the assistants at the Temple School was Ellen Chandler, a youngish teacher from Framingham. Even Louisa's devotion to Abby need not stand in the way of Louisa's attempt to have her own life, if Anna and the loyal (if fickle) Bronson were near.

John Pratt, whom Louisa had come to love as a brother over the ten years of his marriage to Anna, traveled to New York with her and May, accompanied also, it turned out, by Louisa's literary celebrity: on the way an eager boy vendor on the train pressed her to buy *An Old Fashioned Girl*. She told him she didn't care to read it, but he insisted, "Bully book, ma'am! Sell a lot; better have it." John Pratt explained that Louisa had written it, "and his chuckle, stare and astonished 'No!' were great fun." So was discovering the case of champagne sent to their cabin by Waldo and Lidian Emerson's son Edward. Their boat, the French *Lafayette*, was one of the new steamships built after the Civil War and designed for the comfort of the well-heeled hordes of passengers making the Grand Tour.

The route had been well marked, beginning in the 1830s, by the hardier artists and writers who had preceded the new rich of the Gilded Age. The tourists who visited Europe now clung to their *Murray's Handbooks*, the *Fodor Guides* of the day. Undoubtedly Louisa realized that her letters home—lightly fictionalized—could, like Mark Twain's *Innocents Abroad* and her own *Hospital Sketches*, serve as the basis for another best seller. *Shawl-Straps*, named for the popular carpetbags made from the same wool paisley patterns used for shawls, would be its title. She was not planning to be known only as a writer of books for children.*

---

* Louisa might have followed Twain's lead into lucrative travel writing, but Twain followed hers into the children's market with *The Adventures of Tom Sawyer*, published in 1876.

As she always would on ocean voyages, Louisa spent much of her time below deck, an experience she would render in *Shawl Straps*, when a seasick sufferer asks, "If steamers are named the 'Asia,' the 'Russia,' and the 'Scotia,' why not call one the 'Nausea?'" But fandom followed her even to her cabin: a group of little girls "came in a party to call on me, very seasick in my berth, done up like a mummy." In contrast to her own woozy state, she wrote home, May "poked about more, and was liked by all," adding that "there were no beaux except fast N[ew] Y[ork] men, so she had no flirtations." This may have been welcome news to Abby, who joked that May had been engaged twenty-five times. In her own first letter home, May put a wry spin on her report of a couple of days of nausea, calling it a good "spring cleaning" that left her comfortable for the remainder of the trip. Now she and Alice were using their bottles of champagne as stakes in shipboard games of whist.

Twenty-three-year-old Alice Bartlett, an experienced traveler who spoke French and Italian, proved as likable and solicitous as she was adventurous. She had special need of respite. Within the space of three years she had lost her father, her mother, and her younger brother—her only sibling. Like so many Americans in the postwar period, she went to Europe trailing a wake of grief. Thirty-year-old May, liberated from teaching art and helping at home, and thirty-seven-year-old Louisa, exhausted from writing, were also primed for indulgent pleasures.

After a twelve-day voyage they landed in Brest, on the Brittany coast, and by nightfall were settled four miles south, in Morlaix. Louisa wrote home the next day while seated at an open window overlooking the square, "enjoying the queer sights and sounds" as the air resounded from the "rattle of many wooden shoes on the stones." Market women were "selling queer things, among which [were] snails," to buyers who picked out the flesh from the shell with pins. "[May is] in heaven [having] raptures over the gables, the turrets with storks on them, the fountains, people and churches. She is now sketching the tower of St. Melanie, with a crowd of small boys round her enjoying the sight, and criticising the work."

The next day they boarded a ramshackle carriage for Dinan, just south of Saint-Malo on the Breton coast. Louisa's account of the ride is rich with Dickensian characterization, from the humpbacked driver who "ya-hooped" at horses to the garrulous fellow passenger who "gabbled to Alice as only a tipsy Frenchman could, quoted Poetry, said he was Victor Hugo's best friend, and a child of nature."

Louisa judged Dinan the quaintest town she had ever seen. Their elderly whiskered landlady, Madame Costé, welcomed them "with rapture"—*rapture* being a word that came frequently to Louisa when in Europe. Mme. Costé's state of mind could be attributed not only to the recommendation of Mrs. Lodge (who stood with Cabots and Lowells at the apogee of Boston society) but also to the arrival of the celebrated Louisa Alcott herself—as she would discover everywhere she went. Her rooms would have the best views and would be as luxurious as Anna Weld's had been; no servant quarters for Miss Alcott, ever again.

The dollar's standing was as high as Louisa's. Their plummy dose of luxury was costing just three dollars a day for all, Louisa was quick to note. She was still insecure of her future earning power. To her parents she justified the luxury in terms they would approve. "It would be worth that to get the sun and the air alone, for it is like June, and we sit about with open windows, flowers in the fields, birds singing and everything lovely and spring like." In a postscript not meant to be shared with neighbors or cousins, she confided, "This is to be one of our lucky years, and this trip a success if things go on as well as they have begun, for not a single hitch have we had from the time we left Boston. It don't seem possible that a fortnight could do so much, and put us in an entirely new scene."

She later reported two pieces of news. One was the extravagance of ordering a new walking suit of rich, silvery silk from Paris, at only ninety cents a yard; a Parisian dressmaker living in Dinan was making it for her. The other news was that she had found a doctor who seemed to know what her trouble was. Her leg had been acting up until she couldn't bear it. She'd been told of an excellent English doctor in Dinan, and after two solid weeks of misery, finally rushed off to see him one day, and asked for "something to sleep." Her new adviser was Dr. William Kane, "a handsome hearty gray headed Englishman" who had been an army surgeon in India. On learning that Louisa had been an army nurse, he told her he would be honored to cure her. Louisa found the wealthy, sixtyish bachelor kind and good-humored, the older nurturing sort of man Louisa found good company, like Emerson and Thoreau (though Kane was hardly of their stature). Kane became a regular companion; Alice and May called him Louisa's beau and teased her about their supposed romance.

Kane's diagnosis of Louisa's leg pain was rheumatism "in the membrane next the bone," more painful than dangerous. He advised her to keep warm, stay off her feet, and take Iodine of Potash [potassium], and opium to get to sleep. Louisa wrote Anna that she did it all and felt better right away. Perhaps she was helped as much or more by the regular dose of alcohol in which the small amount of potassium was dissolved. Kane also advised Louisa to get plenty of fresh air. "So I take my potash three times a day, drink wine, eat like a pig, and ride when I go out, for it hurts me to walk." The advice proved salutary. "I begin to sleep without opium, and the girls [say] I'm growing fat and rosy." In fact, all three of them were blooming. "I think its the wine. Ha! ha!"

The improvement in her health allowed Louisa to share the pleasures of French provincial life with May and Alice, a giddy pair. Alice "has just grabbed May," Louisa wrote as she closed a letter home, "and cut off a bit of her hair. A. is the strongest and she whacks May around like a doll." A few days later, she noted their preparations for a visit from Kane and his niece, sounding fairly giddy herself. "May is primping and A. is putting on her silk dress. The handsome old doctor is to be fascinated by some of us; it don't matter much which, and then we can travel in style with an M.D. in our train." In the eyes of French readers of *Les Quatre Filles de Docteur March*, its author was greater ornament to the entourage than any M.D. Throughout the trip Louisa was treated like royalty, admired from a respectful distance. After harassment by too-familiar fans in America, European-style celebrity was a great relief.

A report on "the health of her Highness Princess Louisa" two weeks later included an important update.

> Dr. Kane . . . [says] my leg trouble and many of my other woes, come from the calomel they gave me in Washington. He has been through the same thing with an Indian-Jungle-fever, and has never got the calomel out of him. The bunches on my leg are owing to that, for the mercury lies around in a body and don't do much harm until a weak spot appears when it goes there and makes trouble. I don't know anything about it, only [my] leg is the curse of my life.

Kane's account of mercury's action in the body was inaccurate, but his knowledge that mercury had damaging effects was not surprising. At the time Louisa was prescribed calomel, many physicians already considered it therapeutically useless as well as dangerous. In 1863, the surgeon general of the Union army ordered calomel removed from all army hospital supplies, but opposition among doctors (who had nothing else to offer) was so great that the order was never enforced and the use of calomel continued through the end of the war.

Dr. Kane's explanation seemed to ease Louisa's physical and mental suffering, in part from the satisfaction of having a plausible diagnosis, in part from the assurance that she had sacrificed her health for a noble purpose. She also took heart from Kane's story. If iodine of potash had cured him after three months, why shouldn't it cure her? "It is simple, pleasant, and seems to do something to the bones that gives them ease, so I shall sip away and give it a good trial," she declared.

In mid-June the women resumed their travels, heading for Switzerland by way of Tours and Blois. Louisa found the latter dusty and "soldierly"; the military was evidence of the imminent Franco-Prussian War that would break out in July. If the three travelers had planned to visit Paris (which seems likely) and to see Laddie there, the unrest that culminated in the Paris Commune of 1871 would have kept them away. If a letter from Laddie was sent to Blois to warn them off, Louisa would have destroyed it along with the "merry little notes" he had slipped under her door so many years ago. She did record that on retrieving her mail in Blois, she was annoyed to discover two copies of *Moods* from an unauthorized reissue of her novel that A. K. Loring had printed to cash in on her *Little Women* celebrity. Louisa's feeling that she should never have cut *Moods* to suit Loring had not changed. Her sense of violation was so powerful that she took umbrage even at the author's photograph Loring had chosen for the back cover. She declared it "horrid" and sent it "floating down the Loire." That Loring had not sought her consent particularly enraged her: "The dreadful man says that he has a *right to print as many editions as [he] likes for fourteen years!* What rights has an author then I beg to know . . . ? If the law gives over an author and her work to such slaverery [*sic*] . . . I shall write no more books but take in washing, and say adieu to glory." In fact, the edition made a nice sum for Louisa—from buyers who mistook it for a new work.

After Blois the threesome made a one-day stopover in Orléans, where Louisa bought some Joan of Arc mementos for Anna (the two had acted out the martyr's story), then hopscotched across France toward Geneva.

May wrote of "losing her wits" at the sight of the stained-glass windows in Tours cathedral, and of how the "immensity" of both the Le Mans cathedral and Tours struck her with such awe that "it seems disrespectful to enter without falling on ones knees, like all the peasants, and saying a prayer to the good God who put it into the mind of man to make anything so wonderfully beautiful." Louisa thought less of French Catholicism, to judge from the distaste with which she described the "mumbo jumbo" executed by the "red, purple, and yellow priests" they observed at vespers.

Arriving in Geneva felt like a homecoming to Louisa, absent the "Weld incumbrances" of her previous visit, but also without Laddie, who had made it so memorable. The famous Metropole Grand Hotel overlooking the Plaza was as grand as its name, and after two weeks in their traveling suits the three women were glad to change into their best gowns. "We are living in such perfect luxury," May wrote her father, "that Lu often says to me, 'Can this be the poor Alcotts traveling about and doing just as they like?' And it really does seem too good to be true." With Alice eager to visit relatives in Bex, at the opposite end of the lake, and Louisa's memories of nearby Vevey calling, they cut their stay short and took the boat the next morning. By midday they were in their rooms at the Pension Du Rivage, a short walk from Pension Victoria. Louisa had caught a cold during their long trek across France and needed rest when they arrived, but Vevey restored her as few other places could. Revisiting the romantic view, she wrote wistfully, "tis 'morning on the mountains' just now, and it is very sweet for July 2nd."

She looked through mail from home with reassuring news of book sales and requests for new stories, but was in no mood to write anything but replies to letters. She ignored the flood of fan mail and press clippings her mother forwarded at Louisa's expense. "Don't send me any more letters from *so cracked* girls," she wrote back. "The rampant infants must wait." She had been juggling her business affairs with little break since the start of the trip, corresponding with Sampson and Low in London about the English edition of *An Old-Fashioned Girl*, "very handsome, scarlet and gold with gilt edges and type that would delight father," reviewing publishers' statements from Niles, and scanning investment reports that Bronson sent along. The man who had waited for Providence to provide during the first sixty years of his life kept a watchful eye on it when it finally did.

The sense that she had been appropriated for the benefit of others had been a recurring theme since she'd left home, and in midsummer she expressed it in a satirical poem, "The Lay of a Golden Goose," about a poultry yard upstart, product of a "Transcendental nest," whose triumph turns to nightmare as more and more golden eggs are demanded, and at last is forced to flee.

So to escape too many friends,
Without uncivil strife,
She ran to the Atlantic pond
And paddled for her life.

Louisa's sense that she was loved more as a moneymaker than a daughter coalesced in a powerful and harrowing dream that she recounted to her mother in detail. In the dream she had returned to Concord alone and had made her way from the station to the Lexington Road. As she came around the corner, she "found the scene so changed" that she didn't know where she was.

Our house was gone, and in its place stood a grey stone castle with towers and arches and lawns and bridges very fine and antique. Somehow I got into it without meeting any one of you, and wandered about trying to find my family. At last I came across Mr. Moore [the neighbor from whom the Alcotts had bought Orchard House] papering a room, and asked him where his house was? He didn't know me and said "Oh! I sold it to Mr. Alcott for his school . . ." "Where did Mr. Alcott get the means to build this great concern?" I asked. "Well, he *gave* his own land and took the great fortune his daughter left him, the one that died some ten years ago." "So I am dead, am I?" says I to myself, feeling so queerly. ". . . Mr. A has a fine College here," said Mr. Moore papering away again. I went on wondering at the news, and looked into a glass to see how I looked dead. I found myself a fat old lady with grey hair and specs. . . . [Father] didn't know me and I was grieved and troubled at being a Rip Van Winkle. I cried and said I better go away and not disturb anyone, and in the midst of my woe, I woke up.

Louisa was quick to suggest several sources of her "ally-gorry-cal-wision": the "cowcumbers" she had eaten at tea the day before or the real glimpse she'd had of her aging self in a barbershop mirror. She chose not to acknowledge the dream's overwhelmingly elegiac and sacrificial aspects. In the dream her father is young and strong, and surrounded by the kind of frolicking boys Louisa loved to have near. Her father's longings and some of her own—for health, youth, and spirited boys—are fulfilled for him, not her; her fortune makes his dream possible. And even as her value as a provider is confirmed, her real self—the living, breathing "Louy," the brightest, quickest, and funniest of the Alcott girls—is killed off, stripped even of her name. She is simply the Alcott daughter who "had died some ten years ago," confused with her very dissimilar sister Lizzie.

Louisa and May would remain in Vevey for three months while Alice Bartlett visited relatives, watching the town fill with refugees waiting out the Franco-Prussian War, much as Laddie had done five years before during an earlier Polish phase of the great European nationalist movement of the time. Vevey was "full of Spaniards," Louisa wrote home in August, "all plotting and planning some revolution"—and Americans largely oblivious to the armies marching across Europe except as they interfered with travel plans.

Nothing survives in Louisa's journals or letters to suggest whether her hopes of seeing Laddie had brought her to Vevey, but a passage in the article published a few years later as "My Polish Boy" implies that the disappointment was keen.

> Lake Leman will never seem as lovely again as when Laddie and I roamed about its shores, floated on its bosom, or laid splendid plans for the future in the sunny garden of the old chateau. I tried it again last year, but the charm was gone, for I missed my boy, with his fun, his music, and the frank affection he gave his "little mamma," as he insisted on calling the lofty spinster who loved him like a half a dozen grandmothers rolled into one.

Just as no real Laurie awaited Louisa in Vevey, the vibrant young woman who had joyfully celebrated her thirty-third birthday there was also missing. Louisa's time for romance seemed to have passed. Her remaining hope for happiness depended upon unreliable health, a problem she shared with many of her contemporaries compromised by childhoods of poor nutrition—hers was much worse than most—and who suffered chronic or recurring effects of acute diseases for which treatment or cure was unknown.

By September Louisa, May, and Alice were making plans to leave Switzerland as soon as it was safe to travel to spend the winter in warm Italy. Napoleon III had been defeated, Paris was under siege by the Prussians, and all of Europe was in turmoil. They could not be certain how long they would stay in Rome and where they would go afterward. The steady flow of checks from Roberts Brothers meant that no urgent decisions need be made, and Louisa was in no hurry to pick up her pen. The moneymaker informed the family:

> I am afraid I shall not write till I get home, for all I do is scribble odds
> and ends as notes, and dawdle around without an idea in my head. Alice
> says no one does anything in Italy; so after another six months of idle-
> ness, I may get back . . . to work. In the spring, one of us will come home
> to run the machine. I fancy it may be May if I can make up my mind to
> stay, for Alice can't remain without duenna, and I can be one and also
> *pay my own way.*

Louisa's justification for remaining in Europe to chaperone Alice seems disingenuous, given that Alice had originally invited only May to accompany her. The truth seems closer to what Louisa wrote next: "A year of pleasure at A[lice]'s expense [generously supplemented by Louisa] is all May should expect or accept *I* think, and she is ready to fall to again, being grateful for sips of fun. I don't want to stay, but if I'm not tip top by spring, I should feel as if I ought, for fifteen years' mischief cant be mended in twelve months." Part of the mischief that unstinting labor had wrought upon Louisa was her need to rationalize (to herself and to everybody else) rest and pleasure as necessities for health.

Less than two weeks later the trio left for Italy, enjoying "a splendid journey over the Alps and [to Lago] Maggiore by moonlight," followed by sun-soaked "heavenly days." One was followed by a magical evening in Lugano, where their private hotel balcony overlooked the opera house next door and offered a direct view of the stage through an open window. "My Nan can imagine with what rapture I stared at the scenes going on below me," Louisa wrote home, "and how I longed for her as I stood there wrapped in my yellow bed-quilt, and saw gallant knights in armor warble sweetly to plump ladies in masks, or pretty peasants fly wildly from ardent lovers in red tights."

By the time they arrived in Rome in early November, the winter rains had begun, but May was once more "in bliss with lessons, sketching, and her dreams," while Alice, whose relatives kept a house in Rome, slipped into a familiar routine of visits and sightseeing. To Louisa, the eternal city "always oppressed with a sense of sin, dirt, and general decay of all things," though the fault was not entirely Rome's. Iodine of potash had not done the trick after all. "Not well," she admitted, "so saw things through blue glasses." Louisa also confessed that proximity to the Papal See brought out the straight-talking Yankee in her. A month earlier, in the final act of the Risorgimento, the city-state of Rome had been annexed to the new Kingdom of Italy, leaving the pope temporal ruler only of the Vatican. "The Pope," she wrote her father, "sulks in the Vatican pretending to be a prisoner, which pretense deceives no one." The cardinals were just as bad, "seldom seen but go about in close carriages looking very grim and plotting with all their crafty old evils how they may upset the King."

The six-room apartment overlooking Piazza Barberini, rented for six dollars a month, was cozy and warm, a young woman came in daily to cook and clean, and the famous author of *Little Women* was quickly taken up by the expatriate artists' colony. Among her new friends were the actress Charlotte Cushman and her romantic partner Emma Stebbins, a sculptor whose statue of Horace Mann stood outside the Boston State House. (A few years later Stebbins would create one of the greatest works of nineteen-century American sculpture, the angel atop the Bethesda Fountain in Central Park in New York.) A titled crowd also courted Louisa. "The artists were the best company, counts and princes very dull," Louisa opined, although apparently not all of them were: she later traveled in the company of the cultured Baroness de Rothschild, perhaps the richest woman in Europe.

Not long after her arrival in Rome the eminent Miss Alcott was invited to sit for the distinguished painter George Healy, a portraitist whose most recent commission had been Pope Pius IX. The Alcotts were acquaintances of Healy, who was from Boston. Louisa enjoyed the sittings and Healy's gossip about his other famous subjects, among them not only insignificant bishops, cardinals, and royals, but also some of her heroes:

Presidents Pierce and Grant, Abraham Lincoln, and her neighbor Nathaniel Hawthorne.

Healy's portrait is the best depiction of Louisa, more appealing than
later photographs that look self-conscious, frumpy, or sad. Healy's Louisa
is an imposing figure, ascetic, fine-boned, self-possessed, with a slight
(fashionable) frizz to her hair, a vivid flush across her cheeks, and lips set
firmly together as if suppressing a witty, possibly cutting remark. The face
is sharply angled, the prominent nose slightly curved, and the huge dark
eyes stare straight into the viewer's own, intense and serious, like her eyes
in the daguerreotype made in her late teens. Whatever the private
thoughts of the sitter, the result is the portrait of a personage to be reck-
oned with. The portrait, given to Louisa by Healy in exchange for publishing advice for his aspiring novelist daughter, was shipped to Orchard
House and hangs there still. When it arrived, Bronson found it unflattering, "the flesh . . . haggard and the features too elongated for a true lifelike
likeness."

The great flood that inundated Rome three days after Christmas
stirred Louisa to send to the *Boston Daily Evening Transcript* an account
of the city's dramatic transformation. Their apartment was far from the
river, but just to the north the Piazza del Popolo was a vast lake. After
Louisa and May walked a few blocks to the Piazza di Spagna, "It seemed
as if [they] were in Venice," she reported. Her eyewitnessed scenes were
supplemented with the pathetic and thrilling news that "In the Ghetto, at
the Tiber's edge . . . dozens of people drowned in their basements or were
carried away by the rushing waters." Louisa confessed to taking a morbid
pleasure in the calamity. "Being a Goth and Vandal, I enjoy it more than
chilly galleries or mouldy pictures."

Just as the floods receded, Louisa learned—while glancing through an
American weekly published in Rome—that her brother-in-law had died
the month before. John Pratt had been sick for barely a week, and the seriousness of his illness went unrecognized until almost the end.* "You
need not be told what he was to me," Louisa wrote her widowed sister
Anna, or "how I mourn for him, for no born brother was ever dearer. . . .
He did more to make us trust & respect men than anyone I know & so

* There has been speculation about John Pratt's illness, but the cause of his death is not
known. Without antibiotics any infection could have spread quickly and killed him.

with him I lose the one young man whom I sincerely honored in my heart."

To her cousin Lizzie Wells, doing her best to fill in for Anna's absent sisters, Louisa expressed her anguish at being so far away, yet she seemed to be in no hurry to return. "Annie bears her loss so beautifully that it makes it possible to stay away now in order that I may be more useful by & by. But you know how hard it is for me to be even in Rome when my heart is at home & everyday a burden until I can come." She was anxious about Abby's health and spirits as well. Bronson had been on a lecture tour when John died, absent, as he so often was, when Abby needed him. "I ache to go to her," she wrote Wells, "but winter, distance, health & my duty to Alice hold me till April. I think God will keep my Marmee for me because I couldn't bear [not to keep] my promise to close her dear eyes. Annie says she is not well & so I dread another loss before I have learned to bear the last."

She plunged into *Little Men*, "that John's death may not leave A. and the dear little boys in want." The idea that it was up to her to provide for Anna and the boys suited her sense of duty and devotion, as well as her need to be the central figure in her family. "In writing and thinking of the little lads, to whom I must be a father now, I found comfort for my sorrow," she wrote. In no hurry to return to them, she would be an absent father, providing money for their futures.

The new motive energized Louisa as nothing else had in months. Her earlier "scrawls and doodles" had included notes toward a long-promised sequel to *Little Women*, perhaps inspired in part by her powerful dream about returning to Concord to find her father running a school for boys. She picked up the March family not long after the end of *Little Women*. Jo, now the wife of Professor Bhaer, is a mother of two, like Louisa's sister Anna. Jo's children are girl and boy twins, Daisy and Demi; Jo is also surrogate mother to many more boys at the school she named "Plumfield," a close approximation of "Fruitlands." The children Louisa knew best were her nephews; she loved the wildness of boys, and *Little Men* was a bid for their readership. Among her large cast of Plumfield boys some are polite, some gruff, some doted on, and others starved for affection. (However, for what appear to be commercial considerations in the racially unsettled period of Reconstruction, "the little quadroon who sang sweetest of all" in *Little Women* is no longer at Plumfield.) The boys' inspiring tutor, modeled on Thoreau, is an attractive young man who takes nature as his textbook. Though its pastoral setting is more idealized, *Little Men* is every bit as domestic a novel as *Little Women,* full of high jinks, crises, and moral lessons dispensed sweetly but firmly by the wise, Marmee-like woman Jo has become. In *Little Women* Louisa paid homage to Abigail Alcott. *Little Men* is her tribute to Bronson Alcott, whose theories of education and whose long-ago hopes for communal family life come to fruition in Louisa's improved utopia; at Plumfield, unlike Fruitlands, everyone is warm, comfortable, and well fed.

⌒

By February, Louisa was quite enjoying herself. Carnival crowds lined the Corso by night to watch riderless horses race from Piazza del Popolo to Piazza Venezia, and invitations to elegant parties came pouring into the pleasant apartment on the Piazza Barberini. But with *Little Men* almost complete, Louisa decided to start home. Fourteen months was a long time to be away. Alice Bartlett would be leaving Europe, and with her would go any pretense that Louisa was her duenna.

Louisa and May made their way to London, where *Little Men* was scheduled for publication on May 15, three weeks ahead of the American edition. Alice Bartlett sailed on May 11, and after a busy month visiting friends and showing May and the city off to one another, Louisa left her sister behind in London for a half year of study and adventure. Later May would return to the National Gallery to paint copies of Turner that the influential critic and tastemaker John Ruskin would call the best he had seen.

After another rough Atlantic passage haunted by an outbreak of smallpox that spread to her cabin-mate, Louisa reached port in passable health and to a grand homecoming. Thomas Russell, an abolitionist friend of the Alcott family and now the collector at the Boston Custom House, delivered her from the ship to the wharf in his official tug. There Bronson and the publisher Thomas Niles awaited "with a great red placard of 'Little Men' pinned up in the carriage." Fifty thousand copies had been sold before the book was out.

◁━━▷

SIXTEEN

SUCCESS

At Dinan, the first stop on her European trip with May, Louisa had been cautious with money, unsure of her financial prospects. By Geneva, when she found out the size of the checks coming in from continuing sales of the two books of *Little Women*, from her new title *An Old-Fashioned Girl*, and from the unauthorized reissue of *Moods*, she began to realize that she was wealthy. She booked the Metropole, Geneva's best hotel, and in Rome took an expensive apartment in a prime location. On her arrival home, when she saw the hoopla around *Little Men*, she felt sure that the Alcotts would never be in debt again.

Whether she would continue to write at her old pace, or at all, was open to question. She tabled her decision, in order to first take stock of the family's needs. Once they were met, she planned to act on her own need to escape Concord. Her father was no obstacle: Bronson Alcott was thriving on the attention he received as "the father of the little women" and a progenitor of the Transcendental movement. Ellen Chandler's occasional visits to his study for philosophical conversation made him feel young and enthusiastic. May was happily *Studying Art Abroad*, as she would name her little book on the subject, and learning, as its subtitle declared, *How to Do it Cheaply*. Louisa found her widowed sister Anna to be self-possessed and gracious, but thought that "under her sweet serenity is a very sad soul, and she mourns for her mate like a tender turtle-dove."

The truth, as Anna put it in her journal about a year after the death of thirty-seven-year-old John, was neither tender nor sweet.

> I do not feel resigned, and cannot see the justice of the removal of one so well fitted to live as John. I feel so disconsolate at times, so pitiful and wretched, that I cannot bear to think about it, and it makes me feel ashamed to have people praise my resignation. It is not that, but a sort of helpless feeling that I am in the hands of something stronger than myself, that is inevitable, and I must wait and look up and try to see the sun that is there.

Abigail Alcott had aged a great deal. The death of John Pratt, her daughter Anna's mainstay, was matched by the death of her brother Sam May, her rock of strength, the fearless foe of slavery and as Louisa wrote, "our best friend for years." Abby, the youngest of Colonel Joseph May's ten children, was the last survivor of the family. Louisa vowed she would never venture so far from her mother again, but she had made the same vow after her first European trip. Like the resolutions she had made in adolescence, to be "good" and to control her temper, she had made the vows sincerely but had not been able to keep them. Her drive to be independent had been too great.

Louisa herself enjoyed a full month of excellent health on her return. Sitting in the catbird seat vis-à-vis publishers may have had something to do with it. Two days after she reached Concord she polished off a piece of unfinished business in a note to James Fields, the editor of the *Atlantic Monthly*. His blunt response to her request ten years earlier for an assessment of her literary ability—"stick to your teaching"—had burned in her brain ever since. Fields's conviction that Miss Alcott would never succeed as a writer was underlined by his unasked-for loan of forty dollars to start up a school. Fields had been completely wrong, beginning with his prediction that Louisa would succeed at teaching; his forty dollars went down the drain with her last schoolroom. "Once upon a time, you loaned me forty dollars," she wrote him now, "kindly saying that I might return them when I had made 'a pot of gold.' As the miracle has been unexpectedly wrought I wish to fulfill my part of the bargain, & herewith repay my debt with many thanks." She must have been rubbing her palms together in anticipatory glee at Fields's reaction. Louisa was America's biggest literary celebrity now. Mark Twain was well known, and after the publication of *Tom Sawyer* in 1875 his renown, carefully cultivated on the model of Dickens, would rival Louisa's. Dickens and Twain enjoyed the spotlight. They appreciated what it could do for sales of books, and presented themselves well to audiences. While Louisa loved to act, she hated to enact herself. Besides, how could she possibly succeed in the role of Jo March? Fans who found their way to Orchard House were always disappointed (sometimes to the point of tears) to find an old curmudgeon instead of spunky Jo, but Louisa had no sympathy. "It looks like impertinent curiosity to me; but it is called 'fame,' and considered a blessing to be grateful for, I find. Let 'em try it." As a last resort, when no one but she and her mother were home and callers persisted in knocking or lurking, she had a ready defense. Costumed in apron and cap, and armed with the feather duster prop she had handy by the door, she played her own maid. Opening the door a crack, she would shake the feather duster in the face of the would-be intruder, announce indignantly that Miss Alcott was not at home, and slam the door.

If she happened to be outside watering plants with the garden hose when strangers advanced, she restrained a powerful impulse to turn it on them—but found that if she simply turned away they assumed that since the exalted Miss Alcott would never be performing such a menial task, this must be someone else entirely, and walked right past her. Avoiding local friends who showed off by bringing visiting friends and relatives to meet the Alcotts was more difficult. Sometimes she could slip out the back window to hide in the woods behind the house.

After a month in Concord, everything was getting on Louisa's nerves. She developed aches and pains and headaches, and couldn't control her bad moods and wickedly clever tongue. She turned again to morphine to bring on rest and respite. Finally, desperate to escape the family trap, she recalled May from London. "A year and a half of holiday is a good deal," she reasoned in her journal, "she can go back again when I am better." May brought with her a supply of pictures to sell and "interesting tales of the fine London lovers." Louisa left her to run Orchard House with two servants, plenty of money, and an expensive modern furnace. "Mother is to be cosey if money can do it," she said. "She seems to be now, and my long cherished dream has come true, for she sits in a pleasant room, with no work, no care, no poverty or worry, but peace and comfort all about her.... Thank the Lord!"

The royalty checks kept rolling in. In 1871 Louisa took in $7,654 from Roberts Brothers alone. To compare $7,654 in 1871 to today's dollar value is a tricky proposition. In terms of the consumer price index, $7,654 would translate to about $134,000. The GDP (gross domestic product) per capita, however, is a more accurate measure of an individual's economic power. In those terms Louisa was making well over $2 million a year, a better answer to the question of just how rich she was. By any measure, Louisa had enough to equip her father "with warm flannels, neat shirts, gloves, etc . . . , like a gentleman" for his tour of the West. Bronson and Louisa marveled together at the fine array when she supervised his packing. Louisa said, "[We] both laughed over the pathetic old times with tears in our eyes." Bronson had just turned seventy-three.

Louisa's own birthday that year was her fortieth. In the words of her first biographer, Ednah Dow Littlehale Cheney, a friend of the family (and Bronson's companion on those Boston Common walks in the 1850s), "Louisa had accomplished the task she set for herself in youth."

> By increasing toil she had made herself and her family independent; debts were all paid, and enough was invested to preserve them from want. And yet wants seemed to increase with their satisfaction, and she felt impelled to work enough to give up all the enjoyments and luxuries which were fitted to them after the necessaries were provided for. It may be that her own exhausted nervous condition made it impossible for her to rest, and the demand which she fancied came from without was the projection of her own thought.

There were other reasons that kept Louisa writing: she was still cooking up stories that were "knocking at the saucepan lid to get out." She didn't want to be known solely as an author of children's books; she wanted to write one book she could be proud of; she was curious to know how much money she could make. And she simply could not stop writing. Writing was a compulsion. In the next half decade Louisa would publish fifty-four separate titles—many of them stories, travel sketches, articles, or poems, but among them also the novels *Work, Eight Cousins, Rose in Bloom, A Modern Mephistopheles, Under the Lilacs,* and the second and third volumes of *Aunt Jo's Scrap-Bag*. She wrote her hilarious satire of Fruitlands, "Transcendental Wild Oats," in 1873, and tossed off "My Rococo Watch," a story commissioned by the Elgin Watch Company in 1874, probably in a single sitting.

Louisa's enormous literary output is all the more remarkable because her compulsion to write alternated with writer's block. To produce a piece of writing she could either slog determinedly—most of her juvenile writing was produced this way—or fall into the entranced state she called a vortex, as she would composing *A Modern Mephistopheles*, a novel for adults. Either way she would eventually collapse, to be out of commission for months. Was Louisa Alcott, like so many artists, manic-depressive? Certainly her creative pattern and mood swings are consistent with the diagnosis, according to the psychiatrist Kay Redfield Jamison, an authority on manic-depressive, or bipolar, mental illness. The predisposition runs in families. If its location on the genome were known, it would almost certainly be found in the DNA of Abigail Alcott, who threw herself into each new enterprise only to lose steam abruptly. Louisa's existential despair (the six months she spent in bed in 1867, for instance) actually more closely resembles Bronson Alcott's near-catatonic periods that followed episodes of excited vainglorious thinking, especially around the period of Fruitlands.

Nothing continued to stimulate Louisa's drive to write more than money. From the beginning of her career, when she drove her price per story up from five dollars to six dollars and then to ten dollars, she would not be bought for less than the market would bear. Soon after she arrived home from Europe, she turned down Henry Ward Beecher's offer of two thousand dollars for a serial for the *Christian Union*. When he upped the fee to three thousand dollars, and left the book rights to Louisa, she agreed. She couldn't resist a bit of crowing over her successful haggling with Beecher. "T[homas]. N[iles]. said it was a splendid offer as Jean Ingelow* for her story did not get half so much," she wrote Bronson, adding that Niles "was rather taken aback" by the deal, "& felt that others were bidding high for his golden goose." Appropriately enough, she turned to *Success*, the autobiographical novel about the trials of a young woman, which she had started a decade before. At the time, *success* had been the right word for both her and her heroine's objectives. Now that they had

---

* Ingelow's *Off the Skelligs* had just been serialized in a magazine called *Little's Living Age*.

been attained, she renamed the novel *Work*. Louisa understood her story not as a progression toward success but as a series of lessons about the meaning and value of work as the path to an honorable place in the world.

In Boston she established herself in a Beacon Street boardinghouse staffed with uniformed maids, and tried to improve her health. She took brisk walks around the Common. She swore off morphine, deciding that the relief it gave her at night was not worth the dulled spirits it left her in by day. She went to the theater and art shows, and saw friends often, but found that even pleasure was hard. She was much in demand socially and could appear in as much silk yardage as the occasion required. In December, she attended a lavish ball in honor of Grand Duke Alexis and was amused by the sight of the "big blonde boy" dancing with all the pretty young girls and leaving the "Boston dowagers and their diamonds in the lurch." She must have enjoyed being seen in her grandeur by May family connections whose condescension and snubs she had once been compelled to overlook politely. But social life interfered with her writing, and Louisa preferred the stimulation of the intellectual and reform scene anyway—meetings of the Radical Club, and the better plays and lectures.

Sleep was still difficult—it always was when Louisa was writing—and her teeth were troubling her, especially their appearance. After a bout of dental work she boasted, "My mouth is now fair to see, for the ruins are gone & a choice collection of china-ware gleams before the eye." The improvement inspired a comic poem that lamented each pearl lost to the "ruin that Calomel made."

> *They grew in beauty side by side,*
> *they filled one mouth with glee.*
> *Their graves are severed far and wide,*
> *by mount & stream & sea.*
>
> *... The sea, the blue lone sea has one—*
> *it lies where pearls lie deep.*
> *Nuts aboard ship that deed hath done,*
> *I think of it and weep! ...*
> *Farewell my teeth! Of thee bereft,*
> *I know no peace or mirth.*
> *Alas for me if there were left*
> *no dentists upon earth!*

Louisa wrote another of the comic poems that came so easily for the benefit of the Boston Woman's Club, possibly as a good-natured plea for a cessation of breaches of authorial privacy by the kind of literary-minded worshippers who sketched authors in their nightcaps and took photographs of their cats.

Fame, or A Wail Heard at the Woman's Club

Get out your pocket handkerchiefs,
give o'er your jokes and songs,
Forget awhile your women's rights,
and pity authors' wrongs . . .
. . . eager pilgrims penetrate
to their most private nooks,
storm their back doors in search of news,
and interview their cooks . . .
Some April shall the world behold
Embattled Authors stand
With steel pens of the sharpest tip
in every inky hand . . .
Their monuments of ruined books,
Of precious wasted days,
Of tempers tried, distracted brains,
that might have won fresh bays.
And round this sad memorial
Oh, chant for requiem:
Here lie our murdered geniuses;
Concord has conquered them.

Concord's genius Ralph Waldo Emerson used to hasten to his attic when Transcendental tourists loomed, but on a rainy morning in late July 1872 fire was the threat that drove him and Lidian out to the street to sound an alarm. Louisa and May came running from Orchard House to find their hero "wandering about in his night clothes, old coat & no hose," his "dear bald head lightly covered with his best hat, & an old pair of rubbers wobbling on his Platonic feet." While the town's volunteer firemen took charge, May and Louisa managed to save most of the library's valuable books and manuscripts, and carried them home to dry out while the owners, surveying the wreckage on the front lawn, took the whole thing "very coolly & in a truly Emersonian way."

Too much of Louisa's life took place in the domestic arena, where even the high dramas of birth, love, illness, and death were on an intimate scale. An event like Emerson's house fire, though not exactly earth-shattering, lifted her above her concerns with her mother's health and her own aches and pains, and gave her a chance to be courageous. For most of her life Louisa was starved for heightened experiences of the life-endangering kind. Four months after the Emerson fire, she found herself an eyewitness to the calamitous blaze that swept Boston on the night of November 9, 1872. Her taste for lurid spectacle and personal danger was excited as soon as word of the downtown business district conflagration reached her boardinghouse on the other side of Boston Common. She raced out to watch the soaring flames and their dramatic effects. "Trinity Church was beginning to smoke, & all the great granite blocks of stones were melting like ice in the awful heat," she reported, awed by the trans-formation. The behavior of "venerable Beacon Street gentlemen" attempt-ing to rescue inventory from the inferno while plate glass windows melted interested her no less. So did the sound: the fire "created a whirlwind & an awful roar." She saw "blazing boards, great pieces of cloth & rolls of paper flying in all directions falling on roofs & spreading the fire," while "fire men could not go up their ladders the heat was so intense & many were killed by falling walls." The scene was chaotic. Most of the city's horses were unfit for service because of an outbreak of distemper; as a conse-quence, the firefighting equipment had to be pulled by male volunteers hitched into the animals' traces. When water proved useless against the flames, citizens were allowed to blow up buildings in (failed) attempts to create breaks in its path. "The red glare, the strange roar, the flying peo-ple, all made night terrible & I kept thinking of the Last Days of Pompeii," Louisa later wrote to Anna.

Once back in her room, she took in clerks exhausted from rescuing their bosses' account books. She was giving them tea and cake when a friend came to warn that the fire was moving in their direction. Louisa wrapped her manuscript of *Work*, her best dress, a pair of new boots, and some books in an old army blanket and boarded an open wagon to be hauled to safety across the river in Cambridge by men—not horses—in harness.

When the excitement was over and Boston, already struggling to con-tain a smallpox outbreak as well as the horse distemper epidemic, began its massive cleanup, Louisa pushed on with *Work*, now subtitled *A Story of Experience*. Its first installment was due out in weeks. To make copies for three publishers—Beecher of the *Christian Union*, Roberts Brothers in Boston for the American edition of the book, and Sampson and Low in London for the British—she was writing the final draft on impression paper, bearing down so hard that her right thumb was temporarily paralyzed and permanently damaged. She switched to her left hand and continued scribbling in an awkward backhand; part of her self-directed apprenticeship as a writer had been to learn how. She took a brief New Year's holiday break in Newport, but a taste of the excesses of "dinners, balls, [and] calls" left her quite willing to retreat to her quiet room and the solitude of her pen. Newport was not really her kind of place, she had learned.

Staying barely on the near side of physical collapse, Louisa brought the story of struggling Christie Devon to a close. She gives her heroine the love of David Sterling, a man like Thoreau, who shows her the natural world as she has never known it before. (Like Thoreau, who had 706 unsold copies of *A Week on the Concord and Merrimack Rivers,* David has most of the only edition of his unappreciated book.) After Christie and David marry and briefly find bliss, David chooses to fight and die heroically in the Civil War, unaware that he will leave behind a child as well as a wife. The book closes with Christie and her child living in Louisa's earthly, modest version of the celestial city, a quasi-familial household of women who share costs and emotional support. In the group is an African-American, Hepsey, modeled after Harriet Tubman, the fearless rescuer of hundreds of the enslaved, and someone Louisa knew. An unmarried mother and daughter may have been drawn from one of the pregnant strays Abby brought home in her days as a city missionary. The group living situation Louisa describes as a solution to female poverty and loneliness resembles the one in *An Old-Fashioned Girl* and, for that matter, *Little Women*, but Louisa's *Story of Experience* is suitable only for open-minded adults.

Louisa made her deadline but was dissatisfied with *Work* and attributed its shortcomings to interruptions of bad health and family duty. "Should like to do one book in peace, and see if it wouldn't be good," she said, but no sooner was *Work* finished in February of 1873 than the odds against that ever happening increased. Anna came down with pneumonia so severe that Bronson was recalled from his lecture tour, and her sister charged Louisa with raising her children if she were to die. When *Work* came out, the reviews were good and the book sold well—none of

Louisa's books sold fewer than ten thousand copies—but her profit couldn't compare to the windfalls that with much less effort came her way from the juvenile market.

In April Louisa relieved her younger sister of her duties at home after a stint of a year and a half, and as reward sent May off to London with a thousand dollars for another year of art study. Though Concord felt "more like a tomb than ever," Louisa intended to establish a routine of writing and housekeeping. She hadn't minded routine cleaning and washing in the past, and having just completed *Work*, regarded it as honest toil and not beneath her new dignity. Her father liked to see her sweep and dust: "It is gratifying to find that she has lost nothing of her practical cunning while engaged in stories for the million," he noted. But Louisa soon found that housework as a matter of principle held no charms whatsoever, and hired somebody else to do it.

The help that summer gave Louisa plenty of time to be dutiful to her bedridden mother, adjusting pillows and fetching tea. At almost seventy-three, Abby was "never to be our brave energetic leader any more." To leave her side was unthinkable. So was a winter at Orchard House; in October Louisa took all her dependents to Boston instead. She rented adjacent apartments in the South End, one for herself and her mother, and the other for Anna and the boys. Most of the time Abby sat at her window, attentively watching the passing scene. Soon Bronson rejoined the family; he had cut short his annual trip west because a weak national economy was cutting into his bookings. Louisa was paddling her own canoe as she had wished, it was true, but she had a lot of passengers.

Energetic Bronson got busy giving Conversations at clubs around town and lecturing at the Harvard Divinity School in Cambridge, relishing the honor all the more for being a self-educated farm boy. For the first time in twenty years, and almost certainly the last, he and Abby were living in the city. Their winter had an elegiac cast. A tablet in honor of Abby's father had been laid at King's Chapel, where he had sung as a boy and become a deacon. On a Sunday morning in March, Louisa took Bronson and Abby to see the tribute to "Colonel" May. Louisa was touched "to see Father walk up the aisle with the feeble old wife on his arm as they went to be married nearly fifty years* ago." Abby broke down thinking of other times, "when she and her mother and sisters and father and brothers

---

* In fact, it had been not quite forty-four.

all went to church together, and we took her home saying, 'This isn't my Boston; all my friends are gone; I never want to see it any more.'" A few weeks later, when May returned from London, she and Louisa resettled Abby and Bronson in Orchard House, and Louisa returned to Boston alone and with relief.

Over the year her pain and headaches had intensified, and she turned again to morphine. Still, she was getting some work done on a new novel for the lucrative children's market, *Eight Cousins*. At the same time she could practically toss off children's short stories for thirty-five dollars between meals, which was not particularly cost-effective compared to books but kept her name—her "brand"—in front of the public. Except to explain them as a reaction to overwork or worry, she could make no sense of her flare-ups of pain and fatigue. In November of 1874, as she turned forty-two, the symptoms abated as mysteriously as they had come on. By December she felt well enough to finish off *Eight Cousins*. One of Louisa's best books for young adults, *Eight Cousins* is the story of Rose Campbell, a cosseted, recently orphaned heiress sent to live among a boisterous pack of male cousins, eccentric aunts, and an uncle who just happens to espouse some of Bronson Alcott's basic tenets of health—that fresh air is good for Rose and corsets bad. *Eight Cousins* and its sequel, *Rose in Bloom*, are told from the heroine's point of view, one of wealth and privilege, the social position Louisa now shared with most of the people who paid for her books. The two *Little Women* books and *An Old-Fashioned Girl* had asked readers to see through the eyes of the poor; the two books about Rose Campbell asked readers to be good to the poor, and in the process of writing them Louisa's moral tone changed from compassionate to something closer to holier-than-thou. She also took advantage of her soapbox to advocate equal rights and votes for women, dress and diet reform, respect for honest labor (including professional acting), and the works of Henry David Thoreau.

In the meantime, while Louisa toiled, her father was dining out on her fame, "riding in Louisa's chariot" as he called it in a letter recounting his experience at a school in Milwaukee. "After my little story of the famous lady was told in plain terms as the subject allowed scores of hands were stretched, arm over arm, by the gathered group, to take that of 'papa.' . . . What shall poor papa do but bear it gracefully and be himself?"

A few weeks later Louisa accepted an invitation to appear at Vassar College, and she found it impossible to be herself: "Talk with four hundred girls, write in stacks of albums and schoolbooks." She hated the new craze for autographs but complied and even agreed to "kiss every one" who asked her. When the students begged her to make a speech, she replied that she "never had and never intended to make one," so they suggested, in lieu of a speech, she "place herself in a prominent position, and turn around slowly." She did. At the Sorosis Club in New York City immediately afterward, she regaled the members with an account of her Vassar visit and volunteered to revolve for them as well.

That spring of 1875, Concord was preparing to celebrate the centennial of the "shot heard round the world" proclaiming the American Revolution. "Ma's dander is up and she is prancing like an old war horse," Louisa wrote to her cousin Fred May. "[She] coolly begs me to ask the lend of the Hancock punch bowl for the grand Row our unhappy town is to be afflicted with on Monday . . . although it may be like asking for the nose of your noble countenance or the heart out of your manly bosom." The object of Abby's begging was John Hancock's own enormous silver punch bowl, which had served the country on innumerable revolutionary occasions, for what Louisa saw to be shaping up as a mob. Among the expected guests, President Ulysses S. Grant "is to be handed round like refreshment on that day (and from all I learn he's about the only refreshment we are likely to get . . .)." When the hubbub had died down, she wrote to thank Cousin May, and to say how happy she was to be returning the punch bowl, "for I have . . . stood guard over it as if my salvation depended on it."

On the day of the grand speeches, held in a tent pitched near the field where the Minutemen had confronted the British a century before, the women of the town discovered that no accommodation had been made for them, either on the dais or in the audience. Finally they were allowed inside—to stand in the narrow space between the front row of the audience and the speakers' platform, pressed against the muddy boots of the speakers. After delivering his address, President Grant joined the women and soon looked so bored that Louisa longed to offer him a cigar. She watched and fumed as the few venerable Concord women who had been given seats were required to yield them to the female appendages of self-important politicos. As the program went on—and on—the platform began to give way, and the speakers' table with it. Some ventured that the structure collapsed from the weight of the oratory, but Louisa said it was for lack of a suffrage plank. If taken for granted as a mere woman by Concord, which did not appreciate that she did not appreciate it, Louisa Alcott was reaching a new level of renown around the world as foreign-language editions of *Little Women* were published. (The first was in Dutch.) A number of unappealing photographs, circulated as souvenir "cabinet cards," made Louisa recognizable. Soon everywhere she went she was pursued by mobs of "Jo-worshippers." The mass culture of celebrity was so new that it would never have occurred to Louisa to hire someone to protect her from unwelcome intrusions. She had expected fame to confer power and the ability to control her circumstances, but the opposite was proving to be true. In October, arriving late at the Women's Congress in Syracuse with her cousin Charlotte Wilkinson (Sam May's daughter), they were given the only remaining seats, on the stage. Though Louisa "got behind a canvas tree, with a painted fireplace to lean on, and sat as still as a mouse," she was spotted right away. "The stage boxes opposite began to fill up with girls all gazing upon the lady in black," and as soon as the meeting ended, she was besieged by girls. "Finally I had to run for my life with more girls all along the way, and Ma's [mothers] clawing me as I went." On a visit to the theater she was again accosted, this time by a grown woman, who grabbed her hand and effused, "If you ever come to Oshkosh, your feet will not be allowed to touch the ground; you will be borne in the arms of the people! Will you come?" " 'Never,' responded Miss A."

She decided to spend the winter in New York, where she was less likely to find herself the principal attraction at every gathering. She took a room at Dr. Eli Peck Miller's Bath Hotel on West Twenty-sixth Street, which featured a spa that advertised Turkish, Russian, and electric baths, as well as various cures to try for her many ills: the lifting cure, Kidder's Electric-Magnetic Battery, and the Swedish Movement Cure. The improved Turkish bath, according to the hotel's literature, consisted of a progression from the Frigidarium to the Tepidarium to the Suditorium to the Shampooing Room, where Louisa reclined upon a marble couch to receive the benefit of the friction glove.

She also had her head examined (supposedly anonymously), by a phrenologist, a practitioner who claimed to read character by examining the bumps on people's heads. His conclusions were curiously on target despite references to "conjugal love" and motherhood, and it's difficult to believe Louisa was unknown to the examiner.

Faith hope & charity very large . . . has more friends than she wants, bears others' burdens, and lets them impose on her . . . strong sympathy and generosity. . . . Conjugal love very marked . . . a devoted wife and mother. . . . a good nurse . . . adores children and wins their hearts. . . . Loves praise but can go without it . . . has the gift of language, is dramatic and witty. . . . Strong passions but can control them . . . dual nature very marked . . . the spirit is ardent & sometimes headstrong . . . a person who can row against the tide & like it.

Anne and Vincenzo Botta, whose salon on West Thirty-seventh Street Bronson had frequented in 1856, scooped Louisa up as soon as she arrived, and she found herself a regular within a sophisticated world that mixed politics and literature in three or four languages. After an extended conversation there one evening with a Professor Byng, a German ex-consul, she felt as if she'd been to Washington or abroad. "Byng knew Rose and Una [Nathaniel Hawthorne's daughters]," she wrote to Bronson, "and asked about them; also told funny tales of Victor Emmanuel and his Court, and queer adventures in Greece. . . . It is a delightful house," she reported happily, "and I shall go as often as I may." There were also outings to the theater, drives through the new Central Park, and back-to-back engagements, as when Louisa hurried from a seven-course dinner at Mrs. Goddard's to a soiree thrown by the editor of *Harper's Bazaar.*

Louisa felt comfortable as a celebrity in New York, as celebrities still do. "Dr. Holland . . . congratulated me on being a New Yorker. It seems to please folk that I like N.Y. & am not a prim, prejudiced Bostonian. I tell em I don't belong anywhere. . . . [I feel] so well I shall stay on until I am tired of it. . . . I have not an ache to fret over. This, after such a long lesson in bodily ails." But, she assured her father—addressing him as "Dear Seventy-six" in honor of his imminent birthday—"it isn't all play. . . . I'm a thrifty butterfly, and have written three stories . . . [and] have a ballast of work to keep me steady in spite of such fun." She was beginning to get control of fame—the wild stallion she had mounted—and to tame it to good purpose. She would rotate on no more stages but instead use her entrée to see the institutions for the poor and to write affectingly about them, often for an audience of privileged children who might one day have the means to improve them.

With another guest at Miller's Bath Hotel, Sallie Holley, an abolitionist who had turned to teaching people formerly held in slavery, she paid visits to three institutions. The first, in the notorious Five Points area, was the infamous prison known as the Tombs. The second, the Duane Street News-boys' Lodging House for homeless boys, impressed her enough to compel her to make a large contribution. Louisa wrote her nephews describing the huge dormitories filled with "narrow beds with a blue quilt, neat pillow, and clean sheet." Considering the nightmarish alternatives, the 180 young orphans who sheltered on Duane Street for eleven cents a day—six for a bed, five for supper, with schooling and baths thrown in—were the lucky ones. "One little chap, only six, was trotting round as busy as a bee, locking up his small shoes and ragged jacket as if they were great treasures. I asked about little Pete, and the man told us his brother, only nine, supported him and took care of him entirely. . . . Think of that, Fred! How would it seem to be all alone in a big city, with no mamma to cuddle you; no two gran-pa's houses to take you in; not a penny but what you earned, and Donny [Fred's brother Johnny] to take care of? Could you do it?"

Louisa spent Christmas Day at the third institution, an orphanage on Randall's Island, with the Quaker activist Abby Hopper Gibbons. Bear-ing an enormous package of gift dolls, Louisa arrived at the East River in a thick fog to find Mrs. Gibbons and her husband waiting on the dock with all kinds of supplies and a clutch of assorted city officials. Mrs. Gib-bons, wearing the plain Quaker bonnet that she seemed to think gave her license to scold, lit into the officials, outraged by a decision they had made. "The brave little woman was down on 'em in a way that would have made Marmee cry 'Ankore!' [encore] and clap her dress-gloves to rags." The visit was a harrowing experience. Although a group of well-scrubbed orphans curtsied and gave recitations, mistaking Louisa for the "mayoress" they had expected, others lay feebly in their beds in huge wards filled with babies "born of want and sin, suffering every sort of deformity, disease, and pain. Cripples half blind, scarred with scrofula, burns, and abuse," were too awful to describe. They stopped next at the ward for the brain-damaged and insane orphans—called the "idiot house"—where Louisa saw faces and figures she said would haunt her for a long time. The nurses were all pauper women, she wrote her family, and the babies, ac-cording to Mrs. Gibbons, "die like sheep." One of the teachers in the home told Louisa she had worked with Anna at Dr. Wilbur's asylum in Syracuse twenty years earlier. She was "very lady-like, and all devotion to me," Louisa wrote, "but such a life! Oh, me! Who can lead it and not go mad?"

In the course of her three-month stay, Louisa had a taste of New York's best society and worst conditions, strengthening both her commitment to reform and her sense that she could make good use of her celebrity in support of it. If she was sometimes appalled by New York's frivolity and ostentation, she was also exhilarated by its pace and variety. "People are too busy to think & only gossip prospers," she wrote her father. "I shall tire of it by & by," she knew, but for the time being she wanted to enjoy it. In the end she left—as many writers still do—to get back to work.

SEVENTEEN

THE CREAM OF THINGS

She has done her distasteful duty faithfully, and deserved a reward," Louisa said. In September of 1876 she sent May to Paris to continue her art studies, booking her on the Cunard Line's *China* for the ten-day passage that she and George and Anna Weld had made on the same ship eleven years before. Through the eighteen months at home May had worked as hard at painting and drawing as Louisa did at writing, filling orders for decorative panels and sketches, and selling work she had brought back from Europe in 1874. An admired and experienced teacher, May had students in Cambridge, Boston, and Concord, and established the Concord Art Center, where she made casts, sketches, books, and free lessons available to the local youth. "When I become rich and great," May said, "I shall found a school for indigent artists and . . . girls under twenty years of age. I have still thirty more years to work in and think of it, if I am spared." One of her first protégés was already a successful sculptor. Daniel Chester French was a teenage farm boy when May gave him his first set of sculpting tools; his best-known statue would be the enormous seated Abraham Lincoln in the Lincoln Memorial in Washington. French credited May Alcott for encouraging him at the start.

Familiar around town as a golden-curled, graceful figure on her horse, Rosa, May had Anna's even temperament and love of beauty, and Louisa's talent and vivacity. Her irregular features were not as good as Louisa's, according to the boy next door, Julian Hawthorne, who confessed to a terrific crush on her anyway.

May seemed always to be a little bit in love with someone or other, yet she reached her middle thirties still unmarried, and apparently not unhappy about it. Like Anna, May was friendly and easy to love, while Louisa's sometimes cantankerous aspect could leave people choosing to keep their distance. The hard-luck years had wounded and embittered Louisa; May had been sheltered throughout them.

Louisa's belief in May's talent was unwavering and, as it developed, warranted. Still, she was prone to resent her younger sister. "She always had the cream of things," Louisa said of May. She cannot have been entirely happy to learn that soon after May's arrival in Paris, Ladislas Wisniewski was squiring her sister to the sights Louisa and Laddie had visited together ten years earlier, and shopping with May for a watch in the Rue de Rivoli, where he had taken Louisa to pick out a hat.

⁓

That winter Louisa satisfied an ambition simmering since she had read Goethe's *Faust* the year before. A decade earlier her editor at the *Flag of Our Union* had rejected a serial as too sensational; now she holed up at the Hotel Bellevue in Boston for much of January and February to rework the story as *A Modern Mephistopheles*, the sixth title in Roberts Brothers' No-Name series of anonymous works by well-known writers. The guess-the-mystery-author buzz made the series popular and profitable. For Louisa, the chance to escape from writing "moral pap for the young" was irresistible. The story of a soul sold to the devil was deliciously apt as a vehicle.

She gave readers a trio of villains: a handsome young writer who is a fraud, a brilliant older poet who is Satan incarnate, and a treacherous mistress with the charm of a gorgeous reptile. Their virginal victim, Gladys, is nobody's fool, and not long a virgin since she soon marries the supposed poet. Each of the four characters has two faces, giving Louisa a full set of masks to wear—old and young, male and female, good and evil.

The plot of *A Modern Mephistopheles* is as twisted as the villains of the piece. At a critical point the Faust character tempts Gladys with irresistible white candies laced with hashish and served on a dish of tortoiseshell and silver. Released from inhibition, Gladys is transformed: "An inward excitement possessed her, a wild desire to sing her very heart out came over her, and a strange chill which she thought a vague presentiment of coming ill, crept through her blood." Louisa was in rare form in her favorite lurid style: "one Gladys moved and spoke as she was told—a pale dim figure, of no interest to anyone. The other was alive in every fiber, thrilled with intense desire for something, and bent on finding it." The heroine quickly succumbs to "the unconscious stage of the hasheesh dream . . . whose coming none can foretell but those accustomed to its use."

Only "those accustomed to its use" knew the mind-altering powers of hashish, Louisa wrote, indirectly confessing to her own familiarity with the drug. In the privacy of her room, she could try any means of escape available to her, all of them accessible and legal. She was bold enough to drink wine in public, and thought that during her second trip to Europe she sometimes drank too much of it. In a letter to her cousin Abigail Williams May, she inquired as to where to buy beer. Opium knocked out pain to let her sleep, but she was aware of its addictive and ultimately detrimental effects and tried to avoid dependence on it. She knew that with smoking hashish cigarettes "a heavenly dreaminess comes over one, in which [one moves] as if on air. Everything is calm and lovely . . . no pain, no care, no fear of anything, and while it lasts one feels like an angel half asleep."

Abby was not concerned about whether Louisa knew of hashish from books or from life. She only cared that she had written convincingly. She thought that *A Modern Mephistopheles* "surpasse[d] its predecessors in power and brilliancy—and that the author will not easily be recognized." When it arrived in bookstores, the dark theme and brooding characters of the novel, reminiscent of Nathaniel Hawthorne, led the *Atlantic* to speculate that it was the work of Julian Hawthorne. (Louisa had again gotten the better of the *Atlantic*'s dismissive editor James Fields.) The chatter and the guessing amused the book's actual famous author. "It is praised and criticized, and I enjoy the fun, especially when friends say, 'I know you didn't write it, for you can't hide your peculiar style.'" Louisa confined her secret to her immediate family and her journal. She was probably never happier than when successfully in disguise.

Late in February of 1877, Abby had another episode of chest pain and difficulty breathing. Louisa returned to Concord to assess her mother's situation—and Anna's.

Anna and her family had never had a real home. Some of the time they lived in Orchard House, crowded into the small room at the top of the stairs between her parents' and May's bedrooms. They also lived with the boys' other grandparents at the Pratt farm for months at a time and went to Walpole in New Hampshire for the summer, staying in borrowed quarters or subsidized by Louisa. Now Anna told Louisa that she longed for a home of her own, and asked her help to buy it. Here Louisa saw a solution for the whole Alcott family: if Anna had her own house, Abby could move in for the winter, Orchard House could be shut down, and Louisa could be in Boston while Bronson was on a lecture tour and May was in Europe.

The old Thoreau house on Main Street had been on the market since the death of Henry's younger sister Sophia; its availability may have prompted Anna to bring up the idea of buying her own home. The asking price was $5,000, but the house was in need of considerable repair, Louisa pointed out; she offered $4,500, and the offer was accepted. Anna had been able to save about $2,500 of her inheritance from John Pratt (while living on Louisa's royalties from *Little Men*), and Louisa supplied the rest. Anna and her sons moved in right away and got rooms ready for her parents and Louisa to occupy when cold weather set in.

"So [Anna] has *her* wish, and is happy," Louisa wrote. "When shall I have mine? Ought to be contented with knowing I help both my sisters by my brains. But I'm selfish, and want to go away and rest in Europe. Never shall." Now in her midforties, Louisa's resignation to duty was taking on a resentful edge, and as usual, she did not see or recognize any help given her. Anna entertained intrusive fans who hoped for a glimpse of her famous sister. Louisa may not have appreciated how Anna nurtured the family brand too, by replying politely to mail from the gushing fans Louisa hated and refused to acknowledge. One such letter was from a pair of Vassar students forming a Little Women club. These groups had sprung up spontaneously, as had dramatizations of scenes from the book; both provided vehicles for girls to play at being March sisters. Anna carefully

explained to the correspondents that Meg March was the "splendid" product of her sister's imagination.

> [The real] "Meg" was never the pretty, vain little maiden who flirted and
> made herself so charming. But [the real] "Jo" always admired poor plain
> Annie and . . . beautified her . . . saying,—'Dear me girls, we must have
> one beauty in the book,' . . . and no doubt all the 'little women' who read
> of her, admire her just as loving old Jo does. . . . But for all that, she is
> nothing but homely Annie, one of the busy, useful, uninteresting ones.

As cranky as the plague of admirers made Louisa, now and then an
appealing letter slipped past her defenses. Carrie, Maggie, Nellie, Emma,
and Helen Lukens, five sisters from Brinton, Pennsylvania, were journal-
ists and entrepreneurs after her own heart. Their mother had died, and
financial reverses had forced their father to take them out of school. Led
by Carrie and Maggie, the two eldest sisters (the second one, Maggie, like
Louisa, seemed to be the spark and mainstay of the operation), they
started *Little Things*, a family newspaper modeled on the March sisters'
Pickwick Portfolio. After producing three handwritten issues, they persuaded their father to let them typeset it themselves, and in August
1872, they wrote to Louisa to offer her a subscription to their profitable
publication. She accepted, so impressed by their "pluck and perseverance" that she offered to be a contributor for free.

As for herself, she wrote, she heartily believed in women's "right to any
branch of labor for which they proved their fitness. . . . Work is such a beautiful & helpful thing & independence so delightful that I wonder there are
any lazy people in the world." It was as concise a summary of her personal
creed as she could have written, for as everything else fell away, work
freely chosen and pursued remained the one constant in her life.

⌒

May had been working "like a Trojan" all winter, living in Paris's artistic
Pigalle district, near Montparnasse, with two American sisters, Rose and
Kate Peckham. In a portrait by Rose Peckham sent to the Alcotts in Concord, May is a woman of the world, charming and elegant in a fashionable
coat and a feather-trimmed hat that Abby did not like at all. Hat notwithstanding, the portrait was hung in a place of honor in the parlor.

May rejoiced in her disciplined routine in the tiny apartment: up at seven to "slip on L's old flannel gown and in my blue scufflers I take ten steps from my cozy little room to the kitchen." After warming a "pail of chocolate" and dunking in it one of the "little loaves, or rolls, such as only France can produce," she was off to Monsieur Krug's studio on Boulevard Clichy to spend the morning sketching live models (female and male), who posed for the all-women class wearing "only a band around the waist." The three friends were just a five-minute walk to the studio, in May's opinion the best place in Paris for American women, shut out of the most desirable art schools, to study. At noon she ran home for lunch, then returned to Krug's for another four hours of painting. "This week, we have a perfectly superb model," she reported in one of her letters that included her sketch of "an Italian of fine rich color, grand physique, and the head of a god. . . . Wouldn't you call him a beauty? Particularly if you could see him with his head tossed back, eyes raised; he stands like a statue for an hour without moving a muscle; you can't wonder we admire the beautiful creature." She had made enormous progress since drawing the awkward illustrations for the first edition of *Little Women*.

Most evenings, May and the Peckham sisters prepared supper and went to bed early. On occasion they visited the ateliers of well-known artists, or the daughters of the distinguished painter George Healy, but most frequently they went to the beautiful studio of the painter Mary Cassatt. Four years younger than May, the wealthy Pennsylvania-born Cassatt had settled in Paris five years earlier. She was a close friend and artistic colleague of Edgar Degas, and through Degas his friends Claude Monet, Pierre-Auguste Renoir, and Camille Pissarro. Cassatt's work had already been exhibited at several of the prestigious annual Paris Salons.

The parties at Cassatt's studio captivated May. "Statues and articles of *vertu* filled the corners, the whole being lighted by a great antique hanging lamp," May wrote in one of the long letters home. "We sipped our *chocolat* from superior china, served on an India waiter [a kind of tea tray] upon an embroidered cloth of heavy material. Mary Cassatt was charming as usual in two shades of brown satin and rep [a ribbed fabric], being very lively and a woman of real genius."

Four months after her letter, a still-life oil that May had worked on for weeks—and that Mary Cassatt had praised—was accepted at that year's Paris Salon. "Who would have imagined such good fortune, and so strong a proof that Lu does not monopolize all the Alcott talent," she crowed. Knowing Marmee would share her letters, May directed messages to each family member. "Ha! ha! sister, this is the first feather plucked from your cap, and I shall endeavor to fill mine with so many waving in the breeze that you will be quite ready to lay down your pen and rest on your laurels already won." Though her work was but a "simple unpretentious study," she added, and "[wouldn't] look bigger than a postage stamp when hung among so many immense pictures," it was a great distinction, and came with a free pass for the artist and her guests. "So sing for joy, dear Marmee, and be proud of your duckling, won't you?" For her "dear old Lu . . . who loves the artistic side of Paris life so much" (but may not have loved how frequently her name was prefaced with *old*), she recounted the spring opening day of the Salon in every thrilling detail: her escorts, her surprise at knowing so many in the crowd, the many Americans represented, and especially her pride at seeing her painting hung low enough to be almost "on the line," at eye level.

Louisa was proud, too, noting in her journal that May had "no friend at court, and the modest work stood on its own merits." She advised May not to paint "in Millet's later style," at which May "roared over the charmingly assured tone" of what she considered her sister's ignorant remark. May took every opportunity to remind Louisa that she was a recognized artist in her own right. Of May's long letters Abby remarked, "I think she has realized what a sacrifice to me it has been to have her gone so far, and has conscientiously tried to gratify me and her sisters by these frequent and interesting accounts of her progress in art." Perhaps, but perhaps May liked as much the opportunity to boast to the sister who had for so long overshadowed her.

Once back in Concord for the warm weather, on good mornings Louisa took her mother driving to the woods to pick flowers, though Abby could only watch from the carriage. "It keeps her young," Louisa wrote optimistically, "and rests her weary nerves." In early September Abby entered the end stage of congestive heart failure, and Louisa wrote, "The doctor told me it was the beginning of the end."

Bronson came home from visiting relatives in Connecticut, and Louisa devoted herself to her mother, who was ready to die. At Abby's bedside she finished *Under the Lilacs* and wrote a story for her next *Scrap-Bag* collection; by October she was spent from the wear and tear of round-the-clock writing and nursing. "Fearing I might give out, got a nurse and rested a little, so that when the last hard days come I might not fail Marmee, who says, 'Stay by, Louy, and help me if I suffer too much. . . . I promised,'" Louisa said—when had she not?

In November, Louisa and her parents moved into Anna's new home.

The family's long attachment to Orchard House was severed, the house closed up, and Bronson placed under Anna's care in the renovated Thoreau house. His new study, Bronson wrote May, was not as roomy as his old one, "but where Thoreau has sat and written, a humbler scholar will be content." Her mother, Louisa observed, no longer took an interest in anything. She would be moving soon anyway. She wanted to be buried in Sleepy Hollow Cemetery. "To rest among kindred is desirable," Abby wrote, "even if we are insensible to the fact."

Four days before Bronson's seventy-eighth and Louisa's forty-fifth birthday, Abby entered the final stage of her illness. She was not in pain, though she was disoriented and confused Louisa with her own mother. She looked often at a picture of May beside her bed and, waving her hand, bid her youngest daughter good-bye. Turning to Bronson, she said, "You are laying a very soft pillow for me to go to sleep on." He wished her a good journey. Around dusk, as a light rain fell outside, Abby died in Louisa's arms. She was buried at Sleepy Hollow. "[It was] a hard day," reported Louisa, "but the last duty we could do for her; and there we left her at sunset beside dear Lizzie's dust,—alone so long."

Louisa's relief that her mother's suffering had come to an end was quickly overtaken by an almost obliterating grief. "My duty is done, and now I shall be glad to follow her," she wrote a few days after Abby's death, and weeks later, "a great warmth has gone out of life, and there is no motive to go on."

May had moved to London at the end of the summer to study watercolor, and there she struggled with both grief and guilt for not returning: "I have so much to reproach myself with that it seems I can never forgive myself." She ventured a justification: "Perhaps my little triumphs here have given her more pleasure than if I had stayed at home." Louisa replied with a message of love and absolution. "Never mourn that you didn't come. All is well & your work was a joy to Marmee." May's reply was both tart and generous.

> Certainly, dear Lu, you can never be grateful enough that *you* have been the one who could make dear Marmee, and Papa, too, so comfortable and happy these last years . . . for money has done what affection alone could never do, unromantic as it sounds to say so, and you have delighted in making us all happy in our own way, tho' much of your life and health has been sacrificed in doing it.

"Father goes about, being restless with his anchor gone," Louisa wrote to May, but she was equally at a loss for what to do next. "An idle month at Nan's for I can only suffer. Dear Nan is housemother now,—so patient thoughtful and tender; I need nothing but that cherishing which only mothers can give," she maintained, unclear whether Anna could or couldn't give her what she needed. After a long hiatus, Bronson began to schedule Conversations.

In London meanwhile, May had found a different kind of solace. "She has some very *tender friends* near her," Louisa wrote in the new year, alluding discreetly to what the family seems to have known for several months, that May had a serious suitor, one of her fellow boarders in London. Ernst Nieriker was Swiss, held an entry-level position at a bank, and was twenty-one years old to May's thirty-seven. May had an artist's appreciation of Nieriker's physical beauty;* they played chess together; he serenaded her on his violin. "I am not indifferent, my daughter," Bronson had written his youngest a week before Abby's death, "to your social (possible) prospects, and trust entirely to your discretion should you be called to a decision so important to yourself, and family."

Word of the marriage came at the end of March. The ceremony at the Bloomsbury Registry, the bride in a brown silk dress with matching hat and gloves, had been a hasty arrangement, May explained, because Ernst had been offered a job in Paris. They had seized the day rather than part ways until their financial situation improved. Louisa approved her sister's decision and sent a check for one thousand dollars with her good wishes. Louisa had learned the sweetness of self-denial at her mother's knee but did not expect it of her younger sister. Nothing she wrote suggested that May had deserted her, as she had protested when Anna married, or that the banker Ernst's interest in marriage might owe anything to the wealth and generosity of May's famous sister.

The couple settled into a house in the Paris suburb of Meudon. May

---

* Asked to describe Ernst Nieriker, May wrote: "He is slender with broad shoulders, a delicate hand, and very handsome aristocratic foot. He has a beautifully shaped head with a profusion of brown hair curling about the brow, and he parts it in the middle. Large hazel eyes, a handsome nose with proud nostrils and as beautiful a mouth as I ever saw, almost perfect in form with a firm, decided chin below. His throat is round and white as a woman's and he wears an open collar which is very becoming." (Caroline Ticknor, *May Alcott: A Memoir* [Boston: Little, Brown, 1928], 284–85.)

regaled her sisters with details of her enchanting new life, sounding very much like her mother describing her Philadelphia love nest in letters to Sam May thirty-five years before. May was as much in love with European ways as she was with her husband. The pretty little house was surrounded by an exceptionally beautiful garden. From their balcony a view of soaring windmills stood out "against the distant sky, and beyond a glimpse of the winding Seine." May and Ernst had a "magnificent view of Paris with its gilded domes, the buildings of the Trocadero, and the great gates of the 'Champs de Mars.'" Nothing could persuade her to live in Concord again, May wrote, and if Louisa came to visit, she assured her older sister, she too would never want to return. "The charms of the Bois de Meudon are beyond description—it's like opening a portfolio of sketches by Millet! And the air is like champagne."

"How different our lives are," Louisa wrote in her journal. "I so lonely, sad, and sick," and "she so happy, well, and blest."

May was determined to shut her ears to the call of duty. "I do not mean to be hindered by envious people, or anything to divert me from my dream. . . . I never mean to have a house or many belongings but the delightfully free life I do now. . . . It is the perfection of living." May was certain of her course, while Louisa, with Abby gone, could not get her bearings. "I dawdle about, and wait to see if I am to live or die. If I live, it is for some new work. I wonder what?"

One answer was to take up her mother's cause of woman suffrage. In the 1830s Abby and Bronson had been among the first activists in the campaign to extend the franchise to women, but many in the movement had set aside the suffrage issue to work for abolition, hoping that the vote for women would come with emancipation. But the Fourteenth Amendment, passed in 1874, granted the vote only to men. The woman's movement (nineteenth-century parlance for our plural *women's movement*) was regrouping under the banner of Lucy Stone's Woman Suffrage Association. New England women rallied around the campaign for the right to vote as the battle that would lead to complete gender equality under the law; Susan B. Anthony's and Elizabeth Cady Stanton's National Woman Suffrage Association pressed for an equal rights amendment for women that would accomplish legal parity in a single measure. The New England strategy was to start by winning a limited franchise in local town meetings as an opening wedge in a campaign for full voting rights. To minimize opposition, they began by asking that women be permitted to vote only on two local issues in which they were conceded to have expertise: children and education. Massachusetts was considering passing a measure to this effect in 1877. Seeing her goal in sight, Abigail Alcott had declared more than once, "I mean to vote before I die, even if my daughters have to carry me!" The measure passed too late for her mother to fulfill her dream, so Louisa set out in her footsteps to rally the women of Concord to register and vote in the next town election. There was a great deal of confusion about what was required in order to register: proof of literacy, ownership of property, or payment of fees? Some or all of them? Few Concord women intended to register, so during the summer of 1879 Louisa organized reading groups to raise consciousness about the importance of voting, and circulated petitions to encourage registration.

Concord's women showed little interest in Louisa's study sessions, graced though they were by her stellar presence. They hesitated to register "because of 'jelly-making, sewing, sickness or company.'" Louisa "gave them a good scolding & offered to drive the timid sheep (in a van) to the fatal spot where they seem[ed] to expect some awful doom." Louisa proudly wrote in her journal, "was *the first woman to register my name* as a voter." But as she reported in a letter to the *Woman's Journal* in October 1879, out of a hundred eligible women in Concord, by then only seven had done the same. The influential Ellen Emerson had decided not to register, and a number of women followed her example and took their names *off* the voting rolls. "A very poor record for a town which ought to lead if it really possesses all the intelligence claimed for it," Louisa concluded, and signed herself "Yours for reform of all kinds."

When it came to actually voting, some of the twenty-eight who registered claimed that their husbands would not allow them to vote, or that they were unable to form an independent opinion, or that they had too much housework to spare the time. Only twenty women appeared at the town meeting. Concord's men were so unsettled by their presence that they decided to put the school board question at the top of the agenda. With ostensible gallantry, they asked the women to vote first, "allowing" them to leave as soon as their voting was completed. Louisa was the first to break the ice and cast her ballot. After the women had cast their ballots, the men declined to take part in a vote allowed also to women.

The strategy of winning the vote in the "women's" issues of children and education backfired; it was taken as admission that women were not qualified to judge anything else. It would be forty years until women's right to vote was recognized in the Nineteenth Amendment to the Constitution.

To honor her mother, Louisa also thought to write a memoir of Abby, reading through old journals and letters and soliciting recollections from friends. But she made no headway; it was too soon to undertake such a project. However, the awareness that someone would someday be making a similar examination of her own journals prompted her to insert a note asking that they be destroyed after her death.

Bronson was also laid low by the project. As he transcribed Abby's long-ago appeals to relatives, professions of rage and loyalty, and defenses of himself, Bronson's illusions about his marriage and his virtue gave way to a new grief. "These papers admit me, as daily intimacy hardly did, into the very soul of my companion," he confessed.

> And my heart bleeds afresh with the memories of those days, and even long years of cheerless anxiety and hopeless dependence.... I copy with tearful admiration these pages and almost repent now of my seeming incompetency, my utter inability to relieve the burdens laid upon her and my children during these years of helplessness. Nor can I, with every mitigating apology for this seeming shiftlessness, quite excuse myself for not venturing upon some impossible feat to extricate us from these straits of circumstance.

Bronson's conviction of his "helplessness" and "inability" to pull off the "impossible feat" of supporting his family suggests that he was far more debilitated by mental illness than anyone had guessed.

Now, however, Bronson was in a position to choose any project he liked. An 1878 summer visit to Concord by his Midwest followers gave momentum to the fulfillment of a long-held dream. Meeting for two weeks with Bronson, Emerson, and other high-minded Concordians, they laid plans for a Concord School of Philosophy to bring adherents and exponents together at the feet of Bronson Alcott. It would open the following summer.

Louisa looked on amused, glad to see her grieving father engaged in his beloved talk.

She considered a visit to May and Ernst in the autumn but backed out, saying she feared she would become ill on the voyage and prove a burden to May. Her feelings were more complicated than her excuse. She sounded relieved when Anna broke her leg; "there was no one to take her place but me. Always a little chore to be done." Suddenly it was November, her forty-sixth birthday, her father's seventy-ninth, and an eventful year since Abby's death: "May marries; I live instead of dying; Father comes to honor in his old age, and Nan makes her home our refuge when we need one."

Louisa was embarking on a year of good health, although day to day it did not always seem so. Anna's leg healed, her father went on the road, and there was no Marmee to tend. In January she took a room in Boston at the Bellevue for the first time in two years. Persuaded by her friend Maria Porter, she performed her Mrs. Jarley routine for the Old South [Church, where the Boston Tea Party began] Preservation Fund and another charity event, the Author's Carnival. Said Porter:

> It was a famous show,—never to be forgotten. People came from all parts to see Louisa Alcott's Mrs. Jarley, for she had for years been famous in the part whenever a deserving charity was to be helped in that way. Shouts of delight and peals of laughter greeted her original and witty descriptions of the "figgers" at each performance, and it was repeated every evening for a week.

The trouper pulled off the show, but remarked, "A sad heart & a used up body make play hard work I find." When letters arrived from May describing her life of painting, music, and love in a Parisian bower, Louisa thought her sister wise to seize the happy moment—and that it would, inevitably, be a fleeting one.

Louisa longed to visit May and Ernst (despite the dreaded Atlantic crossing), but *Diana and Persis,* a novella for adults written at the Bellevue Hotel early in 1878, hinted at the reason for her hesitation: that she saw the in-law relationship as a dangerous love triangle. She may have recognized the danger of being a third wheel or, worse, a troublemaker in May's marriage.

Diana and Persis is about two artist friends, Diana (a version of Louisa) and Persis, or "Percy" (a version of May), who happily share a studio in Paris, living as May had with her roommates. Diana believes that a devoted artist must renounce romance and motherhood as she has, and hopes Percy will too, so they can stay together. But Percy marries. When Diana visits, Percy's husband, August, feels threatened: Percy and Diana discuss art with such absorption that his wife forgets to refill his coffee cup. August is not self-centered or a villain; in fact, he seems to be another variation of Louisa. He has renounced artistic aspirations and knows "by sad experience how hard the effort is to bind a passionate desire and hold it captive at the feet of duty."

Louisa found it difficult to imagine a married woman operating freely in the world, pursuing art, yet May was doing just that. Two of her paintings, one of an owl and another a portrait of an African woman, *La Negresse*, were accepted at the Salon of 1879. She had works in galleries in France and in England. Louisa could not picture how a mother could divide her attention between her art and her child, either, so when word came from Paris that May was expecting a baby that fall, she had both a happy reason to make the trip and an important function to fulfill in her sister's new family. She could free up May to paint by helping with the baby—Louisa loved babies—and foot some bills so the household could run smoothly. She decided to go as soon as her health improved, if it ever did.

"Very poorly & cross," she wrote as April began. "So tired of being a prisoner to pain. Long for the old strength when I could do what I liked & never knew I had a body." To get around Concord, she bought herself a phaeton, a sporty four-wheeled open carriage, which Bronson also used to ferry visiting philosophers around town in style. Louisa pushed herself to make the best of lovely weather, her little carriage, and her good friends. The mighty engine of her will strained bravely to pull a body heavily freighted with infirmities.

Louisa continued to believe Dr. Kane's 1870 diagnosis, that mercury poisoning from calomel lay at the root of her ills. That diagnosis went unchallenged until 2001, when Drs. Norbert Hirschhorn and Ian Greaves, working with another colleague on a paper about the effects of Abraham Lincoln's mercury-based "blue pills," learned that Louisa Alcott was believed to have died of mercury poisoning. Could they confirm that diagnosis? Greaves and Hirschhorn set out to be Louisa's doctors, compiling a medical history from her writings and reports by others. They noted her excellent health and exceptional vigor before contracting typhoid pneumonia, her treatment with mercury, her recovery, and the symptoms and debility that began about three and a half years later.

Hirschhorn and Greaves classified Louisa's symptoms as headaches ("neuralgia"), joint pain and swelling ("bunches on the leg"), and a welter of gastrointestinal ills: "loss of appetite, nausea, heartburn," also "eructation" (belching) and stomach discomfort. Louisa's intestinal problems overshadowed the others and pointed to gastroesophageal reflux disease, or GERD. Louisa also complained of laryngitis and bronchitis; GERD is a known cause of those symptoms.

Hirschhorn and Greaves found that mercury poisoning was not a plausible explanation for Louisa's symptoms. She did not have the trembling hands or "extreme sensitivity to slights, [and] irrational outbursts of rage" that were known effects of mercury poisoning. Louisa had a temper, but however quick and at times unkind, it always had a cause and a rational target.

The pattern of Louisa's poor health over many years also refuted the mercury poisoning thesis. Mercury causes symptoms only as long as it is taken, and Greaves and Hirschhorn found no evidence that Louisa took mercury after she left the Georgetown hospital. The medical profession knew that mercury was dangerous and ineffective. That knowledge had supported Lincoln's decision to discontinue mercury when he became president. Dr. Kane had been correct about the danger of mercury, but his belief that it never left the body and that the painful "bunches" on Louisa's leg were from dormant mercury was unfounded. Louisa's body would have been free of mercury in a year after treatment, at most, Hirschhorn and Greaves maintain.

What, then, was causing Louisa Alcott's many distressing symptoms? Drs. Hirschhorn and Greaves looked at two theories. Either Louisa suffered from several seemingly unrelated chronic illnesses, or, more likely, all could be explained by one multisystemic disease. If so, which one? Without being able to conduct modern diagnostic tests, Greaves and Hirschhorn wrote, "we can only recall the old professor's teaching: 'Listen to the patient. She is telling you the diagnosis.'" Louisa was "telling" them that she had an autoimmune disease. Exposure to mercury had the potential to trigger an autoimmune response but would not cause the symptoms per se. An autoimmune disease such as syphilis or lupus, on the other hand, could attack Louisa in exactly the miserable ways she described. Discarding syphilis as less probable, the doctors posited lupus as the likely candidate.

Without Louisa their theory could not be proved, and lupus can be difficult to diagnose in any case. But the doctors came very close to clinching the case when Dr. Hirschhorn found a visual clue that had been hiding in plain sight for over a century. As in the best detective fiction, the clue was in the portrait—the only painting of Louisa—by the acclaimed artist George Healy. Louisa had enjoyed sitting for Healy when she came to Rome in 1870 after a run of sunny days in northern Italy. She was less pleased with the portrait, which she described in *Jo's Boys* as notable for the "curious effect of light upon the end of the nose and cheeks as red as the chair she sat in." Jo hung it behind a door.

Hirschhorn was unaware of the passage, but when he saw the painting at Orchard House, he immediately analyzed the curious effect as a rash "sharply demarcated over the upper cheeks and across the bridge of the nose." He saw in it a classic butterfly rash, frequently a first indication of lupus. Often triggered by sunlight, the butterfly rash can easily be mistaken for sunburn and fades the same way. The sun, on those days in northern Italy just before the floods of Rome, quite likely had triggered a butterfly rash that the realistic painter Healy had depicted precisely, not knowing or caring what it signified.

What difference could it have made to Louisa to know a new name for an untreatable disease? She believed her health problems were the consequence of her proud service in the Civil War. She found it comforting to be entitled to say: "As one who gladly gave her dearest possession, health, to serve the good cause I may perhaps deserve a humble place among the women who did what they could." Her health problems were a legitimate and also convenient excuse when she had to—or wanted to—turn away invitations and obligations. As a war veteran, she could not be dismissed as a run-of-the-mill whiner with obscure "female trouble."

Louisa's symptoms were aggravated by stress and somewhat mitigated by the distractions of interesting new experiences and people. Now and then she ventured outings for charity, which she found rewarding and pleasurable. In June of 1879 she accompanied her father in the phaeton to the new Concord prison and amused four hundred inmates by telling them a story. She was so taken with the faces of some young men in the front, who "drank in every word . . . [that she] forgot [her]self & talked away 'like a mother.' One put his head down, & another winked hard, so [she] felt that [she] had caught them, for even one tear in that dry, hard place would do them good." At least one of the men called on her after his release, and she furnished him with a reference to her cousin Sam Greele in Chicago.

With Dr. Laura Whiting Hosmer* Louisa visited the state women's prison at Sherborn, met with its doctor, Lucy M. Hall, and read to the inmates. "A much better place than Concord prison with its armed wardens & 'knock down drag out methods.' Only women here & they work wonders by patience, love, common sense & the belief in salvation for all."

Summer ushered in the first formal session of the Concord School of Philosophy, held in the study at Orchard House, rented for the summer by William Torrey Harris, an educator from Illinois (and later U.S. commissioner of education) who eventually bought the house. "Thirty students, Father the Dean. He has *his* dream realized at last, & is in glory with plenty of talk to swim in. People laugh but will enjoy some new thing in this dull town, & the fresh Westerners will show them that the culture of the world is not in Concord." However delighted to see the local snobs get their comeuppance, she had little patience with the "swarms [of] budding philosophers" the school attracted. "They roost on our step like hens, waiting for corn," she complained. "If they were philanthropists I *should* enjoy it, but speculation seems a waste of time when there is so much real work crying to be done. Why discuss the Unknowable till our poor are fed & the wicked saved?" At the end of the summer, Louisa escaped to the shore for a week with Dr. Hosmer and returned ready to begin the serial *Jack and Jill*, based on the adventures of Concord's youth. She had none of her own left to write about, and knew the current crop had different pastimes. She made it her business to learn what they were.

In the spring one doctor encouraged Louisa to make the trip to see May and be at the birth of her child, but by autumn friends, family, and a different doctor had convinced her that she would only add to her sister's worries if she arrived in Paris ill from the stress of the trip. The decision released the sense of foreboding that lay just beneath the surface. She

---

* Dr. Hosmer, a widow with a practice in Concord, was one of several women of Louisa's acquaintance who had earned medical degrees despite powerful resistance to their inclusion in the profession. They treated few men other than the charity cases that were a large component of their practices. Louisa seems to have asked Dr. Hosmer's medical opinion only informally.

knew she would wish she had gone. Instead she again rented a room at the Bellevue for a month and sat down to finish *Jack and Jill*.

⁓

On November 8, word arrived that May had given birth to a baby girl. The baby was named for Louisa and immediately nicknamed Lulu. "All doing well. Much rejoicing. . . . Ah, if I had only been there! Too much happiness for me." A month later the news from Paris was unsettling. The baby was thriving, but May was not; she had contracted postpartum fever. "The weight on my heart is not all imagination," Louisa wrote. "She was too happy to have it last, & I fear the end is coming." Unable to help her sister, she was frantic with worry and self-accusation. "Such a tugging at my heart to be by poor May alone so far away," she wailed. "This is a penance for all my sins." Bronson returned from the West to be with the family and to worry about the outdated news in letters sent days before by Ernst or his sister Sophie. On the last day of 1879, Anna was in Boston and Bronson was haunting the post office when one of the servants summoned Louisa: Mr. Emerson was waiting for her in the parlor. "I found him looking at May's portrait, pale & tearful with the paper in his hand. 'My child, I wish I could prepare you, but alas, alas!' [T]here his voice failed and he gave me the telegram." Ernst Nieriker had sent the message to Emerson rather than to the family in hopes that he might soften the blow. Louisa was touched by the kindness but not surprised by the telegram's contents; "[I read] the hard words as if I knew it all before." Louisa had to relay the news of May's death twice, to Bronson and to Anna when each returned, "a very bitter sorrow for all."

In every way, this death was Louisa's cruelest blow. The loss of so much happiness ended so soon confirmed her darkest view of life. Ernst Nieriker would have the baby to console him. Nothing could comfort the Alcott family. Louisa was left with painful regret. "I shall never forgive myself for not going even if it put me back. If I had lived to see her & help her die, or save her, I should have been content." In letters that followed, she would learn that in her delirium, May had spoken of "'getting ready for Louy,' & asked if she had come."

May had headed into childbirth with foreboding equal to Louisa's, and the presence of mind to anticipate its all-too-frequent outcome. "If I die when baby comes," she wrote her family, "don't mourn for I have had as much happiness in this short time as many [have had] in twenty years."

She prepared trunks containing treasures for Louisa and Anna and for Ernst's sisters, brought her diary up to date, even chose her burial place. Most significant of all, she asked that her daughter be turned over to Louisa to bring up. Ernst would obey May's wishes "sacredly," wrote Louisa. So would she: "I see now why I lived. To care for May's child & not leave Annie all alone."

EIGHTEEN

MORE COURAGE AND PATIENCE

Louisa was going to be a mother at age forty-seven. For ten months she waited for her child to arrive, not quite able to believe that a baby, and not her sister, would be coming off the steamship. She could not "make it true that our May is dead, lying far away in a strange grave." But the plans were made, the steamship tickets bought, the nursery prepared. Ernst Nieriker did not dispute his late wife's wishes. He was planning to go to Brazil to try to forget his wife and child, to start a new life, and to make his fortune.

Louisa sought relief in hard work, writing the final episodes of *Jack and Jill* "with a heavy heart" and the "hope the grief did not get into them." It did. *Jack and Jill* is full of loss and grief, specifically grief in children, so commonplace in Louisa's time. Like the nursery rhyme, the book begins with Jack suffering a serious head injury while sledding. It ends with the death of Jack's best friend, Ed Devens. The story stays out of Ed's sickroom, focusing instead on the children who come around after school, at first expecting to see their pal within days, and at last understanding that they never will. As narrator, Louisa anticipates parental objection to a scene of such pathos: "since even the . . . most guarded child cannot escape some knowledge of the great mystery, is it not well to teach them . . . that affection sweetens sorrow, and a lovely life can make death beautiful?" A scene between Jack and his brother, grief-stricken by the loss of their friend, could be Louisa's image of the Pratt brothers' reaction to their father's death: "There was such a sympathetic choke in Frank's voice that Jack felt comforted at once, and when he had had his cry out, ... he let Frank pull him up with a bear-like but affectionate hug, and sat leaning on him as they talked about their loss, ... and resolving to love one another very much hereafter." *Jack and Jill*'s dark story is a warning to youth that grief lies ahead, and an admonition to cherish one another.

Louisa was emotionally spent. She turned down *St. Nicholas* magazine's request for another serial. "Reality makes romance seem pale & flat now," she lamented. She also put away *Diana and Persis*, her tale of May's romance, her own jealousy, and the conflict between love and art. Louisa's argument that motherhood was fatal to artistic ambition had proved true, disastrously in May's case, and Louisa had no taste for completing and publishing it. As she had during her sister Lizzie's last illness, Louisa turned to poetry. "Our Madonna" commemorates May's life as a progress through art to the crowning achievement of motherhood.

> *. . . A mother folding in her arms,*
> *The sweet supreme success*
> *Giving a life to win a life,*
> *Dying that she might bless.*
> *Grateful for joy unspeakable,*
> *In that brief, blissful past:*
> *The picture of a baby's face,*
> *Her loveliest and last . . .*

Bronson Alcott could not comprehend the terrible news of a second daughter's death. He wrote poetry, too. Bronson's "Love's Morrow" is less a memorial poem than a characteristically self-involved chart of his grief.

> *I wake in tears and sorrow:*
> *Wearily I say,*
> *"Come, come fair morrow,*
> *And chase my grief away!"*
> *Night-long I say, "Haste, haste, fair morrow,*
> *And bear my grief away!"*
> *All night long,*
> *My sad, sad song.*

Louisa reviewed her papers, as she had before and would again, this time probably for glimpses of May as much as from her professed feeling that "one should be ready to go at any moment." She "sorted old letters and burned many. Not wise to keep for curious eyes to read, and gossip-lovers to print by and by. My journals were all burnt long ago in terror of gossip when I depart and of unwise use of my very frank records of people and events." In fact she did not burn all her journals but seemed determined to obliterate her private writings bit by bit, to sacrifice the selves she had so often addressed in the margins of her earlier entries.

In March, a large box of May's things arrived from France, material evidence for Louisa that her sister's death was a fact. May had selected the contents herself before she gave birth, anticipating that she might not survive it. Louisa was glad to have "all that is left us of this bright soul, but the baby soon to come. Treasures all." Among them "in one of her own sepia boxes [was] her pretty hair tied with blue ribbon." Louisa's relief to have emblems of May to mourn infuses her description of "a sad day & many tears dropped on the dear dress, the blue slippers she last wore." They were the same blue slippers that May had shuffled into on chilly Paris mornings in her art student days. Wearing May's fur-lined bed jacket felt like having her sister's arms around her and gave Louisa solace. The many paintings May sent soon adorned the walls of the old Thoreau home, now Anna's. Some were familiar from letters filled with sketches and anecdotes of days spent painting. Bronson, Louisa, and Anna—the Alcott family remnant—could imagine May pondering her next stroke, brush at the ready. They could see the great progress May had been making.

To raise Louisa May Nieriker was more than just a motive to go on. Louisa viewed it as a duty and also a joy. At Anna's house a nursery awaited the ten-month-old baby that May had wanted to call Lulu. A nurse, Mrs. Giles, had been dispatched to Europe with everything the child might need, and a ticket for Ernst Nieriker's sixteen-year-old sister to accompany her back. Sophie Nieriker would stay several months to be a familiar presence and to help with Lulu. On September 19, 1880, Louisa stood watching on the Boston wharf as passengers debarked; each time she saw someone with a baby, she wondered "if that was mine."

At last the Captain appeared, & in his arms a little yellow-haired thing in white, with its hat off as it looked about with lively blue eyes. . . . I held out my arms . . . only being able to say her name. She looked at me for a moment, then came to me saying "Marmar?" in a wistful way, & nestling close as if she had found her own people & home at last, as she had, thank Heaven!

Later Louisa would write to Maggie Lukens, "[May's spirit] is about her baby I feel, for out of the innocent blue eyes sometimes come looks so like her mother's that I am startled, for I tended May as a child as I now tend Lulu." Anna had the same feeling about her niece, for the same reason. Bronson delighted in walking his granddaughter through his garden to spy on birds. Lulu was balm for the whole family.

Ernst's sixteen-year-old sister Sophie turned out to be delightful, helpful, and eager to know her niece's relatives. Louisa made her the heroine of a story, "Sophie's Secret," where the "fine manners, foreign ways, and many accomplishments," along with "a quick temper" and plain dress, set her apart from the rude if beruffled American girls. Only the character Fanny, a version of young Louisa, "a slender brown girl . . . with her hair streaming in the wind . . . always took her part, and helped her."

Louisa treated the family to a winter in Boston, renting a cousin's house on Pinckney Street on Beacon Hill, and getting a piano for Sophie to play. Bronson, at eighty still in the peak of health, was off on a seven-month tour of the West, giving a speech every day, and on some days two.

"Devote myself to [Lulu]," Louisa wrote, "and find life much brighter." Like many new mothers, she recorded Lulu's every milestone and threw a first-birthday celebration worthy of her parents' devotion to festivities, with the material abundance of the Gilded Age substituted for the pine boughs and homemade presents of her own childhood. Like her mother, Lulu had a talent for pleasing. She sang "Up! Bow wow, Mama Da," then from her pile of new dresses, dolls, and toys selected a picture book to study, "like a true artist's baby." She favored the illustrations of Randolph Caldecott and Kate Greenaway, the greats of the day.

Motherhood so absorbed Louisa the next year that she made only four journal entries and wrote to editors mostly to explain why she was rejecting their pleas for new work. "Baby is well, thank you," she wrote in midsummer to the editor Mary Mapes Dodge,* who apparently had not

---

* The author of *Hans Brinker: or, The Silver Skates* (1865), Mary Mapes Dodge was the editor of *St. Nicholas* magazine.

inquired. Dodge had caught up with Louisa at Nonquitt, a resort community on Buzzards Bay near the offshore island of Martha's Vineyard.
Nonquitt would become the summer haunt of Lulu and her cousins Fred
and John Pratt. In the autumn Louisa wrote the persistent Mrs. Dodge
again, this time making her point more bluntly.

> Dear Distracted Editor,
>
> I will try. Can a mortal woman say more? The reason why I have re-
> fused before is that since I stopped writing my over taxed nerves have
> given me little trouble, & the care of Baby has been just the right work
> for me. For her sake as well as my own, I have held off from the pen,
> knowing that if I once took it up the old hurry & worry would come on,
> & I should be as fractious as a teething child.

She could afford the sabbatical. In 1881 alone, Roberts Brothers printed
almost thirty-five thousand copies of her earlier titles, reflected in a January payment of nearly four thousand dollars. Seeing that she needn't
write something new to generate income, Louisa bought back the copyright to *Moods* from the publisher A. K. Loring, who had gone bankrupt.
Of all her adult fiction, *Moods* had been her favorite, and she had never
accepted the shortened version that she believed had spoiled the original
work. Now she revised the book, but whatever intention she may have
begun with, ultimately she did not restore *Moods* as an unconventional
novel of ideas. Instead she reframed it for her teenage audience. In an introduction to the new edition she said she had cut some chapters, restored
others, and trimmed "as much fine writing as could be done without de-
stroying the youthful spirit of the little romance." She gave the story a
new, happy ending: in this one Sylvia Yule resumes her marriage to the
Emersonian Geoffrey Moor, having learned that "love and duty go hand
in hand." In her new introduction she denied that marriage had ever been
the subject of the book, for "a girl of eighteen could know but little" about
marriage. "At eighteen," she states, "death seemed the only solution to
Sylvia's perplexities," but "thirty years later" the author sees that life's
compromises can be for the best, and her "heroine meets a wiser if less
romantic fate."

The 1882 revision of *Moods* is regarded as Louisa's last work of adult
fiction, and as a correction of the first version, but more than either it is a
betrayal of the work. *Moods* as originally written *was* about marriage, as

Louisa had said at the time. And at the time she wrote *Moods* she was not a girl of eighteen but a woman of twenty-eight, although twice in the introduction she makes that claim in furtherance of an attempt to convert the book from a daring adult novel to one that could pass for juvenile fiction. Louisa had been pigeonholed as a writer for children and had long felt trapped by the typecasting, but with the advent of Lulu, she seems to have accepted it. She gave up her wish to write one book she could be proud of, not realizing that in *Little Women* she had written that book. Between her poor health, her preoccupation with her young child, and the lure of a market she had already cornered, her decision, if it was that, is understandable. After *Little Women* was published, she actually never again wrote a first draft of a novel for adults. *Work* was a revision of *Success*, which she had begun to write and then put aside before she started *Moods*. *A Modern Mephistopheles* was based upon *A Long Fatal Love Chase*, a thriller written immediately after her return from her first European trip and rejected as too sensational for publication at the time.

After 1882, when Louisa picked up her pen it was not to write the ambitious novel *Moods* had once been, but little tales for Lulu, or letters and articles to further the causes of woman suffrage and temperance. Temperance was considered a feminist issue; domestic violence and economic hardship were the demonstrable results of men's excessive drinking. (The addiction of many women to opiates was rarely acknowledged, much less cited as a threat to families, although of course it was one.) While she was never a teetotaler, Louisa was concerned with daredevil drinking among her teenage readers, and in *Rose in Bloom* she drew for them a cautionary tale in the tragic death of a sympathetic young man. Worried about "young Americans, gentlemen as well as farmers & mill hands," she helped organize Concord's first temperance society.

⌒

At two and a half, Lulu went through the ordeal of teething. Louisa devoted hours to distracting her, telling "stories by the dozen," playing "lambs, piggies & 'tats' [cats] [to] soothe her little woes." But Louisa found it hard to tolerate the noise her niece made, and she often felt impatient and on edge. The incessant demands of motherhood were too much, and hired help was usually worse than none; few nurses met her standards or the challenge of boisterous Lulu, who was something of a hellion. "I don't think I was afraid of the devil. I was a little devil myself,"* Lulu would say more than ninety years later.

⁓

Every month seemed to bring the death of another of her father's generation, Louisa noted after the funeral of Wendell Phillips, where she squeezed in between Mr. and Mrs. Frederick Douglass.† Some of the older sages were gone but not dead. Mr. Emerson had been declining for years. At the funeral of Henry Wadsworth Longfellow, Emerson was so confused by the open casket that he returned for a second look, asking, "Where are we? Whose house is this? And who is the sleeper?" A few weeks later he caught pneumonia, sure to be fatal to a frail elderly man in that era.

Bronson made a final visit to his dearest friend in the big white house just down the Lexington Road. After the 1872 fire it had been rebuilt exactly as before. From his sickbed, Louisa reported, Emerson "held [Father's] hand looking up at the tall, rosy old man, & saying with that smile of love that has been father's sunshine for so many years, 'you are very well, Keep so, keep so.' After father left he called him back & grasped his hand again as if he knew it was for the last time & the kind eyes said 'Good by, my friend.'"

⁓

Louisa spent the first half of the 1880s on successive tours of duty: to Bronson, to Anna, to her nephews, to Lulu, to friends, and to her publishers. "Shall never live my own life," she wrote in her journal. Duty took

---

* "afraid of the devil": The late Madelon Bedell, author of *The Alcotts*, interviewed Louisa May "Lulu" Nieriker Rasim in Switzerland in 1975, when Lulu was ninety-six years old. After almost a century of disuse, her English no longer came naturally. Bedell had, in fact, been warned that Lulu no longer remembered very much of the language of her childhood, but the writer made the trip to Switzerland anyway. Lulu died four months after Bedell's interviews took place. Madelon Bedell herself died before completing the second volume of *The Alcotts*. These quotations from her transcription of the interviews are published here for the first time. (Bedell Papers, Orchard House.)
† Frederick Douglass (1818–95), orator, author, suffragist, and publisher, had worked with Wendell Phillips in the Boston antislavery movement; Frederick's wife, Anna Murray Douglass (c.1813–82), was a Baltimore free black woman who had helped him to escape slavery.

Louisa to Concord in July of 1882 to help out with the annual session of her father's School of Philosophy. The town was a carnival of strangers seeking wisdom—Louisa called them "M. Fullers in white muslin & Hegels in straw hats"—and locals taking their money for rooms and carriage rides. Louisa and Anna had four hundred callers at the Orchard House school headquarters that month. The sisters preferred running a house (or as Louisa called it, a hotel) to being bored at the formal sessions held in the structure in the side yard built for the purpose in 1880. Its style, unique to Bronson Alcott, is best described in an oxymoron, Rustic Gothic. Its one room was as hot as the air exhaled by the expositors of pet theories and bearers of cultural tidings within. Louisa turned out a comic verse inspired by the scene.

> *Philosophers sit in their sylvan hall*
> *And talk of the duties of man,*
> *Of Chaos and Cosmos, Hegel and Kant,*
> *With Oversoul well in the van;*
> *All on their hobbies they amble away,*
> *And a terrible dust they make;*
> *Disciples devout both gaze and adore,*
> *As daily they listen and bake!*

October of 1882 found a relieved Louisa back in Boston at the Bellevue—now an apartment hotel—with nineteen-year-old Fred Pratt and seventeen-year-old Johnny. Fred was studying flute at the Conservatory of Music while his brother attended Chauncy Hall School, tuitions undoubtedly paid by Aunt "Wee," or "Weedy," as she was called. Louisa said she missed Lulu, but peace and quiet were essential to writing.

With Lulu in Concord, Bronson's study can't have been very quiet, but he was writing too—dozens of sonnets, most of them tributes to the people most important to his life. At eighty-two, he was improving as a writer. Although Bronson Alcott rates no higher than the third rank of poets, his sonnets are interesting as contemporary portraits of Emerson, Thoreau, Abby, and many others in his circle. Not among the best is the sonnet to Louisa, but it repays trudging through its lines to see the light it throws upon Bronson's admiration and love for Louisa. Not the easy, natural feeling he gave to his other daughters, his affection for her is like a medal, bestowed for good conduct. Louisa's demonstration of her bravery and sacrifice in the Civil War, her hard work making a fortune, and her devotion to family finally earned his approval. Like the other poems, this sonnet has no title, but it has always been called "Duty's Faithful Child."

When I remember with what buoyant heart,
Midst war's alarms and woes of civil strife,
In youthful eagerness thou didst depart,
At peril of thy safety, peace, and life,
To nurse the wounded soldier, swathe the dead,—
How piercèd soon by fever's poisoned dart,
And brought unconscious home, with bewildered head,
Though ever since, mid languor and dull pain,
To conquer fortune, cherish kindred dear,
Hast with grave studies vexed a sprightly brain,
In myriad households kindled love and cheer;
Ne'er from thyself by Fame's loud trump beguiled,
Sounding in this and the farther hemisphere,—
I press thee to my heart as Duty's faithful child.

In Boston, Louisa's lucrative and popular literary pursuits supported her father's high-minded and obscure forays into letters. Mary Mapes Dodge's repeated appeals for a serial finally propelled Louisa to work on *Jo's Boys*, the last of the March family stories. The book had been planned first for publication as a serial and promised to Niles after that, but Louisa dropped it after May's death; like her artist sister, she painted from life. Louisa could establish that Marmee had died, but for bright, vivacious Amy to die was as unacceptable fictionally as May's death had been in real life. The author would explain to her readers, "Since the original of that character died, it has been impossible for me to write of her as when she was here to suggest, criticise, and laugh over her namesake." In *Jo's Boys*, May/Amy is enshrined with her husband and daughter in a home "full of unostentatious beauty and comfort" called Parnassus, after the Roman home of the Muses. She is an artist, "one of those who prove that women can be faithful wives and mothers without sacrificing . . . [their] special gift."

Now, less for Dodge than for Niles who had always been kind and honest in his dealings with her, Louisa would try to write *Jo's Boys*. She had barely begun when Bronson suffered a crippling stroke. In an instant, her hale, handsome father was changed into a helpless wreck.

In letters detailing her father's condition, mostly in replies to the cadre of women who had worshipped at his Conversations, Louisa expressed the wish, and the expectation, that her father would not live long. As the cause of his debility, she blamed overwork. "The 40 sonnets he wrote last winter & the 50 lectures at the school were too much for a man of 83 ... now poor father pays the penalty of breaking the laws of health." Actually it was Louisa who paid her father's penalty for the stroke, by having to take on his care.

Lulu remembered her grandfather as "a beautiful old man. His profile was serene. . . . He . . . had been paralyzed, and couldn't talk with me." With his right side useless, Bronson Alcott never penned another word. He had written, some would say, enough. His fifty-two volumes of journals were nearby, bound elegantly at Louisa's expense as a gift, but he could only admire, not read them. Toward the end of 1882 there was some progress: Bronson regained his speech and with it his original Connecticut Yankee accent. His thinking—or the expression of it—was garbled, however. Louisa reported that he made "very queer remarks, the sublime and the absurd so mixed that one must laugh even with tears in the eyes." Sometimes Bronson talked in his sleep, "& seem[ed] to be lecturing." Louisa recorded some of his utterances: " 'True godliness is the ideal.' 'The devil is never real, only truth,' and the mystifying 'I am taking a predicament.' " On November 29 "he was dimly conscious of his birthday though he was sure his age was *twenty-three* instead of eighty-three." Louisa was fifty and truly middle-aged. She had responsibility for the generation before her own and also for the one that came next.

Someone to bathe, feed, dress, and undress Bronson was urgently needed. Louisa spent much of January 1883 hiring and firing incompetent nurses who sat by the fire drinking tea. She could do better herself, she knew, but hadn't the desire or the stamina. In February, at last finding a trustworthy helper—Lulu remembered "a man nurse, who dressed [Bronson] and undressed him, put him to bed like a child"—she fled to Boston for a week of respite. In March she got away again, this time absconding with Lulu and a maid to the Bellevue for a month. Louisa bought the three-year-old a canary and took her to meet people. She wanted them to know May's child, perhaps to be sure her niece could feel the support of an extended family as she had done, however mixed with unkindness. She had Lulu's picture taken by William Notman, the premier portrait photographer of the day, and indulged Lulu's and her own weakness for fine clothing. "I was always very well dressed as a child," Lulu would remember, in particular her "little hats, a peaky hat, and a pom-pom all around." She had twenty-five dresses at a time, and her aunts always "went to first class shops" to buy her clothes. Louisa enjoyed lavishing money and attention on her niece. Devoting herself to her father, on the other hand, was distressing and unrewarding, and the back-and-forth between Concord and Boston in shifting combinations of Pratts and Alcotts was exhausting. No wonder that a friend of Louisa's said that she "spoke of herself as one destined to fill vacant niches, being a wife to her father, a husband to her widowed sister, and a mother to her little niece."

⁓

By September 1883, they were all together back in Concord, at Anna's house on Main Street. The crowded quarters and the combination of invalid Bronson and toddler Lulu set off competition for Louisa's attention. Christmas brought out the worst. Writing to her cousin Lizzie Wells, Louisa confessed that between her "two babies" she felt "like a nursing ma with twins. Father is jealous of L. & she doesn't like me to kiss him before her, & it is funny to see them frown at one another. . . . Funny but not fun. I run to & fro till legs & head are tired out." On New Year's Day of 1884 Lulu threw a royal tantrum. Louisa responded miserably: "[I] solemnly spank[ed] my child. . . . Her bewilderment was pathetic, & the effect, as I expected, a failure. Love is better, but also endless patience." Louisa could supply endless love, but not patience.

"Oh, Aunt Louisa took me in hand," Lulu told the Alcott biographer Madelon Bedell. "I hope she spanked me very often. I needed it. I was a spoiled child and all my governesses when they were engaged by Aunt Louisa were told not to touch me." After nine decades, Lulu's memories of her Alcott aunts remained vivid. "Anna was a perfect angel. I've never known anybody so sweet. . . . She never got angry with anybody. She loved everybody." Lulu described Louisa as tall and thin, with "dark hair . . . and a lot of hair. Aunt Anna had a lot of hair, but it was grey. Aunt Anna had a soft voice. . . . I thought angels must be like that. Aunt Louisa was more like a man, so strong, and I think her voice rang out, whereas Aunt Anna was just like a dove. Aunt Anna I remember was very serene. Aunt Louisa was the one who was nervous . . . and yet I felt I could do anything I liked."

That June, almost seven years after the Alcotts had left it, Louisa sold Orchard House to their tenant, her father's friend William Harris, and happily used the money to buy a summer cottage at Nonquitt. At the end of the month she went there with Lulu and John, their preferred Pratt brother (Lulu would recall Fred as stolid and distant), and the newest nanny. John and his friends formed a drama group to perform under the expert direction of his seasoned aunt, Lulu hero-worshipped her older cousin and played with other little girls, and Louisa repaired and decorated the first house she had ever owned. She loved that it had no kitchen; how they dined is unknown, but they probably had prepared food delivered to them from a hotel next door.

⌒

The new year of 1885 found Louisa living in Boston unencumbered by Alcotts or Pratts, in a position to shape her own life as she wanted—and she tried. She attended the opera and spent evenings with friends, but pain got the better of pleasure. Her bitter prophecy was proving true: "When I had the youth, I had no money; now I have the money I have no time; and when I get the time, if I ever do, I shall have no health to enjoy life." Her right arm and hand ached too much to hold a pen, so she was even denied her salvation—work.

Determined to try every possible cure, no matter how seemingly outlandish, she sought out Anna Newman, a Mind Cure practitioner. Mind Cure, mesmerism,* and the new religion of Christian Science constituted the alternative medicine of the day; all held that the mind was the key to health. (Before his stroke, Bronson had spent some time in Lynn with the founder of Christian Science, Mary Baker Eddy.)

Louisa was skeptical of Mind Cure but was quite taken with it at first. The treatments seem to have been guided meditations that relied upon the power of suggestion for results. In a letter to Maggie Lukens that

---

* Mesmerism, named after its inventor, Franz Anton Mesmer, a German physician of the late eighteenth century, was essentially what we now call hypnotism. Mesmer also called it "animal magnetism" and believed that it involved a magnetic fluid present in the body.

winter of 1885, Louisa described a session: "The patient sits quietly with shut eyes, & the Dr the same, for fifteen minutes in silence. . . . I feel very still then very light, & seem [to be] floating away on a sea of rest. Once or twice I seemed to have no body. . . . I felt as if I trod on air & was very happy & young for some hours." But soon she quit. Thirty treatments, she wrote, "made no more impression on me than a moonbeam," and she concluded that a treatment that claimed to cure cancer but couldn't even cure a headache had to be bogus. She was still ". . . very lurchy when I walk," she wrote, "and dizzy when I stoop"; but with no remedy "I go on as before."

She had resumed correspondence with Maggie Lukens after a lapse of ten years, long after the Lukens sisters had stopped publishing *Little Things*, the magazine inspired by the *Pickwick Portfolio* produced by the March sisters in *Little Women*. One of Maggie Lukens's sisters had died, and Maggie sought comfort as well as advice about leaving home. "You speak of "'breaking away,'" Louisa replied cautiously. "If it can be dutifully and wisely done I think girls should see a little of the world, try their own powers. . . . Young people need change." Louisa hoped to see her if she "[took] flight from the nest," renewing her invitation of five years before, and signed "with much love and sympathy to all I am, dear Maggie, your friend as always, L.M. Alcott."

In her reply Maggie apparently wrote that she was questioning her religion, and asked Louisa about her faith. Louisa answered at length, describing her churchless upbringing, finding God in nature, and happiness in duty—or trying to. "Freedom was always my longing, but I have never had it, so I am still trying to feel that this [her obligation to family members] is the discipline I need." The postscript to this letter comes as a surprise: "The simple Buddha religion is very attractive to me, & I believe in it."

The next letter to Lukens describes Louisa's conception of the "great Hereafter" and reveals her belief in past lives. "I seem to remember former states before this . . . & in my next step I hope to leave behind many of the trials that I have struggled to bear here. . . . This is my idea of immortality. An endless life of helpful change, with the instinct, the longing to rise, to learn, to love, to get nearer the source of all good . . . as we climb into the clearer light, the purer air, the happier life which must exist." When Louisa was a girl, around the time of the Fruitlands debacle, her father had been accused of being a Buddhist and had denied it, but now

Buddhism seemed to catch Louisa's attention and to help her through her earthly trials.

She passed most of the winter of 1885 alone on Chestnut Street in Boston, visiting friends, reading, sewing, and writing letters, though none survive that are as intimate and frank as those addressed to Maggie Lukens. To a fan who peppered her with a long list of questions she brusquely replied, "Miss Alcott does not usually answer any letters from strangers because she has a lame hand & it is impossible for one busy woman to answer the questions of many curious people." Then she answered them anyway, by number.

1. My father only is living.
2. *Laurie* was a real boy . . .
5. I do not sell my pictures . . .
6. *Amy*'s real daughter *Lulu* is not like me. Amy is dead . . .
9. Meg is alive & Jo, & Teddy [Laurie/Laddie] who lives in Paris . . .

To Lucy Stone, editor of the *Woman's Journal*, Louisa affirmed her support for the publication's readership, "those who are giving lives to the emancipation of the white slaves of America," and granted the use of her name though not her time. Louisa's writing for girls was her feminist platform, and a strong one. From Nonquitt later that summer, she wrote Niles to suggest that they combine some recent stories with tales she had invented for Lulu to produce a book to market at Christmas. *Lulu's Library* could be the first of a series for the youngest children. Recycling was the best she could do. It had taken Louisa two or three months to write each volume of *Little Women*. *Jo's Boys* would take seven years.

It was imperative to come up with a better plan for the family; to that end, she signed a two-year lease for a house at No. 10 Louisburg Square in Boston, the most fashionable neighborhood on Beacon Hill. The rent— $1,650 for two years—struck her as high, but the house was spacious, furnished, and big enough for her entire extended family. For someone who liked freedom and her own company, the new plan was a tremendous sacrifice. Louisa vowed she would "try to bear the friction & the worry" a lot of people always brought her.

Everyone else was pleased by their benefactor's choice—Bronson happy in his new room, Lulu charmed by her big sunny nursery. "I could see the [Charles] river from my window," she remembered, "and down in the yard . . . one beautiful chestnut tree" that budded out spectacularly in spring. Her cousins Fred and John were on top of the world, as was their mother, able to enjoy Boston for the first time in her adult life. Louisa, a former servant, now employed ten servants herself. Although her aunts were raised as vegetarians, Lulu remembered that "they always had splendid meals, a great deal of meats, splendid roast beefs." Louisa was determined that Lulu would be well nourished; in the Gilded Age that meant eating great quantities of meat.

Afraid to write and perhaps bring on an attack, for a while Louisa devoted herself to her niece and her father. Virtue went unrewarded; she got sick anyway. Plans for *Jo's Boys* were spinning in her brain; she argued to her doctor that if she could only get her ideas down on paper she would be able to rest. He was persuaded to let her try for half an hour a day. Within a few days she was back in bed. A week later she got up, not to write but to take care of Lulu, who had a cold.

Warmer weather inexplicably brought the gift of renewed health. In June of 1885 Louisa took a vacation in the mountains of New Hampshire and for the first time in seven years wrote for a sustained period. She tore off fifteen chapters of *Jo's Boys* in three weeks. On the last page she confessed that it was "a strong temptation to the weary historian to close the present tale with an earthquake which should engulf Plumfield and its environs so deeply in the bowels of the earth that no youthful Schliemann* could ever find a vestige of it." She relented, however, and continued, "But as that somewhat melodramatic conclusion might shock my gentle readers, I will refrain, and forestall the usual question, 'How did they end?' by briefly stating that all the marriages turned out well." She spelled out the merited fate of every character, then bowed out gracefully: "And now, having endeavored to suit everyone by many weddings, few deaths, and as much prosperity as the eternal fitness of things will permit, let the music stop, the lights die out, and the curtain fall forever on the March family."

Louisa didn't think much of *Jo's Boys*, but she understood that given the pent-up demand it would sell, and she needed a lot of money to keep the family luxury liner afloat. Roberts ran off two ten-thousand-copy

---

* Heinrich Schliemann had rediscovered the ancient city of Troy a decade earlier. His discovery was the first evidence that Homer's *Iliad* was based in fact, which created tremendous excitement.

printings in quick succession and urged the golden goose to begin another novel immediately.

⌒

With the publication of *Jo's Boys, and How They Turned Out*, editors of
magazines suddenly felt renewed hope for new stories, as did Louisa,
briefly. But on some unknown date in 1886, she gave her mind permission to rest and be reconciled with her literary fate in a poem titled "To
My Brain." Like most of her verse, it was not written for publication.

> *Rest, weary brain, thy task is done,*
> *The Burden of the day is past;*
> *Thy wage is earned and freely paid,*
> *Thy holiday begins at last . . .*
> *. . . Rest, and rejoice in thy one gift.*
> *For sure it is a happy art*
> *To conquer fate, win friends and live,*
> *Enshrined in many a childish heart.*

"If possible [I mean] to keep up until after Christmas, and then I am
sure I shall break down," she wrote to a friend, Maria Porter, and did just
that. When Porter stopped by Louisburg Square with a gift, Louisa
showed her the Christmas tree and seemed in good spirits. But on New
Year's Day Porter found her in bed at a nursing home in nearby Roxbury.
The "Saint's Rest," as Louisa dubbed it, was run by her friend Dr. Rhoda
Lawrence and financed in part by Louisa; she had foreseen her own need
for professional care. She had suspended her life many times to nurse
Lizzie, Abby, Bronson, Anna, Lulu, and her nephews, believing in the
comfort of a family member nearby, but when she became bedridden,
there was no one to reciprocate. "Feeble & sick, away from home &
worn out with the long struggle for health," she wrote. "Have had many
hard days but few harder than this. Say my prayers & try to see many
mercies."

She spent much of 1887 at Dr. Lawrence's retreat, feeling *sick & blue,*
cross, or *discouraged*—the words that recur almost daily in her brief
journal entries. Exhaustion often reduced her comments to a mere *ditto,*
although now and then a wry philosophical comment breaks through:
"Patience is having her perfect work," she noted in mid-January. "Hope

she likes the job better than I do." In verse she prayed for "Courage and Patience."

> *Courage and patience, these I ask,*
> *Dear Lord in this my latest strait;*
> *For hard I find my ten years' task,*
> *Learning to suffer and to wait.*

From her invalid's bed she planned her nephew Fred's wedding, mapped out an excursion in Boston with Lulu, and played with a new idea for a novel. As always Louisa's complaints were various and confusing, but her gastrointestinal troubles were the worst. Her diet had dwindled to monotonous doses of "geum"—a popular plant-based remedy for indigestion—and cream, with now and then a few oysters, which rarely sat well, and small doses of red meat that she chewed but did not swallow. She diligently tracked the miserable state of her bowels using a discreet code—X for enema, *Job* for a successful bowel movement—but the facts could not be interpreted in any useful way. In the six months between October 1886 and March 1887, she lost twenty-five pounds.

In the hours confined to her bed, Louisa read, wrote letters, and sewed. When she was too tired, Dr. Lawrence read to her. She saw little of Lulu but sent affectionate letters filled with advice and encouragement. "I suppose tomorrow p.m. you will go off to the theatre as fine as any young lady. Take a fan, & if you get hot & tired go out and walk between the acts. There is water & a W.C. in the ladies room to the left as you leave the parquette, tell Miss H.* Then you will be fresh & comfy for the rest."

She made the most of any renewal of strength, going into the city to visit Lulu, attending a lecture, or running errands. She tracked Lulu's lessons, her outings, and her (unimpressive) progress in school. "I hated schools," Lulu recalled as an old woman. "I hated all the teachers." She described herself as a "very bad scholar": "Very bad. You know, I didn't grab so quickly. I was very slow in grabbing the *meaning* of things." Louisa was more concerned that Lulu spent too much time with cranky old people, and didn't like the nanny trying to rein in the natural activity of a small child. "I know how she feels," the former dynamo commented.

---

* A Mrs. Hall was helping Anna run 10 Louisburg Square.

Despite regular visits from Anna and the boys and Fred's fiancée, Jessica Cate, Louisa could not help but feel lonely, depressed, and discouraged. A good day merited underlining or an exclamation point. "Spirits good. A ray of hope!"

By July of 1887 Louisa concluded that "hope and patience seem in vain." She updated her will. She made arrangements to adopt John as a legal heir to bequeath her copyrights. On September 1, she made a prophecy: "The end is not far off. The Drs see it, & I feel it." Citing her doctor's instructions to "eat or die," she noted that she "might as well die."

"Death never seemed terrible to me," she had written to Maggie Lukens. In her journal she wrote, "Life was always a puzzle to me, and gets more mysterious as I go on. . . . It's all right, if I can only keep brave and patient to the end."

Louisa's fifty-fifth birthday was the first she'd spent away from her father in years, but Lulu's visit made up for it. She arrived bearing armloads of presents from Anna and friends—plus flowers, and a drawing by May of the salon in Paris where she and Ernst had been so happy. Louisa looked at the room full of gifts and marveled that she had inspired them. They were little consolation for her loneliness.

On good days she was still willing to believe in miracles. New Year's Day of 1888 was "a happy day & great contrast to Jan. 1st of last year. Then I was ill & hopeless & sad. Now though still alone & absent from home I am on the road to health at last." But she was not well enough to attend her nephew Fred's wedding to Jessica Cate several weeks later.

Every few days Louisa managed to make the half-hour trip to Louisburg Square to see Bronson. Installed on a sofa in the parlor, his right side immobile, her father was too weak to speak more than the occasional word. Most of the day he was half-awake or half-asleep, but always calm, his eyes more serene and blue than ever. For six years he had clung to life beyond all expectations, outliving all the other Transcendentalists. On his most recent birthday, his eighty-eighth and her fifty-fifth, Louisa had saluted his personal pilgrim's progress in a poem, "The Last of the Philosophers." It had the unmistakable whiff of a eulogy written in anticipation of the funeral.

On March 1, 1888, Louisa paid her father what she believed would be her final visit. Anna was there, and Maria Porter happened to be visiting when Louisa arrived. "The sight of her thin, wan face and sad look shocked me," Porter said, "and for the first time I felt she might be hopelessly ill." She described the parting of father and daughter that followed:

> Kneeling by his bedside, she took his hand, kissed it, and placed in it pansies she had brought, saying "It is "Weedy" (her pet name). Then after a moment of silence she asked: "What are you thinking of, dear?" He replied, looking upward, "Up there; you come too!" Then with a kiss she said, "I wish I could go," bowing her head as if in prayer. After a little came the "Good-by," the last kiss, and like a shadow she glided from the room.

Louisa's diary entry for that day is more matter-of-fact: "Fine. In to see Papa. Very sweet and feeble. Kissed me and said "Come soon." Smelt my flowers and asked me to write him a letter. Nearly gone. A[nna] very dear . . . Met Mrs P[orter]." March 2, 1888, is a capsule-sized version of so many of her days, tiny doses of the accustomed activities of her life: "Write letters," she reported, and "Pay Ropes $30, Notman 4." She sewed—on this day a red flannel dress for a poor baby. "Write a little," referring to a children's story she was working on. She also noted an anticipated visit from her niece—"L[ulu] to come."

The quiet resignation described by the rich and famous fifty-five-year-old invalid in a Roxbury nursing home was far distant from the boundless hopes and energy recorded by the twelve-year-old Concord girl on an autumn morning years before. On that long-ago day at Hillside Louisa had awakened before her parents and her three sisters and quietly slipped outdoors. She returned, ecstatic, to write in her journal:

> I had an early run in the woods before the dew was off the grass. The moss was like velvet, and as I ran under the arches of yellow and red leaves I sang for joy, my heart was so bright and the world so beautiful. I stopped at the end of the walk and saw the sunshine out over the wide . . . meadows.
>
> It seemed like going through a dark life or grave into heaven beyond.

A very strange and solemn feeling came over me as I stood there, with no sound but the rustle of the pines, no one near me, and the sun so glorious, as for me alone. It seemed as if I *felt* God, and I prayed in my heart that I might keep that happy sense of nearness all my life.

"I have," she had written on the page many years later, "for I most sincerely think the little girl 'got religion' that day when dear mother Nature led her to God."

The next day, March 3, Maria Porter sent Louisa a note, enclosing a photograph of May. Anna also wrote. Louisa answered Anna's letter first, saying she had a crushing pain in her head, with a "weight like iron." To Maria Porter she sent thanks for May's picture, and expressed her hope that her father would die soon "after his long & innocent life." In such a situation, Louisa believed, "sorrow has no place." In a postscript she said she planned to stay a year at Dr. Lawrence's rest home, "& then I am promised twenty years of health. I don't want so many. I hold on for others, & shall find time to die some day, I hope."

The "weight like iron" in Louisa's head intensified. Then she became feverish. She asked if she had meningitis. Dr. Lawrence thought not. A few hours later Louisa sank into a coma. Anna and her son John were sent for. Louisa briefly recognized John, then fell back unconscious again. Anna kept watch all that day. On the morning of March 4 she was still there when word came from Louisburg Square that Bronson had died. Despite the need to make arrangements for his funeral and burial, Anna continued her vigil at Louisa's side. Dr. Green examined Louisa and told Anna that her sister had suffered a stroke or, as he referred to it, "apoplexy."* She might recover, or not. Anna wrote a friend to cancel a visit to Concord; Dr. Lawrence expected her to stay by Louisa until there was a change for better or worse. "So I still wait—and hope—or try to hope—this awful sorrow may be spared me now." There was no change,

---

* Current medical opinion confirms this diagnosis. Lupus can cause kidney damage, which can lead to high blood pressure, which can lead to a stroke. Even if Hirschhorn and Greaves's diagnosis of lupus is not correct, the account of Louisa May Alcott's death is consistent with stroke.

but Anna had to return to Louisburg Square to prepare for their father's funeral the following day.

Sometime early the next morning, March 6, 1888, Louisa died. She did not know that her father had died two days before. There was no one by her side.

~⧳~

HOW THEY TURNED OUT

Mourners who arrived at the funeral ceremony for Bronson Alcott were met, as Ednah Cheney put it, "with the startling intelligence, 'Louisa Alcott is dead.'" Many of them returned to 10 Louisburg Square two days later for the same kind of intimate gathering. Louisa's poem to her father, "The Last of the Philosophers," was read at Bronson's service, and "Duty's Faithful Child," his poem to Louisa, was read at hers, along with Louisa's tribute to her mother, "Transfiguration." Lulu was not present at either observance but remembered, "[Louisa's] coffin was carried out from Louisburg Square by Fred and John, her two nephews, and then a musician whom she had given money to make a career, I've forgotten his name now. And who was the fourth one?"

Two days after Bronson's burial next to Abby in Sleepy Hollow, Louisa went to her final resting place, at the foot of the graves of her parents, as she had requested in her will, to "take care of them as she had done all her life." Later a small stone with the initials L.M.A. and the dates 1832–1888 was placed at its head; at the foot was a stone reading only "Louisa M. Alcott," set flat against the ground. According to her right as a war veteran, a small American flag would always fly there. But preferable to picturing Louisa May Alcott in an afterlife eternally in service to parents and country is to imagine her reaping the reward she described on her twenty-third birthday: "[for playing] the small part already given me, and acting that well, [mixing] the tragedy and comedy of life so wisely that when the curtain falls I can jump up as briskly as the stage dead do, and cheered by the applause of my little audience here, go away to learn and act a new and better part in the Lord's theatre, where all good actors are stars." Or set free in another, better life, as she liked to believe she would be.

Louisa May Nieriker—Lulu—would recall the Alcotts as "*large,* as the French say, *très large.*" In English, *large* in this sense roughly translates as "bigger than life" and connotes generosity and moral integrity. With the deaths of Bronson and Louisa May Alcott, the days of family greatness came to an end. On March 1, 1888, when Louisa paid her last visit to Bronson, the Alcotts were a cohesive social unit; less than a week later, they were a handful of individuals with no patriarch (Bronson) or head of household (Louisa). Frederick Pratt was a serious married man of twenty-five and John a lighthearted twenty-three; then there were Anna and Lulu.

Lulu was eight years old when her Aunt "Wee" died. Neither Louisa's nor Bronson's deaths made a great impact, since both of them were invalids in the years Lulu knew them best. Her deepest attachment was to Anna. Madelon Bedell found it ironic that Lulu barely remembered the aunt whose series of story anthologies, *Lulu's Library,* had ensured that she herself would be remembered so well that Bedell would seek her out in Europe to learn the rest of her story. After Louisa's and Bronson's deaths, the little girl still had the most important things; Anna, her cousin John, and her vast collection of dolls.

She had to part with the dolls within the year, when Ernst Nieriker asked that his daughter be sent back to her family in Switzerland. He had lived only briefly in Brazil, without notable success. Nieriker's was a reasonable claim, but difficult for Anna to accept, and impossible for his daughter to understand. The child knew no German or French, was unacquainted with her father, and had no wish to leave everything she knew for what must have seemed like the moon.

Anna pleaded to keep Lulu, but Nieriker insisted, and Anna had to yield. She and her son John Pratt, now legally John Pratt Alcott, traveled with Lulu to Europe, consoling her along the way for the loss of most of her dolls. Once in Switzerland, Anna Alcott was as charmed by Ernst Nieriker as May had been. John was smitten by Ernst's young sister Ida, who was taking on Lulu's care. When Anna and John left after nine happy months, Ida and John were engaged. Lulu remembered waving a casual, cheerful good-bye, oblivious to the near-certainty that she would never see her aunt again. She told Madelon Bedell that Anna Alcott Pratt was the greatest woman she had ever known. Of the many American and Swiss women who took care of her, Lulu saw Anna alone as a mother. She liked her aunt Ida, but Ida was too young for the role.

The harmony between the Nieriker and Alcott-Pratt families was short-lived. Ida Nieriker soon forgot John Pratt, married somebody else, and ran off to Manila. The division of Louisa's estate did not go well either. In repossessing Lulu, Ernst Nieriker apparently acted from financial as well as paternal motives. "We were four heirs, Aunt Anna, Fred and John [and myself]," Lulu told Madelon Bedell. By the terms of the will, Ernst's daughter was to have a quarter of the estate of about $200,000. "My father thought that I didn't get sufficient, and I'm sorry to say that he was a man who was a little bit on money." Nieriker claimed half of Louisa's fortune for his daughter and put her smack in the middle of the dispute: "He dictated to me nasty letters, and of course it wasn't right, it was *not right*. . . . [He] wrote horrid letters to my darling Aunt Anna. . . . He called her terrible names and [said] that it wasn't right that I didn't get half. Half! The will was absolutely fair." Lulu never mentioned exactly how the estate was settled, but did say that later there was bad blood when Fred objected to John's adopted son inheriting any money or rights to Louisa's works. John resisted, but eventually went along with his stern brother's resolve. If you asked Lulu, the devil could be right here on Earth, in the form of money.

The person of no Alcott blood who benefited most from Louisa's fortune was Ernst Nieriker, who spent his daughter's money to support his entire household. As one of nine children of a court clerk, he had never had much, and the cigar store he opened with a brother in Zurich was just a store, not an ongoing cash cow as Louisa's books were until the copyrights ran out in the 1920s.

Anna Alcott Pratt died in 1893, at the age of sixty-two. She had become so identified with the character of Meg March that she signed letters with that name, and published a collection of the plays she had written with Louisa as *Comic Tragedies, by Meg and Jo*. That she was the model for Meg March of *Little Women* was enough to make Anna's death (though not the cause of it) worthy of note in the *New York Times*. Lulu was "sure she would have lived longer if they hadn't had that fight about this nasty money."

Lulu, nine years old when she was repatriated to Switzerland, found it difficult to start over among strangers whose language she didn't know. When she reached twenty-one she returned to Boston and Concord, possibly intending to resettle in the area. She remembered two aspects of

her turn-of-the-twentieth-century visit. The first was hearing all her Alcott relatives and friends assert her striking resemblance to the blonde,
blue-eyed mother she had never known. Madelon Bedell, on the other
hand, said the ninety-six-year-old Lulu wore the face of Bronson Alcott.*
Perhaps in her old age Lulu's features grew more like her grandfather's.

Lulu's other strong recollection of her return to New England was of
meeting, in Concord, Harry Hosmer, probably a relative of Cyrus Hosmer,
who six decades before had dared her aunt Louisa to jump off the highest
beam of the barn and carried her home with two sprained ankles. Hosmer
visited Lulu every evening, and they were expected to marry, Lulu said,
but she returned to Europe and young Hosmer died of tuberculosis soon
after. In 1903, at age twenty-five, Lulu married Emil Franz Rasim, a wine
merchant, over her father's objection. Lulu told Madelon Bedell that Ernst
Nieriker's reason for standing in the way of the marriage was that Louisa
May Alcott's money would go with his daughter. It did, and with it her
relationship to him, it appears. Emil Rasim and Louisa May Nieriker had
one daughter, Ernestine May Rasim, known as Erni.

Every other year, on the anniversary of Anna Alcott's marriage to John
Pratt, the ceremony is reenacted at Orchard House. The current John Pratt,
who could double for his ancestor John Pratt, often plays the groom; once a
visiting Swiss Nieriker relative stood in for Anna Alcott. May never intended to return from Europe and never has; her remains were not brought
back to Concord from Paris, although there was talk of it. Louisa had
placed in the family plot in Sleepy Hollow a small stone with May's name
and dates of birth and death, possibly for Lulu to visit—or for herself, to
make the Alcott family plot seem complete. A number of May's paintings
and sketches are still in Switzerland with descendants of Ernst Nieriker,
who made May so happy when he was a romantic youth of twenty-one.
Given his later actions, it's hard not to wonder whether Ernst knew from
the start that May's sister was a wealthy woman. He does not seem to have
known his wife's true age. When Madelon Bedell went to the cemetery in

---

* Bedell met Lulu on a stormy night in woodsy mountains. With the electricity out, the
ancient visage of the last person who had known the Alcotts emerged from the dark by
candlelight. Bedell described the interview beautifully in her introduction to *The Alcotts: Biography of a Family* (New York: Clarkson Potter, 1980), her wonderful account
of the family's early years. Several unpublished chapters of Madelon Bedell's projected
second volume are among her papers at Orchard House.

Paris where May is buried, she found her listed as thirty-two at the time of her death; actually her next birthday would have been her fortieth.

⌒

The "little romance" with Ladislas Wisniewski that "couldn't be" had some repercussions. Louisa and Laddie corresponded—infrequently, Louisa said—for at least five years after their fortnight in Paris. Only one letter survived, and that only in a brief quotation by Louisa in "My Boys." In it Laddie wrote that Paris was *stupide* without Louisa, asked her help in translating some obscure English phrases in *Vanity Fair* that he thought must be prison argot ("Nubble your dad and gully the dog"), and regretted that the faulty English of his expressions of love and regard would make Louisa *ridicule* rather than take them to heart. Using a pet name, he hinted to Louisa, "One day [you might] see your *Varjo* in *Amérique,* if I study commerce as I wish." In September of 1872, in fact, Louisa wrote to Maggie Lukens, "My Polish boy, Laddie (or Laurie), has turned up in New York alive and well with a wife and 'little two daughters' as he says in his funny English. He is coming to see me, and I expect to find my romantic boy a stout papa, the glory all gone. Isn't it sad?" No account of this meeting exists, if it ever occurred. Wisniewski and his family wound up stranded financially in the United States, and in October of 1873 Louisa had Roberts Brothers issue a check for four hundred dollars for their fares back to Europe, designating the money as payment to Wisniewski for providing the model for Laurie—a face-saving gesture, perhaps. He popped up again five years later to show May Alcott around Paris. The last glimpse of Laddie in Louisa's life story is in a newspaper column among the Alcott papers in Houghton Library. The unidentified publication may be a church newsletter; the author of the column, Bernard Carpenter, was a popular minister who contacted Laddie in Paris shortly after Louisa's death. Laddie seems to have been quite open with Carpenter. He gave an account consistent with Louisa's: he had married and had children; become rich; lost everything in the Vienna Crash of 1873; tried his luck in the United States; was rescued by Louisa. He resettled in Paris, where by the time of Louisa's death he had become rich again.

⌒

Louisa had requested that all her papers be burned, but Anna Pratt delayed. She disposed of some and entrusted the rest to Ednah Dow Littlehale

Cheney, the social activist, writer, and family friend who in the 1850s had often met Bronson Alcott for early morning walks on the deserted Boston Common. Mrs. Cheney used the papers to research and publish two books within the year: *Louisa May Alcott: The Children's Friend*, and *Louisa May Alcott: Her Life, Letters and Journals*. The popular *Louisa May Alcott: The Children's Friend* presented Louisa minus the rough edges, as the genteel spinster Aunt Jo. Louisa had invented the image herself and "built the brand" in *Aunt Jo's Scrap-Bag*, a series of six books published annually during the Christmas gift season. Ednah Cheney's book perpetuated an image of the author that was so fixed and limited it eventually became an icon. The real woman behind *Little Women*—the Louisa Alcott who wrote pulp fiction and could be the life of the party—was buried with its author. Cheney's other book, the brief biography *Louisa May Alcott: Her Life, Letters and Journals*, is more a commentary on a selection from Louisa's letters and journals than a biography, although her insights are true as far as they go, which is not very. She and Anna Pratt excised from the various journals and letters whatever they thought detrimental. Worst of all, Cheney did not return many of the papers she consulted, leaving contemporary scholars only Cheney's own selective transcriptions as sources.

From 1888 until 1950 there was no full-length biography of Louisa May Alcott, not surprising given her utter lack of critical cachet. Her readers never knew or cared. Cynthia Ozick's childhood encounter with Alcott can stand for them all: "I read *Little Women* a thousand times. Ten thousand! I am Jo in her 'vortex'; not Jo, exactly, but some Jo-of-the-future. I am under an enchantment." The list of literary careers of women inspired by Louisa May Alcott is too long to name more than a selection; among them are Ursula Le Guin, Gertrude Stein, Bobbie Ann Mason, Simone de Beauvoir, and J. K. Rowling.

There is a card game called "Authors." The male writers are Mark Twain, Charles Dickens, William Makepeace Thackeray, Robert Lewis Stevenson, William Shakespeare, James Fenimore Cooper, Washington Irving, Nathaniel Hawthorne, Henry Wadsworth Longfellow, Sir Walter Scott, Alfred Lord Tennyson, and Edgar Allan Poe. There is only one female: Louisa May Alcott.

NOTES

ABBREVIATIONS

PEOPLE

ABA Amos Bronson Alcott
AMA Abigail May Alcott
LMA Louisa May Alcott
RWE Ralph Waldo Emerson
SJM Samuel Joseph May

SOURCES

HAP Alcott Pratt Collection, Houghton Library, Harvard University
HMC Houghton Library, Harvard University, miscellaneous collections
Journals *The Journals of Louisa May Alcott*, edited by Joel Myerson and Daniel Shealy; Madeleine Stern, associate editor
Letters *The Selected Letters of Louisa May Alcott*, edited by Joel Myerson and Daniel Shealy; Madeleine Stern, associate editor
Letters of ABA *The Letters of A. Bronson Alcott*, edited by Richard Herrnstadt
LMA: LW, LM, JB *Louisa May Alcott: Little Women, Little Men, and Jo's Boys*, edited by Elaine Showalter
Selected Fiction *Louisa May Alcott: Selected Fiction*, edited by Daniel Shealy, Madeleine Stern, and Joel Myerson

Occasionally the spelling and punctuation of quotations have been altered for ease of reading and consistency.

PAGE   **PROLOGUE: BEHIND A MASK**

1 "magically the book": Pennie Azarcon de la Cruz, "How Jo Met Jo and Finally Found Her Groove," *Sunday Inquirer Magazine*, 29 March 2008. http://blogs. inquirer.net/sim/category/books-that-changed-one-life/ (accessed 29 March 2008).

2 Beverly Hills: Judith Rossner, *His Little Women* (New York: Summit Books, 1990).

2 Allende's Chile: Marcela Serrano, *Hasta Siempre, Mujercitas* (Chile: Planeta, 2004).

2 Upper West Side: Katharine Weber, *The Little Women* (New York: Farrar, Straus and Giroux, 2003).

2 "Fifteen-year-old-Jo": LMA, *LMA: LW, LM, JB*, 10.

2 "full of spirit and life": Frederick L. H. Willis, "From *Alcott Memoirs* (1915)," in *Alcott in Her Own Time*, ed. Daniel Shealy (Iowa City: University Press, 2005), 177.

3 "a strange combination": John S. P. Alcott, "The 'Little Women' of Long Ago (1913)," in ibid., 135.

4 "rich, famous, and happy": LMA, "Recollections of My Childhood," in *Louisa May Alcott: An Intimate Anthology*, New York Public Library collectors' edition (New York: Doubleday, 1997), 9.

4 "Lived in my mind": LMA, 2 January 1887, *Journals*, 287.

4 "A happy world": LMA, 3 January 1887, ibid.

                    ONE: FIT FOR THE SCUFFLE OF THINGS

5 "a fine foundation . . . on my birthday (33)": ABA to Colonel J. May, 29 November 1832, ABA, *Letters of ABA*, 19.

5 "On a dismal November day": LMA to ABA, 28 November 1855, LMA, *Letters*, 13.

6 "I was the youngest": AMA, Autobiography, AMA Fragments, shelf mark: 59 M-311 (2)-(19), HAP.

6 "She adored her husband": Ibid.

7 "a fair-haired boy": Samuel Joseph May, *Memoir of Samuel Joseph May* (Boston: Roberts Brothers, 1873). Digital reprint, University of Michigan Library, 5.

7 "was a good child": AMA, Autobiography, AMA Fragments.

7 "I may yet earn": AMA to Eliza May Willis, July 1819, AMA Memoir, shelf mark: 59 M-306 (28), HAP.

7 "a cheerful habit": SJM to AMA, 13 June 1819, ibid.

7 "If I incur the epithet": AMA to Colonel and Dorothy S. May, 10 October 1819, ibid.

9 "under the trees": LMA, "Eli's Education," from *Selected Fiction*, 338.

10 "I found . . . an intelligent": AMA, 5 August 1828, AMA Memoir.

10 "views on education": Ibid.

10 "soon saw the indication": SJM, *Memoir*, 123.

10 "I have never been so taken": Ibid., 122.

11 "An interesting woman": ABA, 2 August 1828, *The Journals of A. Bronson Alcott*, ed. Odell Shepard (Boston: Little, Brown, 1938), 11.

11 "I have been conquered": AMA, AMA Fragments, 1828–29.

11 "All was openness": ABA, 2 August 1828, *Journals of ABA*, 12.

11 "I have something to live for": AMA in Honoré Willsie Morrow, *The Father of Little Women* (Boston: Little, Brown, 1927), 67.

11 "avoid him as much": AMA, 5 August 1828, AMA Memoir.

12 "a very respectable effort": ABA, 28 September 1828, *Journals of ABA*, 12.

12 "We are unwilling": ABA, 1 June 1828, ibid., 9.

12 "[Father] must approve . . . for his own": AMA, 5 August 1828, AMA Memoir.

12 "I cannot look with complacency": ABA, quoted in AMA, 20 April 1829, ibid.

12 "I will modify it": AMA quoted in ABA, 29 April 1829, ibid.

12 "delicately sketched": AMA, AMA Fragments, 1828–1829.

12 "Mr. Alcott's visits": Colonel J. May to AMA, 6 July 1829, AMA Memoir.

12 "I have something to love": AMA to SJM, August 1828, Family Letters, 1828–61, HAP.

13 "I hope we may": AMA to Lucretia May, 15 June 1830, ibid.

13 "Man and woman": ABA, "Psyche: An Evangele; in four books," bMS Am 1130.10(6), 17, HAP.

13 "He is moderate": AMA to SJM, August 1828, Family Letters, 1828–61.

13 "peculiarly amiable disposition . . . introduction to existence": ABA, "Observations on the Life of My First Child [Anna Bronson Alcott] During Her First Year," HAP.

14 "Behold the babe!": ABA, "Psyche," in Odell Shepard, *Pedlar's Progress: The Life of Bronson Alcott* (Boston: Little Brown, 1937), 143.

14 "with a beautiful serpentine walk . . . painted white": AMA to SJM, 22 May 1831, Family Letters, 1828–61.

14 "We hardly earn": AMA to SJM 25 August 1831, ibid.

15 "one of those periods of mental depression": ABA, 26 July 1842, *Journals of ABA*, 145.

15 "a fine fat creature": ABA to Anna Alcox, 29 November 1932, *Letters of ABA*, 18.

15 "first for a proper quantity": LMA to ABA, 28 November 1855, *Letters*, 13.

15 "a spritely, merry little puss": AMA to SJM, 20 February 1833, Family Letters, 1828–61.

15 "fit for the scuffle": ABA, "Researches on Childhood," bMS Am 1130.10(9), HAP.

15 "unusual vivacity": ABA, "Louisa's First Year," 267, HAP, and in Madelon Bedell, *The Alcotts: Biography of a Family* (New York: Clarkson Potter, 1980), 66.

15 "active, vivid, energetic": Ibid., 315, HAP.

15 "power, individuality, and force": Ibid., 192, HAP.

15 "with the measure of pockets": AMA to Jane Haines, 9 April 183[3], Memoir ABA.

16 "the most eccentric man": Charles Godfrey Leland, *Memoirs*, in Shepard, *Pedlar's Progress*, 162.

16 *"amazed* beyond measure . . . an era in society": Elizabeth Peabody to Mary Peabody, 17–22 July 1834, Henry W. and Albert A. Berg Collection, New York Public Library, Astor Lenox and Tilden foundations.

TWO: THE LAW OF MIGHT

18 "Louisa shed a few tears . . . every part of speech": ABA, "Observations on the Spiritual Nurture of My Children," shelf mark: bMS Am 1130.10 (6), 21, HAP, and in Morrow, *The Father of Little Women,* 111–13.

21 "V . . . sssssssssssss": ABA, "Spiritual Nurture," 91.

21 "Mr. Alcott asked . . . faithfulness": Elizabeth Peabody, *Record of a School: Exemplifying the General Principles of Spiritual Culture* (Bedford: Applewood Books, 2005), 2.

21 "Boston feels more like a sepulchre": AMA to SJM, 2 September 1834, Family Letters, 1828–61.

22 "Do you want . . . want to be good": ABA, "Researches on Childhood," 273–76.

22 "She hesitated . . . she understood me": Ibid., 116.

22 "There is a self-corroding nature . . . to every attack": ABA, 20 November 1835, Journal, Autobiographical Collections, 1834–39, MS AM 1130.11(3), HAP.

23 "I told her she must stop": ABA, "Spiritual Nurture," 110.

23 "It has a little head": ABA, "Psyche," 49–50.

24 "I don't love . . . God won't love me": Ibid., and Bedell, *The Alcotts,* 102.

25 "comfort . . . poor slaves": LMA, "Recollections," in *An Intimate Anthology,* 3.

25 "By some oversight": LMA, in "Sketch of Childhood, by Herself," in Ednah Dow Littlehale Cheney, *Louisa May Alcott: Her Life, Letters and Journals* (New York: Gramercy Books, 1995), 13.

25 "the whole celebration": ABA, 28 November 1835, *Journals of ABA,* 70.

26 "Louisa having her sister . . . on her cheek!": ABA, "Spiritual Nurture," 161.

26 "Louisa, . . . result of her temerity": ABA, 12 May 1836, in Morrow, *The Father of Little Women,* 157–58.

26 "Her violence is at times . . . tempted to pinch me": Ibid.

26 "that Louisa's untamable spirit": ABA, 1 February 1836, ibid., 154–55.

26 "vegetable production": LMA, May 1859, *Journals,* 95.

26 "Louisa's spirit . . . affluent nature": ABA, 12 May 1836, Morrow, *The Father of Little Women,* 156–58.

26 "love, kindness": ABA, 24 June 1837, ibid., 159.

27 "discipline . . . amplitude": ABA, 12 May 1836, ibid., 158.

27 "neat light parlor . . . life is now": Elizabeth P. Peabody to George Francis Peabody, 18 June [1836], Robert L. Straker, Collections of Mann and Peabody Letters, Antiochiana, Antioch College, Yellow Springs, Ohio.

27 "It was really delightful": Elizabeth P. Peabody to Mary T. Peabody, 25 March 1836, Berg Collection, New York Public Library.

27 "No pen can do any justice": Elizabeth Peabody to Mary Peabody, Summer 1835?, MM Berg Collection MN micro, New York Public Library, 1020.

28 "We are now going to speak . . . pearl fishers": ABA, *How Like an Angel I Came Down: Conversations with Children on the Gospels*, ed. Alice O. Howell (Hudson: Lindisfarne Press, 1991), 1.

28 "NATHAN. I don't see . . . Jesus Christ's": Ibid., 67–68.

28 *quicken*: Ibid., 59.

28 *conceive*: Ibid., 50.

28 "How is the body made? . . . shaped to the eyes?": Ibid., 73–74.

29 "Don't you know Mrs. Alcott came into my room": Elizabeth P. Peabody to Mary T. Peabody, n.d., *Letters of Elizabeth Palmer Peabody, American Renaissance Woman*, ed. Bruce Ronda (Middletown, CT: Wesleyan University Press, 1984), 157ff. For more detail see Megan Marshall, *The Peabody Sisters: Three Women Who Ignited American Romanticism* (Boston: Houghton Mifflin, 2005), 542n. Marshall's book is a superb account of the period as seen through the eyes of the Peabody sisters.

29 "Miss Peabody left": ABA, "Bronson Alcott's 'Journal for 1836,' " ed. Joel Myerson, 64, Autobiographical Collections, HAP.

29 "I love everybody": LMA, Cheney, *Louisa May Alcott*, 6.

29 "[Louisa's] *force* makes me retreat . . . Mr. Alcott's spirit": Sophia Peabody to Mrs. William Russell, 25 July 1836, Memoir, 1878, HAP; also in Bedell, *The Alcotts*, 125.

29 "unusual degree of excitement": ABA, 13 April 1837, Diary, in F. B. Sanborn and William T. Harris, *A. Bronson Alcott: His Life and Philosophy*, 2 vols. (New York: Biblo and Tannen, 1965), 1:221.

29 "expect this book": SJM to ABA, 1835, in Morrow, *The Father of Little Women*, 191.

29 "A more indecent and obscene book": Clipping, *Courier*, ABA, Autobiographical Collections, 123.

29 "Radically false": Clipping signed "Nathan Hale," *Daily Advertiser*, n.d., ibid.

30 "either insane or half-witted": Clipping, signed "Joseph T. Buckingham," *Courier*, n.d., ibid.

30 "an ignorant and presuming charlatan": Clipping, *Courier*, n.d., ibid.

30 "one third absurd": Clipping, n.d., letter signed "Buckingham," ibid. A pencil note in the hand of ABA identifies Norton as the author of these words.

30 "the palmy times": Margaret Fuller Ossoli, *Memoirs of Margaret Fuller Ossoli*, vol. 1 (BiblioBazaar, 2007), 152.

30 "imposition of the adult mind": Elizabeth Peabody, "Mr. Alcott's Book and School," *Christian Register and Boston Observer*, 29 April 1937, in Marshall, *The Peabody Sisters*, 326.

30 "wise" and "simple": RWE, *The Journals and Miscellaneous Notebooks of Ralph Waldo Emerson*, ed. William H. Gilman et al. (Cambridge, MA: Harvard University Press, 1960–82), 5:98–99.

30 "[a man] who grows upon me": RWE, *Letters of Ralph Waldo Emerson*, vols. 1–6, ed. Ralph L. Rusk (New York: Columbia University Press, 1939), 2:29.

30 "I hate to have all the little dogs barking": Ibid., 61–62.

30 "the clamor and misapprehension . . . in the street": ABA, April 1837, *Journals of ABA*, 88.

30 "At one time the excitement threatened a mob": ABA, March 1837, ibid., 87.

31 "She wasn't a wilfully . . . street might see": LMA, "Poppy's Pranks," in *Aunt Jo's Scrap-Bag,* vol. 6 (Boston: Roberts Brothers, 1885), 124.

31 "a big dog . . . repent at leisure": LMA, "Sketches of Childhood," in Cheney, *Louisa May Alcott,* 28.

31 "On the impetuous stream of instinct": ABA, "Spiritual Nurture," 204–6.

THREE: THE TOPSEY TURVEY GIRL

32 "You have seen . . . 'visionary' ": AMA to SJM, 23 April 1837, Sanborn and Harris, *A. Bronson Alcott,* 1:231–32.

33 "My wife is a capital nurse": RWE to ABA, 27 July 1837, ibid., 229.

33 "We are as poor as rats": AMA to SJM, 3 October 1837, Family Letters, 1828–61.

33 "Mr. A is of good comfort"; "Poverty presents": Ibid.

34 "I care less for this world": AMA to SJM, 22 April 1838, ibid.

34 "She got so wild . . . danger was the fun": LMA, "Poppy's Pranks," in *Aunt Jo's Scrap-Bag,* 6:141.

35 "I spent three days with Emerson . . . life and nature": ABA, June 1838, *Journals of ABA,* 101.

35 "fitness for publication": Ibid.

35 "When he sits down to write": RWE in Sanborn and Harris, *A. Bronson Alcott,* 256.

35 "I judge the counsel wise": ABA, June 1838, *Journals of ABA,* 102.

35 "It never was so dark": AMA to Mrs. Anna Alcott, 9 May 1838, AMA Memoir.

36 "What ideas . . . 'corn in the ear' ": Peabody, *Record of a School,* 91.

37 "first . . . boy, to whom I clung . . . at this bottom": LMA, "My Boys," in *Selected Fiction,* 315–16.

37 "[I am] living by talking . . . jump for joy": ABA to Mrs. Anna Alcott, 18 March 1839, *Letters of ABA,* 41.

38 "snuggled in sofa corners": LMA, "My Boys," in *Selected Fiction,* 316.

38 "some passages . . . plain fact": ABA, 2 February 1839, *Journals of ABA,* 114.

38 "Death yawns at me": ABA, 5 February 1839, ibid., 115.

38 "I did something very naughty . . . up to the foe": LMA, "My Boys," in *Selected Fiction,* 316.

38 "one little boy said": Peabody, *Record of a School,* 94.

38 "Peanuts and candy": LMA, "My Boys," in *Selected Fiction,* 316.

38 "No boy could be my friend": LMA, "Recollections," in *An Intimate Anthology,* 5.

39 "full grown": AMA, AMA Fragments.

39 "My thrill of hope": ABA, August 1841, *Journals of ABA,* 119.

39 "ride the cows": LMA, "My Boys," in *Selected Fiction,* 317.

39 "she has had several spells": Miss. C in Providence to AMA or ABA(?), Cheney, *Louisa May Alcott,* 7.

39 "She is a beautiful little girl": Ibid.

39 "[so] you can read it": ABA to LMA, December 1839, *Letters of ABA,* 45.

39 "You want to see us all": Ibid.

40 "I collected several poor children"; "full of sympathy": LMA, "My Boys," in *Selected Fiction,* 317.

40 "You shall see us . . . some new feeling": ABA to LMA, December 1839, *Journals of ABA*, 45.

40 "I often wish I had": LMA, 23 December 1844, *Journals*, 48.

40 "this bud of a son": ABA, 7 April 1839, MS Journal, HAP.

41 "My patrons": ABA, Autobiographical Index, HAP.

42 "This dolly . . . her little mamma": LMA, "Poppy's Pranks," in *Aunt Jo's Scrap-Bag*, 6:143.

42 "You are Seven years old": ABA to LMA, 29 November 1839, *Letters of ABA*, 43.

42 "the worst child": LMA, "My Boys," in *Selected Fiction*, 317.

FOUR: WILD EXUBERANT NATURE

44 "in rapture . . . admiration": AMA to Colonel Joseph May, 5 April 1840, AMA Memoir.

44 "could make birds": LMA, *Little Men*, in *LMA: LW, LM, JB*, 644.

45 "The Naughty Kitty-Mouse . . . absurd demands": Ibid., 614.

45 "I think no man": RWE, 8 December 1839, *Selections from Ralph Waldo Emerson: An Organic Anthology*, ed. Stephen E. Whicher (Cambridge, MA: Riverside Press, 1960), 133.

46 "to get his living": RWE to Thomas Carlyle, 31 March 1842, *The Correspondence of Emerson and Carlyle*, ed. Joseph Slater (New York: Columbia University Press, 1964), 320.

46 "Every new experience . . . with its lot": AMA to SJM, 5 April 1840, Family Letters, 1828–61.

46 "I place myself . . . whensoever I may": ABA to SJM, 6 April 1840, *Letters of ABA*, 47.

47 "Cy was a comrade . . . aversion to pork": LMA, "My Boys," in *Selected Fiction*, 318.

47 "We dramatized the fairy tales": LMA, "Recollections," in *An Intimate Anthology*, 6.

47 "always very busy": Lydia Hosmer Wood, "Beth Alcott's Playmate: A Glimpse of Concord Town in the Days of *Little Women* (1913)," in Shealy, *Alcott in Her Own Time*, 164–65.

48 "a new periodical": AMA to Hannah Robie, 26 April 1840, AMA Memoir.

48 "Dial on time": ABA in Fredrick C. Dahlstrand, *Amos Bronson Alcott: An Intellectual Biography* (Rutherford, NJ: Fairleigh Dickinson University Press, 1982), 182.

48 "cold, vague . . . do not like them": RWE to Margaret Fuller, *Letters RWE*, 2:276.

48 "Neither the butcher": AMA to SJM, October 1833, Family Letters, 1828–61.

48 "quite grand": Margaret Fuller to RWE, May 31, 1840, Margaret Fuller, *The Letters of Margaret Fuller*, ed. Robert N. Hudspeth, 5 vols. to date (Ithaca, NY: Cornell University Press, 1983).

48 "Engage in nothing"; "The popular genesis": ABA, *The Dial: A Magazine for Literature, Philosophy, and Religion* (J. Monroe), 1841, 85.

48 "Gastric Sayings": *Boston Transcript*, 1840, ABA, Autobiographical Collections.

48 "a train of 15": *Boston Post,* 1840, ibid.

48 "While he talks": James Russell Lowell, 1840, ibid.

49 "I had no beans": LMA, *Little Men,* in *LMA: LW, LM, JB,* 618.

49 "My Dear Louisa": ABA to LMA, 21 June 1840, *Letters of ABA,* 49.

50 "Tomorrow I enter": ABA to SJM, 29 July 1840, ibid., 51.

50 "the Newness": Clara Endicott Sears, *Bronson Alcott's Fruitlands with Transcendental Wild Oats* (Cambridge, MA: Riverside Press, 1915; reprint, Boston and New York: Houghton Mifflin), 19.

50 "Why so much talk"; "why are men": AMA to SJM, 26 April 1840, AMA Memoir.

50 "Do bear this in mind": AMA to SJM, 30 August 1840, ibid.

51 "No one will employ": AMA to SJM, November 1840, ibid.

51 "Two passions strong divide": ABA to LMA, 29 November 1840, *Journals of ABA,* 54.

51 "I am so weary": AMA to SJM, 24 January 1841, AMA Memoir.

52 "I cannot see": AMA to SJM, 24 January 1841, Family Letters, 1828–61.

52 "My father did *not* love me": AMA, February 1841, AMA Memoir.

52 "secured by my Executors": Estate inventory, will of Joseph May, Probate Court Records, docket number 32792, Suffolk County, Massachusetts.

52 "If I am despised": AMA, "From the Diary," February n.d., 1841, AMA Memoir.

52 "We have in no wise": AMA to SJM, 15 April 1841, Family Letters, 1828–61.

53 "My girls shall have trades": AMA to SJM, 4 April 1841, ibid.

53 "To the First Robin": LMA, *The Poetry of Louisa May Alcott* (Concord, MA: Louisa May Alcott Memorial Association, c. 1977), 1.

53 "I miss you . . . and field": ABA to Anna Alcott, 14 May 1841, *Letters of ABA,* 56.

53 "slipped into the brook": LMA, "Poppy's Pranks," in *Aunt Jo's Scrap-Bag,* 6:132.

54 "If it were not": LMA to Mary Mapes Dodge, 2 December 1874, *Letters,* 188.

FIVE: MAN IN A BALLOON

56 "Here is a fine person": RWE, *Journals of Ralph Waldo Emerson,* ed. Edward Waldo Emerson and Waldo Emerson Forbes, 10 vols. (Boston: Houghton, Mifflin, 1909–14), 8:29.

56 "Child, he is dead": LMA, "Reminiscences of Ralph Waldo Emerson," in *The Sketches of Louisa May Alcott: With an Introduction by Gregory Eiselein* (New York: Ironweed Press, 2001), 209.

56 "tedious Archangel": RWE, Journal, Autumn 1842, *Selections from RWE,* 126.

56 "You might spend the summer": RWE to ABA, 12 February 1842, copied by ABA in ABA Autobiographical Collections.

56 "What shall I say . . . of discourse": RWE, *Journals and Miscellaneous Notebooks,* 8:210–15.

57 "rare moral courage": William Lloyd Garrison to Dr. John Bowring M.P., 8 May 1842, in *Letters of ABA,* 66.

57 "I am summoning": AMA, 1 April 1842, Diary, 1841–44, HAP.

57 "wife, children, and friends": Ibid.

57 "A philosopher is a man": LMA to Ednah Dow Littlehale Cheney, 1878(?), in Cheney, *Louisa May Alcott*, 228.

57 "how naturally man's": AMA, 1 April 1842, Diary.

57 "feeling sick and sad": AMA, 6 March 1842, Journal, HAP.

58 "father going off to England": LMA, 14 September 1843, *Journals*, 45.

58 "as ill as it was": Thomas Carlyle to RWE, London, 29 August 1842, in Emerson and Carlyle, *Correspondence*, 329.

58 "venerable Don Quixote": Ibid., 326.

58 "crazy or sound asleep": Robert Browning to Alfred Donnett, 30 September 1842, in Emerson and Carlyle, *Correspondence*, 329n.

58 "bent on saving the world": Thomas Carlyle to RWE, London, 29 August 1842, in ibid., 326.

58 "Work! Work!": ABA, 5 July 1842, *Journals of ABA*, 163.

58 "I am enjoying": AMA, 8 July 1842, Diary.

59 "Wedlock! blessed union": ABA, "Psyche."

59 "If you ask where evil": Charles Lane in Alcott House Scripture, "Formation," Shepard, *Pedlar's Progress*, 325.

59 "Dearest . . . Guests to our Wedding": ABA to AMA, 2 August 1842, *Letters of ABA*, 88.

59 "I think of you": ABA to Anna, Louisa, Elizabeth, and May Alcott, 15 July 1842, ibid., 88.

59 "Father dear": AMA, 20 June 1842, Journal.

59 "peculiarities and moods": AMA, 26 July 1842, ibid.

60 "ebullition . . . so happy": AMA, 23 October 1842, ibid.

60 "effort to initiate . . . human regeneration": ABA and Charles Lane, *Dial*, July 1843.

60 "Mr. Lane does not": RWE,"The English Reformers," in *Uncollected Prose, Dial Essays*, 1842, http://www.emersoncentral.com/english_reformers.htm (accessed January 29, 2009) and in Shepard, *Pedlar's Progress*, 345.

60 "no prophet of the future": Charles Lane to William Oldham, 9 September 1843, from William Harry Harland, "Bronson Alcott's English Friends," unpublished essay, Fruitlands Museum, Harvard, Massachusetts.

60 "off the railroad of progress": Charles Lane to William Oldham, 29 September 1843, in Sears, *Bronson Alcott's Fruitlands*, 116.

60 "cockerels": RWE, *Journals and Miscellaneous Notebooks*, 8:404.

61 "bottomless imbeciles": Thomas Carlyle to RWE, London, March 11, 1843, in Emerson and Carlyle, *Correspondence*, 338.

61 "[For] a founder of a family": RWE, 19 November 1842, *Journals and Miscellaneous Notebooks*, 8:300–301.

61 "His countenance": Lydia M. Child to Augusta King, 19 September 1843, Cynthia H. Barton, *Transcendental Wife: The Life of Abigail May Alcott* (Lanham, MD: University Press of America, 1996), 95.

62 "the school part": LMA, 20 November 1843, *Journals*, 47.

62 "Circumstances most cruelly": AMA, 29 November 1842, Journal.

62 "stupidly obtuse . . . speculation and discussion": Ibid.

63 "Mrs. A. has passed": Charles Lane to William Oldham, 30 November 1842, in Sears, *Bronson Alcott's Fruitlands*, 121.

63 "I sought . . . any such emblem": ABA to LMA, 29 November 1842, *Letters of ABA*, 92.

63 "I live, my dear daughter": Ibid.

63 "Left Concord to try": AMA, 24 December 1842, Journal.

64 "bounteous stores": LMA *Eight Cousins* (New York: Penguin, 1995), 238.

64 "I left home toil-worn": AMA, 1 January 1843, ibid.

64 "less tenacious": AMA, 4 January 1843, ibid.

64 "opportunity for the children": AMA, 15 January 1842, ibid.

64 "You are most certainly . . . thy brother, Charles": Charles Lane to AMA, 30 January 1843, letter pasted into AMA Journal, January 1843, HAP; also in Bedell, *The Alcotts*, 201.

65 "A truly kind and fraternal note": AMA, February 1843, Journal, HAP; also in Bedell, *The Alcotts*, 202.

65 "day of some excitement": AMA, 17 January 1842, Journal, HAP.

65 "Thus were we spared": Ibid.

65 "The gentlemen discussed": AMA, 22 January 1843, ibid.

65 "simple dinner which Mr. Alcott": ABA, 22 January 1843, *Journals of ABA*, 151.

65 "chess, morris, backgammon": LMA, *Little Men*, in *LMA: LW, LM, JB*, 622.

66 "Our purposes . . . wisdom and purity": ABA to a Friend, 15 February 1843, *Letters of ABA*, 99.

66 "Am greatly beset": AMA, 23 January 1842, Journal.

66 "a picture for you": AMA, 12 March 1843, microfilm, Concord Free Public Library.

67 "I do not see anyone": Charles Lane to William Oldham, 1 May 1843, in Sears, *Bronson Alcott's Fruitlands*, 18.

67 "the prospect from the highest part": Charles Lane to William Oldham, 31 May 1843, in ibid., 14.

67 "entitle transcendentalism:" Ibid., 15.

68 "Mr. Lane paid me a long visit": RWE to HDT, 10 June 1848, in Franklin B. Sanborn, "The Emerson-Thoreau Correspondence: The *Dial* Period," *Atlantic Monthly*, May 1892.

SIX: TRANSCENDENTAL WILD OATS

69 "On the first day of June": LMA, *Transcendental Wild Oats and Excerpts from the Fruitlands Diary*, introduction by W. H. Harrison (Boston: Harvard Common Press, 1981), 25.

69 "and he brought his son": Ibid., 65.

70 "I ran in the wind": LMA, 14 September 1843, *Journals*, 45.

70 "I felt sad at the thought": Anna Alcott, 6 June 1843, in Sears, *Bronson Alcott's Fruitlands*, 86–87.

70 "I told mother . . . 'your loving mother'": LMA, 29 November 1843, *Journals*, 47.

70 "Friday, Nov. 2nd . . . lessons—L.M.A.": LMA, 2 November 1843, ibid., 46.

70 "Sunday, [Sept.] 24th . . . the same at fifty,—L.M.A.": LMA, 24 September 1843, ibid., 45.

71 "whose peculiar mission": LMA, *Transcendental Wild Oats*, 32.

71 "believing that language": Ibid., 42.

71 "persecuted for wearing": Palmer's grave is in Evergreen Cemetery in Leominster, MA.

71 "idea of reform consisted": LMA, *Transcendental Wild Oats*, 31.

71 "in two plates . . . perpetual picnic": Ibid.

71 "We are cleaning": AMA to Hannah Robie, 10 June 1843, Family Letters, 1828–61.

71 "To this rare library": LMA, *Transcendental Wild Oats*, 37.

72 "Walked over our little territory": AMA, 4 June 1843, Journal.

72 "The prospect . . . perturbation of 10 years": AMA to SJM, 14 June 1843, Family Letters, 1828–61.

72 "Mr. Alcott is . . . like his mind": Charles Lane to William Oldham, 16 June 1943, in Sears, *Bronson Alcott's Fruitlands*, 26–27.

72 " 'Each member' ": LMA, *Transcendental Wild Oats*, 34–35.

73 " 'We shall spade it' ": Ibid., 33–34.

73 "I rose at five": LMA, 1 September 1843, *Journals*, 45.

73 "worm-slaughter": LMA, *Transcendental Wild Oats*, 49.

73 "Vegetable diet . . . melody itself": LMA, 2 November 1843, *Journals*, 47.

74 "This was Lizzie's . . . oak leaves": Anna Alcott, 24 June 1843, in Sears, *Bronson Alcott's Fruitlands*, 93.

74 "And Father's friends": Ibid., 96.

74 "A rose of Fruitland's": Ibid., 97.

74 "The sun and the evening sky"; "there is as much merit": RWE, 4 July 1843, *Journals and Miscellaneous Notebooks*, 8:433.

74 "The right people": AMA to Charles May, 6 November 1843, Family Letters, 1828–61.

74 "Occasionally he took his walks abroad": LMA, *Transcendental Wild Oats*, 45.

75 "not a spiritual being": Charles Lane to William Oldham, 16 June 1843, in Sears, *Bronson Alcott's Fruitlands*, 26.

75 "A second irrepressible being": LMA, *Transcendental Wild Oats*, 42–43.

75 "They defied each other": RWE, 1844, "New England Reformers."

76 "by no means satisfied": Charles Lane to William Oldham, in Sears, *Bronson Alcott's Fruitlands*, 26.

76 "This morning after breakfast": Isaac Thomas Hecker, 12 July 1843, in ibid., 77–78.

76 "a noble horse": AMA to SJM, 30 August 1840, Family Letters, 1828–61, HAP; also in Barton, *Transcendental Wife*, 71.

76 "I had a music lesson": LMA, 14 September 1843, *Journals*, 45.

76 "Miss P. is gone": LMA, 20 November 1843, *Journals*, 47.

76 "Miss Jane Gage . . . forbidden fruit": LMA, *Transcendental Wild Oats*, 46–48.

77 "Shall I sip tea": Ibid., 51.

77 "We had a dinner": LMA, 28 August 1843, *Journals*, 44.

78 "Father and Mr. Kay": LMA, 4 August 1843, ibid., 43.

78 "Transcendentalest [*sic*] . . . inquiring into our principles": *Harvard Shaker Society Journal*, in *Transcendental Wild Oats*, 65fn.

79 "Visited the Shakers"; "There is a servitude": AMA, August 1843, in *Pedlar's Progress*, 372.

79 "I don't know": Lydia Maria Child to AMA, late summer 1843, in Martha Saxton, *Louisa May Alcott: A Modern Biography* (New York: Farrar, Straus and Giroux, 1995), 144.

79 "When I woke up": LMA, 8 October 1843, *Journals*, 46.

80 "Dearest Mother": LMA to AMA, 8 October 1843, *Letters*, 3.

80 "I shall be very lonely": LMA, 12 October 1843, *Journals*, 46.

80 "It is concluded . . . *acts worse*": AMA to SJM, 4 November 1843, Family Letters, 1828–61.

81 "I do not allow": AMA to SJM, undated, probably late December 1843, ibid.

81 "Your letter was duly received": AMA to SJM, 11 November 1843, Family Letters, 1828–61.

81 "Mr. Lane thought": Ibid.

81 "alone and naked . . . separation is possible": Charles Lane to William Oldham, 26 November 1843, in Sears, *Bronson Alcott's Fruitlands*, 123–24.

82 "In the evening": LMA, 20 November 1843, *Journals*, 47.

82 "Father read to us . . . all together": LMA, 10 December 1843, ibid., 47.

82 "Christmass Rimes": LMA, 25 December 1843, ibid., 48.

83 "I am content with what I have": Ibid., 50.

83 "I mean to take my cubs": AMA to Hannah Robie, 12 March 1844, AMA, Memoir.

83 "Concluded to go to Mr. Lovejoy's": AMA, 1 January 1844, Journal.

83 "load of goods to Mr. L's": AMA, 6 January 1844, ibid.

83 "The arrangements": AMA, 7 January 1843, ibid.

84 "Very sad, indeed": RWE, April 1844, *Journals and Miscellaneous Notebooks*, 9:86.

84 "Silently he lay down": LMA, *Transcendental Wild Oats*, 57.

84 "In the early dawn": Ibid., 60.

84 "Yesterday, having ate": AMA to SJM, 11 January 1843, Family Letters, 1828–61.

85 "I wish I was rich": LMA, 8 October 1843, *Journals*, 46.

85 "To Mother": LMA, "To Mother," in *The Poetry of Louisa May Alcott*, 2.

85 "I wrote in my Imagination Book": LMA, undated 1843, *Journals*, 51.

SEVEN: THE HAPPIEST YEARS OF MY LIFE

87 "quite comfortable": AMA, 6 March 1842, Journal.

87 "Our home is humble . . . himself to God!": AMA, 24 April 1844, ibid.

87 "As sure as the sun . . . gay pranks": Annie M. L. Clark, "From *The Alcotts in Harvard* (1902)," in Shealy, *Alcott in Her Own Time*, 118–19.

88 "brief and tragical experience": LMA to Anna Marie Lawrence, 3 February 1865, *Letters*, 107.

88 "got mad . . . immediately hanged!": Clark, "From *The Alcotts in Harvard* (1902)," in Shealy, *Alcott in Her Own Time*, 121.

88 "how it did smell!": LMA, "Poppy's Pranks," in *"Aunt Jo's Scrap-Bag*, 6:101.

88 "swift as an antelope": "Blue Juniata" (Bright Alfarata), by Marion Dix Sullivan, http://books.google.com/books?id=XMPFEmlqDJ18C&pg=PA245&dq=Bright+Alfarata#PPA245.M1 (accessed 26 January 2009).

89 "We christened a favorite nook . . . Princess Royal": Frederick L. H. Willis, "From *Alcott Memoirs* (1915)," in Shealy, *Alcott in Her Own Time*, 171.

89 "No matter how weary . . . had a care": Ibid., 172.

89 "strangely out of place . . . charmingly practical": Ibid., 173.

89 "Emerson will nurture a wiser . . . led last winter": AMA to SJM, 6 October 1844, Family Letters, 1828–61.

90 "Mr. A's inclinations": Ibid.

90 "My dear Fire . . . butter-in-a-churn": LMA to Sophia Gardner, 23 September 1845, *Letters*, 4.

90 "It is very important . . . entire satisfaction": SJM to RWE, 22 December 1844, Lexington, MA, HAP.

90 "happiest years": LMA, "Recollections" in *An Intimate Anthology*, 6.

91 "Mr. Emerson . . . cheap as dirt": AMA to SJM, 8 June 1845, Family Letters, 1828–61.

91 "a citizen of the town": Clara Gowing, "From *The Alcotts as I Knew Them* (1909)," Shealy, in *Alcott in Her Own Time*, 134.

91 "On the opposite side": Ibid.

91 "Though comparatively disregarded now"; "he was pledged . . . Nature cannot spare him": Henry David Thoreau, *Walden; Or, Life in the Woods* (New York: Houghton Mifflin, 1893), 417.

92 "[At Sandy] Pond where we found": LMA to Sophia Gardner, 23 September 1845, *Letters*, 3.

92 "often shocked her sensitive sister": Gowing, "From *The Alcotts as I Knew Them* (1909)," in Shealy, *Alcott in Her Own Time*, 134.

93 "Augustus! Oh, my Augustus! . . . sad history": LMA, "My Boys," in *Selected Fiction*, 318–20.

93 "It was visited almost daily . . . Louisa was herself": Gowing, "From *The Alcotts as I Knew Them* (1909)," in Shealy, *Alcott in Her Own Time*, 136.

93 "a game of cards . . . 'Mr. Smack'": Ibid., 137.

94 "Ah, Louis, Why art thou here? . . . free thee from his power!": Anna Bronson Pratt, "*Comic Tragedies*" (Boston: Roberts Brothers, 1893), 19, http://books.google.com/books?id=Q4M0AAAAMAAJ&printsec=titlepage&source=gbs_summary_r&cad=0#PPA3,M1 (accessed 28 January 2009).

94 "Louisa is so interesting": Anna Alcott, 1 September 1845, *Little Women Letters from the House of Alcott*, ed. Jessie Bonstele and Marion de Forest (Boston: Little, Brown, 1914), 131.

94 "Jo [Louisa] and Meg [Anna] . . . nothing but the name": Anna Alcott Pratt, "*Comic Tragedies*," 8–12.

95 "very quiet and gentle": AMA to SJM, 9 August 1845, Family Letters, 1828–61.

95 "I wish we could be together": LMA, January 1845, *Journals*, 56.

95 "I am so cross"; "Read *The Heart of Mid-Lothian*": Ibid., 55.

95 "I found this note . . . L.M.A.": Ibid.

95 "Your temperament is a peculiar one . . . ranking among the best": AMA, 24 November 1845, Journal.

96 "BRONSON: How can you get what you need . . . [She never got it. L.M.A.]": LMA, January 1845, *Journals*, 55–56.

96 "very faithfully": ABA, April 1846, *Journals*, 175.

96 "My Louy, I was grieved . . . passion is over": AMA to LMA 1846, in Cheney, *Louisa May Alcott,* 29.

96 "I encourage her writing . . . young and tender heart": AMA to SJM, 18 April 1845, Family Letters, 1828–61.

96 "I was very dismal"; "Despondency . . . smile through the darkest hours": LMA, January 1845, *Journals,* 56.

97 "A Sample of our Lessons . . . Love of Cats": Ibid., 55.

98 "I have been thinking": LMA to AMA, 1845, *Letters,* 6.

98 "I have at last got . . . my dear mother": LMA, March 1846, *Journals,* 59.

99 "My Kingdom . . . And dare to take command": LMA, "My Kingdom (1845)," in *The Sunny Side: A Book of Religious Songs for the Sunday School and the Home,* ed. Charles W. Wendte and H. S. Perkins, in Gloria T. Delamar, *Louisa May Alcott and "Little Women"* (Lincoln, NE: Universe, 2001), 207–9.

100 "I once thought all minds in childhood": ABA, March 1846, *Journals of ABA,* 173.

100 *"Oh! May this Pen":* AMA, 24 November 1846, *Journal,* in Bedell, *Alcotts,* 239.

100 "Two devils": ABA, March 1846, *Journals of ABA,* 173.

101 "sentimental": LMA, "Recollections," in *An Intimate Anthology,* 8.

101 "broad-shouldered": LMA, *Work,* 175.

101 "not dry facts": LMA, *Work,* 183.

101 "I used to venture . . . and Carlyle": LMA, "Reminiscences of RWE," in *The Sketches of Louisa May Alcott,* 210.

101 "Browsing over Mr. Emerson's library . . . I liked it very much": LMA, 9 October 1847, *Journals,* 60.

101 "The door opened . . . he had found me": Bettine von Arnim, *Goethe's Correspondence with a Child,* http://www.hedweb.com/bgcharlton/bettina-goethe.html.

102 "[I was] at once fired": LMA, "Recollections," in *An Intimate Anthology,* 8.

103 "I don't see who is to clothe and feed us": LMA, January 1845, *Journals,* 56.

103 "in a state of sad mental imbecility . . . paying our debts": AMA to SJM, 2 November 1846, Family Letters, 1828–61.

104 "retirement, agreeable occupation": AMA to SJM, 29 February 1848, ibid.

104 "the fancy stores": Ibid.

104 "Make no arrangements for them . . . any effort at all": ABA, quoted in AMA to SJM, 13 February 1848, Family Letters, 1828–61.

104 "Three little fairies . . . all so sad?": LMA, *Flower Fables* (Echo Library, 2007), http://books.google.com/books?id-TYQ79KSNLVAC (accessed 29 January 2009), 9–10.

104 "a natural source . . . She knows their angels": RWE to Charles J. Woodbury, in Charles J. Woodbury, *Talks with Ralph Waldo Emerson* (Kessinger, 2006), 100–01.

105 "I begin to wonder": AMA to "My Beloved Family," 27 May 1848, Family Letters, 1828–61.

105 "Louisa in the lane running . . . drenched in tears": Ibid.

105 "My friends begin to value . . . 'make their nests in him'": RWE, *Journals and Miscellaneous Notebooks,* 11:51.

106 "It was an anxious . . . see if I won't!": LMA, "Recollections," in *An Intimate Anthology*, 9.

EIGHT: HEAVEN'S SO FAR AWAY

107 "the happiest years": LMA, "Recollections," in *An Intimate Anthology*, 6.

107 "Since coming to the city": LMA, May 1880, *Journals*, 61–62.

107 "a caged sea-gull": LMA, "Recollections," in *An Intimate Anthology*, 10.

108 "Walking-dress and mantilla": http://www.history.rochester.edu/godeys/0-1-50.htm (accessed 24 October 2008).

108 "In the street": LMA, May 1850, *Journals*, 61.

109 "Lord Hamilton's stately home": LMA, *The Inheritance* (Boston: Penguin, 1995), 3.

109 "Here and there rose an old gray tower": Ibid.

109 "the cold neglect, the crude": AMA to "Dear Cousin," undated, probably 1852, AMA Memoir.

110 "treated with too much severity": AMA, April 1850, "Missionary Report," HAP.

110 "the sharks of lust": AMA, 24 January 1849, AMA Fragments, HAP; also in Barton, *Transcendental Wife*, endnote 14 for chapter 6.

110 "I can't talk to anyone": LMA, May 1850, *Journals*, 62.

112 "which was filled with original tales": LMA, *Little Women*, in *LMA: LW, LM, JB*, 105.

112 "Oh my kitty": LMA, *Olive Leaf*, July 15, 1849, HMC; also in Bedell, *The Alcotts*, 297.

112 "report card . . . Abba bad": Ibid.

113 "the brimming fount of family": ABA, "The Return," in Shepard, *Pedlar's Progress*, 389.

114 "Quite dejected, feeble": ABA, 27 May 1850, *Journals of ABA*, 231–32.

115 "Best American and Foreign Help": Printed announcement dated Boston, August 14, 1850, pasted in AMA Memoir; also in Bedell, *The Alcotts*, 282.

115 "It was not fit work": LMA, 1852, *Journals*, 67.

115 "Anna would find much to enjoy": Caroline Sturgis Tappan to AMA, 28 May 1850, Alcott Family Letters, 1850–55, vol. 5, HAP.

115 "We had small pox": LMA, May 1850, *Journals*, 62n.

116 "very hard . . . over my dinner": Ibid., 63.

116 "Her unhappiness was such a weight": Caroline Sturgis Tappan to AMA, June 1850, Alcott Family Letters, 1850–55.

116 "School is hard work"; "Anna wants to be an actress": LMA, August 1850, *Journals*, 63–64.

117 "He possessed an impressive nose"; LMA, "How I Went Out to Service," in *Selected Fiction*, 461.

117 "stately old mansion . . . along the walls": Ibid., 463–65.

117 "a passive bucket": Ibid., 468.

118 "charming room"; "Infinitely": Ibid., 469.

118 "The roughest work": Ibid.

118 "This experience of going out to service": Maria S. Porter, "Recollections of Louisa May Alcott (1892)," in Shealy, *Alcott in Her Own Time*, 64.

118 "I fondly hoped was": LMA, "How I Went Out to Service," in *Selected Fiction*, 471.

119 "great bundle of goodies"; "Mother broke down entirely": LMA, 2 January 1853(?), *Letters*, 7.

119 "Christmas won't be": LMA, *Little Women*, in LMA: LW, LM, JB, 1.

119 "Don't you wish": LMA, "How It All Happened," in *Aunt Jo's Scrap-Bag*, 6:39.

119 "go round each Christmas": Ibid., 40.

120 "second girl"; "I needed the change": LMA, 1853, *Journals*, 69.

120 "My home-child": AMA to Elizabeth Alcott, 8 August 1853, Family Letters, 1928–61.

121 "Put on your bonnet and cloak": AMA to Anna Alcott, 18 November 1853, ibid.

121 "It seems as if": AMA to ABA, 19 November 1853, ibid.

121 "Betty . . . had a little romance": LMA, 1853, *Journals*, 69.

122 "There was once a beautiful . . . youthful days": Anna Alcott Pratt to "Julia" and "Alice," two Vassar girls, 20 January 1871, "A Letter from Miss Alcott's Sister about 'Little Women' (1871)," in Shealy, *Alcott in Her Own Time*, 18–19.

122 "I think she feels better"; "I think Anna and Lizzie": AMA to ABA, 29 November 1853, Family Letters, 1928–61.

122 "Louisa feels stronger and braver": AMA to ABA, 19 November 1853, ibid.

123 "Louisa is to give a Masquerade Ball": AMA to ABA, 29 November 1853, ibid.

123 "Mother flew down, crying . . . funny old jacket"; LMA, 1854, *Journals*, 71.

123 "I began to see": Ibid.

124 "Whatever beauty is to be found": LMA, 25 December 1854, *Letters*, 11.

124 "The principal event of the winter": LMA, 1 January 1855, *Journals*, 73.

125 "I was prouder": LMA, 1866 note added to 1 January 1855 journal entry, ibid.

NINE: THE INDEPENDENT FEELING

126 "People began to feel": LMA, April 1885, *Journals*, 73.

126 "Oronthy Bluggage": Ibid., 74.

126 "'Alcott Sinking Fund,'" LMA to Anna Alcott, November 1858, *Letters*, 38.

127 For a chronological bibliography of LMA's works, see Delamar, *LMA and "Little Women,"* 299–300.

127 "seeing the woods": LMA, June 1855, Walpole, NH, *Journals*, 75.

127 "the smell of the fresh earth": Ibid.

128 "the gayest of the gay": July 1855, Ibid.

128 "always in demand": Frank Preston Stearns, "From *Sketches from Concord and Appledore* (1895)," in Shealy, *Alcott in Her Own Time*, 83.

128 "superior histrionic ability": *Boston Commonwealth* (18 March 1865, p. 2), in introduction by Madeleine Stern, *Journals*, 15.

129 "great idiot asylum": LMA, September 1855, *Journals*, 75.

129 "I think it is but right . . . not of this world": LMA to ABA, 28 November 1885, *Letters*, 13–14.

130 "I can make up": Ibid., 14.

130 "After being on the stage": Ibid.

130 "only one of many . . . ambitious spirit": LMA, *Work*, 37.

130 "would make a clever actress": Ibid., 39.

130 "If I had beauty": Ibid., 38.

130 "she had little beauty": Ibid., 39.

130 "The Sisters' Trial": in LMA, *Selected Fiction*, 216–22.

132 "I suppose you see": LMA to Charlotte Wilkenson, 2 January 1853, *Letters*, 8.

132 "E. Wells married S. Greele": LMA, September 1866, *Journals*, 153.

132 "Dear Eliza, perhaps": LMA to Eliza Wells, 19 March 1858, *Letters*, 33.

133 "great yellow placards": LMA, January 1856, *Journals*, 78.

133 "Sewed a great deal . . . down on Sundays": LMA, March 1856, *Journals*, 78.

133 "last effort to leave . . . checkered by her duties": AMA to SJM, 4 May 1856, Family Letters, 1828–61.

134 "caught from some poor children . . . anxious time": LMA, June 1856, *Journals*, 79.

134 "dark valley of selfish impropriety": AMA to ABA, 14 December 1856, Family Letters, 1828–61.

134 "as money is the principle": LMA to Miss Seymour, 21 September, *Letters*, 16.

135 "I took my little talent . . . good will and sympathy": LMA to Anna Alcott, 2 November 1856, ibid., 18–19.

135 "be independent of everyone . . . good will & sympathy": Ibid., 20.

136 "a straw-colored supercilious lady . . . hoarse and worn out": LMA to Anna Alcott, 6 November 1856, ibid., 21–22.

137 "the air and bearing": LMA, *Little Women,* in *LMA: LW, LM, JB*, 264.

137 "Aunt March is no one": LMA, Letters

137 "I think I shall come out . . . rough and tumble world": LMA to ABA, 29 November 1856, *Letters,* 26.

138 "shopping excursion . . . your hustle": LMA to Anna Alcott, December 1856, ibid., 28.

138 "a handsome silk gown . . . talk like other people": Ibid., 29.

138 "eight cents in the bank": Ibid., 30.

138 "[It is] hard work": LMA, 18 December 1856, *Journals*, 82.

139 "They seem specifically sent": AMA to ABA, 14 December 1856, Family Letters, 1828–61.

139 "a glad surprise": AMA to ABA, 20 February 1855, ibid.

139 "I have done what I planned": LMA, May 1857, *Journals*, 85.

139 "Oh, my sister, passing from me": LMA, *Little Women,* in *LMA: LW, LM, JB*, 443–44.

140 "too heavy . . . pretty hair gone": LMA, 14 March 1858, *Journals*, 89.

140 "perhaps want of more cheerful society": AMA to Louisa and Anna Alcott, 29 September 1857, in Saxton, *Louisa May Alcott*, 214.

140 "It seems to me that the system": AMA to SJM, 25 August 1857, Family Letters, 1828–61.

141 "the case is a critical one": ABA to Anna, Louisa, and May Alcott, 27 August 1857, *Letters of ABA*, 250.

141 "he is never happy": LMA, August 1857, *Journals*, 85.

141 "The people are kind": LMA, October 1857, ibid., 86.

141 "Find Betty a shadow": Ibid.

142 "No written words . . . from Lizzie": Alfred Whitman, "[Reminiscences of 'Laurie'] (1901 and 1902)," in Shealy, *Alcott in Her Own Time,* 106.

142 "I entered the house": Ibid., 107.

142 "For two days": LMA, 14 March 1888, *Journals,* 88–89.

143 "A few moments after the last breath came": Ibid., 89.

143 "she is well at last": LMA to Eliza Wells, 19 March 1858, *Letters,* 32.

143 "You must take my place, Jo": LMA, *Little Women,* in *LMA: LW, LM, JB,* 444.

144 "So the first break comes": LMA, 14 March 1888, *Journals,* 89.

TEN: NATURE MUST HAVE A VENT

146 "I was to do Widow Pottle": LMA, June 1858, *Journals,* 90.

147 "all the nooks . . . unexpected places." Lydia Maria Child to Mrs. S. B. Shaw, 1876, *Letters of Lydia Maria Child* (Boston and New York: Houghton Mifflin, 1882), 240.

147 "All seem to be glad": LMA, August 1858, *Journals,* 90.

147 "on my usual hunt": Ibid.

148 "Last week was": LMA to the Alcott family, October 1858, *Letters,* 34.

148 "a bonny bride": LMA, *Work,* 123.

148 "Something white swept by": Ibid., 124.

148 "My fit of despair": LMA, October 1858, *Journals,* 90.

149 "came a note . . . you stood it": Ibid., 91.

149 "bore herself proudly": ABA to AMA, 4 December 1858, *Letters of ABA,* 282.

149 "This past year . . . do something": LMA, November, 1958, *Journals,* 91–92.

150 "Take it, Basil": LMA, "Love and Self-Love," in *Selected Fiction,* 75.

150 "I take pride": ABA to AMA, 23 December 1858, *Letters of ABA,* 286.

151 "no boy could be my friend": LMA, "Recollections," in *An Intimate Anthology,* 315.

151 "grand sum of $35 . . . I shall get a second-hand carpet": LMA to Anna Alcott, November 1858, *Letters,* 38.

151 "I have been through . . . a boy's wrath"; "Lets you and I go . . . Will you go?": LMA to Alfred Whitman, 27 October 1858, *Letters,* 38.

151 "Walked from Concord": LMA, May 1859, *Journals,* 95.

152 "Never till I'm sick": LMA, *Little Women,* in *LMA: LW, LM, JB,* 164.

152 "We are boiling over with excitement": LMA to Alfred Whitman, 8 November 1859, *Letters,* 49.

153 "The execution of Saint John": LMA, December 1859, *Journals,* 95.

153 "There blossomed forth": LMA, "With a Rose, That Bloomed on the Day of John Brown's Martyrdom," in *The Poetry of Louisa May Alcott,* 11, and in the *Liberator,* January 20, 1860.

153 "if it was not a translation": LMA, November 1859, *Journals,* 95.

153 "I felt much set up": Ibid.

154 "Mr.——won't have 'M.L.'": LMA, February 1860, ibid., 98.

154 "with Nan as the heroine": LMA, March 1860, ibid.

154 "I thought that honor": LMA, May 1860, *Journals,* 100.

154 "found Louisa putting a small wreath"; "Lizzie's memory inviolate": Anne Brown Adams, "[Louisa May Alcott in the Early 1860s]," in Shealy, *Alcott in Her Own Time*, 9.

155 "bereaved family"; "washing dishes": LMA to AAP, 25(?) May 1860, *Letters*, 54.

155 "had a natural dignity"; "event and worshipped": Ibid., 55.

155 "a funny lover who met me"; "haunt[ing] the road": LMA, April 1860, *Journals*, 98.

155 Mr. Condit: ancestry.com, Condit Family Genealogy Entries: 12997, ID: I06659, Name: Sears Byram CONDIT (from "Condits and Cousins—Volume 6"). Sears B. Condit learned the trade of hatmaking in New Jersey and went to Boston in 1855. After two years he went into business for himself and continued in the same business for fifty years.

155 "She consulted her mother": Cheney, *Louisa May Alcott*, 64.

155 "I have decided it be best": LMA to Mr. Condit, n.d., Houghton Library, Harvard University, HAP.

156 "where she and her mate . . . my own cause": LMA, June 1860, *Journals*, 99.

156 "new neighbors . . . this vast town": LMA to Adeline May, July(?) 1860(?), *Letters*, 57.

156 "Genius burned so fiercely . . . it *had* to be done": LMA, August 1860, *Journals*, 99.

157 "will touch it up": LMA, October, 1860, *Journals*, 100.

157 "This must be a frivolous . . . a discontented mind": LMA to AAP, c. August(?) 1860(?), *Letters*, 58.

157 "as if a gale . . . Thoreau Alcott & Co": LMA to Louisa Greenwood Bond, 17 September [1860] *Letters*, 60.

157 "good gown . . . what I felt": LMA, December 1860, *Journals*, 100.

158 "She is one of the fortunate": LMA, November 1860, *Journals*, 100.

158 "More luck for May"; "What shall I do": LMA to AAP, after 17 December 1860, *Letters*, 61–62.

158 "A quiet Christmas": Ibid.

ELEVEN: I'VE OFTEN LONGED TO SEE A WAR

159 "A most uncommon . . . and a bonnet": LMA, January 1861, *Journals*, 103.

159 "From the 2d to the 25th": February 1861, ibid., 103–4.

160 "Every few weeks": LMA, *Little Women*, in *LMA: LW, LM, JB*, 283–84.

160 "Mother pronounced it wonderful . . . your metaphysics?": LMA, February 1861, *Journals*, 104.

160 "Even if it never comes to anything": Ibid.

161 "the manliest man . . . in every gesture": LMA, *Moods*, ed. and introduction by Sarah Elbert (New Brunswick, NJ: Rutgers University Press, 1996), 36.

162 "past thirty . . . their true level": Ibid., 144. The author is grateful to Sarah Elbert for pointing out to her that Faith Dane is modeled upon Margaret Fuller.

163 In response to criticism that the Sylvia-Warwick-Moor love triangle was not possible, Louisa replied, "I know them to be *possible* as I have seen them more than once" (LMA to Mr. Ayer, 19 March 1865, *Letters*, 109).

163 "scarce thirty years of age . . . tale of woes": ABA, 9 February 1847, *Journals of ABA*, 190.

163 "Fugitive slaves were sheltered": LMA, "Recollections," in *An Intimate Anthology*, 8.

163 "write on the hearth": Ibid.

163 "surrounded with chains . . . protection and sympathy": ABA, 4 April 1851, *Journals of ABA*, 243.

164 "I shall be horribly ashamed": LMA, 1851, *Journals*, 65.

164 "I've often longed . . . I have my wish": LMA, April 1861, ibid., 105.

164 "a sight to behold . . . birds of prey": LMA to Alfred Whitman, 19 May 1861, *Letters*, 64.

164 "who poke each others eyes out": Ibid.

164 "A sad day . . . times like these": LMA, April 1861, *Journals*, 105.

165 "Are you going to have a dab": LMA to Alfred Whitman, 19 May 1861, *Letters*, 65.

165 "I long to be a man . . . those who can": LMA, April 1861, *Journals*, 105.

165 "sewing violently": LMA to Alfred Whitman, 19 May 1861, *Letters*, 64.

165 "very martial": LMA, May 1861, *Journals*, 105.

165 "Wrote, read, sewed": LMA, November/December 1861, ibid., 106.

165 "Stick to your teaching": LMA, May 1862, ibid., 109.

165 "Mrs. Stowe, Fanny Kemble": LMA to Alfred Whitman, 6 April (1862), *Letters*, 73.

165 "Hate to visit . . . push one into": LMA, February 1862, *Journals*, 108.

166 "A wasted winter . . . sell my hair to do it": LMA, April 1862, ibid., 109.

166 "I won't teach": Ibid.

166 "not many days": ABA, 4 May 1862, *Journals of ABA*, 346.

166 "Henry would not have . . . it was Henry": LMA to Sophia Ford, 11 May 1862, *Letters*, 74.

166 "has made a stir": LMA, May 1862, *Journals*, 109.

167 "I saw . . . 'Louisa Alcott'": Rebecca Harding Davis, "From *Bits of Gossip* (1904)," in Shealy, *Alcott in Her Own Time*, 124.

167 "she never had any troubles": LMA, May 1862, *Journals*, 109.

167 "They are easy to 'compoze'": LMA to Alfred Whitman, 22 June 1862, *Letters*, 79.

168 "At twenty-five . . . accept the fact": LMA, *Little Women*, in *LMA: LW, LM, JB*, 467.

168 "Decided to go to Washington . . . some new way": LMA, November 1862, *Journals*, 110.

169 "If you intend to be smashed": LMA to Edward J. Bartlett and Garth Wilkinson James, 4 December 1862, *Letters*, 82.

169 "Nurses don't need nice things": LMA, November 1862, *Journals*, 110.

169 "We had all been full": Ibid.

169 "So I set forth": Ibid.

169 "to face the president": LMA, *Hospital Sketches* (Boston: Applewood Books, 1986), 8.

169 "full of hope": LMA, December 1862, *Journals*, 110.

169 "The boat is new . . . fulfill my destiny": LMA, *Hospital Sketches*, 18.

169 "mist wreaths": Ibid., 19.

170 "old place"; "big, dirty, shippy": Ibid., 20–21.

170 "should enjoy": Ibid., 21.

170 "for no journey": Ibid., 22.

170 "We often passed . . . at the North": Ibid., 22–23.

170 "made the fields . . . as we passed": Ibid., 23.

170 "carriages were rolling": Ibid.

170 "and a very trying quantity": Ibid., 24.

170 "some not so inappropriate . . . wounds could christen it": Ibid., 28.

170 "in the grey dawn"; "They've come": Ibid., 25.

171 "Having a taste . . . home again": Ibid., 27.

171 "All was hurry": Ibid., 28.

171 "ragged, gaunt": Ibid.

171 "If she had requested me": Ibid., 29.

171 "manfully . . . Irishman": Ibid.

172 "the merciful magic . . . best they might": Ibid., 37.

172 "seemed to regard . . . surgical seamstress": Ibid., 36.

172 "The expression . . . among the wounded": Angel Price, "Whitman's *Drum Taps* and Washington's Civil War Hospitals," http://xroads.virginia.edu/~CAP/hospital/whitman.html.

172 "a somewhat sudden plunge . . . 'yourn in haste'": LMA, *Hospital Sketches*, 38.

172 "Beds to the front of them": LMA, in *The Poetry of Louisa May Alcott*, 16.

172 "I never began . . . heart sick & worn out, I like it"; "grumble and shiver"; "breed a pestilence": LMA, January 1863, *Journals*, 113.

173 "Quotes Browning copiously": Ibid., 115.

173 "night side . . . house to themselves": Ibid., 114.

173 "duty room . . . a shroud": LMA, *Hospital Sketches*, 41.

175 "A most attractive face"; "child's eyes . . . secret of content": Ibid., 49.

175 "There's not the slightest hope . . . leave it to you": Ibid., 50.

175 "Straightway my fear vanished": Ibid., 51–52.

175 "'This is my first battle' . . . returned elsewhere": Ibid., 54, 58.

176 "Sharp pain": LMA, January 1863, *Journals,* 115.

176 "Hours began to get confused": LMA, *Hospital Sketches*, 77.

177 "Dream awfully . . . likely to do": LMA, January 1863, *Journals,* 115.

177 "Horrid war . . . he to give": ABA, 18 January 1863, 353.

TWELVE: WHERE GLORY WAITED

178 "It was most fortunate . . . at the hospital": ABA to Anna Alcott Pratt, 25 January 1863, *Letters of ABA*, 332.

178 "in the firm belief": LMA, 21 January 1863, *Journals*, 116.

178 "I beg you will not": ABA to Anna Alcott Pratt, 25 January 1863, *Letters of ABA*, 332.

178 "Poor Louy left": AMA to SJM, 1863, MS Am 1130.0(28), HAP; also in John Matteson, *Eden's Outcasts: The Story of Louisa May Alcott and Her Father* (New York: Norton, 2007), 285.

178 "[their] contribution": ABA to Anna Alcott Pratt, 25 March 1863, *Letters of ABA*, 336.

178 "The most vivid . . . 'Lie still, my dear' ": LMA, 21 January 1863, Journals, 116–17.

179 "I appealed . . . worshipping the Devil": Ibid.

179 "very busy . . . hadn't come": Ibid., 117.

179 "tending to millions": Ibid.

180 "queer, thin . . . wits inside": LMA, February 1863, ibid.

180 "no end of rubbish": LMA, March 1863, ibid., 118.

180 " 'Good news!' . . . 'wouldn't be a girl' ": Ibid.

180 "I must go down . . . ever your admiring": LMA to Anna Alcott Pratt, 30 March 1863, *Letters*, 83.

181 "beautiful & new"; "To go very near death": LMA, April 1863, *Journals*, 118.

181 "a big, loveable": Julian Hawthorne, "[Memories of the Alcott Family] (1922 and 1932)," in Shealy, *Alcott in Her Own Time*, 189.

181 "white, tragic mask . . . could not speak": Ibid., 195.

181 "They thought them witty": LMA, April 1863, *Journals*, 118.

181 "fluent and sparkling": *Boston Evening Transcript,* 4 June 1863, in *Louisa May Alcott: The Contemporary Reviews*, ed. Beverly Lyon Clark (Cambridge: Cambridge University Press, 2004), 9.

181 "The reader is": *Waterbury American,* quoted in the *New York Tribune,* 5 September 1863, in ibid., 10.

181 "one of the raciest . . . fresh and deeply interesting": *Roxbury Journal,* quoted in advertisement in the *Commonwealth,* 2 October 1863, in ibid., 9.

182 "I cannot see why": LMA to Mary Elizabeth Waterman, 6 November 1863, *Letters*, 95.

182 "[*Hospital Sketches*] showed me": LMA, 1863, *Journals*, 124n.

182 "one-legged lad . . . read it like": LMA to Annie Adams Fields, 24 June [1863], *Letters*, 84.

182 "[It is] altogether superior": Sophia Hawthorne to Anne Fields, 14 June 1863, Boston Public Library Special Collections, cited in Saxton, *Louisa May Alcott*, 262.

182 "We sighing said": "Thoreau's Flute," in *The Poetry of Louisa May Alcott*, 15.

183 "It was printed, copied": LMA, May 1863, *Journals*, 119.

183 During this period she left home for Boston to give six charity performances for the Sanitary Commission as the Dickens character Mrs. Jarley. At times she moved in with Anna at the Pratt household, especially when Anna was ill, to substitute for her sister as mother, keep house, and be her nurse. For two weeks she and May visited a family in Gloucester, a fishing town and resort on Cape Ann, a resort area.

184 "All my dreams . . . to lend a hand": LMA, October 1863, *Journals*, 121.

186 "he was not brought home . . . peculiar one throughout": LMA, May 1864, ibid., 130.

186 "in a pomp": RWE, 24 May 1862, *Journals and Miscellaneous Notebooks,* 15:59–60, in Baker, *Emerson Among the Eccentrics*, 448.

186 "I thought there was a tragic element . . . the painful solitude of the man": Ibid., 449.

187 "I slept no more . . . came out now": LMA, October 1864, *Journals*, 132.
187 "small, stupid": LMA, November 1864, ibid., 133.
187 "saw, heard & talked": LMA, December 1864, ibid.
187 "like the Queen . . . literary youth": LMA, January 1865, *Journals*, 139.
187 "quick fancy": *Commonwealth*, 7 January 1865, in Clark, *Contemporary Reviews*, 28.
187 "not unlike Goëthe's *Elective Affinities*": Ibid.
188 "Some fear it isn't moral": LMA, February 1865, *Journals*, 139.
188 "The grand mistake . . . can always conquer": *Boston Evening Transcript*, 21 January 1865, in Clark, *Contemporary Reviews*, 30.
188 "maiden reformers": *Springfield Daily Republican*, 4 January 1865, in ibid., 40.
188 "the inevitable *cavaliere* . . . ignorance": *North American Review*, July 1865, in ibid., 35.
188 "*Moods* is not"; "Perhaps I was over bold": LMA, 18 February 1865, *Letters*, 108.
189 "Alcott brains seem": LMA, March 1865, *Journals*, 139.
189 "grand jollification": LMA, April 1865, ibid., 140.
189 "a fine little lad": LMA, June 1865, ibid.

THIRTEEN: A LITTLE ROMANCE

190 "everyone said . . . when [she] came back": LMA, July 1865, *Journals*, 141.
191 "burly guard . . . life that we have": LMA to ABA, 31 July 1865, *Letters*, 111.
191 "got into a novel": LMA, August 1865, *Journals*, 141.
191 "The English . . . and asked questions": LMA, "Up the Rhine," in *The Sketches of Louisa May Alcott*, 165.
191 "There is no use . . . artist can attain": Ibid., 166.
192 "suit & serve"; "many would have done": LMA, August 1865, *Journals*, 142.
192 Anna Weld eventually married: *The Louisa May Alcott Encyclopedia*, ed. Gregory Eiselein and Anne K. Phillips (Westport, CT: Greenwood, 2001), 342.
192 "My absence seems": LMA, September 1865, *Journals*, 143.
192 "Who was Goethe": Ibid., 147n.
192 "most romantic place": LMA, October 1865, ibid., 144.
192 "white Alps of Savoy"; "pleasant, well kept . . . quarters of the world": LMA, "Life in a Pension," in *The Sketches of Louisa May Alcott*, 173.
193 "with a thin, intelligent face"; "he cast wistful glances"; "the heat": LMA, "My Boys," in *Selected Fiction*, 321.
193 "a weakness"; "warmed to him at once": Ibid.
193 "It was impossible . . . pleading eyes": LMA, "Life in a Pension," in *The Sketches of Louisa May Alcott*, 177.
194 "the barrier": LMA, "My Boys," in *Selected Fiction*, 322.
194 "though he often . . . 'beast of English!'": Ibid., 323.
194 "romances, like the roses": LMA, "Life in a Pension," in *The Sketches of Louisa May Alcott*, 183.
194 "splendid plans": LMA, "My Boys," in *Selected Fiction*, 323.
194 "a pile of merry little notes": Ibid.
194 "wheedlesome": Ibid., 325.

194 "'ma drogha'"; "in the tenderest manner": Ibid., 325–26.
195 "his sweetest airs . . . as the time goes on": LMA, November 1865, *Journals*, 145.
195 "[Although] we jokingly agreed": LMA, "My Boys," in *Selected Fiction*, 323.
195 "& went back to V[evey] disconsolate . . . our troubles": LMA, December 1865, *Journals*, 145.
195 "Anna troubled . . . both worried": Ibid.
196 "whim, selfishness": LMA, 1885 insert to entry November 1865, ibid., 148n.
196 "tired of doing nothing": LMA, December 1865, ibid., 145.
196 "a dull Christmas": Ibid., 148n.
196 "tired of the fashionable": LMA, January 1866, ibid., 149.
196 "tired of it": LMA, February 1886, ibid., 150.
196 "young Germanized": Ibid., 155n.
196 "a tedious month . . . Conceited but better than no one": March 1866, ibid., 150.
197 "queer times": Ibid., 155n.
197 "every facility . . . desire in England": ABA to LMA, 18 March 1866, *Letters of ABA*, 390.
197 "My twelve years' seniority": LMA, "My Boys," in *Selected Fiction*, 325.
198 "only all that . . . year of travel": LMA, "My Boys," in *Selected Fiction*, 324.
198 "in the best of the French . . . under the balcony": Ibid.
198 "At his gift of cologne": Ibid., 327.
198 "Did she ever have a love affair?": Julian Hawthorne, "[Memories of the Alcott Family] (1922 and 1932)," Shealy, *Alcott in Her Own Time*, 193.
199 "the penny boats": LMA, "London Bridges," in *The Sketches of Louisa May Alcott*, 244.
199 "the intricacies": LMA, "The Maypole Inn: A Place of Holiday Stories," in ibid., 270.
199 "the Zoo to hunt": LMA, "London Bridges," in *The Sketches of LMA*, 244.
200 "Peter Taylor and his wife": Moncure Daniel Conway, *Autobiography: Memories and Experiences of Moncure Daniel Conway* (Adamant Media, 2001), 51.
201 "The youth and comeliness": LMA, 21 September 1867, in *Boston Commonwealth*, in LMA, *Journals*, 155n.
201 "I dont care a pin": LMA, 1870, *Letters*, 148n.
201 "As Paradise Lost": LMA to Ellen Conway, 15 April [1866], ibid., 113n.
201 "very free & jolly"; "dining late & resting": LMA, June 1865, *Journals*, 152.
201 "youth of an inquiring turn": LMA, "London Bridges," in *The Sketches of Louisa May Alcott*, 245.
201 "a capital guide": Ibid.
201 "[we] struck into a pretty . . . right or wrong"; "fourteen miles": LMA, "The Maypole Inn," in ibid., 272.
201 "On the evening": "London Bridges," in ibid., 245.
202 Blackfriars Bridge: By the time Louisa visited London, the original 1760 Blackfriars Bridge had been demolished. A new bridge, under construction, was opened in 1869. Louisa and C—— walked along a temporary wooden bridge erected next to the old site. It is described in Cruchley's *London in*

1865: A Handbook for Strangers, 1865 as "well worth a visit. . . . The footway is divided for a to-and-fro stream of passengers; and there are three intersecting paths for crossing from one to the other. Gas mains, pipes, and lamps are provided for both the ways." No niches are mentioned, but as the site was famous for fine views, it seems that small areas alongside and out of the flow of foot traffic were provided at regular intervals. http://www.victorianlondon .org/thames/blackfriarsbridge.htm.

202 "for the poor . . . path to heaven": LMA, "London Bridges," in *The Sketches of Louisa May Alcott*, 247.

FOURTEEN: WE REALLY LIVED MOST OF IT

203 "behind hand when the money-maker": LMA, August 1866, *Journals*, 152.

203 "debt more than the devil": LMA, August 1867, ibid., 158.

204 "a woman of thirty at least"; "if actresses"; "I'll not fail": LMA, "Behind a Mask," in *Behind a Mask: The Unknown Thrillers of Louisa May Alcott*, ed., Madeleine Stern (New York: William Morrow, 1975), 11–12.

205 "sorry yet glad": LMA, November, 1866, *Journals*, 153.

205 "thin, sad, hungry & dirty"; "No one else"; "had a fine . . . end of em": Ibid., 154.

205 "At Nice till May": LMA, 1866, Notes and Memoranda, *Journals*, 154.

205 "Louisa Alcott has been": Ibid., 160n.

205 "Sick from too hard work . . . used up generally": LMA, 1867, ibid., 157.

206 "for bills accumulate": LMA, August 1867, ibid., 158.

206 "Niles, partner of Roberts": LMA, September 1867, ibid.

207 "going to camp out"; "hospitable and healthy": LMA, October 1867, ibid.

207 "I am in my little room": LMA, January 1868, ibid., 162.

207 "Keep all the money I send . . . his clothes getting shiney?": LMA to AMA, January 1868, *Letters*, 113.

207 "white and sweet"; "a good omen": LMA, January 1868, *Journals*, 162.

207 "older-sisterly advice"; "woke up prancing": LMA, ibid., 163.

208 "the top of his illustrious head . . . 'And all as tall as you?' ": LMA, 15 January 1868, ibid., 163.

211 "I hoped it would make me soft": LMA, "Perilous Play," in *Plots and Counterplots: More Unknown Thrillers of Louisa May Alcott*, ed. Madeleine Stern (New York: William Morrow, 1976), 315.

211 "Rose, we have been near death": Ibid.

211 "We brooded over Johnny": LMA, 18 January 1968, *Journals*, 163.

211 "the busy, useful, independent spinsters . . . lives for them and is content": "Happy Women," in *Alternative Alcott*, ed. Elaine Showalter (New Brunswick, NJ: Rutgers University Press, 1989), 203–6.

212 "to dream of flannel": LMA, 14 February 1868, *Journals*, 165.

213 "They want a book . . . us personally and pecuniarily": ABA to LMA, 19 February 1868, *Letters of ABA*, 427.

214 "The Sisters' Trial," 215; "A Modern Cinderella," 228; LMA, in *Selected Fiction*. "Two Scenes in a Family," LMA in appendix B: Early Sketches by the Alcott Sisters, in *Journals*, 338.

214 "Marmee [Abby], Anna, and May all approve": LMA, May 1868, *Journals*, 165–66.

215 Civil War period: See Sarah Elbert's *Hunger for Home* for a full discussion of Alcott's place in cultural history.

215 fictionally speaking, unworkable: The author is grateful to the novelist Geraldine Brooks for this insight.

215 "*'Young Women,'* or something of that sort": LMA to Thomas Niles, June 1868, *Letters*, 116.

215 "thought it *dull*": LMA, June 1868, *Journals*, 166.

216 "Christmas won't be Christmas": *LMA: LW, LM, JB*, 7.

216 "Not a bit sensational": LMA, 26 August 1868, *Journals*, 166.

217 "Bronson Alcott's daughter": *Boston Daily Evening Transcript*, 30 September 1868, in Clark, *Contemporary Reviews*, 61.

217 "the restless and confused . . . with the four sisters": *Springfield Daily Republican*, 21 October 1868, in ibid., 62.

217 "natural, human children . . . 'think' or 'suppose.' ": *National Anti-Slavery Standard*, 21 November 1868, in ibid., 65.

217 "Capital . . . is not a Christian book": *Ladies' Repository* (Boston), December 1868, 472, in ibid., 66.

217 "Don't put [it] in the Sunday School library": *Zion's Herald*, 22 October 1868, in ibid., 172.

217 "the majority . . . spiritless property": *Eclectic Magazine*, November 1868, 1414, in ibid., 64.

217 "pleasant notices and letters . . . to please anyone": LMA, 30 October/1 November 1868, *Journals*, 167.

218 "Girls write to ask"; "Publishers . . . insist on having people": LMA to Elizabeth Powell, 20 March 1869, *Letters*, 125.

219 "I am so full of my work": LMA, 17 November 1868, *Journals*, 167.

219 "My birthday": LMA, 29 November 1868, ibid.

219 "up in the garret": LMA, *Little Women,* in *LMA: LW, LM, JB*, 465.

219 " 'Jo' on the next lid, scratched and worn": Ibid., 503.

220 "Jo laid her head down": Ibid., 465.

220 "the finest Turkish baths"; "the second passenger elevator": Mary F. Eastman and Helen Cecelia Clarke Lewis, *The Biography of Dio Lewis: Prepared at the Desire and with the Co-operation of Mrs. Dio Lewis* (Fowler and Wells, 1891), 125. Original from Harvard University Digitized 27 January 2006. http://books.google.com/books?id=J67qXsLvJOQCcad=0 (accessed 26 January 2009).

220 "Had a queer time whisking up": LMA, December 1868, *Journals*, 168.

221 "There were slow boys": LMA, *Little Women,* in *LMA: LW, LM, JB*, 511–12.

221 "The Professor suddenly began to sing": Ibid., 514.

221 "headaches, cough, and weariness": LMA, January 1869, *Journals*, 171.

221 "who don't seem to be grown up . . . 'on a Sunday night' ": LMA to Ellen Conway, 9 February 1869, *Letters*, 123.

222 "every penny that money can pay": LMA, January 1869, *Journals*, 171.

222 "very poorly": LMA, April 1869, ibid.

222 "Afraid to get into a vortex": Ibid.

222 "People begin to come and stare": Ibid.
223 "If people knew how O.F.G.": LMA to Alcott Family, 13 [14] May [1870], *Letters*, 135.
224 "Kate King, the authoress . . . to be the fashion, just then": LMA, *An Old-Fashioned Girl* (New York: Puffin Books, 1996), 242–43.
224 "beware of popularity": Ibid., 245.
224 "Fanny took a good look": Ibid., 246.
225 "rainy day, and no debts": LMA, August 1869, *Journals*, 172.

FIFTEEN: HAPPY BEFORE I DIE

226 "Gentlemen: Many thanks for the check": LMA to Roberts Brothers, 28 December 1869, *Letters*, 129.
226 "I'll be rich, and famous": LMA, "Recollections" in *An Intimate Anthology*, 9.
226 "half a dozen devoted beings": LMA, April 1870, *Journals*, 174.
227 "Bully book, ma'am": Ibid.
228 "If steamers are named the 'Asia,'": LMA, *Shawl-Straps: A Second Series of Aunt Jo's Scrap-Bag*, vol. 2 (Boston: Roberts Brothers, 1885), 15.
228 "came in a party to call": LMA, April 1879, *Journals*, 174.
228 "poked about more": LMA to AMA, 14 April 1870, *Letters*, 130.
228 "enjoying the queer sights . . . criticising the work": Ibid.
228 "ya-hooped": LMA to AMA, 17 April 1870, *Letters*, 131.
229 "It would be worth that . . . entirely new scene": Ibid., 132.
229 "something to sleep": LMA to Alcott Family, 13 May 1870, ibid., 135.
229 "in the membrane": Ibid.
230 "So I take my potash . . . Ha! ha!": LMA to Anna Alcott Pratt, 25 May 1870, *Little Women Abroad: The Alcott Sisters' Letters from Europe, 1870–1871*, ed. Daniel Shealy (Athens, GA: University of Georgia Press, 2008), 58.
230 Alice "has just grabbed May": LMA to Alcott Family, 13 May 1870, *Letters*, 136.
230 "the health of her Highness Princess Louisa": LMA to Alcott Family, 30 May 1870, ibid., 136.
231 "It is simple, pleasant": Ibid.
231 "horrid"; "floating down the Loire": LMA to AMA, 24 June[–2 July], 1870, ibid., 138.
231 "The dreadful man": LMA to Alcott Family, 1 June 1870, ibid., 142n.
232 "it seems disrespectful": May Alcott to the Alcott Family, 17 June 1870, *Little Women Abroad*, 98.
232 "mumbo jumbo"; "red, purple, and yellow priests": LMA to AMA, 24 June 1870, *Letters*, 140.
232 "Weld incumbrances": Ibid., 139.
232 "We are living in such perfect luxury": May Alcott Nieriker to ABA, 20–21 June 1870, *Little Women Abroad*, 108.
232 "'tis 'morning on the mountains'": LMA to AMA, 24 June[–2 July], 1870, *Letters*, 142.
232 "Don't send me any more letters": LMA to AMA, 21 August, 1870, ibid., 148.
232 "very handsome, scarlet and gold": LMA to Anna Alcott Pratt, 4–9 June 1870, *Little Women Abroad*, 81.

233 "Golden Goose": LMA, "The Lay of a Golden Goose," in *The Poetry of Louisa May Alcott*, 25.

233 "found the scene so changed"; "Our house . . . I woke up": LMA to AMA, 21 August 1870, *Letters*, 146.

234 "full of Spaniards . . . all plotting": Ibid., 147.

234 "Lake Leman will never seem": LMA, "My Boys," in *Selected Fiction*, 323.

235 "I am afraid I shall not write": LMA to the Alcott Family, September 1870, *Letters*, 152.

235 "A year of pleasure": Ibid.

235 "a splendid journey over the Alps": LMA, October 1870, *Journals*, 175.

235 "My Nan can imagine": LMA to the Alcott Family, 20 September 1870, *Letters*, 151.

236 "in bliss"; "always oppressed with a sense of sin"; "not well": LMA, 10 November 1870, *Journals*, 175.

236 "The Pope . . . sulks"; "seldom seen": LMA quoted by ABA to Mrs. Adams, 7 January 1871, *Letters of ABA*, 530.

236 "The artists were the best company": LMA, 10 November 1870, *Journals*, 175.

237 "the flesh . . . haggard": ABA, 17 June 1870, *Journals*, in Saxton, *Louisa May Alcott*, 309.

237 "seemed as if [they] were in Venice": LMA to Unknown Recipient, 29 December 1870, *Letters*, 154–55. (The recipient is possibly Daniel Noyes Haskell, editor of the *Boston Daily-Evening Transcript*, which published it 3 February 1871.)

237 "You need not be told": LMA to Anna Alcott Pratt, December(?) 1870(?), ibid., 153.

238 "Annie bears her loss": LMA to Elizabeth Wells, 9 January 1870, ibid., 159.

238 "that John's death"; "In writing and thinking": LMA, 1871, *Journals*, 177.

239 "with a great red placard": LMA, June 1871, ibid., 178.

SIXTEEN: SUCCESS

240 "under her sweet serenity": LMA, June 1871, *Journals*, 178.

241 "I do not feel resigned": *Anna Alcott Pratt*, 19 March 1871, Journal, HAP.

241 "our best friend for years": LMA, July–September 1871, *Journals*, 179.

241 "Once upon a time": LMA to James T. Fields, 3 July 1871, *Letters*, 160.

242 "It looks like impertinent curiosity": LMA, August 1872, *Journals*, 183.

242 "A year and a half of holiday": LMA, November 1871, ibid., 179.

242 "Mother is to be cosey": Ibid.

243 "with warm flannels"; "[We] both laughed": LMA, November 1872, *Journals*, 183.

243 "Louisa had accomplished the task": Cheney, *Louisa May Alcott*, 186.

243 "knocking at the saucepan": LMA to Mary Mapes Dodge, 13 April 1886, *Letters*, 297.

244 manic-depressive illness: "The evidence, taken as a whole does not irrefutably show, but is consistent with, the strong likelihood that Louisa May Alcott suffered from a form of manic-depressive illness." Kay Redfield Jamison, e-mail to John Matteson, 16 August 2006, in Matteson, *Eden's Outcasts*, 305.

244 "T[homas]. N[iles]. said . . . golden goose": LMA to ABA, 29 November 1872, *Letters,* 173.

245 "big blonde boy . . . in the lurch": LMA, December 1871, *Journals,* 180.

245 "My mouth is now fair . . . no dentists upon earth": LMA to Louisa Wells(?), 1871(?), *Letters,* 164.

245 "They grew in beauty . . . no dentists upon earth!": LMA to Louisa Wells(?), 1871, *Letters,* 163–64.

246 "Fame, or A Wail . . . Concord has conquered them": LMA, *The Poetry of Louisa May Alcott,* 28.

246 "wandering about . . . Emersonian way": LMA to Louisa Wells, 27(?) July 1872, *Letters,* 166.

247 "Trinity Church was beginning to smoke . . . days of Pompeii": LMA to Anna Alcott Pratt, 10(?) November 1872, ibid., 169–70.

248 "dinners, balls [and] calls": LMA, *Journals,* 187.

248 Thoreau owned 706 unsold copies of *Walden:* http://www.thoreausociety.org/ _resources_works.htm.

248 "Should like to do one book": LMA, February–March 1873, *Journals,* 187.

249 "more like a tomb than ever": Ibid., 189.

249 "It is gratifying": ABA, 9 June 1873, *Journals of ABA,* 435.

249 "never to be our brave": LMA, June–July 1873, *Journals,* 188.

249 "to see Father . . . want to see it any more": LMA, March 1874, ibid., 192.

250 "riding in Louisa's chariot": LMA, January 1875, ibid., 196.

250 "After my little story . . . and be himself?": ABA to LMA, 4 February 1875, *Letters of ABA,* 646.

251 "Talk with four hundred girls . . . kiss every one": LMA, February 1875, *Journals,* 196.

251 "never had . . . around slowly": Anonymous, "LMA Visits the Sorosis Club in 1875," *New York Graphic,* 18 December 1875, 374, in Shealy, *Alcott in Her Own Time,* 20.

251 "Ma's dander is up . . . manly bosom"; "is to be handed round": LMA to Frederick W. G. May, 20 April 1875, *Letters,* 191–92.

251 "for I have . . . depended on it": Ibid., 21 April 1875, *Letters,* 192n.

252 Louisa "got behind a canvas tree"; "Presently the stage boxes"; "Finally I had to run": LMA to ABA, 18 October 1875, ibid., 198.

252 "If you ever come to Oshkosh": LMA, September–October 1875, *Journals,* 196.

252 This description of Dr. Miller's Bath Hotel is derived entirely from Madeleine B. Stern, *Louisa May Alcott: A Biography,* 240–41.

253 "Faith hope & charity": "Phrenological Examination of L.M. Alcott," in *Signature of Reform,* ed. Madeleine Stern (Boston: Northeastern University Press, 1975), 48.

253 "Byng knew Rose . . . often as I may": LMA to ABA, 26 November 1875, *Letters,* 201.

253 "Dr. Holland . . . bodily ails": LMA to AMA, 1–2 January 1876, ibid., 215.

253 "Dear Seventy-six . . . such fun": LMA to ABA, 26 November 1875, ibid., 201.

254 "narrow beds"; "One little chap . . . Could you do it?": LMA to Frederick and John Pratt, 4 December 1875, ibid., 203.

254 "die like sheep . . . not go mad?": LMA to the Alcott Family, 25 December 1875, ibid., 210–12.

255 "People are too busy": LMA to ABA, 12–13 December 1875, ibid., 207.

SEVENTEEN: THE CREAM OF THINGS

256 "her distasteful duty": LMA, September 1876, *Journals*, 201.

256 "When I become rich and great": May Alcott, in Caroline Ticknor, *May Alcott: A Memoir* (Boston: Little, Brown, 1928), 165.

257 "She always had the cream of things": LMA, April 1878, *Journals*, 209.

257 "moral pap": LMA, January/February 1887, *Journals*, 204.

258 "An inward excitement": LMA, *A Modern Mephistopheles* (New York: Book-of-the-Month Club, 1995), 174–75.

258 "the unconscious stage": Ibid., 177.

258 "a heavenly dreaminess": LMA, "Perilous Play," in *Selected Fiction*, 118.

258 "surpasse[d] its predecessors": Ticknor, *May Alcott,* 189.

258 "It is praised": LMA, April 1877, *Journals*, 209.

259 "So [Anna] has *her* wish": Ibid., 204–5.

260 "[The real] 'Meg' was never the pretty": Anna Alcott to two Vassar students, 1871, Concord Free Public Library Special Collections.

260 an appealing letter: This account of the Lukens sisters and their publication, including quotations, is derived entirely from the original research and writing of Daniel Shealy of the University of North Carolina, Charlotte, in his article "The Growth of Little Things: Louisa May Alcott and the Lukens Sisters' Family Newspaper," *Resources for American Literary Study* 30 (2006): 160–77.

260 "pluck and perseverance . . . in the world": LMA to the Lukens Sisters, 23 August 1872, *Letters*, 168.

260 "like a Trojan": LMA, January/February 1877, *Journals*, 204.

260 "slip on L's old flannel gown . . . the beautiful creature": May Alcott to AMA, 1876, in Ticknor, *May Alcott*, 141–42.

261 "Statues and articles . . . real genius": May Alcott to Alcott Family, November 1876, ibid., 151–52.

261 "Who would have imagined . . . won't you?": May Alcott to AMA, 18 April 1877, ibid., 192–93.

262 "dear old Lu . . . on the line": May Alcott to LMA, 1877, ibid., 198–99.

262 "no friend at court": LMA, April 1877, *Journals*, 204.

262 "in Millet's later style"; "roared over the charmingly assured tone": Ticknor, *May Alcott*, 203.

262 "I think she has realized": AMA, 1877, Journal, in ibid., 177.

262 "It keeps her young": LMA, May, June 1877, *Journals*, 205.

262 "The doctor told me": LMA, September 1877, ibid.

262 "Fearing I might give out": LMA, October 1877, ibid., 205.

263 "but where Thoreau": ABA to May Alcott, November 1877, *Letters of ABA*, 703.

263 "To rest among kindred": AMA, 1877, Journal, in Ticknor, *May Alcott*, 176–77.

263 "You are laying a very soft pillow": LMA, November 1877, *Journals*, 206.

263 "[It was] a hard day": Ibid.

263 "My duty . . . no motive to go on": Ibid.

263 "I have so much to reproach myself": May Alcott to Alcott Family, 1878, in Ticknor, *May Alcott,* 252.

263 "Never mourn": LMA to May Alcott, 25 November 1877, *Letters,* 225–26.

263 "Certainly, dear Lu": May Alcott to LMA, 1878, in Ticknor, *May Alcott,* 255.

264 "Father goes about . . . only mothers can give": LMA, January 1878, *Journals,* 209.

264 "She has some very *tender friends*": Ibid.

264 "I am not indifferent": ABA to May Alcott, 18 November 1877, *Letters of ABA,* 703.

265 "against the distant sky . . . like champagne": May Alcott Nieriker to Alcott Family, Spring(?) 1878, in Ticknor, *May Alcott,* 266.

265 "how different our lives . . . well, and blest.": LMA, April 1878, *Journals,* 209.

265 "I do not mean to be hindered": May Alcott Nieriker to Alcott Family, 1878, in Ticknor, *May Alcott,* 267.

265 "I dawdle about": LMA, April 1878, *Journals,* 210.

266 "I mean to vote": LMA quoting AMA to Lucy Stone, 1 October 1873, *Letters,* 178.

266 "because of 'jelly-making' "; Louisa "gave them a good scolding": LMA, September 1879, *Letters,* 235.

266 "was *the first woman*": LMA, July 1879, *Journals,* 216.

266 "A very poor record": LMA, October 1978, *Letters,* 238.

267 "These papers admit . . . straits of circumstance": ABA, 10–14 June 1878, *Journals of ABA,* 490.

268 "there was no one": LMA, June/July 1878, *Journals,* 210.

268 "May marries": LMA, November 1878, ibid.

268 "It was a famous show": Porter, "Recollections of LMA (1892)," in Shealy, *Alcott in Her Own Time,* 67.

268 "A sad heart": LMA, January 1879, *Journals,* 213.

269 "by sad experience": LMA, *Diana and Persis,* Sarah Elbert edition (New York: Arno Press, 1978), 122.

269 "Very poorly & cross": LMA, April 1879, *Journals,* 214.

269 "blue pills": Norbert Hirschhorn, Robert G. Feldman, and Ian A. Greaves, "Abraham Lincoln's Blue Pills," *Perspectives in Biology and Medicine* 44, no. 3 (Summer 2001); 315–32.

270 "neuralgia . . . extreme sensitivity": Norbert Hirschhorn and Ian A. Greaves, "Louisa May Alcott: Her Mysterious Illness," *Perspectives in Biology and Medicine,* 50, No. 2, 255.

270 "we can only recall": Ibid., 254.

271 "curious effect of light": LMA, *Jo's Boys,* in *LMA: LW, LM, JB,* 842–43.

271 "sharply demarcated": Hirschhorn and Greaves, "Louisa May Alcott: Her Mysterious Illness," 250.

271 "As one who gladly": LMA to Mr. Rand, 23 October (n.y.), *Letters,* 339.

271 "drank in every word": LMA, June 1879, *Journals,* 215.

272 "A much better place": LMA, October 1879, ibid., 217.
272 "Thirty students": LMA, July 1879, ibid., 216.
272 "swarms [of] budding": LMA, August 1879, ibid.
273 "All doing well": LMA, November 1879, ibid., 217.
273 "The weight on my heart . . . penance for all my sins": LMA, December 1879, ibid., 218.
273 "I found him . . . very bitter sorrow for all": Ibid.
273 "I shall never forgive": Ibid.
273 " 'getting ready for Louy' ": LMA, 1 January 1880, ibid., 223.
273 "If I die": LMA, 31 December 1879, ibid., 219.
274 "sacredly": LMA, 1 January 1880, ibid., 223.
274 "I see now why I lived": LMA, 31 December 1879, ibid., 219.

EIGHTEEN: MORE COURAGE AND PATIENCE

275 "make it true that our May is dead": LMA, February 1880, *Journals*, 224.
275 "with a heavy heart"; "hope the grief": Ibid.
275 "since even the . . . most guarded child . . . death beautiful": LMA, *Jack and Jill* (Boston: Little, Brown, 1999), 232.
276 "There was such a sympathic choke . . . very much hereafter": Ibid.
276 "Reality makes romance": LMA, May 1880, *Journals,* 225.
276 "Our Madonna": LMA, *An Intimate Anthology,* 153.
276 "Love's Morrow": ABA, *Sonnets and Canzonets,* 79.
277 "one should be ready to go": LMA, February 1880, *Journals,* 224.
277 "sorted old letters": LMA, August 1885, ibid., 262.
277 "My journals were all burnt": LMA to Louise Chandler Moulton, 18 January 1883, *Letters,* 267.
277 "all that is left . . . she last wore": LMA, March 1880, *Journals,* 224.
277 "if that was mine . . . thank Heaven!": LMA, September 1880, *Journals,* 227.
278 "[May's spirit] is about her baby": LMA to Maggie Lukens, 14 February 1884, *Letters,* 280.
278 "fine manners, foreign ways": LMA, "Sophie's Secret," in *Selected Fiction,* 364–67.
278 "Devote myself": LMA, "Notes and Memoranda 1880," in *Journals,* 229.
278 "Up! Bow wow . . . artist's baby": LMA to ABA, 10 November 1880, *Letters,* 250.
278 "Baby is well": LMA to Mary Mapes Dodge, 6 August [1881], *Letters*, 254.
279 "Dear Distracted Editor": LMA to Mary Mapes Dodge, 13 February 1882(?), ibid., 257–58.
279 "as much fine writing"; "less romantic fate": LMA, *Moods,* 225.
280 "young Americans": LMA, March 1882, *Journals,* 223.
280 "stories by the dozen"; "lambs, piggies . . . soothe her little woes": LMA, April 1882, ibid., 233.
280 "I don't think I was afraid of the devil": Louisa May Nieriker Rasim (1879–1975), interview with Madelon Bedell, 1975. This and all quotations from Louisa May Nieriker Rasim ("Lulu") are to be found in Madelon Bedell's transcription of the interviews and are published here for the first time (Bedell Papers, Orchard House).

281 "Where are we?": Gay Wilson Allen, *Waldo Emerson: A Biography* (New York: Viking Press, 1981), 668.
281 "held [Father's] hand": LMA, April 1882, *Journals,* 233–34.
281 "Shall never live": LMA, May 1883, ibid., 239.
282 "M. Fullers": LMA, July 1882, ibid., 235.
282 "Philosophers sit": LMA, "The School of Philosophy," in Delamar, *Louisa May Alcott and "Little Women,"* 121.
283 "Duty's Faithful Child": ABA, *Sonnets and Canzonets,* 73.
283 "Since the original": LMA, Preface, *Jo's Boys,* in *LMA: LW, LM, JB.*
283 "full of unostentatious": Ibid., 820.
283 "one of those who prove": Ibid.
284 "The 40 sonnets": LMA, November 1882, *Journals,* 236.
284 "very queer remarks": LMA to Mary Preston Stearns, 26 November 1882, *Letters,* 264.
284 "& seem[ed] to be lecturing": LMA, December 1882, *Journals,* 236.
284 "he was dimly conscious": LMA to Mary Newbury Adams, 5 December 1882, *Letters,* 264.
285 "spoke of herself": Lurabel Harlow, *Louisa May Alcott: A Souvenir* (Boston: Samuel E. Cassino, 1889), Special Collections, Concord Free Public Library, Concord, MA.
285 "two babies": LMA to Elizabeth Wells, 9 October 1883(?), *Letters,* 273.
285 "[I] solemnly spank[ed]": LMA, January 1884, *Journals,* 243.
286 "When I had the youth": LMA, January 1874, *Journals,* 191.
287 "The patient sits": LMA to Maggie Lukens, 15 March 1885, *Letters,* 287.
287 "made no more impression": LMA, March 1885, *Journals,* 252–53.
287 "very lurchy": LMA to Laura Hosmer, 16 March 1885, *Letters,* 288n.
287 "You speak of 'breaking away'": LMA to Maggie Lukens, 5 February 1884, ibid., 276. Fifty years later, Maggie Lukens visited Orchard House, by then a museum.
287 "Freedom was always my longing . . . I believe in it": LMA to Maggie Lukens, 5 February (1884), ibid., 279–80.
287 "I seem to remember . . . which must exist": LMA to Maggie Lukens, 14 February 1884, ibid., 279–80.
288 "Miss Alcott does not": LMA to Mary E. Edie, 11 January 1885, ibid., 285.
288 "those who are giving": LMA to Lucy Stone, 31 August 1885, ibid., 291.
288 "try to bear the friction": LMA, October 1885, *Journals,* 264.
289 "a strong temptation": LMA, *Jo's Boys,* in *LMA: LW, LM, JB,* 1063–64.
290 "Rest, weary brain": LMA, "To My Brain," in *The Poetry of Louisa May Alcott,* 44.
290 "If possible [I mean] to keep up": Porter, "Recollections of LMA," quoted in Shealy, *Alcott in Her Own Time,* 71.
290 "Feeble & sick, away": LMA, 1 January 1887, *Journals,* 287.
290 "Patience": LMA, 14 January 1887, ibid., 288.
291 "Courage and Patience": LMA, "Courage and Patience," in *The Poetry of Louisa May Alcott,* 43.
291 "I suppose tomorrow": LMA to Lulu Nieriker, March 1887, *Letters,* 306–7.
291 "I know how she feels": LMA, 6 April 1887, *Journals,* 296.

292   "Spirits good": LMA, September 1887, ibid., 313.
292   "hope and patience": LMA, July 1887, ibid., 306.
292   "The end is not far off": LMA, September 1887, ibid., 311.
292   "eat or die": Ibid.
292   "Death never seemed terrible": LMA to Maggie Lukens, 14 February 1884, *Letters,* 279.
292   "Life was always a puzzle": LMA, January 1874, *Journals,* 191.
292   "a happy day": LMA, January 1888, ibid., 327.
292   "The Last of the Philosophers": Poem in Delamar, *Louisa May Alcott,* 138.
293   "Kneeling by his bedside": Porter, "Recollections of LMA," in Shealy, *Alcott in Her Own Time,* 72.
294   "weight like iron": Ibid., 73.
294   "after his long . . . sorrow has no place": LMA to Maria S. Porter, 4(?) March 1888(?), *Letters,* 337.
294   "& then I am promised": Ibid.
294   "So I still wait": Anna Alcott Pratt to Anna Ricketson, 4 March 1888, HMC, HAP.

EPILOGUE: HOW THEY TURNED OUT

297   "with the startling intelligence, 'Louisa Alcott is dead' ": Cheney, *Louisa May Alcott,* 267.
297   "Transfiguration": LMA, in *The Poetry of Louisa Alcott,* 43.
297   "take care of them": LMA in Cheney, *Louisa May Alcott,* 268.
297   "[for playing] the small part": LMA to ABA, November 1855, *Letters,* 15.
299   "about $200,300": $200,301 in 1888 would amount to about $4.5 million in 2007, using the consumer price index as the gauge. If we use the nominal GDP per capita, the equivalent figure would be close to $40 million. Samuel H. Williamson, "Six Ways to Compute the Relative Value of a U.S. Dollar Amount, 1790 to Present," MeasuringWorth, 2008. http://www.measuring worth.com/uscompare/ (accessed 29 January 2009).
300   Lulu died in 1975: www.xanth.de/alcott/lulu_e.htm. NB: This Web site is not part of any institution; it is the work of a German enthusiast of Alcott. On it is a photograph of Lulu's grave in the small town of Reutlingen, near Stuttgart, Germany.
301   "One day [you might] see your *Varjo*": LMA, "My Boys," in *Aunt Jo's Scrap-Bag,* 1:22.
301   "My Polish Boy": LMA, 20 September 1873, *Letters,* 178.
302   From 1888 until 1950: Madeleine B. Stern's *Louisa May Alcott: A Biography* revealed its subject in her true dimensions for the first time, and broke the news of the discovery of the thrillers, although the stories themselves were not republished until the 1970s, when they sparked a wave of feminist interest in Alcott. Madeleine B. Stern (1912–2007) herself was a woman of greatness and the person most responsible for the recognition of Louisa May Alcott as a major American writer.
302   "I read *Little Women*": Cynthia Ozick, *Art and Ardor: Essays by Cynthia Ozick* (New York: Knopf, 1983), 303.

SELECTED BIBLIOGRAPHY

Alcott, Bronson. *Concord Days*. Philadelphia: Albert Saifer, 1962.

———. *How Like An Angel Came I Down: Conversations with Children on the Gospels*. Edited and abridged by Alice O. Howell. Hudson, NY: Lindisfarne Press, 1991.

———. *The Journals of A. Bronson Alcott*. Selected and edited by Odell Shepard. Boston: Little, Brown, 1938.

———. *The Letters of A. Bronson Alcott*. Edited by Richard L. Herrnstadt. Ames, IA: Iowa State University Press, 1969.

———. *Sonnets and Canzonets*. Boston: Roberts Brothers, 1882.

———. *Tablets*. Boston: Roberts Brothers, 1868.

Alcott Family Tree. http://genealogy.about.com/od/famous_family_trees/a/lou isa_alcott.html (accessed 29 January 2009).

Alcott, Louisa May. *Alternative Alcott*. Edited by Elaine Showalter. New Brunswick, NJ: Rutgers University Press, 1989.

———. *Aunt Jo's Scrap-Bag*. Volume 6, "Poppy's Pranks." http://books.google.com/books?id=xM4QAAAAYAAJ&printsec=titlepage#PPA40,M1 (accessed 29 January 2009).

———. *Aunt Jo's Scrap-Bag*. Volume 2, *Shawl-Straps*. Boston: Roberts Brothers, 1885.

———. *Behind a Mask: The Unknown Thrillers of Louisa May Alcott*. Edited by Madeleine Stern. New York: William Morrow, 1975.

———. *"Comic Tragedies: Written by "Jo" and "Meg" and Acted by the "Little Women."* Foreword by Meg (Anna Alcott Pratt). Boston: Roberts Brothers, 1893. http://books.google.com/books?id=Q4M0AAAAMAAJ&printsec=titl epage&source=gbs_summary_r&cad=0#PPA3,M1 (accessed 29 January 2009).

———. *Diana and Persis*. Sarah Elbert, ed. New York: Arno Press, 1978.

———. *Eight Cousins*. New York: Penguin, 1995.

————. *Flower Fables.* Echo Library, 2007. http://books.google.com/books? id=TyQ79KsnLVAC (accessed 29 January 2009).

————. *From Aunt Jo's Attic: Stories of Intrigue and Suspense.* Edited by Madeleine B. Stern and Daniel Shealy. Boston: Northeastern University Press, 1993.

————. *Hospital Sketches.* Boston: Applewood Books, 1986.

————. *The Inheritance.* Boston: Penguin, 1995.

————. *Jack and Jill.* Boston: Little, Brown, 1999.

————. *The Journals of Louisa May Alcott.* Edited by Joel Myerson and Daniel Shealy. Madeleine Stern, associate editor. Boston: Little, Brown, 1989.

————. *L. M. Alcott: Signature of Reform.* Edited by Madeleine Stern. Boston: Northeastern University Press, 2002.

————. *The Lost Stories of Louisa May Alcott.* Edited by Madeleine B. Stern and Daniel Shealy. New York: Citadel Press, 1993.

————. *Louisa May Alcott: An Intimate Anthology.* New York Public Library Collectors' Editions. New York: Doubleday, 1997.

————. *Louisa May Alcott: Little Women, Little Men, and Jo's Boys.* Edited by Elaine Showalter. New York: Literary Classics of the United States, 2005.

————. *Louisa May Alcott on Race, Sex, and Slavery.* Edited with an introduction by Sarah Elbert. Boston: Northeastern University Press, 1997.

————. *Louisa May Alcott: Selected Fiction.* Edited by Daniel Shealy, Madeleine Stern, and Joel Myerson. Athens, GA: University of Georgia Press, 2001.

————. *Louisa May Alcott Unmasked: Collected Thrillers.* Edited by Madeleine Stern. Boston: Northeastern University Press, 1995.

————. *A Modern Mephistopheles.* New York: Book-of-the-Month Club, 1995.

————. *Moods.* Edited by Sarah Elbert. New Brunswick, NJ: Rutgers University Press, 1996.

————. *An Old-Fashioned Girl.* New York: Puffin Books, 1996.

————. *The Poetry of Louisa May Alcott.* Concord, MA: Louisa May Alcott Memorial Association, c. 1977.

————. *Plots and Counterplots: More Unknown Thrillers of Louisa May Alcott.* Edited by Madeleine Stern. New York: William Morrow, 1976.

————. *Rose in Bloom.* Boston: Little, Brown, 1995.

————. *The Selected Letters of Louisa May Alcott.* Edited by Joel Myerson and Daniel Shealy. Madeline Stern, associate editor. Boston: Little, Brown, 1987.

————. *The Sketches of Louisa May Alcott.* Introduction by Gregory Eiselein. New York: Ironweed Press, 2001.

————. *Transcendental Wild Oats and Excerpts from the Fruitlands Diary.* Introduction by W. H. Harrison. Boston: Harvard Common Press, 1981.

————. *A Whisper in the Dark: Twelve Thrilling Tales by Louisa May Alcott.* Edited by Stefan Dziemianowicz. New York: Barnes and Noble, 1996.

————. *Work: A Story of Experience.* New York: Penguin, 1994.

Baker, Carlos. *Emerson Among the Eccentrics.* New York: Penguin, 1997.

Barton, Cynthia H. *Transcendental Wife: The Life of Abigail May Alcott.* Lanham, MD: University Press of America, 1996.

Bedell, Madelon. *The Alcotts: Biography of a Family.* New York: Clarkson Potter, 1980.

————. "Louisa and Her Sisters: The Alcotts, Vol. 2." Draft, eight chapters. Orchard House, Concord, MA.

Brook Farm. http://www.vcu.edu/engweb/transcendentalism/ideas/brhistory.html (accessed 29 January 2009).

Brooks, Van Wyck. *New England: Indian Summer, 1865–1915.* New York: Dutton, 1940.

Brown, Amy Belding. *Mr. Emerson's Wife.* New York: St. Martin's, 2005.

Charlton, Bruce G. *Editorial Preface to the English translation of Goethe's Correspondence with a Child by Bettina von Arnim—1837.* http://www.hedweb.com/bgcharlton/preface-bettina.html (accessed 29 January 2009).

Cheney, Ednah Dow Littlehale, ed. *Louisa May Alcott: Her Life, Letters and Journals.* New York: Gramercy Books, 1995.

———. *Reminiscences of Ednah Dow Cheney (Born Littlehale).* Boston: Lee and Shepard, 1902.

Clark, Beverly Lyon, ed. *Louisa May Alcott: The Contemporary Reviews.* Cambridge: Cambridge University Press, 2004.

Dall, Caroline Healey. *Daughter of Boston: The Extraordinary Diary of a Nineteenth-century Woman.* Boston: Beacon Press, 2005.

Delamar, Gloria T. *Louisa May Alcott and "Little Women": Biography, Critique, Publications, Poems, Songs and Contemporary Relevance.* Lincoln, NE: iUniverse, 2001.

Dumond, Dwight Lowell. *Antislavery Origins of the Civil War in the United States.* Ann Arbor: University of Michigan Press, 1960.

Eiselein, Gregory, and Anne K. Phillips. *The Louisa May Alcott Encyclopedia.* Westport, CT: Greenwood, 2001.

Elbert, Sarah. *A Hunger for Home: Louisa May Alcott's Place in American Culture.* New Brunswick, NJ: Rutgers University Press, 1987.

Emerson, Ralph Waldo. *The Heart of Emerson's Journals.* Edited by Bliss Perry. New York: Courier Dover, 1995.

———. *Selections from Ralph Waldo Emerson.* Edited by Stephen E. Whicher. Cambridge, MA: Riverside Press, 1960.

———. *The Spiritual Teachings of Ralph Waldo Emerson.* Introduction by Robert Richardson. Edited by Richard Geldard. Great Barrington, MA: Lindisfarne Books, 2001.

Foster, Shirley. *American Women Travellers to Europe in the Nineteenth and Early Twentieth Centuries.* http://www.baas.ac.uk/resources/pamphlets/pamphets.asp?id=27 (accessed 29 January 2009).

Francis, Richard. *Transcendental Utopias: Individual and Community at Brook Farm, Fruitlands, and Walden.* Ithaca, NY: Cornell University Press, 1997.

Handlin, Oscar. *Boston's Immigrants: 1790–1880.* Cambridge, MA: Harvard University (Belknap) Press, 1991.

Hawthorne, Nathaniel, *The Blithedale Romance.* New York: Modern Library, 2001.

Hirschhorn, Norbert, Robert G. Feldman, and Ian A. Greaves. "Abraham Lincoln's Blue Pills." *Perspectives in Biology and Medicine* 44, no. 3 (Summer 2001): 315–32.

Hirschhorn, Norbert, and Ian A. Greaves. "Louisa May Alcott: Her Mysterious Illness." *Perspectives in Biology and Medicine* 50, no. 2 (2007): 243–59.

James, Laurie. *Outrageous Questions: Legacy of Bronson Alcott and America's One-Room Schools.* New York: Golden Heritage Press, 1994.

Kaplan, Justin. *Walt Whitman.* New York: Simon and Schuster, 1980. Reprint, New York: Perennial Classics, 2003.

Marshall, Megan. *The Peabody Sisters: Three Women Who Ignited American Romanticism.* Boston: Houghton Mifflin, 2005.

Matteson, John. *Eden's Outcasts: The Story of Louisa May Alcott and Her Father.* New York: Norton, 2007.

May, Samuel Joseph. *Memoir of Samuel Joseph May.* Boston: Roberts Brothers, 1873. Digital reprint, University of Michigan Library, 2005.

McFarland, Philip. *Hawthorne in Concord.* New York: Grove Press, 2004.

Meigs, Cornelia. *Invincible Louisa: The Story of the Author of Little Women.* Boston: Little, Brown, 1968.

Morris, Roy, Jr. *The Better Angel: Walt Whitman in the Civil War.* New York: Oxford University Press, 2000.

Morrow, Honoré Willsie. *The Father of Little Women.* Boston: Little, Brown, 1927.

New York Times, obituary of Louisa May Alcott, March 7, 1888. http://www.ny times.com/learning/general/onthisday/bday/1129.html (accessed 29 January 2009).

Nieriker, May Alcott. *Studying Art Abroad, and How to Do It Cheaply.* Boston: Roberts Brothers, 1879.

Peabody, Elizabeth. *Letters of Elizabeth Palmer Peabody, American Renaissance Woman.* Edited by Bruce Ronda. Middletown, CT: Wesleyan University Press, 1984.

———. *Record of a School: Exemplifying the General Principles of Spiritual Culture.* Bedford, MA: Applewood Books, 2005.

Perrin, Pat, ed. *The Underground Railroad: Life on the Road to Freedom.* Carlisle, MA: Discovery Enterprises, 1999.

Richardson, Robert. *Emerson: The Mind on Fire.* Berkeley: University of California Press, 1995.

Riis, Jacob. *How the Other Half Lives.* http://books.google.com/books?id=zhcv_ oA5dwgC&printsec=frontcover&dq=How+the+Other+Half+Lives&ei=Ev6R SYmmJZHaMd6dhaUK (accessed 29 January 2009).

Sanborn, F. B., and William T. Harris. *A. Bronson Alcott: His Life and Philosophy.* 2 vols. New York: Biblo and Tannen, 1965.

Sargent, Mary Elizabeth. *Sketches and Reminiscences of the Radical Club of Chestnut Street, Boston.* http://books.google.com/books?id=qS1HAAAAIAAJ&pri ntsec=frontcover&dq=Sketches+and+Reminiscences+of+the+Radical+Club+ of+Chestnut+Street,+Boston&ei=rf6RSYDRBJvWzAS3nfmdBg (accessed 29 January 2009).

Saxton, Martha. *Louisa May Alcott: A Modern Biography.* New York: Farrar, Straus and Giroux, 1995.

Schultz, Jane E. *Women at the Front: Hospital Workers in Civil War America.* Chapel Hill, NC: University of North Carolina Press, 2004.

Sears, Clara Endicott. *Bronson Alcott's Fruitlands with Transcendental Wild Oats.* Cambridge, MA: Riverside Press, 1915. Reprint, Boston and New York: Houghton Mifflin.

The Secret Six (Harpers Ferry conspirators). http://www.law.umkc.edu/faculty/ projects/ftrials/johnbrown/secretsixdetails.html (accessed 29 January 2009).

Shealy, Daniel, ed. *Alcott in Her Own Time*. Iowa City, IA: University Press, 2005.

———. "The Growth of *Little Things*: Louisa May Alcott and the Lukens Sisters' Family Newspaper." *Resources for American Literary Study* 30 (2006): 160–77.

———, ed. *Little Women Abroad: The Alcott Sisters' Letters from Europe, 1870–1871: Louisa May Alcott and May Alcott*. Athens, GA: University of Georgia Press, 2008.

———. "Louisa May Alcott's Juvenilia." In *The Child Writer from Austen to Woolf*, edited by Christine Alexander and Juliet McMaster. Cambridge: Cambridge University Press, 2005.

Shepard, Odell. *Pedlar's Progress: The Life of Bronson Alcott*. Boston: Little, Brown, 1937.

Sklar, Kathryn Kish, ed. *Women's Rights Emerges Within the Antislavery Movement, 1830–1870*. Boston: Bedford/St. Martin's, 2000.

Stern, Madeleine B. *Louisa May Alcott: A Biography*. Norman, OK: University of Oklahoma Press, 1950. Reprint, New York. Random House, 1996.

———. *Louisa May Alcott: From Blood and Thunder to Hearth and Home*. Boston: Northeastern University Press, 1998.

Stern, Madeleine B., and Leona Rostenberg. *Old Books, Rare Friends: Two Literary Sleuths and Their Shared Passion*. New York: Main Street Books, Doubleday, 1997.

Thoreau, Henry D. *The Illustrated Walden with Photography from the Gleason Collection*. Edited by J. Lyndon Shanley. Princeton: Princeton University Press, 1973.

Ticknor, Caroline. *May Alcott: A Memoir*. Boston: Little, Brown, 1928.

von Arnim, Bettine. *Goethe's Correspondence with a Child*. http://www.hedweb.com/bgcharlton/bettina-goethe.html (accessed 28 January 2009).

Whicher, Stephen E., ed. *Selections from Ralph Waldo Emerson: An Organic Anthology*. Boston: Houghton Mifflin, 1957.

Whitman, Walt. *Specimen Days*. Boston: D. R. Godine, 1971.

Willis, Dr. Frederick L. H. Willis. *Alcott Memoirs*. Boston: Richard G. Badger, 1915.

Wilson, Ellen. *Margaret Fuller: Bluestocking, Romantic, Revolutionary*. New York: Farrar, Straus and Giroux, 1977.

Wineapple, Brenda. *Hawthorne: A Life*. New York: Random House, 2003.

Woodbury, Charles J. *Talks with Ralph Waldo Emerson*.

ACKNOWLEDGMENTS

I am deeply grateful to the people who made the writing of this book possible, rewarding, and even pleasurable:

On the publishing side, ICM agent Jennifer Joel, for her indispensable expertise; editor Jack Macrae and associate editor Supurna Banerjee of Henry Holt and Company, who shepherded the manuscript with kindness and expertise; and copy editor Vicki Haire, for her meticulous reading.

I could not have completed this book without the help of the renowned Alcott scholars who generously shared their knowledge and insight: the late Madeleine Stern and the late Dr. Leona Rostenberg; Sarah Elbert; John Matteson; Joel Myerson; and Daniel Shealy. Megan Marshall, biographer of the Peabody sisters, was also a helpful advisor. Jan Turnquist, executive director of Louisa May Alcott's Orchard House, generously shared her extensive knowledge of the Alcott family, the contents of the archives, and the house itself. I never met the late Madelon Bedell, but her important book about the Alcott family and her diligent research and drafts of five chapters on Louisa Alcott (made accessible to me by her husband, Bob Bedell, and her daughter Jane Bedell) played a crucial role in my own work. Julie Bogart catalogued the papers, making them appreciably more navigable.

Thanks to line editor Lorraine Bodger, for her keen mind and sharp pencil, and to Jan Nicholson, for turning my scribbles into legible documents. Ann Banks could always be counted upon to give counsel and good leads.

I'm indebted to the distinguished writer Martha Fay for contributions to this book in all its stages.

My boundless gratitude goes to Nancy Porter, my fellow producer and the director of the film *Louisa May Alcott: The Woman Behind Little Women*. She put her talent, intelligence, and unstinting effort into this book from conception to finish.

Finally, love and thanks go to my adorable husband, Tony Kahn, and my affectionate son, Andrew Kahn, for propping me up on the home front, enduring occasional neglect, and cheering me on through it all.

INDEX

ABOUT THE AUTHOR

Harriet Reisen's interest in Louisa May Alcott dates to her marathon reading of Alcott's eight children's novels after her mother presented her with a copy of *Little Women*. Over the past twenty years, what began as a passion for the subject of Louisa May Alcott developed into a film biography for PBS's *American Masters* and this book. Reisen has worked as a journalist, a lyricist, in public television as a writer and producer, and as a contributor to public radio.